THE
BOOKS OF ENOCH
REVEALED

"*The Books of Enoch Revealed* is an epic work of history that highlights Churton's virtuosity in meticulously analyzing the theology of the texts and the historicity of their journey from biblical antiquity to our era. The Enochic texts present a maze of complexity, both historically and theologically. Tobias Churton is one of the few living scholars capable of disassembling and reassembling all the moving parts without losing any along the way."

MITCH HOROWITZ, PEN AWARD–WINNING AUTHOR OF
OCCULT AMERICA AND *MODERN OCCULTISM*

"A fantastic new addition to our understanding of the Book of Enoch and its connection to the Watchers, Nephilim, the patriarchs Enoch and Noah, and the angels of heaven. It shows the text's origins, its influences, and its impact on the early Christian world before its eventual banishment into oblivion and its eventual rediscovery by Scottish Freemason James Bruce in the eighteenth century. An essential addition to the mysteries bookshelf."

ANDREW COLLINS, AUTHOR OF
KARAHAN TEPE AND *FROM THE ASHES OF ANGELS*

"Tobias Churton has produced an encyclopedic summary of the myth, history, and importance of the Books of Enoch. Once relegated to the back shelves of libraries and ignored by mainstream academia, Enochic works and all associated with them have become the topic du jour. With their discussions of angels, demons, apocalypticism, spiritual revelations, heavenly realms, and hermetic, alchemical, and magical potencies, there is something for everyone in Enochic lore. Dive deep and enjoy!"

MARK STAVISH, FOUNDER AND DIRECTOR OF
THE INSTITUTE FOR HERMETIC STUDIES AND AUTHOR OF
EGREGORES AND *THE PATH OF FREEMASONRY*

THE
BOOKS OF ENOCH REVEALED

The Wicked Watchers, Metatron, and
the Fruits of Forbidden Knowledge

TOBIAS CHURTON

Inner Traditions
Rochester, Vermont

Inner Traditions
One Park Street
Rochester, Vermont 05767
www.InnerTraditions.com

Cataloging-in-Publication Data for this title is available from the Library of Congress

ISBN 978-1-64411-925-9 (print)
ISBN 978-1-64411-926-6 (ebook)

Printed and bound in China by Reliance Printing Co., Ltd.

10   9   8   7   6   5   4   3   2   1

Text design by Priscilla Baker and layout by Virginia Scott Bowman
This book was typeset in Garamond Premier Pro with Gitan Latin, Myriad Pro, and Futura used as display typefaces

To send correspondence to the author of this book, mail a first-class letter to the author c/o Inner Traditions • Bear & Company, One Park Street, Rochester, VT 05767, and we will forward the communication.

Scan the QR code and save 25% at InnerTraditions.com. Browse over 2,000 titles on spirituality, the occult, ancient mysteries, new science, holistic health, and natural medicine.

Contents

Foreword

By Jeffrey J. Bütz

If you have been looking for the best book to read about the enigmatic biblical patriarch Enoch and the truly fantastic writings attributed to him, please know that you have come to the right place. *The Books of Enoch Revealed* is all you will need as it thoroughly covers every aspect of this fascinating subject. In response to interest in Enoch among fundamentalist Christians over the last century (who have filtered the writings of Enoch through their varied apocalyptic beliefs about the Second Coming), quite a number of books have been written about Enoch, most however from a very limited perspective. In contradistinction, the book you are about to read is a most welcome, even-handed, and scholarly assessment of these fascinating ancient texts, which are still of importance today despite the taint of both religious fundamentalism and off-beat esotericism that has often surrounded them. The taint of illegitimacy that has assigned Enoch to the status of an apocryphal or pseudepigraphic writing is rather sad, for as you will see the writings of Enoch greatly influenced both the earliest Christians amidst the persecutions they faced, as well as first-century Jews facing the greatest persecution in their history. Enoch could speak to them both, and still speaks to many today, in turbulent political times.

Tobias Churton has stated that his goal in writing *The Books of Enoch Revealed* is for it to be the most comprehensive and up-to-date presentation of these apocryphal writings, covering their history, current scholarly evaluations of their origins and import, and the influence of these writings from ancient times to the present. While that may seem an overwhelming goal, as the reader will soon discover, Churton has succeeded brilliantly. He covers in detail everything that has been discovered about these documents from the fascinating story of their historical transmission and the perspectives of early rabbis and church fathers, to the most recent scholarly perspectives, as well as sharing his own insightful analysis of the surprising influence these writings have had throughout history as well as the modern era.

Tobias Churton is a prolific author and very well-informed about the areas in which he writes. I have personally followed his work since his first groundbreaking books and television documentaries about the Gnostics appeared back in the late 1980s to widespread acclaim. Since then, Churton has written over two dozen books as well as numerous musical and theatrical works. I have found him to be a most careful researcher and writer, and the depth of time and labor he has put into his latest book is obvious. I am honored to have been asked to write a Foreword to this important work.

What I most appreciate about Churton's work is his ability to distill the best of current scholarship and brew it together with his own unique perspectives as an expert in the types of esoteric literature in which the Enochic writings have had such an influence. It is fascinating that the apocryphal book of 1 Enoch, while only considered scripture by the Ethiopian Tewahedo Orthodox Church, has had religious, spiritual, and even political influence on modern religion and culture far beyond the relatively small group of people who even know of its existence. This is best seen in current popular fascination with the biblical Nephilim and the Enochic Watchers. Here we can plainly see the astonishing impact of these ancient writings on today's technological, yet still superstitious culture with these stories of angels mating with human women to produce a hybrid race influencing the extraterrestrial speculations of writers such as Erich Von Däniken and helping create a popular new zeitgeist based on earthly visitations not of angels, but of ancient astronauts. Unfortunately, it is from such sources that too many people have been introduced to a heavily distorted understanding of Enoch. And herein lies the great value of *The Books of Enoch Revealed,* which presents a sober scholarly evaluation of these writings while not shying away from discussion of their important esoteric influence and impact on popular culture.

Of most interest to me personally is Churton's extensive discussion of the influence of the Enochic writings on the writers of the New Testament—from the gospel writers themselves, to Paul and the writers of the Johannine literature, and especially, of course, the book of Revelation. His extensive citing of the specific parallels between Enoch and the New Testament plainly shows the huge influence that Enoch had on not only the writers of the New Testament, but most likely Jesus himself. Looking objectively, one cannot come away from Churton's astute analysis without seeing that the Enochic worldview had to have had a major influence upon Jesus's own well-known apocalyptic vision.

Further, Churton examines the importance of the Enochic writings for the Qumran community and the Essene sect, by which time the reader will likely be overwhelmed at the extensive influence of Enoch. And lest one think Churton's presentation is an exaggeration, his assessment is backed up by no less a scholar than Princeton's James Charlesworth, who holds the Enochic writings to be nothing less than, "the Second Temple period's most important collection." That is a truly stunning statement. And, as you will see, Tobias Churton provides stunningly exhaustive evidence to back up Charlesworth's proclamation. All of which raises the question: Why were these vital and important writings not included in any canon of either Judaism or Christianity except one? The answers await you within.

But beyond my own personal interests in the Judeo-Christian tradition, Churton goes much further, enlightening us on the surprisingly widespread influence Enoch has had on many other traditions, from earliest Jewish mysticism to earliest Islam, from leading intellects of the Renaissance to modern esoteric sects and movements such as Rosicrucianism, Freemasonry, and occultism. None of this should be surprising since the books of Enoch recount how Enoch was not only taken up to heaven but was there appointed guardian of all the celestial treasures, made chief of the archangels, and the immediate attendant at the throne of God where he was taught all secrets and mysteries.

Please now allow Tobias Churton to take you on a guided journey into the heavenly realms, a spiritual voyage of discovery to examine a cosmic worldview shared by many Jews and Christians two millennia ago, later rejected by most Jewish and Christian leaders, but which has had a rather startling resurrection in the 21st century amidst another time of apocalyptic hopes and fears. You could have no better guide into these realms than Tobias Churton. In my estimation, what you are about to read is nothing less than an academic and spiritual *tour de force*.

THE REV. JEFFREY J. BÜTZ, M.DIV., S.T.M.

Jeffrey J. Bütz holds a master of divinity degree from Moravian Theological Seminary and a master of sacred theology degree from the Lutheran Theological Seminary at Philadelphia where he wrote his groundbreaking thesis on James the brother of Jesus under the late John Reumann. Ordained in the Lutheran Church, he has standing in both the E.L.C.A. and the United Church of Christ and served as pastor of both churches from 1994 until his retirement in 2022. During that time, he was also a professor of religion and philosophy at Pennsylvania State University. He is the author of two influential books—*The Brother of Jesus*, which has received critical acclaim as the best book on Jesus's brother James, and *The Secret Legacy of Jesus*, which has been called "the new definitive work on Jewish Christianity." He has helped make groundbreaking archaeological discoveries in Jerusalem as part of the Mount Zion Archaeological Expedition and has been a leader and participant in many inter-religious dialogue groups.

Preface

Why be interested in the books of Enoch?

Champion of Enoch studies at Princeton Theological Seminary, James H. Charlesworth, remarked in 2005 that during the 1970s, theology didn't take the Book of Enoch seriously. Today, theology *does* take Enoch seriously. Currency in academe, however, has hardly reached the intelligent layperson. This book is intended to fill that gap—and fill it well. Evidence for Enoch's remarkable endurance is revealed by tracing the extraordinary story of how, from the second century BCE right through to our own time, the books of Enoch have been received.

Many of us will welcome insight into how belief in a coming era of salvation, judgment and destruction of evil—the familiar apocalyptic package—came about. Investigating Enochic prophecy gives us the lens to see the illuminating picture in perspective. Challenging to many inherited ideas, the texts may at first appear strange, but closer acquaintance reveals surprisingly familiar territory; the books of Enoch "ring bells."

Enochic tradition also illuminates the primary aspiration of mysticism: ascension to the source of the universe and all being—"heaven," culminating in the glory of God's presence.

Proceeding, we gain insight into the notion and origin of *evil*, as understood by religious men in the Second Temple period (ca. 538 BCE–70 CE). We see the first flowering of what would become a key component of Christianity revealed as a Second Temple–era Jewish project: an apocalyptic "last-chance saloon" before God's coming to judge his creation and institute a new one.

Many readers will find Enochic tradition profoundly compelling because it prefigures and enlightens our understanding of the spiritual framework and itinerary of the Jesus movement of the first and second centuries CE. Enochic writings reveal the subtlety, complexity, urgency, and curious logic of late–Second Temple Judaic thought, casting light upon what we know of the origins and authentic meaning of Christianity.

Recent years have witnessed a surge of references to Enoch on the internet. Much of the interest has focused on a supposition that the Book of Enoch (1 Enoch) has been hidden for some two thousand years, and that its apparent revelation in our times constitutes a sign disclosing knowledge of an imminent end of the world. Speculation on the Enochic myth of fallen angels and "nephilim" has also linked Enoch to von Dänikenesque scenarios of extraterrestrial knowledge supposedly seeding a remote past with promise of bearing perilous fruit in our own times.

The Books of Enoch Revealed clarifies the field, confuting many errors of understanding of history and ideas. I hope readers share my conviction that sober fact, responsibly researched and clearly presented, is more truly sensational than un- or misinformed speculations with stridently overconfident interpretations of ancient texts.

Taking all this into account, *The Books of Enoch Revealed* aims to be the world's most comprehensive, up-to-date, single-work presentation of the Enochic field, based firmly on the research and discoveries of the world's leading scholars of the subject from late antiquity to the present day.

Last but not least, we may ask: What is the *spiritual* value of Enoch? While this is not a question entirely congenial for scholars careful to avoid "value judgments," it *is* a question people may ask for themselves. My hope is that by furnishing readers with the first and only informed aggregate of the best scholarship available on Enoch, this book may enable you to enjoy that question—along with many others—including questions such as: *Should the Book of Enoch be included in canonical scripture, as it has been for centuries . . . in Ethiopia?*

PART ONE

Out of Ethiopia

ONE

Bruce

While empty to the eye, extraordinary things come out of the wilderness. On December 20, 1772, a few days after his forty-second birthday, a bedraggled, near-starving Scottish-born explorer emerged from Upper Egypt's burning desert into the shades of Barjurah, close to the Nile's bank, 360 miles south of Cairo. Leaving his exhausted master to rest, Michael, the explorer's Greek servant, hastened to nearby Farshut, seeking help from a community of Capuchin fathers. The Capuchins bluntly informed Michael that his master was dead, drowned in the Red Sea three years before. In Barjurah, meanwhile, the village's hospitable Muslim Sheikh Hagi Ishmael delighted in finding the explorer alive and cheerfully acceded to the infidel's request for two loaves of bread and some rice.

That James Bruce, bright, open-faced laird of Kinnaird in Sterlingshire, had suffered murder, death by drowning, or a narrow escape from a pitiable end had been rumored among officials throughout Bruce's five-year-long search for the source of the Nile. As Bruce wryly observed of Farshut's Capuchin monks tasked with bringing Egyptians and Ethiopians into the Roman Catholic fold, a rooted aversion to their mission received no "increase in keenness" when they heard Bruce's account of what he'd seen as a guest of Ethiopia's emperor Tekle Haymanot II. Bruce's last few years' sojourn in Abyssinia's distant capital Gondar had been anything but uneventful.[1]

Before retiring exhausted to a brief hermit's life, young, handsome, and cultured Tekle Haymanot had endured a seven-and-a-half-year reign (1769–1777) scarred by murderous scheming and merciless combat among Ethiopia's princes, warlords, and senior clergy. Given Abyssinia's instability, Bruce's returning alive to Egypt was itself somewhat miraculous; the Capuchin fathers expected no such graces.

A week's recuperation and a well-needed shave at Farshut did little to restore the demeanor of this wealthy descendant of Robert the Bruce, Scottish king and hero of Bannockburn (1274–1329). James Bruce hadn't seen a shirt for fourteen months. Chafing under a waistcoat of coarse, brown wool, his trousers—of like material—only escaped falling down thanks to a rough woolen girdle wrapped repeatedly about the waist. The girdle also supported Bruce's two silver-mounted English pistols and a crooked Abyssinian knife with rhinoceros horn. While a red Turkish cap protected his head, Bruce's agonized feet, bereft of shoes and stockings, were pocked with holes from inflammations suffered in the desert.

Weakened further by residual pleurisy, Bruce and Michael boarded a Cairo-bound vessel—probably the familiar dhow of Nile-borne traffic—at, or near, Nagaa Hammadi, a few miles south of the Jabal al-Tārif's sandstone cliffs, at whose feet in 1945 Muhammad Ali al-Sammān and his brothers would discover the famous "Nag Hammadi Library" of fourth-century Gnostic codices while digging—as they claimed—for fertilizing birdlime (*sabak*).

Close to ancient Thebes, the Thebaid region would acquire exceptional repute for discoveries of precious, late antique papyri. Here Bruce purchased what came to be called the "Bruce Codex," supposedly unearthed amid a ruined monastic structure near Medinet Habu, a day's camel ride south of Nag Hammadi, a hamlet just south of the larger Nagaa Hammadi. The caves that pierce the Jabal al-Tārif—not far from Faw Qibli's ruined Pachomian monastery to the west—once sheltered Christian hermits, and in ancient times the Jabal's other caves served as tombs. The Thebaid's old grave sites have yielded rich pickings for archaeologists—though seldom by accident; grave-robbing means substantial business, and the presence of a collector like Bruce would hardly have passed the miscreants' notice.

Bruce had a sharp eye for artifacts. The *Bruce Codex* (*MS. Bruce 96*; Bodleian Library, Oxford, since 1848) contained seventy-eight leaves of approximately fourth-century CE papyrus, inscribed on both sides in Sahidic Coptic. Calling itself *The Book of the Great Logos corresponding to Mysteries*, the longest section, illustrated with Gnostic cryptograms and diagrams, reveals the "living Jesus" instructing his apostles on the mystery of forgiveness of sins and the baptism of the spirit. He also recommends "crucifying the world," rather than being crucified by it, and tells of the spirit's ascent through hostile *archons*—dark, angelic "rulers"—to the "Treasury of the Light." A figure named "Jeu" (*Ieou*), described as the "true God," projected by the eternal Father, has access to the Father's "treasuries" in the highest heaven. From these, Jeu emanates further realms of intelligent spiritual principles. The word "treasury" in relation to high heaven is also significant to the Book of Enoch, but even more significant is the appearance of the word "watchers" applied to angels in chapter six of the *First Book of Jeu*:

> This is his character. He [Jeu] will set up a rank corresponding to the treasuries, and will place it as watchers at the gate of the treasuries which are those which stand at the gate as the three . . . [text missing] This is the true God.[2]

In 1892, German Coptologist Carl Schmidt identified the *Book of the Logos* with "Books of Jeu" mentioned in the parallel Gnostic collection *Pistis Sophia*. Known as the *Askew Codex* after Dr. Anthony Askew who purchased it, this work appeared for sale in London in 1772 or 1773—was it another of Bruce's finds? An incomplete text from another scribe's hand in the *Bruce Codex* is called *Untitled Apocalypse*. It concerns the spirit's ascent through those *archons* that in gnostic cosmology seek to entrap souls devoid of spiritual knowledge. Redemption from the fatal world (symbolized as water) by the *new wine* of the "living Jesus's" spiritual baptism is the dominant theme of these impressive, didactic texts.*

---

*See Schmidt, *The Books of Jeu and the Untitled Text in the Bruce Codex* (1978).

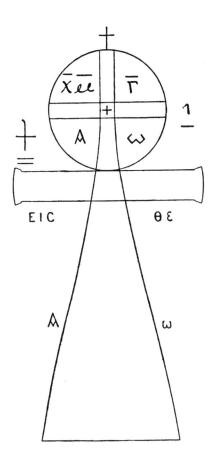

Fig. 1.1. Gnostic Cross from the Bruce Codex.

• • •

Sailing northward down the Nile, Bruce noted docking at the ancient textile-making city of Akhmim (formerly Panopolis)—once home to third-century alchemist Zosimos of Panopolis. In the nineteenth century, Akhmim hosted excavations of graves that brought to light numerous rare papyri, including the only known Greek version of parts of the Book of Enoch.*

Having befriended an Egyptian Christian, or Copt, who collected taxes from predominantly Christian villages near Akhmim, Bruce sailed on, returning at last to Cairo in mid-January 1773, about the time Captain James Cook became the first European explorer to cross the

*See pages 180–85.

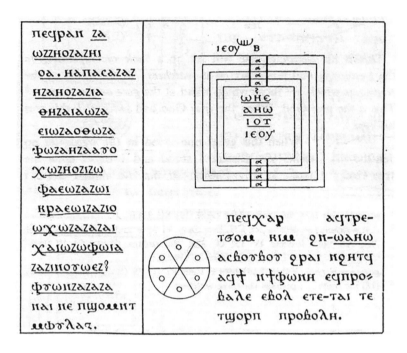

Fig. I.2. Gnostic diagram from the Books of Jeu.

Antarctic circle. His feet still a mass of sores, Bruce avoided the worst of Cairo's hot streets by mounting an ass and traveling at night, desperately trying to keep his feet from scraping the earth.

Brusquely summoned from the St. Victor convent to the palace formerly held by Bruce's old friend Ali Bey al-Kabir, Bruce entered the luxurious apartments of the latter's son-in-law, Mahomet Bey Abou Dahab (1735–1775). Abou Dahab had assumed power after falling out with his father-in-law when commanding Egypt's army against the Ottomans in Syria the previous year; he would shortly connive in Ali Bey's death in Cairo.

Notwithstanding his beggarly appearance, Bruce's tact and exceptional manners made a good impression on the Bey, even encouraging him to issue a *firman* to establish a new trading agreement with East India Company merchant ships at Jidda. The English merchants were about to forgo the trade after the local sheriff enforced extortionate duties, demanding a "present." Bruce himself declined all financial assistance, despite the Bey's offering a handsome purse. In the future, Bruce

Fig. 1.3. *Ali Bey, Sultan of Egypt* (1728–1773),
by Johann Andreas Nothnagel (1729–1800).

would justly claim other benefits to British trading relations with Egypt,
including better maps of the Red Sea and precise instructions on how
to secure advantageous contact with the Bey and his ministers, which
earned, he noted, no official recognition despite his being interviewed
by Prime Minister Lord North. North, at the time, was more concerned
with imposing an incendiary tax on tea imported into the American
colonies. Such frostiness was not shared by the Bey who, before leaving
to battle with al-Kabir, informed Bruce that his filial opponent had told
him the English were a uniquely remarkable people, something he now
recognized, since only such a country could have produced so many
great and able men yet permitted one as superior in skill, courage, and

judgment as James Bruce to spend his life not as leading merchant or state minister, but in the private—and politically irrelevant—pursuit of exploration and knowledge.

Bruce's ship departed for Cyprus just as Alexandria erupted in startling flashes of musket fire—signals of Egypt's latest tumble into instability. Leaving the troubled zone, but soon threatened by severe storms and a leak off Derna, the vessel's captain approached Bruce's bed and asked in French how many of "these things" Bruce had loaded on to the ship.

"What things?"

"Dead men," replied the captain. Convinced Bruce's trunks carried corpses, the crew had conspired to jettison the lot—and would again if conditions worsened. Offering keys to the trunks, Bruce declared that should they find a single corpse, they could throw them all overboard. Opening two, the captain was satisfied, and when a storm arose close to Malta, the threat to Bruce's precious cargo passed—fortunate for our story, for had the crew succumbed to fear, we should have no story to tell.

After three weeks, Bruce arrived at Marseille, and with him, among many other treasures of knowledge, were four copies of a collection of prophecies entitled the *Mäṣṣäfä Henok Nabiy* ("Book of Enoch the Prophet") in the Ethiopian language of Ge'ez, which, while included in the Ethiopian Church's Bible—sitting before Job in their Canon—had, as far as anyone knew, only been known in the West in fragmented quotations for a thousand years. As a result, the Book of Enoch had become the most legendary, sought-after text in the world.

Precisely what else Bruce brought back in those suspect trunks will never be known for sure. Certainly he returned to Europe with detailed, extensive accounts and drawings of all he'd seen, from ancient Egyptian statues and artifacts, to flora and fauna, dietary information, birds and animals, maps, histories and legends, and a barometer, weather, and temperature reading for every single day of his two-year sojourn in Abyssinia, still valuable today for those wishing to construct a climate picture (in East Africa at least) before records for the wider world beyond the continent were recorded.

A child of the rational "Enlightenment" in the benevolent spirit

Fig. 1.4. James Bruce by Pompeo Batoni, 1762.

of contemporary Freemasonry, Bruce felt duties to science and civilization to banish superstitious fantasy with cool, rational explanations based on observation and logic. While feeling a like duty of service to his country—describing himself as "English" throughout the account of his travels, and referring to the United Kingdom as "England"—he was far from bigoted when perceiving customs alien to his own. He made frequent, poignant contrasts and observations of states of mind encountered among Christians and Muslims; Bruce was a man who liked to think decency would become universal once barnacles of past error were revealed as baseless.

Thanks to discoveries made in the Vatican Library by Professor Gabriele Boccaccini,[3] we now know Pope Clement XIV was the first recipient of Bruce's largesse. The pope handed Bruce's presentation copy of The Book of Enoch the Prophet to archaeologist Monsignor Leonardo Antonelli (1730–1811) in whose library at Rome's Palazzo Pamphilij on Piazza Navona it was examined by orientalist Agostino Giorgi (1711–1797), who compared passages to Enoch fragments preserved in Byzantine churchman George Syncellus's eighth-century

Chronographia—then chief quotation-source for Enochic prophecy. Giorgi wrote to Antonelli before April 1775:

> Most venerated Monsignor.
> In asking your most illustrious and revered Lordship the grace of having in my hands for a few days the famous Ethiopic manuscript believed to be the book of Enoch, I had in my heart only the desire to find in it (within the limits of my abilities) all or at least part of the fragments of this apocryphal book cited by the ancient Church Fathers and then again amply corrected and edited by George Syncellus, as we read today in the pseudepigraphic codex of the Old Testament, among the works of Albert Fabricius [see pages 18-19]. (Vatican Library; Vat. Eti. 71).[4]

Still unpublished, Giorgi's translation examples stand among three first efforts to render the Ethiopian text into a European language. "It would be good," Giorgi concluded, "to have the translation of the whole manuscript; but I am neither capable nor patient of this fatigue; which would require of me a very long waste of time."[5] Unfortunately, Bruce's reputation for showy boasting and a well-publicized demand for a duel over a disputed love compounded skepticism among Italy's educated elite. As Boccaccini puts it: "Reasons of expediency led Bruce himself to remain silent about his trip to Rome and his gift to the Pope."[6]

Disappointment must have gone very deep, coloring Bruce's later attitude to the book. He'd made great efforts to frame his gift for maximum effect, as Ted M. Ehro has recently revealed in his chapter "James Bruce's Illusory 'Book of Enoch the Prophet.'"[7] Ehro shows how the work's title was inserted at Bruce's behest to make it resemble a stand-alone "book" suited to European expectations, and as "a special Ethiopian supplement to the Protestant Old Testament."[8] In fact, Enoch's prophecy was simply part of the Ethiopian Old Testament, which Bruce, at Gondar, had had specially transcribed *separately* from Enoch. In Bruce's original manuscript purchase of Enoch near Adwa (almost certainly Bruce MS 74), it was one among twenty Old Testament books. Bruce refrained also from having *apocryphal* books copied, presumably to emphasize Enoch's canonicity, his selected copies generating his own vision of an Ethiopian Old Testament. According to Ehro, "The illusion was perpetuated by foreigners, first and foremost Bruce, who evidently wanted an independent, free-standing book to bring home, even though it seldom circulated as such in the native context."[9] Bruce had reason to present Enoch as an extraordinary work of great rarity, being wise to a skepticism among European scholars fueled by purported "books of Enoch" vaunted as the missing book in the past, while many doubted a composite text existed. Hence, as Ehro says, the title "The Book of Enoch the Prophet" was born, despite authentic Ethiopian copies having no title page, with indications of the text following being either "Enoch"; "of Enoch"; or "of Enoch the prophet."[10] As Ehro notes: "It is not surprising that Bruce kept the original manuscript of Enoch acquired at Adwa for himself since the broader contents of the codex formed an integral section of the Old Testament that he had compiled."[11]

Next to receive a presentation copy of "The Book of Enoch the Prophet" was King Louis XV of France. News of its placement in the Royal Library soon crossed the Channel to London where Polish-born orientalist Carl Gottfried Woide (1725–1790) was hot on the case.

Pastor to Dutch Reformed communicants at the Queen's Chapel, St. James's Palace, Westminster, and to German Lutheran communicants at their wooden chapel at St. James's—both chapels administered by the Chapel Royal—Woide was, on Prime Minister Lord North and Bishop George Lowth of Oxford's recommendation, financed by King George III to hasten to Paris with letters from the secretary of state to ambassador to the French court Lord Stormont to request access to Enoch. Woide's subsequent paper on the Ethiopic Enoch was heard by the Society of Antiquaries on March 10, 1774. According to Bruce, "a translation of the work was brought over; but, I know not why, it has nowhere appeared."[12] Forty-seven years later, Rev. Thomas Laurence— the complete work's first recorded translator—asserted that Woide did not make a *translation*, but a *transcription* of it.[13]*

---

*Laurence noted that Woide's papers, including his Enoch material, had become property of the Delegates of Oxford's Clarendon Press. Evidence reveals only Woide's attempting to translate a few detached passages into Latin. According to Laurence, Woide's knowledge of Ge'ez was rudimentary, attention to it interrupting his study of Sahidic Coptic.[14]

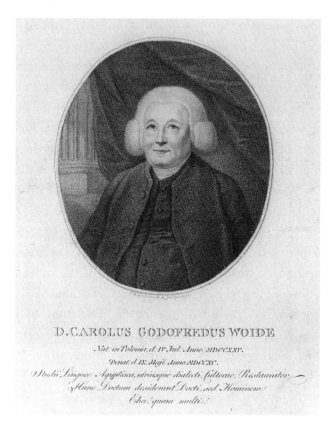

Fig. 1.5. Charles Gottfried Woide (1725–1790);
engraving by Francesco Bartolozzi (1791).

After twelve years absence, Bruce was back in London June 21, 1774. Nine days later, he attended an evening audience with King George III and Queen Charlotte. Meanwhile, German orientalist Johann David Michaelis (1717–1791) included a section on Enoch drawn from Woide's research in the sixth installment of his *Orientalische und Exegetische Bibliothek*, representing, as Ariel Hessayon notes, "the first printed discussion of Ethiopic Enoch in Western Europe."[15] An October 1774 letter from Woide to Michaelis concerning Bruce's Ethiopic Bible collection indicates Woide's hoping Bruce would soon confide when he would translate Enoch. A wary Bruce was annoyed at the French royal librarian's giving Woide access, and feared Woide's receiving credit for presenting Enoch to the world.[16] Such concerns encouraged Bruce to maintain *he* would attend to Enoch's translation. His efforts were not encouraging. Having received sample translations, French intellectual Journu de Montagny responded to Bruce on November 15, 1775:

> Your seventh chapter of Enoch surpasses the understanding of the present age. . . . The antediluvian prophet, whom you are about to introduce into Europe, will not succeed . . . I should be very much delighted to converse with the author of that book. . . . How much nonsense, magic, divination, and priestcraft, should I discover in those ages! . . . The humour of drowning mankind, in order to preserve them from being eaten, deserves particular notice.[17]

Hearing nothing more of Bruce's translation, Montagny wrote again four months later. Ariel Hessayon reckons Montagny's light attitude had stung Bruce into abandoning his efforts, despite claiming to Scottish anatomist William Hunter in February 1776 he'd completed half of it. While that's possible, Hessayon thinks it more likely he'd managed chapter 7 as indicated in Montagny's November letter, since that chapter could be checked against Syncellus's Greek excerpts available in Latin and English.[18] As to Bruce's competence, Egyptologist Henry Salt's *Voyage to Abyssinia* (1814; 334–35) records Bruce's acquaintance at Gondar testifying that when Bruce arrived, he couldn't speak the Tigré tongue, and knew little Amharic. Recognizing Ge'ez characters, his knowledge was limited. Nevertheless, familiarity with the country improved his knowledge.[19]

There is a somewhat ironic twist to Bruce's gifting Pope Clement XIV and, subsequently, King Louis XV with copies. Within twenty years of Bruce's return, the power of both papacy and monarchy would be broken in France by a revolution dizzy with so-called Enlightenment rhetoric employed to justify destroying traditional order. When in 1790 Bruce came to address publicly the subject of Enoch in his *Travels*, shortly after France's revolution began, he noted he'd only got so far as the first section before feeling repulsed by what he took as its superstitious, irrational, and, to him, risible legend. Its alleged prophetic origin he asserted as being of unorthodox "Gnostic" (ca. second century CE), *not* antediluvian, provenance. While apparently cloaking his dismissive attitude in the dress of Montagny's jest, he practically blocked translation possibilities by asserting a right in the matter. Putting Enoch's translation effectively in escrow, he perhaps repaid negative reactions to his efforts.

A century and a half before, when speculation about the existence, authority, and possible contents of Enoch was at its height in Europe, Enoch's arrival would have stirred a scholarly, and possibly popular, sensation, but the relatively new epistemological mood within the British establishment denied it such a reception. In the wake of revolution and Napoleon's rise, a solidifying orthodoxy that entailed repugnance for what was denigrated as "religious enthusiasm," coupled with a collective frowning upon what we might call creative, or in any way innovative theology, quickly relegated the book to purely antiquarian interest, which, it should be said, was nonetheless considerable among churchmen and gentry. Had it been possible to peruse Enoch in translation, there would have been noticeable interest in appropriate journals, such as *The Gentleman's Magazine*, as well as among scholars. A rationalist antiquarian himself, Bruce, however, did nothing to allay declivity of interest.

As Hessayon has observed, "by retaining two copies of Ethiopic Enoch for more than seventeen years he ensured that no one else in the British Isles other than Woide could complete a translation unless they too journeyed to Paris,"[20] where in 1800, Antoine Isaac, Baron Sylvestre de Sacy (1758–1838), France's leading Arabist and Persian scholar, would attempt to match parts of the Ge'ez manuscript with Syncellus's excerpts, a task left incomplete.

On June 4, 1788, Bruce presented his penultimate copy to Scottish divine, John Douglas (1721–1807), recently appointed bishop of Carlisle "as a token of his respect and Gratitude," urging him to place it "in any Collection at Oxford, he may think proper."[21] Thus it came to Oxford's Bodleian Library where it languished, untranslated, for a further thirty-three years.

Gems often go undiscovered and unlauded because, whilst in plain sight, they remain unseen; the blind lead the blind—or is it rather that such discoveries might prove troublesome to encrusted orthodoxies?

TWO

A Long Time Coming

*And Jared lived an hundred sixty and two years, and he
begat Enoch:*
*And Jared lived after he begat Enoch eight hundred years,
and begat sons and daughters:*
*And all the days of Jared were nine hundred sixty and two
years: and he died.*
And Enoch lived sixty and five years, and begat Methuselah:
*And Enoch walked with God after he begat Methuselah
three hundred years, and begat sons and daughters:*
*And all the days of Enoch were three hundred sixty and five
years:*
*And Enoch walked with God: and he was not; for God took
him.*

(GENESIS 5:18–24)

*And Enoch also, the seventh from Adam, prophesied of
these, saying, Behold, the Lord cometh with ten thousands of
his saints,*
*To execute judgment upon all, and to convince all that are
ungodly among them of all their ungodly deeds which they
have ungodly committed, and of all their hard speeches
which ungodly sinners have spoken against him.*

(JUDE VV. 14–15)

Educated at Bath grammar school, Wiltshire, Richard Laurence was twelve when James Bruce returned to England in 1773. Graduating B.A. from Corpus Christi College, Oxford, in 1782, Laurence was made doctor of canon law in 1794 and deputy professor to his distinguished brother, French Laurence, when the latter was appointed Regius Professor of Civil Law at Oxford in 1796. Before returning to Oxford himself, Richard Laurence served as Anglican minister to two Wiltshire parishes while further pursuing studies of theology and canon law. Subsequent acquisition of oriental languages led to Laurence's appointment as Regius Professor of Hebrew and canonship of Christ Church, Oxford, in 1814; he was fifty-four. Five years later, Laurence's translation from an Ethiopic manuscript of the Christian pseudepigraphical *Ascension of Isaiah* (generally dated to the second century CE) was published in Oxford and dedicated to prime minister and radical reform opponent, Lord Liverpool, the dedication placing Laurence firmly in the antiradical, high Anglican-conservative camp. In 1821, the university press printed Laurence's translation of *The Book of Enoch the Prophet: An Apocryphal Production, supposed to have been lost for ages; but discovered at the close of the last century in Abyssinia; now first translated from an Ethiopic Ms. in the Bodleian Library.*

As Laurence's Bampton Lectures of 1804 had shown dutiful dedication to the Anglican Church's Thirty-Nine Articles of belief—by demonstrating error in Calvinist and Unitarian understanding of them—it's no surprise that the first English translation of the Book of Enoch is described on its title page as an "apocryphal production." That meant that Enoch could not be used in formulating Christian doctrine; that is, in England at least, Enoch would not receive scriptural authority as it had in Abyssinia—there was to be no religious innovation. Nor was there any fanfare when university press agent and Oxford bookseller Joseph Parker, and Messrs. Rivington, booksellers to the Society for Promoting Christian Knowledge of 62 St. Paul's Church-Yard, London, published Laurence's translation.

Laurence's "Preliminary Dissertation" to his translation informs that this "apocryphal" book was "known until the eighth century of the Christian era; after which it seems to have sunk into complete obliv-

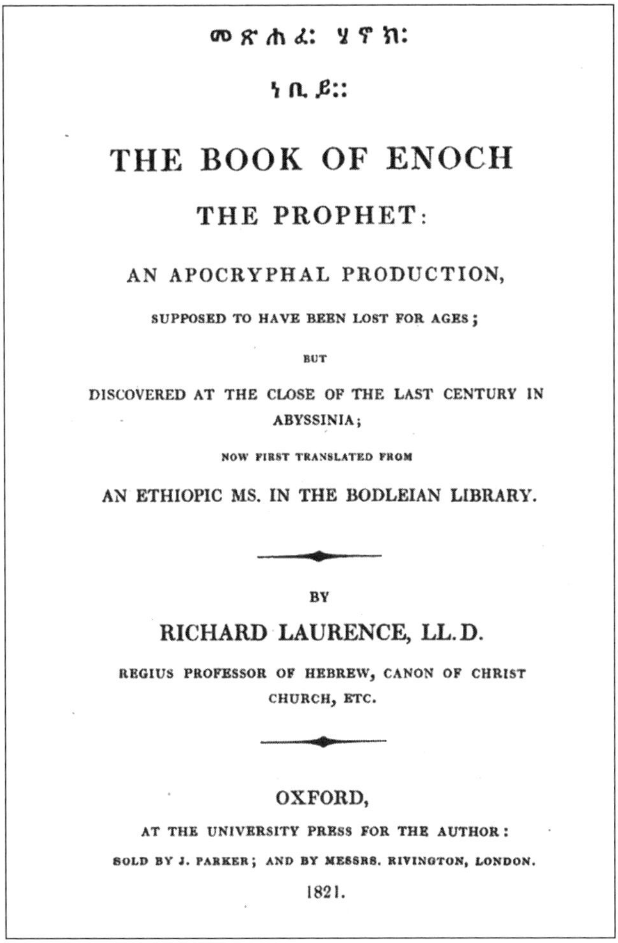

 መ ጽ ሐ ፈ: ሃ ፖ ክ:

ነ ቢ ይ::

THE BOOK OF ENOCH

THE PROPHET:

AN APOCRYPHAL PRODUCTION,

SUPPOSED TO HAVE BEEN LOST FOR AGES;

BUT

DISCOVERED AT THE CLOSE OF THE LAST CENTURY IN
ABYSSINIA;

NOW FIRST TRANSLATED FROM

AN ETHIOPIC MS. IN THE BODLEIAN LIBRARY.

———◆———

BY

RICHARD LAURENCE, LL.D.

REGIUS PROFESSOR OF HEBREW, CANON OF CHRIST
CHURCH, ETC.

———◆———

OXFORD,

AT THE UNIVERSITY PRESS FOR THE AUTHOR:

SOLD BY J. PARKER; AND BY MESSRS. RIVINGTON, LONDON.

1821.

Fig. 2.1. First edition of *The Book of Enoch the Prophet,*
translated by Rev. Richard Laurence.

ion."[1] He then relates how a "considerable fragment" of it was found by French Calvinist scholar Joseph Justus Scaliger (1540–1609) in the then unprinted *Chronographia* of George Syncellus (or Synkellos). Scaliger published Syncellus's extracts in his notes on Eusebius's Chronography and Canons. However, as Syncellus's extracts did not contain the highly significant passage from Enoch quoted uniquely as divine prophecy in the New Testament Epistle of Jude (vv.14–15), there was doubt as to whether Syncellus had in fact quoted from the same work as the apostle.

The subject caught the attention of some of the finest theologians and orientalists in Europe.

Laurence cited Hamburg Gymnasium theologian Professor Johannes Albertus Fabricius's *Codex Pseudepigraphus Veteris Testamenti*, 1:160–224, as the best account of authors, including church fathers (the study of whom is called "patristics"), who had alluded or quoted from the "celebrated apocryphal production" before it was lost. Notable patristic authors and works referring to Enoch's prophecy included Justin Martyr, Irenaeus, Tertullian, Clement of Alexandria, Origen, Hilary of Poitiers, Jerome, and the pseudepigraphical *Testaments of the Twelve Patriarchs*, all reproduced by Fabricius in either Greek or Latin. Their words were followed by Syncellus's copious quotations. Fabricius (1668–1736) also named and quoted from numerous relatively recent continental scholars who referred to Enoch, such as Joseph Scaliger, Guillaume Postel, Johann Heinrich Hottinger, Hugo Grotius, Joannes Ernestus Grabe, French priest Richard Simon, Bishop Brian Walton, and Hebraist Johannes Drusius. Fabricius also quoted from Job Ludolf's *Historia Aethiopica* (vol. 3, Frankfurt, 1681, 387) where Ludolf (1624–1704) related how, having been assured an Ethiopian manuscript of Enoch had arrived in Paris's Royal Library, brought from Egypt and purchased by astronomer and antiquary Nicolas-Claude Fabri de Peiresc (1580–1637), he rushed to inspect it, only to be disappointed by a manuscript of unrelated "fable and superstition."[2]

After referring to Enoch's importance to Jewish mystical and kabbalist works such as the celebrated thirteenth-century collection, the *Zohar* or "Book of Splendour," Fabricius gave a list of works by twenty chiefly seventeenth- and eighteenth-century theologians and orientalists who discussed Enoch. Among them, if we omit the scholars mentioned above, we find Jacques Boulduc, Johann Georg Dorsche, Johann Heinrich Heidegger, Johann Heinrich Hottinger, Pierre Jurieu, Athanasius Kircher, Peter Lambeck, Ioachim Johann Mader, August Pfeiffer, Jacob Friedrich Reimmann, Johann Andreas Schmidt, Scipione Sgambati, and Johannes Heinrich Ursinus.[3]

As Gabriele Boccaccini has observed, Laurence was as unaware of

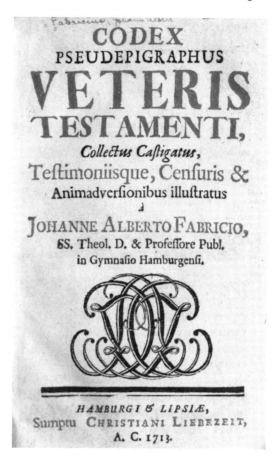

Fig. 2.2. *Codex Pseudepigraphus Veteris Testamenti*
by Johannes Albertus Fabricius,
Hamburg and Leipzig, Christiani Lieberzeit, 1713.

sixteen-year-old Daniele Manin's 1820 study of Enoch as Manin was apparently unaware of Bruce's Enoch manuscript.[4]

Young Manin, from a prominent Jewish-Italian family who'd converted to Christianity, was in Venice when he finished his *Degli Egregori*—concerning Enoch's Book of the Watchers section. Manin concluded the book was neither antediluvian nor written by Enoch, despite the early church having considered it scripture—that is, before revelation of its "lies."[5] Believing it written in apostolic times in Greek, Manin dismissed it as irrational, as had leading Italian liberal economist, philosopher, and historian Pietro Verri (1728–1797), after lunching with Bruce in Milan in March 1774.[6] Manin had no excuse for not mentioning Bruce and his manuscript since Bruce's Italian sojourn (1773–1774) was widely reported. However, as Boccaccini has shown, Bruce's reputation in Italy for overstartling statements and hot-headedness had sidelined him from serious consideration, while Bruce's gift to the pope remained buried in Antonelli's library until philologist Angelo Mai bought it for the Vatican Library around 1825 as an Ethiopian manuscript of "unknown origin"—too late for Manin's precocious research effort.[7]

Laurence considered that his own analysis of the Ethiopic text and comparison with the Syncellus fragments and other Greek and Latin citations, such as those in Irenaeus and Tertullian,* proved beyond doubt that a Greek version, from which Laurence deduced the Ethiopic was a translation, was essentially the same work employed by St. Jude when Jude quoted prophet Enoch in his canonical epistle, the details of which we shall duly examine.

What Laurence did *not* suspect was that a Greek version may have been different from the constituents of Enoch as originally composed. In the first 1821 English edition, Laurence treated the Book of Enoch as a single work from its inception. He would later alter his opinion—1 Enoch (there are two, much later "books of Enoch") is a collection of works written over two, perhaps three hundred years, with a majority of scholars currently accepting that all Enoch's components existed by the very early first century CE while the largest number of components existed before 100 BCE. Laurence also noted that the Ethiopic versions Bruce brought back did in fact differ between themselves in minor ways, such as passages being included under adjacent chapters, while the Bodleian Library manuscript lacked the short preface that opened the Paris manuscript.

---

*Irenaeus "directly alluded" to an embassy of Enoch to the angels, which is not in Syncellus (Irenaeus, *Opera*, ed. Grabe, 319). According to Laurence, Tertullian (*Opera*, ed. Paris, 1664, 87), makes a "direct and distinct quotation" from the Book of Enoch's chapter 97:7–8.[8]

As a pillar of the Church of England, Laurence was understandably quick to guard against any supposition that the work had ever held canonical authority, writing: "It seems to have been always enumerated among the apocryphal books of Scripture."[9] This statement is a little disingenuous, highlighted by the word *seems*. In fact, there *was* no universally agreed official canon of Christian scripture when Irenaeus was writing (ca. 180 CE). Certain works today's churches take as canonical were disputed over, most notably, the Gospel of John, among others including the "Revelation" ascribed to St. John the Divine. Furthermore, the meaning of the word *apocryphal* meant to theologians of Irenaeus's time a "secret" or "hidden" book for a cognoscenti, rather than, necessarily, or by definition, a work unsuitable for formulating doctrine, or lacking authority. It has also been conjectured that a work was apocryphal if its true origin and author was hidden. Tertullian did not see Enoch as apocryphal. As far as he was concerned, if St. Jude regarded Enoch's prophecy as valid—namely, inspired directly by God—Christians had no right to defer, regardless of the question of how antediluvian Enoch's work could have survived that very Flood the book itself prophesies. Indeed, the issue of tracing a work to its author by word of tradition, written or spoken, expressed in long usage, was the usual criterion of respect for scripture. Secret books (sometimes called "apocryphons") associated with gnostic groups for example, were dismissed by orthodox writers not only because their doctrines deviated from acknowledged gospels and apostolic epistles, but because despite claimed attributions to secret teachings uttered by Peter, Paul, Thomas, John, Philip, Mary, Judas, or Jesus himself, the works appeared to detractors as novel and untraceable in tradition. To orthodox eyes then, apocryphal works stood midway between authoritative scripture and rejected apocryphons and pseudepigraphical (false authorship) gospels.

Laurence does note that in Tertullian's work *On Idolatry*, Enoch's prophecy was ascribed to "providence of the Holy Spirit," though in his work *On Feminine Apparel*, Tertullian allowed Enoch was not acceptable to *everyone*; Jewish authorities did not admit it, a resistance often partially ascribed to its usefulness to Christians, which argument testifies implicitly to Enoch's acceptability to at least some

Christians. Jewish rejection of the work from *its* canon (when established) couldn't overcome, for Tertullian, the overriding, God-willed support of St. Jude.

Aware of the question's prickly nature, clergyman Laurence had to admit that neither Irenaeus nor Clement of Alexandria alluded to "its apocryphal character" but Laurence then cited church father Origen at the beginning of the third century whose *Contra Celsum* cast doubt on Enoch's divine inspiration, while Origen elsewhere ambiguously allowed that some, holding it sacred, might disagree (see pages 172–73). Laurence forewent to mention that fourth-century bishop Epiphanius of Salamis regarded Origen as a fount of Arian and other heresies!

Laurence correctly noted that Alexandria's bishop Athanasius, whose festal letter of 367 CE provided a synopsis of thirty-seven authoritative New Testament scriptures for Egyptian churches and monasteries, believed Enoch apocryphal, but Athanasius also spent much of his ecclesiastical career exiled because he opposed Arius, which is to say, there was still no definitive, universally binding canon for the whole church. Athanasius's position on the trinity only became official at the Council of Constantinople in 383, a decade after his death. Nailing down canon and orthodoxy became an issue when Roman emperors took direct interest in the church. Applying state law to these issues ensured Enoch could no longer occupy an ambiguous position; it was either in, or out. Whatever support it might have had by the fifth century failed to trump post-Athanasian doctrinal legalism. Thus we find church father Jerome (ca. 342 or ca. 347–420), who translated the Hebrew scriptures into Latin rather than from the commonly used Greek Septuagint, regarded Enoch as apocryphal. Laurence then jumped to the beginning of the *ninth* century when Enoch *was* definitely apocryphal to the church as a whole, according to Nicephorus, Patriarch of Constantinople's Catalogue. Outside the Roman and Byzantine pale, Ethiopia did not enter the reckoning.

Possibly troubled by ambiguity, Laurence shifted his position to whether *modern* (1821) scholarship could ever allow Tertullian's arguments, say, to gain the upper hand and overturn the judgment of over a millennium of ecclesiastical authority. He noted that Enoch's "allusions to the Lord, or rather to the Son of Man, exalted on his throne of glory and of judgment by the Ancient of Days, may demonstrate, that it was written after the *Book of Daniel*; but not, surely, that it was the production of Enoch before the flood."[10] Furthermore, Laurence argued that just because St. Jude found *one* quotation useful does not guarantee approval of the whole book. Likewise, Laurence argued, St. Paul's reference to several pagan poets in his letters does not mean the apostle recommended *all* their works for Christian digestion. Apart from the fact that St. Jude believed all true prophecy including Enoch's came *from God*, not opinion, what Laurence could not get to grips with was *why* St. Jude found in Enoch a familiar quotation to employ, and why he expected his audience to take it as decisive—and here Laurence had to face the question of where the book might have originated, and among which people.

Laurence believed the book's author—"if indeed it were the work of one and the same person" (pg. xx of Laurence's "Preliminary Dissertation")—was a Jew, following Scaliger who, on the basis of Syncellus's Greek extracts, deduced the Greek was translated from Hebrew. Laurence bolstered this view by reproducing several quotations from the mystical commentary on Genesis found in the *Zohar*, which, being also in Hebrew, supposed its references to a "book of Enoch" were also in that language. If nothing else, these quotations suggest something of Enoch's having enjoyed a hidden life within Jewish mystical circles beyond Christian usage, for the bulk of the *Zohar* collection—first printed as a whole in 1558—is generally accepted as part-authored and edited by thirteenth-century kabbalist sage Moses de León.

> "The holy and the blessed One," it is said, "raised him (Enoch) from the world to serve him, as it is written, *For God took him*. From that time a book was delivered down, which was called the Book of Enoch. In the hour that God took him, he shewed him all the repositories above; he shewed him the tree of life in the midst of the garden, its leaves and its branches. *We see all in his book*.
> (Sefer ha-Zohar 'al ha-Torah, vol. 1., *Parashah* p. 37, Mantua, 1559; Christ Church, Oxford, MA. 7.11.)

> We find in the Book of Enoch, that after the holy and blessed One had caused him to ascend, and shewed him all the repositories of the superior and inferior kingdom, he shewed him the tree of life, and the tree respecting which Adam had received a command; and he shewed him the habitation of Adam in the garden of Eden.
> (Sefer ha-Zohar 'al ha-Torah, vol. 2, *Parashah*, p. 55, Mantua, 1559.)

Laurence was right to link the references to the heavenly repositories or treasuries, and to the tree of life, to the Book of Enoch's chapters 16 to 37, with the tree of life appearing in chapter 31. This does not prove the *Zohar*'s compiler had access to the work translated by Laurence, but Laurence was prescient to surmise that Enoch's words available to the *Zohar* could have been written in Aramaic, the language Laurence most associated with kabbalist texts.[11]

Laurence posited an ingenious hypothesis to explain *where* it was written based on a text in Enoch's chapter 71 where the day and night hours are divided by a proportion of twelve to eighteen parts—equivalent to our sixteen to twenty-four. If we look, argued Laurence, for a country where a day of sixteen hours is likely, and allow for minor divisions after the vernal equinox, we find a location of approximately 45 degrees north latitude and no higher than 49 degrees north latitude where the longest day is sixteen hours, taking us to northern districts of the Caspian and Euxine seas. Laurence speculated that its "author" came from a tribe Assyrian King Shalmaneser V carried away and "placed in Halah and in Habor by the river Goshan, and in the cities of the Medes" (2 Kings 17:6) in the 720s BCE, who never returned from captivity. These place-names have been identified with Colchis and the Iberian kingdom—mostly modern Georgia, northeastern Turkey, and northern Armenia.

As to when it was written, Laurence had no doubt it was pre-Christian. Its contents demonstrated it could not have been written before the Babylonian exile of Jews (ca. 597–538 BCE) as chapters 83 to 90 provide a symbolic list of kings ("shepherds") from the first King Saul through to foreign monarchs from the period of Persian domi-

Fig. 2.3. *The Zohar*, Mantua, 1558 (Library of Congress).

nation to that of the Seleucids who followed Alexander the Great. There then follow symbolic references to the Maccabees who revolted against the Greek Seleucids to establish the Hasmonean dynasty, replaced finally by Herod the Great. Laurence reckoned Enoch to be a product of early in his reign, which began its uninterrupted course in 37 BCE. A reference in Enoch to Parthians also helped Laurence with dating, for he noted the Parthians were unknown to history before 250 BCE. Having invaded Syria in 41 BCE, they entered Jerusalem the following year and imposed Jewish Hasmonean Antigonus in place of John Hyrcanus against Herod—possibly alluded to in Enoch chapter 54—while in 36 BCE the Parthians drove Mark Antony's forces from Syria.

Laurence was in no doubt that this apocryphal work, while not in his judgment a rock for the faith, had its uses. Its heady descriptions of the "Son of Man" as being pre-existent, along with exciting and reassuring descriptions of the work of the "Messiah," "Elect One," and "Son of God," for Laurence gave an idea of Jewish expectations existent before Jesus. Opponent of sectarian or nonconformist faith, Laurence was happy to report that these references contradicted the views of Unitarians that no Jew, before Christian doctrines were construed, ever thought of the messiah as pre-existent. He even intuited from Enoch an implicit trinity of divine "lords" involved in creation.[12] He ended his dissertation with the thought that despite its mixing fable and invention, it was yet able to transport the reader "far beyond the flaming boundaries of the world,"[13] that is, it might offer a glimpse of eternity.

Published shortly before his death, Laurence's preface to his translation's third edition (Oxford, 1838, iii–iv), praised the Rev. Edward Murray's *Enoch Restitutus*, a work that attempted to "separate from the Books of Enoch the Book quoted by St. Jude." Murray's book seems to have been the first to divide Enoch formally into separate works, having coined titles for these works similar and sometimes identical to divisions familiar to scholars today, though it must be said Murray's insightful attempt has long been superseded.

Laurence's own view on whether the book might have been a collection rather than a unified work had undergone modification by the time his third edition was published in 1838. On page xx of the "Preliminary Dissertation" introducing the first 1821 edition he had only alluded to what for him at that time was a vague, rather questionable possibility that "different parts of the book itself might have been composed at different periods." Indeed, Laurence only made this suggestion to explain how it might have been that Johann Ernst Grabe (1666–1711), chaplain of Christ Church, Oxford, in his *Spicilegium SS. Patrum, ut*

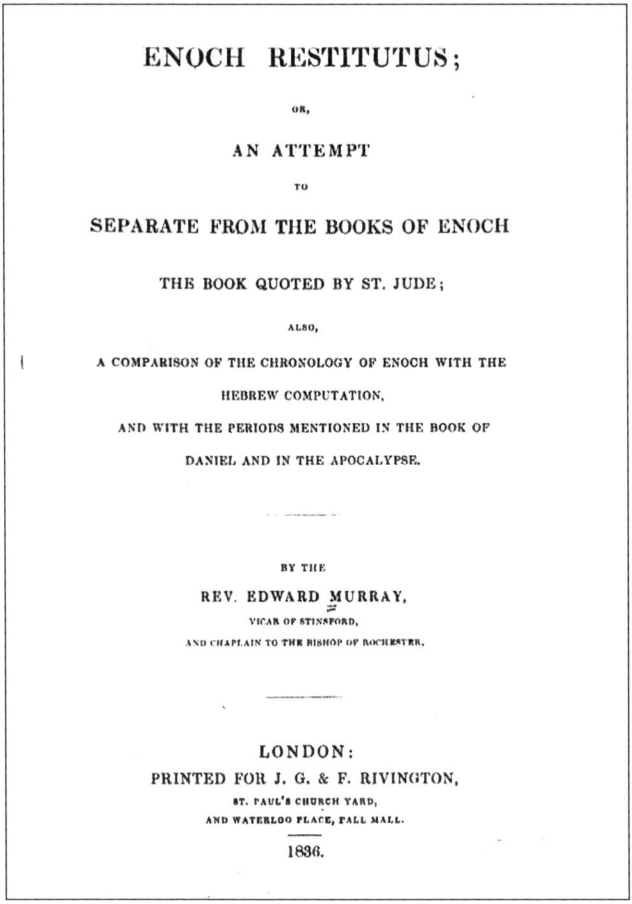

ENOCH RESTITUTUS;

OR,

AN ATTEMPT

TO

SEPARATE FROM THE BOOKS OF ENOCH

THE BOOK QUOTED BY ST. JUDE;

ALSO,

A COMPARISON OF THE CHRONOLOGY OF ENOCH WITH THE

HEBREW COMPUTATION,

AND WITH THE PERIODS MENTIONED IN THE BOOK OF

DANIEL AND IN THE APOCALYPSE.

BY THE

REV. EDWARD MURRAY,

VICAR OF STINSFORD,

AND CHAPLAIN TO THE BISHOP OF ROCHESTER.

LONDON:

PRINTED FOR J. G. & F. RIVINGTON,

ST. PAUL'S CHURCH YARD,

AND WATERLOO PLACE, PALL MALL.

1836.

Fig. 2.4. *Enoch Restitutus* by Rev. Edward Murray (London: Rivington, 1836).

et haerticorum conjectured that Hellenistic Jewish historian Eupolemus (ca. 158/7 BCE) quoted from Enoch in passages Eusebius took from Alexander Polyhistor (early first century BCE), that is, at a time long *before* Laurence reckoned the book first appeared, which he'd concluded was early in Herod the Great's reign.

In Laurence's third edition preface (Oxford, 1838, iii–iv) he reproduced the possibility of multiple elements with more conviction, allowing that parts of Enoch seemed to be different tracts on different subjects, and that a vision of the Flood was evidently attributed to Noah, not Enoch. This reservation, he wrote, had been amplified in his mind by Rev. Murray's *Enoch Restitutus*, which attempted to "separate from the Books of Enoch the Book quoted by St. Jude."

Fig. 2.5. Only known image of Archbishop Laurence, from a
small miniature taken "furtively" by a "lady of the family" when
in his seventy-fifth or seventy-sixth year; from *Poetical Remains
of French Laurence . . . and Richard Laurence*, Dublin, 1872.

Laurence called this book, by the bishop of Rochester's chaplain, a
"work of much conjectural ingenuity, and of considerable research" (at
pg. iv). Laurence also recognized the work on Enoch undertaken by
French orientalist Silvestre de Sacy and German orientalists Wilhelm
Gesenius and Andreas Gottlieb Hoffmann since his book's first
appearance.

Laurence insisted his translation was only a beginning,* and
while now too old to do more, he believed publication of an accurate

---

*Especially, Laurence maintained, as the Ethiopic manuscript was Oxford University
property, and he was not permitted to take it home, having to study it at the Bodleian
Library under constraints.

Ethiopic language version vital to further a study yet in its infancy. He also expressed disappointment that while Hoffmann had used his (Laurence's) book to introduce Germans to Enoch in German, it was still, in 1838, only Hoffmann's *intention*, not accomplishment—as Laurence had been led to believe—to undertake a scholarly version of the Ethiopic text. Laurence also noted that when Hoffmann's German translation had appeared in 1833, the savant imagined Laurence had withdrawn his edition from circulation due to ecclesiastical pressure, his having been archbishop of Cashel in Ireland since 1822!—such was Hoffmann's explanation for Laurence's work's scarcity in Germany. In fact, Laurence's translation was simply out of print in 1833, a circumstance encouraging the archbishop to arrange a second edition. Four years later, in 1837, Laurence heard a large order for more copies had been received from America. This led him to authorize the third, 1838, edition.

Richard Laurence, Archbishop of Cashel, died on December 28, 1838. Buried in Dublin's Christ Church cathedral vaults, Laurence deserves great credit for, as he put it, waking the Ge'ez manuscript from sleep on the shelves of Oxford's Bodleian Library.

THREE

1 Enoch

Let's familiarize ourselves with the book that assumed permanent residence in the Ethiopian Orthodox Tewahedo Church's canon at an unknown date after 330 CE, but which was certainly in place by the fifteenth century. A collection of five works, plus some relatively minor additions by different authors, the first composition may derive from as long ago as the fourth century BCE, while most specialists believe the latest work (the Parables or Similitudes of Enoch) appeared between the very late first century BCE and early first century CE.

After a brief five-chapter introduction, we enter the following books, listed here not in the order of the Ethiopic Enoch,[1] but in what is generally regarded as the order in which they first appeared.

> The Book of the Watchers (chapters 6–36; ca. 300 BCE or ca. 200 BCE)
> The Astronomical Book (chapters 72–82; after 300 BCE?)
> Dream Visions (chapters 83–90; after 200 BCE or after 164 BCE)
> The Epistle of Enoch (chapters 91–105; ca. 100 BCE?)
> The Similitudes or Parables of Enoch (chapters 37–71; first century BCE/CE?)[2]

Chapters 106–7 and chapter 108 are considered additions. The former is from a separate work on Noah, related thematically to Enoch's prophecy of the Flood as God's first judgment on the corruption that overtook his creation. Similar Noachic fragments are to be found apparently inserted into the Parables (chapters 54 to 55:2 and 60).

A Note on Translation

Before we summarize in the order above the Ethiopic Enoch, we need a note on translation.

Laurence's English translation was superseded, by dint of accuracy and access to alternative manuscripts, by Robert Henry Charles's translations of 1893 and 1912. Still the most widely disseminated—and stylish—English translations, we shall generally employ Charles's 1912 version. Scholars today, however, pay first call either to original language manuscripts (in Aramaic, Ge'ez, and Greek) or to more recent translations by George Nickelsburg (2001; Nickelsburg and VanderKam, 2012), Michael Knibb (1978), Ephraim Isaac (1983), or to Siegbert Uhlig's German translation of 1984. These have all benefited from ancient Aramaic fragments of Enochic books (excluding the Parables) found among the Dead Sea Scrolls in the 1950s, a Greek version, and fresh Ethiopian disclosures, such as Lake Tana Manuscript 9 (fifteenth century).

Enrichment of textual sources does carry limitations, however. As Mirjam Judith Bokhorst and Elena Dugan have noted in recent papers, assumptions about an "original text" can frustrate attempted reconstructions of fragmentary and variant sources.*

Regarding philological restoration of tiny fragments, Elena Dugan sees poor methodology in assuming a fragment indicates presence of a known text (perhaps in another language). *Absence* may ultimately tell more than assumed presence; textual history may be more involved than we think.

---

*Mirjam Judith Bokhorst (Martin Luther University Halle-Wittenberg, Germany) "Opportunities and Limitations of a Synoptic Approach in Editing and Translating, Exemplified by 1 Enoch 22"; and Elena Dugan (Phillips Academy–Andover, Massachusetts) "New Philology and the Discovery of New Works: Enoch in the First-Century CE." Both papers were delivered at the Enoch Seminar Webinar, June 26, 2023.

Assessing past editing and translation of 1 Enoch, Mirjam Judith Bokhorst examined translations that represent an eclectic hybrid text, from variant sources, but that historically never existed in one of the source languages. Examples include Nickelsburg and Uhlig's translations. Seeing methodological inadequacies in the hybrid text, Bokhorst notes how Nickelsburg, for example, while using the Greek of Codex Panopolitanus, chose to change the Greek for "circles" in 1 Enoch 22:8 to the more widely extant (in Ge'ez) "hollow places," while also relying on Ethiopic Group 2 manuscripts when an Aramaic fragment was unclear. Isaac and Knibb's translations were, Bokhorst asserts, almost arbitrarily based on one textual witness, either because it closely approximated a postulated final text or offered a perceived trustworthy text for criticism. Finding these methods unequal to accommodating all textual evidence, Bokhorst sees greater historical value in a synoptic approach, with variants placed side by side. However, she recognized that Ethiopian churches and monasteries hold more than a hundred Enoch manuscripts, so a synoptic approach would be impractical in their case.

The simple fact is that there *is* no universally valid translation reflecting an "oldest version." Being already a collection of Enochic sources edited over many years, our oldest Ethiopic Enoch comes from the fifteenth century, and we don't know when its constituents arrived at that stage, only that sections have been found in considerably older manuscripts.

Glaring weaknesses in R. H. Charles's translation I shall highlight, while employing Nickelsburg's translation where it affords significant information.

Introduction (chapters 1–5)

The first five chapters of 1 Enoch were most likely written after 200 BCE. They introduce the main theme of Enochic narratives: the commission given Enoch by God to announce salvation of "the elect" through a cataclysmic intervention in which "the eternal God will tread upon the earth" (1:4)—whether treading figuratively or actually is unclear.* Certainly, the world will shake, and quake, and this "day of tribulation" will generate great fear, especially among the "Watchers." Crucial to the Enochian *weltanschauung*, these beings are understood in Enochic texts as angels whose consequential evil is their barbed offering to humanity.

It is presumed readers know something about Enoch already.† Announced here only as a "righteous man, whose eyes were opened by God" to whom the angels had shown the "vision of the Holy One in the heavens," it may be the case that readers already knew Genesis 5's brief account of Enoch where he appears in the Sethite genealogy of antediluvian patriarchs. That account places Enoch seventh in the generations from Adam, and because Enoch "walked with God," "God took him" (5:24). Enochic writings understand this remarkable phrase as indicating Enoch did not die. For being incorruptibly righteous and intimate with God's will, he was permitted ascent to heaven while alive, a privilege allowing him to play an extraordinary role in the salvation of the righteous, and the wicked's final punishment and destruction, for Enoch is uniquely at liberty to explore the heavens and their inner workings, to see causative relations to earthly processes, and to communicate what he has seen. If human beings on earth with their limited perception suffer vexation through not understanding what is happening to them, leading them to doubt whether the judge of all the earth will do right, Enoch *does* understand. He can "tell it like it is."

Genesis is usually thought to have been compiled from much older material, edited and reworked during the sixth century BCE, perhaps during the forced exile of leading Judean families to Babylon, or at some stage after the official return of survivors and progeny around 538 BCE. It is possible the first Enochic text was not reliant on Genesis, or at least the version familiar to us; Enoch may represent

---

*Nickelsburg has "and the eternal God will tread from thence on Mount Sinai [having 'come forth from his dwelling']." Nickelsburg, *1 Enoch 1*, 142.
†The name in Hebrew may be transliterated Hh N Kh, pronounced *Chanokh* (soft *ch*, like lo*ch*, possibly from the root *hanak*: to train, dedicate, devote, or initiate. The meaning may then be "dedicated."

an independent tradition. Enochic texts may even have been consulted and possibly censored in a late stage of constructing, or restructuring Genesis, or it may be that Genesis and the first Enochic text enjoyed common source material. As Genesis 5 and 6 now stand, it should not be presumed that the earliest Enochic text, the Book of the Watchers, was intended as an interpretation or expansion of Genesis narratives, though the balance of views favors the idea that Genesis preceded the Book of the Watchers, while its root mythos perhaps existed already. One thing is clear: there was no "canon" of Jewish religious writings when Genesis was compiled. In the world of Second Temple or pluralistic "Middle" Judaism (between the return from Babylonian exile and the destruction of Herod's temple in 70 CE), different Jewish parties favored certain texts and interpretations over others, as circumstances and convictions dictated.

A key qualification of Enoch's purpose appears in what is now the introductory chapter to the collection: "from them [angels in heaven] I heard everything, and from them I understood as I saw, but not for this generation, but for a remote one which is for to come" (1:2). This important caveat places the Enochic message not in antediluvian times purely—though the Flood is seen typically as the *first act* and *type* for God's final judgment against evil—but in the period of apocalyptic prophecies. Apocalyptic revelations may be considered symptomatic of a long crisis of faith, and faith in wisdom, that apparently gripped at least a portion of the sages of Israel, especially after Near Eastern governance fell largely to Greek generals and confederates who inherited the empire won by their late commander, Alexander the Great, who died in Babylon in 323 BCE.

While return from exile in Babylon in 538 BCE had been prophesied as a glorious event, a holy exodus from captivity, sanctified as a direct act of divine salvation to usher in a golden age, evidence indicates the ensuing two centuries saw internal divisions and humiliations amid an Israel fragmented and alienated from its glory days, dominated by Persian satraps who exploited divisions and taxed the people, while desultory attempts to rebuild Jerusalem's temple aroused controversy. Still, there was some familiar continuity while Persia predominated. Collapse of Persian control in Judea, Samaria, and Syria after Alexander of Macedon's conquests added further frustrations, with Palestine ruled by the Greek Ptolemies from Egypt, until Antiochus III "the Great" defeated Ptolemy V's army in 200–198 BCE. Antiochus's successor Antiochus IV "Epiphanes," angered by opposition to his appointing Hellenizer Menelaus as high priest in Jerusalem, banned the Jewish religion outright. Installing an image of Zeus in the temple, and sacrificing a pig before an image of Moses, Antiochus insisted priests eat swine. A bloody revolt led by Judas Maccabeus ("the Hammer") restored the temple but initiated further long-term partisan conflict.

Into this maelstrom of acute challenge to the national faith—"*Will not the Judge of all the earth do right?*" (as Abraham asked God, or himself, in Genesis 18:25)—came a ringing voice of comfort, at least to the suffering righteous. While most people today see an apocalypse as something awful, the word properly means salvific information "out of hiding," namely, God's primordial plan for Israel and all creation. If *men* couldn't discern the wood of salvation from the trees of crisis, poverty, violence, and fear, then divinely inspired prophets could. Prophecies of Isaiah, Jeremiah, Ezekiel, and others were scoured for clues as to God's itinerary, and new prophecies emerged with the emphasis on prediction. The Book of Daniel with all its seductive quasi-historical symbolism was likely composed during the Maccabean revolt. Its contents relate to important elements of Enochic composition, which appear as remarkable fruit of the need to know why justice seemed remote and hope in hope so tortuously trying.

Enoch is privy to the tablets of God's will, inscribed in heaven. The Enochic message is that God planned before time all that has, and will, come to pass, and, if one interprets all aright, the end-time of corrupted creation is close: God will intervene and finally extinguish evil. All that is asked of the believer is to choose righteousness. Hidden from the world with the secrets in heaven, righteous Enoch had communicated to select progeny eventual fulfillment of God's will. That communication was revealed in book form to reassure sufferers of creation's unfolding finale.

Chapter 1 paints a rosy picture for the righteous, the "elect." While everything on earth will perish, the righteous will be protected: "light shall appear unto them and he will make peace with them" (1:8). The next verse is exactly that to appear in the Epistle of Jude, arguably written in the 50s or 60s CE, and quite possibly the sole work left by Jesus's brother Juda (Greek: *Ioudas* or "Judas").

And behold! He cometh with ten thousands of His holy ones
To execute judgment upon all,
And to destroy all the ungodly:
And to convict all flesh
Of all the works which they have ungodly committed,
And of all the hard things which ungodly sinners have spoken
against Him. (1 Enoch 1:9)

Different in style, chapters 2–5 begin like a panegyric on Nature's wonders as expressions of divine wisdom. Hearers are encouraged to observe the regularity of the stars and planetary orbits, the steady courses of rivers, the dependability of the seasons, the renewal of growth in springtime, and the fruit to come. Nothing in nature deviates from God's commandments. It sounds like a classic wisdom text—nature follows its interior laws—but then cometh the punch! Such obedience to God's express wisdom as is natural to the natural world is absent in men, rebels against God's order, giving themselves over to hardness, avarice, and violence. While the wicked will suffer curses, the righteous will know mercy, forgiveness, peace, forbearance, light, wisdom, and eternal gladness, for they shall "all live and never again sin," and will not die from God's wrath, but their "joy shall be multiplied" (5:9).

The Book of the Watchers

For man-of-reason James Bruce, the Book of the Watchers' account of angels descending to earth appeared both absurd and repulsive, disinclining him to penetrate further into the book he at first tried to reveal to the wider world. Perceptions change. Today, many persons inured to the von Dänikenesque speculation of aliens, mythologized as gods to our ancestors, coming with dangerous knowledge from other worlds in early human history, may see the Book of the Watchers as myth encoding some folk-memory of far distant extraterrestrial-cum-terrestrial events. It is, however, uncertain whether the writer or writers of the book intended the account—which may very well be a twist on earlier, possibly Babylonian, myths—to be seen as literal history. It resonates more as visionary, symbolic history: a pictorial parable to shed light on an underlying truth about the human condition in terms picturable, albeit alarming, to ordinary intelligence, but perhaps with an inner, privileged meaning for those able to see it. A problem here is that we do not know who the intended audience of the Watchers myth was. Was it open to anybody, or was its status that of esoteric text for a cognoscenti, to be treated with reserve, not bandied about in uninitiated circles? I personally favor this latter view, especially given its rarity as a quotation source in the Second Temple period, and proximity to religious "party" texts among the Dead Sea Scrolls.

In 1977, scholar and co-translator of 1 Enoch George W. E. Nickelsburg dated the myth around rebel angel Shemihazah (variantly spelt "Semjaza," "Semiazaz" or "Semyay") to the early Hellenistic period: a response to the turmoil of the Diadochoi (Alexander the Great's successors), the lustful angels even parodying Greek leaders' claim to divine parentage. John J. Collins (Yale University) was skeptical of trying to read history from the text, believing it open to multiple interpretations. David W. Suter (St Martin's University, Washington) has suggested the myths reflected anxiety about the impurity of Levite priests, as highlighted in Second Temple Jewish texts, the Testament of Levi, and the Damascus Document. Most scholars see the myth as pre-Daniel (before 164 BCE).[3]

The Book of the Watchers reveals how corrupting evil came to flourish in God's creation. It declares what God has done, and would do, about it. Such appears the book's prime intention. Evil's source and humanity's ultimate destiny, good and bad, relate to a world beyond. How do we know? *Enoch* knows, because he "walked with

God" and communicated his knowledge to the righteous: evil will be defeated in time, while in time, even evil has its uses, paradoxical though it appears.

Something else comes over clearly from the start of the narrative. The writer sees with penetrating, almost overwhelming vividness the sheer power of erotic attraction to feminine beauty, strong enough even to alter the balance of a created order, and to deviate from its path even an eternal being. Untrammelled lust means disorder.

Opening with the statement that human beings have multiplied, it becomes increasingly apparent to angels watching from above that human daughters are startlingly beautiful, magnetically attractive, indeed so arousing to "angels, the children of the heaven," that they experience a kind of frenzy. Beside themselves with passion, they "saw and lusted after them" (6:1). Thus, intense tremors of sexual curiosity in heaven set the ball rolling—downward.

In her recent article, Rivka Nir of Israel's Open University has emphasized that the rebel angels of the Book of the Watchers bring *desire* to humans. Normal procreation ceases with the angels' descent to earth. Knowing about sexual pleasure, they corrupt humans with knowledge of cosmetics and jewelry that tempt men, while the angels' lust generates "giants." As Nir points out: "Sexual knowledge resides in heaven."*

---

*Rivka Nir, "Sexual Desire in the Book of the Watchers (1 Enoch 6–36) and the New Testament Exhortation to Sexual Abstinence" (2021), discussed at the Enoch Seminar Webinar, June 28, 2023. Nir thinks the letter to the Colossians 3:5–6 (generally attributed to St. Paul) alludes to the myth of the fallen angels: "Mortify therefore your [physical] members which are upon the earth; fornication, uncleanness, inordinate affection, evil concupiscence, and covetousness, which is idolatry: For which things' sake the wrath of God cometh on the children of disobedience." She also believes the Book of the Watchers explains both Christian revulsion at fornication, and the idea of Christians becoming angels, or like angels, to dwell in heaven, as expressed in Luke 20:34–36: "The children of this world marry, and are given in marriage: But they which shall be accounted worthy to obtain that world, and the resurrection from the dead, neither marry, nor are given in marriage: Neither can they die any more: for they are equal unto the angels; and are the children of God, being the children of the resurrection." This doctrine is still problematic for Christians and others.

Shemihazah, leader of the besotted angels, urges his fellows to choose wives and beget children from the beautiful women of earth, concerned only that he'll carry sole blame and suffer solitary judgment for it. He needn't have worried: so excited are his two hundred confederates and their leaders that they promise a mutual pact to prosecute the plan together. Descending en masse to snow capped Mount Hermon—on what is now the Israeli-Lebanese border—they swear, with mutual curses for pact-breakers, which fact, the narrative says, explains the mountain's name. Under chief Semiazaz—a change of spelling (spellings of the angels vary in Bruce's Bodleian Library copy)—the names of the guilty "chiefs of tens'" may be transliterated as Arakiba, Rame'el, Kokabi'el, Tami'el, Rami'el, Dan'el, Ezeqe'el, Baraqijal, Asa'el, Armaros, Batar'el, Anan'el, Zaqi'el, Samsape'el, Satar'el, Tur'el, Jomja'el, Sari'el (it will be noted that a name is missing from the Bodleian manuscript).*

Having had their way with human women, the angels bring knowledge properly left in heaven. They teach charms and enchantments, cosmetics and chemistry, cutting of roots and poisonous uses of plants and, as a result of transgressive miscegenation, the women give birth to giants thousands of feet high. The giants take everything men give them, and when there's no more, they eat human beings and vent their wrath on every kind of living thing, cannibalizing even each other.

While "the earth laid accusations against the lawless ones" (7:6) Azaz'el (a variant of Asa'el) sows the seeds of warfare on earth by teaching men how to make swords, knives, shields, and breastplates. Familiarizing them with the metals of the earth, and their working, Azaz'el introduces vanities for women with mascara, bracelets, jewelry, antimony, and coloring tinctures (the basis of alchemy). The effect on humans is to lead them thoroughly astray with fornication, corruption, and godlessness. While Shemihazah teaches enchantments or magic,

---

*Derived from Aramaic, the names mean, starting with Shemihazah in the order given above: "My Name has seen"; "The earth is power"; "Burning heat of God"; "Star of God"; *Tamiel* is unknown; "Thunder of God"; "Judge of God"; "Lightning-flash of God"; "Lightning of God"; "God has made"; "of Hermon"; "Rain of God"; "Cloud of God"; "Winter of God"; "Sun of God"; "Moon of God"; "Mountain of God"; "Day of God"; "God will guide."[4] You would not surmise their villainy from their names.

Baraqijal imparts astrology; Kokabel, astronomy; Ezeqe'el, cloud-lore; Araq'el, the signs of the earth; Shamsi'el, the signs of the sun; and Sari'el, the course of the moon. And the cries of men for help rise to heaven (10:4).

Hearing the plea, "holy ones" Michael, Uriel, Raphael, and Gabriel intercede with the "Lord of lords, God of gods, King of kings" (9:3) over the disaster on earth. The good angels speak to the "God of the ages," acknowledging that he made all things and sees all things, and therefore knows what Azaz'el and Shemihazah have done, revealing the "eternal secrets" preserved in heaven to those unfit for them (9:6).

The Most High sends Uriel to deliver a message to Noah that he hide himself: a deluge is coming to destroy the earth. Raphael is ordered to bind Azaz'el, make a chasm in the desert and cast him into it, covered with jagged rocks, that he abide in darkness there "for ever and ever" (10:5). On the "day of the great judgment," he will be cast into fire. Raphael is charged with healing the earth "that all the children of men may not perish through all the secret things that the Watchers have taught their sons" (10:7). There follows a crucial passage: "And the whole earth has been corrupted through the works that were taught by Azaz'el: *to him ascribe all sin*" (10:8; my italics). This could mean that sin entered the world only through the Watchers, for the text has nothing to say about Adam and Eve's sin, nor Cain's against brother Abel, as Genesis relates.

Readers will notice we've moved from leader Shemihazah to leader Azaz'el. Scholar Kim Papaioannou, from Cyprus, has looked into what are plainly different traditions regarding fallen angels, combined in 1 Enoch.* In chapter 6, Azaz'el is secondary to "Semyay" (as Papaioannou prefers), the one who looked down from heaven to experience sexual attraction, whereas from chapter 7 the leader is Azaz'el, a name that will dominate Watchers discourse in other Enochic texts, as well as appearing in Leviticus 16:8 as one of two male scapegoats in the Jewish Atonement ritual. Azaz'el's role imparting corrupting knowledge is not so clearly sex motivated as Shemihazah's, who brings defilement to earth. After Enoch is asked to announce judgment on the Watchers,

---

*See Papaioannou's article "The Sin of the Angels in 2 Peter 2:4 and Jude 6," *Journal of Biblical Literature* 140, no. 2 (2021): 391–408.

Azaz'el receives a separate sentence for injustice and sin, being cast into a desert pit until final judgment. Papaioannou concludes it's clear that different fallen angel narratives existed in Jewish tradition, being pivotal to the degeneration of the antediluvian state. Two angelic chief stories were conflated and integrated in a single work.

Returning to our 1 Enoch, Gabriel disposes of the Watchers' giant offspring by making them war on one another. Instead of the "eternal life" hoped for, their span is limited to five hundred years. Michael is commanded to bind Shemihazah and his associates, compelling them to see their unclean misbegotten sons destroy one another, after which they'll be bound fast in the earth's depths for seventy generations till the "day of their judgment" (10:12), then hurled into the "abyss of fire," in which tormenting prison they'll be forever confined (for angels exist eternally). Anyone condemned will be bound with them always, and all evil works will end so that "the plant of righteousness and truth" will appear, and the days of the righteous and their abundant progeny shall be completed in peace (10:16).

It takes till chapter 12 before Enoch appears in the Book of the Watchers, and one senses that we're getting a retelling, a variant scheme of events—this time with Enoch—of what we've seen already. We're told he's been hidden, his business to do with the Watchers and the "holy ones" (12:1). These are the good Watchers, and they tell him to go to the Watchers who've left heaven and "defiled themselves with women" (12:4) and tell them that because of the destruction they've wrought upon the earth, they shall "have no peace or forgiveness of sin" (12:5). Enoch announces this to Azaz'el, then to all the others, and they're mighty scared. They beseech "scribe of righteousness" Enoch to write their petition and deliver it to the Lord, for they're too ashamed to raise their eyes heavenward. They desire forgiveness and a reprieve from punishment.

Enoch pens the petition before departure for Dan, a little southwest of Mount Hermon. The setting of Dan for this scene will gain in significance as our story progresses. A deep cleft in the rock, close to the Damascus Road, was thought to be the gushing spring of the holy river Jordan. Sitting down by the "waters of Dan," Enoch reads the petition again, but falls asleep, whereupon he dreams a dream that sore judgment awaits the "sons of heaven." This he announces when he finds them weeping at "Abellsjail" between Lebanon and Seleser. He tells them of the vision experienced while asleep, that he ascended to heaven, summoned by clouds and enveloped in a rising mist, and found a wall of crystals with tongues of fire. He entered the fire and came to a crystal house, with a ceiling of stars and fiery cherubim between lightnings and a heaven as clear as water. He entered a second house with floor and ceiling of fire, and lightnings and cherubim of indescribable magnificence. In the midst was a throne, like crystal, with wheels like the shining sun. Streams of blinding fire came from beneath it. The "Great Glory" was seated in raiment brighter than any sun and whiter than any snow (14:20). Enoch is prostrate, eyes cast down, but the Lord calls him, approvingly, and tells him he should tell the Watchers that it's their job to intercede for men, not men to intercede for them. Having been holy, spiritual, and "living the eternal life" (15:6) they are now defiled with women, and the blood of flesh, lust for which has forfeited them their high privileges. Crucially, the Lord informs Enoch that whereas the giants were born of a mix of spirits and flesh, destruction of bodies will leave them evil spirits on earth, afflicting humankind, hating them. It was spirits consorting with flesh that brought about this abject role. The spirit belongs to heaven; only evil spirits are bound to earth. When the judgment comes in fullness of time, these evil spirits will share final fate with the sinful Watchers and the godless.

Enoch's final message to the Watchers must be: "You shall have no peace" (16:4).* This characteristic phrase appears elsewhere in Enoch with regard to *all* people condemned by righteous judgment, which might suggest a primary parabolic intention behind the story, either at inception or in its development over time.

• • •

---

*Is this perhaps a root idea and context behind these words of Matthew's gospel (10:34–36) attributed to Jesus? "Do not think that I have come to bring peace to the earth; I have not come to bring peace, but a sword. For I have come to set a man against his father, and a daughter against her mother, and a daughter-in-law against her mother-in-law; and one's foes will be members of one's own household."

Chapters 17–19 constitute a truly amazing tour of the infinitudes shown Enoch by angels acting as guides: stunning landscapes, seascapes, fire-scapes, to all the "treasuries" from which the powers of nature draw energy and movement, to the causes of winds and seas and mountains, the cornerstone of the earth, the "pillars of heaven" described as winds. Wind seems to symbolize invisible energies that hold and link all in their order. At times we cannot tell whether we are in the farthermost regions of the unseen earth or in heavenly mansions: the two are integrated, the lower world drawing on the providential energies of the higher. The language is rich, visionary, evocative, and also specific, sparkling, elemental, and transcending of ordinary imaginings. Seeing "stars like seven burning mountains" Enoch's hosts tell him the "horrible place" he sees about him is the end of heaven and earth, lifeless, a place become a prison "for the stars and the host of heaven" who have failed to come forth at their appointed times; they are bound for ten thousand years until their guilt has expired (18:13–16). Uriel tells Enoch that the transgressive Watchers will "stand" there until the final judgment: all those who have taught men to sacrifice to demons as though they were gods (implying the godless "pagans" of the nations), while the defiled women "shall become sirens." "And I, Enoch, alone saw the vision, the ends of all things: and no man shall see as I have seen" (19:2–3). Here are the ancient roots of Dante's *Inferno* and *Purgatorio*.

Enoch is next taken west where an extraordinarily high, hard rock mountain towers, and within which plunge four hollow chasms, deep and dark. Raphael explains their depth is purposed to accommodate all souls of the human dead: an underworld holding place until the appointed day of judgment (22:1-3). Enoch hears the voices of the dead pleading their case, and in particular the voice of Abel, begging a judgment against the seed of Cain, that it be obliterated from among men forever. There are separated chasms to divide the righteous from sinners. For a time it is true the righteous must live in proximity to the sinners, but in the end the righteous will not be slain. Hearing this, Enoch blesses the "Lord of righteousness," that is: the Judge of all the earth is shown to do right, even when the world cannot see it (22: 8–14).

Enoch is then shown a flowing current of burning fire linked to the lights of heaven, and afterward seven mountains of arresting mineral luminescence. The seventh, bounded with trees, is like a throne, and by it a tree of fragrance unparalleled, and fruit uneaten—a tree like a palm but like no other. What is it? Michael tells Enoch this is the throne on which the "Holy Great One" will sit to judge "when He shall come down to visit the earth with goodness" (25:3). The fruit of the tree is reserved for the holy and righteous: "food to the elect: it shall be transplanted to the holy place, to the temple of the Lord, the Eternal King" (25:5). The fragrance will enter the marrow of their being, and they will live long lives on earth, like Enoch's ancestors, and nought evil will touch them. Enoch again blesses the God who has promised to give such bounties.

"Yea, I travelled very much," says Enoch, having been taken from mountain, to ravine, to underground streams, beneath the mountains, and farther and farther, among great rocks, bare and massive. In one part are trees in abundance, in another, austere rock. Uriel informs Enoch that the bare place is "accursed" for all those who blaspheme the Lord or declare of God's glory "hard things" (27:2). Here in the valley, bleak and bare will the righteous witness their judgment, as the merciful bless the Lord of Glory, Eternal King. These things Enoch sees in the west; in the east he is shown a mountain range in a desert, and then a place fed by water from above, with aromatic trees fragrant with frankincense and myrrh. He travels to another valley, full of water and cinnamon, then to groves of trees producing nectar: sarara and galbanum. Other trees are full of stacte like almond trees, which, when burnt, issues a surpassing fragrance. Then farther east, over mountains to the Erythraean Sea (Gulf of Aden to Horn of Africa), then flying over mountain summits of pepper and cinnamon, over the angel Zoti'el to the "Garden of Righteousness" containing the great tree of wisdom whose fruit is wisdom to the wise. Raphael tells Enoch this is the tree from which his ancestors Adam and Eve "learnt wisdom and their eyes were opened, and they knew that they were naked and they were driven out of the garden" (22:6). This telling is notable for its positive view of the fruit, not as agent of catastrophe, but of enlightenment. That they were driven out seems almost an afterthought!

He then travels to the ends of the earth, seeing manifold kinds of wildlife, to where the heavens are supported and the portal to heaven opens. Seeing how the stars "come forth" he records the astronomical phenomena and their measurement. Uriel helps with inscribing the information about the heavenly bodies' courses, laws, and governing beings (23:4).

In the north he is shown three heavenly portals whence derive winds, hail, and tempests. One portal is for good, the others blow ill winds and damage and destruction. Rain and dew issue from portals in the south, at the ends of the earth—at which point, the Book of the Watchers is curtailed.

The Astronomical Book

The next component of the Ethiopic Book of Enoch is generally held to be the Astronomical Book (chapters 72–82), and had it held to this order, the book would follow logically, for the Book of the Watchers ends with Enoch and Uriel committing meteorological and astronomical science to writing. Chapter 72 announces what follows plainly as "The Book of the courses of the luminaries of heaven," and it is apparent that the book was intended to be seen as one composed from Enoch and Uriel's writings. According to Klaus Koch (Hamburg University), the work depends on the Akkadian *MUL.APIN*, the Babylonian astronomical text considered composed around 1000 BCE, with latest copies dated ca. 300 BCE. Koch also sees in the Enoch figure borrowings from the "tradition around Emmeduranki."[5] Emmeduranki was seventh on Sumer's king list (as Jude 14 described Enoch as "seventh from Adam"). As "En-men-dur-ana," pre-Sumerians saw him as ancestor from whom priests of the sun god should be descended. Assumed to heaven, like Enoch, Emmeduranki was king of Sippar, a city associated with solar worship.

The account of laws governing the astronomical realm in 1 Enoch begins with the sun. Its settings and rising at different times are detailed. The phases of the moon follow (chapter 73), and it is important to note this order, for as we shall see, those to whom the work was most dear held to a solar calendar as opposed to the lunar calendar of adversaries in Jerusalem (see 74:12 where the lunar year is criticized). Both Greeks and Babylonians used calendars based primarily on lunar phases; Egyptians used a solar calendar of 365 days with three 120-day seasons, followed by an intercalary period of five days. In this context we might also observe that Enoch's age in Genesis is said to be 365 years, the number of days in the solar year,* which plots the year according to the sun's relation to the stars, not from the phases of the moon (twelve full lunar cycles making 354 days).

Chapter 76 gives us Enoch's vision of twelve portals at the ends of the earth through which winds blow to the four quarters. Four of the portals bring winds seen as a blessing; the other eight bring harmful winds with drought, locusts, and desolation in their trail. The good gifts include dew, fruitfulness, and prosperity. Chapter 77 details the distribution of rivers and seas upon the earth, while the following chapter describes the names and properties of sun and moon, which are considered alike in circumference, as would seem natural to the observer on Earth observing the moon's waxing and waning.

Chapter 79 begins with the words: "And now, my son . . ." which suggests it might have come from another text where Enoch addresses son Methuselah. However, Enoch in verse 6 describes *his* teacher as Uriel, archangel and chief of the luminaries, and it may be Uriel who is addressing Enoch as "my son" (see also 81:1).

Chapter 80 again seems like an addition, for while it is linked thematically, the emphasis is now on the perversion of the natural courses for which men's sins are responsible. "And all things on the earth shall alter" (80:2). This might be music to the ear of the climatologist today who attributes climate change to human error, but it would be a rum

---

*1 Enoch gives the solar year as 364 days. This is because it divides the year into four seasons of exactly thirteen weeks: two months of thirty days, followed by one month of thirty-one to mark the season's end (making four intercalary days per year). The objection that after twenty-five years the calendar would have a season coming a month early can be rectified by intercalation: adding an extra week every seventh year (in the manner of a sabbatical or rest), and adding a week every fourth group of seven years, that is, every twenty-eighth year.

thing if our scientists attributed such alterations to fornication, blasphemy, and idolatry rather than excessive use of fossil fuels and the like. At least industry would be relieved, as its executives sought alternative means of relief! Enoch envisions crop failure, drought, the moon's phases disrupted, excessive sunlight, errors in astronomical observation, and—with increase in evil—punishment so "as to destroy all" (80:8).

"And he said unto me: 'Observe, Enoch, these heavenly tablets, And read what is written thereon, And mark every individual fact.'" So opens chapter 81, penultimate chapter of the Astronomical Book. Enoch marks the tablets' contents well, and finds in them all mankind's deeds, and all deeds yet to be done. The destiny of the world is prewritten; God knows all that will occur. Heaven will never know the anxiety of not knowing the outcome of events. No wonder heaven is peaceful! "Blessed is the man who dies in righteousness and goodness" (81:4).

There follows the enactment of Enoch's special commission. He is set on earth by "seven holy ones," right by his own front door in fact, and instructed to declare everything to Methuselah, "and show to all thy children that no flesh is righteous in the sight of the Lord, for He is their Creator" (81:5). Despite righteous rejoicing and the sinner's certain demise, "those who practise righteousness shall die on account of the deeds of men, And be taken away on account of the doings of the godless" (81:9).*

The chapter ends plaintively, like the voice of *another* better-known prophet acquainted with sorrows: "And in those days they ceased to speak to me, and I came to my people, blessing the Lord of the world" (81:9). Is Enoch another *type* for the prophet "not without honour save in his own country"? (cf. Isaiah 53:3; Matthew 13:57).

Chapter 82 begins with Enoch entreating Methuselah to care for the books he has written to instruct successive generations. This wisdom, he says, will bring more pleasure than good food to those who understand it: "And those who understand it shall not sleep, But shall

---

*cf. Matthew 10:22: "And ye shall be hated of all men for my name's sake: but he that endureth to the end shall be saved." Also Luke 21:12: "But before all these, they shall lay their hands on you, and persecute you, delivering you up to the synagogues, and into prisons, being brought before kings and rulers for my name's sake."

listen with the ear that they may learn this wisdom," (82:3) for, as he continues in a style we may recognize: "Blessed are all the righteous, blessed are all those who walk in the way of righteousness and sin not as the sinners"—sinners who ignore the solar calendar's astronomical wisdom Enoch now teaches, believing it a holy, angelic revelation. The calendar is, furthermore, an expression of the same computation of time that will ensure final judgment occurs at the precise hour, with all deeds reckoned according to it. It is not simply a matter of an alternative authority for calculating months and years; it is *the* calendar by which men may compute, if they understand it, God's providence on earth, and certain hope in its dénouement: the vanquishing of sin's power to disrupt the heavens by gainsaying God's will. Countering such authority means opposing the "thousands" led by leaders of every aspect of power that make the year possible (82:10–14). The powers' angelic leaders who divide the seasons are named: Milki'el, Hel'emmelek, Mel'ejal, and Nar'el, and further hierarchies of leaders of a thousand are also named. These are presumably the thousands that will come in power to judge the transgressors of heavenly order, angelic and human.

Dream Visions (chapters 83–90)

The order of the books' logic implies that having expressed the heavenly order in its visible manifestation and through reference to invisible energies (invisible to ordinary men, that is) that sustain it, and having indicated the order's authority, including the *names* of its angelic authorities, it follows for Enoch to inform Methuselah how, in course of time, preordained events will lead to the judgment of those who've broken faith with the heavenly order, before that order is reset, or rather, led into its next glorious phase. Wisdom it is to fear God first, and to know the *times*. For in ancient Jewish wisdom, *everything has its time*, even if such transcends human understanding. All is done according to a heavenly calendar to which human beings would be well advised to attune themselves. Enoch shows how—for *he* walks with God—his wisdom is inscribed for all generations to see. In this sense, *apocalyptic*—adjective, not noun, note—wisdom is an intended summation of wisdom brought explicitly to bear on the problem of evil manifest in innocent suffering and guilty prosperity. In this aspect, wisdom is simply *knowledge* (rather than blind faith) in the *times*; interpreting them aright being the province of the wise, while failure to do so is to fall out of wisdom—and he who trips on *that* stone shall be broken,* for, as Enoch has seen, wisdom is the cornerstone of all.

Having been shown heaven and earth, we are now invited to see what Enoch has seen with the inner eye of vision. We must expect symbolic language for what the book's author believes is truth conveyed in symbols.

According to the first verses of *Dream Visions*, Enoch's first two visions occurred before Methuselah's birth: one when still learning to write (much later traditions ascribed writing's *invention* to Enoch), the other before marriage. In the first he was at grandfather Mahalalel's house. Envisioning heaven's collapse, he was borne off and fell to earth, which became an abyss of topsy-turvy elements: mountains suspended, trees uprooted. "The earth is destroyed," he cried. Alarmed, Mahalalel woke him up and asked Enoch to make supplication, that the Lord save a remnant of humanity and not annihilate the whole earth. Enoch composed a prayer for the generations of the earth. Venturing out and seeing the sun and moon in good order, he praised and thanked the Lord. This great prayer of thanks and praise includes his knowledge that "now the angels of Thy heavens are guilty of trespass" and God's wrath abides on the "flesh of men" until judgment day (84:4). In words reminiscent of the paternoster: "And thy power and kingship and greatness abide for ever and ever . . . And all the heavens are thy throne for ever, And the whole earth thy footstool for ever and ever" (84:2)—to which we may wish to add "Amen."

The second vision Enoch relates occurred before marrying Methuselah's mother Edna. Often called by scholars "the Animal Apocalypse," it tells the world's history to the messianic kingdom's establishment, with protagonists appearing in animal form, the kind familiar to any Eastern farmer: bulls, heifers, cows, sheep, oxen.

---

*cf. Matthew 21:44; Daniel 2:34.

The Watchers' descent is presented as a first star falling from heaven, followed by a host of stars joining the first. These stars become bulls and pasture with the oxen (86:1–3). The bulls uncover their "privy members" "like horses" and impregnate the cows, producing elephants, camels, and asses (the Giants). All earth's children flee the ensuing bloodbath.

Enoch envisions seven archangels "like white men" (87:2). Three take Enoch to heaven, out of harm's way, so that he may see all taking place below him. Four archangels stone and bind the bestial stars on earth, committing them to an earthly abyss.

Noah is then presented as one "born a bull but became a man," instructed by a white bull, given a secret by the four archangels. This man builds a vessel. Enoch envisions waters pouring from heaven above upon the earth. After the destruction of the wicked angels' progeny, chasms open in the earth. The waters subside and flow into them. Other than the white bull (Noah), three bulls emerge, one white, one red, one black: the sons of Noah and the foundation of the world's races.

Further zoological imagery tells the story from chapter 89 to the children of Israel's exodus from Egypt. They are presented as sheep, harassed by wolves—the surrounding nations, Egypt particularly. But the sheep follow the Lord. "And the Lord of the sheep went with them, as their leader, and all His sheep followed Him: and his face was dazzling glorious and terrible to behold" (88:22). The wolves drown in the exodus miracle of the parting of the waves. The sheep are led to a goodly land and settle. We are led to the period of the Judges as a story of conflicting beasts while some of the sheep's eyes were opened but at other times closed (89:41). The sheep's enemies are now typified as dogs, wild boars, and foxes. Eventually, a little sheep becomes a ram: a prince and leader of the sheep, resulting in a temple, a house for the "Lord of the sheep" (88:50).

Next comes the division of the Solomonic kingdom into Judah and Israel. For failing to keep faith with the Lord of the sheep, apostates are delivered unto lions and tigers, wolves and hyenas who tear them apart for their sins. Eventually the wild beasts burn the tower and demolish the house of the Lord of the sheep: this is the great catastrophe that precedes exile in Babylon.

Returning from exile, "three of those sheep" turned back and attempted to rebuild the fallen house, but their offering is described as "polluted" (89:73).

Chapter 90 takes us from Alexander the Great to Graeco-Syrian domination. "Thirty-five shepherds" (high priests) attempt to pasture the sheep. Dogs, eagles, and kites descend to peck at the sheep's eyes. From verse 6 we enter the period of Maccabean revolt against the Seleucids. Despite oppression, one of the lambs develops a horn, and despite the ravens and kites and vultures doing the utmost, the lamb's horn prevails: Judas Maccabeus, founder of the Hasmonean dynasty of priest-kings.

Attacks upon the sheep do not cease, but then comes the Lord of the sheep in wrath, and all who see him flee. A throne is "erected in the pleasant land" (90:20) and the Lord of the sheep sits thereon with the "sealed books" open before Him. He proceeds to judge the fallen stars. Seventy shepherds who'd exceeded their authority and killed more sheep than instructed follow the "stars" into the abyss.

The old temple ("house"; 90:28) is dismantled—pillars, beams, and ornaments, taken to a place in the south, whereupon Enoch sees a new house brought by the Lord of the sheep, greater than any house before it, with pillars and ornaments all new. And all the beasts of the earth fall down and do homage to the sheep now gathered at the new house. The three figures in white who had taken Enoch before, take Enoch's hand and place him among the sheep of whitest wool before the judgment seat, whereon the Lord of the sheep rejoices at the faithful remnant. And all who had been destroyed or dispersed come to the house, "the beasts of the field, and all the birds of the heaven." The sword given to the sheep is brought to the house and sealed. And all the sheep are called, but the house does not hold them. And the eyes of all are opened, and it is seen that the house is large, broad, and very full.

Enoch sees a white bull born, with large horns, and all the beasts of the field fear and petition him. "And I saw," says Enoch, "till all their generations were transformed, and they all became white bulls" (90:38), of which the first becomes a lamb that grows into a great animal with black horns, and the Lord of the sheep rejoices over it.

Such is the vision Enoch sees before marrying Methuselah's mother, seen in his sleep, and on waking leads him to weep "for everything shall come and be fulfilled" and all the deeds of men would come as he had seen.

The Epistle of Enoch (chapters 91–105)

Methuselah is called with his brethren to hear Enoch's message. He wants to show them "everything that shall befall you for ever" (91:1).

"Let not your spirit be troubled on account of the times; For the Great and Holy One has appointed days for all things" (92:1). This is the epistle's wisdom for which we should now be well prepared. It addresses a real anxiety felt by intended hearers. The righteous are told they will "arise from sleep" and "walk in eternal light" (92:3–4). Sin will forever perish in darkness. Methuselah's brethren and progeny must walk in uprightness and avoid the double-hearted despite increase in violence, apostasy from God, transgression, and impurity. These will be met with punishment and wrath. In that day, heathen idols will be abandoned and their temples burnt with fire (91:9). The rising from sleep of the righteous who'll be granted wisdom that will rise with them seems to refer to a resurrection, while the unrighteous, the violent will perish by the sword.

An "Apocalypse of Weeks" follows, as Enoch takes his cue from "the books" taken from the heavenly tablets (93:1). Having surveyed suggested dates of composition, Nickelsburg favors a date shortly before the Maccabean revolt, though it could be as late as 125 BCE. He considers it either an epitome of the Animal vision, or a source for it, noting reference to it in the book of Jubilees (composed ca. 125 BCE or 168 BCE).[6]

World history is divided into periods called "weeks." This idea seems to stem from insight into the relativity of time—a hundred years to a human is as nothing to God, who, transcending time, deals with time's magnitude in a manner belittling human life-spans. Enoch says he was born seventh (from Adam) in the first week. The divisions of time and numbers in the apocalypse are always based on significant numbers seven and ten (especially 7 x 10). The second week sees the rise of unrighteousness. The third brings Noah, whose posterity is to be "the plant of righteousness for evermore" (91:5). The law is given in the fourth week (Moses is not named—but then neither was Noah or any historical figure). The fifth week sees the temple's completion. The sixth week sees the godless forsaking wisdom.

The emphasis on "wisdom" tells us much about the writer's religious standpoint. Wisdom literature, the work of sage-scribes, distinguished itself from legal and historical Jewish literature.

The "house of dominion" is burnt in the sixth week and "the whole race of the chosen root shall be dispersed" (91:8). This suggests the writer's forebears may have joined the Babylonian exile (beginning 597 BCE) that took Judah's leading Jewish families and enslaved a proportion of its population (Nebuchadnezzar destroyed Jerusalem and the temple in 587 BCE). When the Persians permitted Jews to leave Babylon in 538 BCE, many settled in the north of what had been the old northern kingdom of Israel, including Samaria and Galilee, which territory included Dan at its most northern edge. The region may arguably have provided an alternative religious power base to that in Jerusalem.

The seventh week brings an "apostate [Nickelsburg has 'perverse'[7]] generation" (93:9) which means people who've abandoned Jahveh for foreign gods. This may cover Persian domination after the exile, the Greek invasion of 332 BCE, followed by Egyptian Ptolemaic rule until 200 BCE, after which the Seleucids dominated until Judas Maccabaeus cleansed the temple in 164 BCE. The period saw a pro-Seleucid Jerusalem faction.

At the seventh week's end, we are told the "elect righteous of the eternal plant of righteousness" will receive "sevenfold instruction concerning all His creation" (93:10). An eighth week will see the righteous given a sword and to it will be delivered the sinners. The righteous will acquire "houses" and an everlasting house will be built for "the Great King of glory" (93:13). The works of the godless will vanish from the earth in the ninth week as righteous judgment is revealed, and the world will face destruction. In the seventh part of the tenth week, the great eternal judgment will occur "amongst the angels" (v.15). Does this refer to the wicked Watchers? We cannot be sure. The first heaven will depart and disappear to be replaced by a new heaven, and "all the powers of the heavens shall give sevenfold light" (93:16). This done, there will be many weeks of goodness and righteousness extending infinitely.

Enoch then admonishes his listeners to walk in the paths of peace despite sinners who will attempt to evict wisdom from the world so she finds no dwelling as temptations increase (95:5). There follows a powerful litany of "Woes": "Woe to those who build unrighteousness and oppression . . ." "Woe to those who build their houses with sin . . . Woe to you, ye rich, for ye have trusted in your riches . . ." (94:6–11). More Woes come in chapter 95 for those who promulgate anathemas that cannot be reversed; for bearers of false witness; for those who requite neighbors with evil; for persecuting sinners—and yet more "Woe unto ye's" in chapter 96 for those whose riches make them appear righteous; those devouring the finest wheat, drinking copiously while treading on the lowly; for the deceitful, blasphemous, and those who've forsaken the "fountain of life" (96:6); for the mighty who oppress the righteous. Destruction is coming to them all. Oppressed sufferers need not fear: "For healing shall be your portion, And a bright light shall enlighten you, And the voice of rest ye shall hear from heaven" (96:3).*

There is more "Woe" in chapter 97 for sinners who live either in mid-ocean or dry land—the "dry land" may refer to foreign or collaborationist landowners who've driven poor farmers into the marshes, such as the Hula marshes south of Dan and toward the Tyrian coast. Those who've acquired wealth through unrighteous practices can expect a weight of woes. Pride themselves they may on high staff numbers and full granaries, but the wealth will not last, flowing away like water before them: a fine metaphor.

Chapter 98 looks at the vanity of men in fancy clothes who adorn

---

*For the twelve "Woes" in these three chapters of 1 Enoch, Matthew 23 can show eight. One may speculate that were we to swap "Woes" between the texts, there would be little interruption in tone or sense to either, except that Matthew's Jesus aims his woes specifically at scribes and Pharisees condemned as "hypocrites," though hypocrisy is clearly an object of Enoch's prophetic ire as well.

themselves "like women" (98:2). Those who dress in gold, silver, and purple (the imperial Roman color) can expect to be poured away like water too. They'll go down like their possessions, without wisdom, in shame, and slaughter, and destitution, with their spirits cast into the fiery furnace (v.3).

Arguably in contradistinction to the attribution of sin on earth to the Watchers in the eponymous book, sin is laid in verse 4 at men's door: "Even so sin has not been sent upon the earth, But man of himself has created it, and under a great curse shall they fall who commit it." If a woman is barren, it is the consequence of her deeds (v.5). All sins are recorded in heaven, and ingenious attempts to hide them are vain. Woe unto such fools, for their folly will ensure their end. Woe also to the obstinate of heart who refuse to see all good things enjoyed on earth come from God, placed in abundance for the good of humankind. The righteous will have no mercy for those who've taken good things from their mouths; thieves can expect to be slain.

Woe to those who rejoice in the tribulations of the righteous; they will not even be buried. No hope of life will come, no peace will be had among those denying the words of righteousness, who write down lies and godless thoughts. They shall "have no peace" (98:16) and death will come suddenly to them. Woe is poured out upon those who pervert words of truth and "transgress the eternal law" (99:2). According to Nickelsburg, this is the only explicit reference to the Mosaic covenant/ Torah in the whole Enochic corpus—if indeed that's what "eternal law" denotes—which observation highlights significant questions.[8]

A recent paper by Daniel Schumann (Tübingen University, Germany) probes prophecies of an elect people, delivered from oppression, in Isaiah 65, the Damascus Document* (CD A 3:1–20) and 1 Enoch 1:3, 8; 93:2, along with the practical absence of Mosaic law and covenant in 1 Enoch. Schumann believes this absence reflects uneasy relations between groups of priests and more apocalyptically minded Jews in the third and second centuries BCE. The apocalyptists were perhaps sages familiar with the court, or possibly communities in northern Galilee or even the Nile Delta's Jewish temple (or both; see pages 219-21.). According to Schumann, "the authors of the Book of Watchers

---

*See pages 95, 99.

(1 En 1–36) and the Epistle of Enoch (92–105) separate Israel into a small remnant of righteous people on the one hand, and a majority of sinners on the other, thus focusing on the election of a small group and its individuals instead of Israel as a covenantal people."*

I should add that "righteousness" in 1 Enoch is generally measured by overall positive resistance to evil derived from the Watchers rather than conscious performance of Mosaic commandments. Given Enoch's antediluvian context, righteousness is practically equated with *innocence*, being rooted in the uncorrupted state of God's chosen. Thus, Enoch is permitted to see God's paradise, approaching *from above* the tree of knowledge of good and evil without risk. God's promise is essentially heard in the heart, not from ink. This emphasis may have impacted upon early Christian understanding.

As Tyler Stewart has recently proposed, St. Paul's letter to the Galatians (3:19) assumes Enoch's story of transgressive angels, in that evil undermines and overcomes attempted law-observance, leaving people in sin and need of atonement.† Paul is aware God's "promise" to Abraham preceded Moses and was not annulled by Moses (Galatians 3:18). In verse 19, the law is seen as pragmatic, a secondary protection from evil, lest people suffer confusion (by evil) about what acts are wrong: "Wherefore then serveth the law? It was added because of transgressions, till the seed [of salvation] should come to whom the promise was made; and it was ordained by angels in the hand of a mediator." Whatever was originally intended by the latter phrase, Paul's argument involves a fundamental logic of salvation resonant with the Epistle of Enoch's—perhaps derived from it or from circles where it was recognized that evil's *essential* cause was spiritual, not behavioral. Where the wicked angels worked through the lusts of the body (defiling the will), the pristine promise of faith, manifest, for Paul, in Christ, allows crucifixion of the flesh, with Christ, opening the door to salvation: an eternal covenant. While Paul's Christology was shaped by the Damascus Road, his presuppositions were

---

*"Making Sense of Silence: How to Read the Lack of Covenantal Terminology in Early Enochic Literature in a 3rd and 2nd Century BCE Judean Context," delivered at the Enoch Seminar Webinar, June 28, 2023.

†*The Origin and Persistence of Evil in Galatians* (Tübingen: Mohr Siebeck, 2022).

Jewish, his view of the angels, Enochic. Indeed, in a recent talk about his book *Paul's Three Paths to Salvation* (2020), Gabriele Boccaccini stated that "Paul is an answer to an Enochic problem."*

The "Enochic problem" centered around what was to be done in the final judgment with certain kinds of sinners, on account of the perception of evil as something capable of undermining right-action, even when willed, flesh being weak, with evil defiling both will and flesh. Was there any chance of repentance; could sinners be forgiven and saved from eternal judgment on their acts? Returning to the Epistle of Enoch (chapter 99), we quickly dive into a scenario where this problem has not been answered.

In the coming "unceasing bloodshed," worshippers of impure spirits who seek help from them, or from idols, shall receive none. Their hearts' fear will render them blind; their folly makes them godless. "For they shall have wrought all their work in a lie, And shall have worshipped a stone: Therefore in an instant will they perish" (99:8). In the coming days, fathers will slay their sons, and their sons' sons. While sinners will be gathered from the secret places by angels for execution of judgment, holy guardian angels will be appointed over the righteous and holy, to guard them "as the apple of an eye" (100:5). Though the righteous sleep a long sleep, they've naught to fear, for the "children of the earth shall see the wise" and understand the words of "this book" (105:6). No one will buy themselves salvation from judgment. Sinners should look to the sailors who naturally fear when at sea, for all their possessions are vulnerable to violent waves, but as the Lord made the sea, he made all forces of nature, and though the "sinners fear not the Most High" (101:9) their eyes will be opened to all fear when too late to avert it, for the rain and the dew and the snow and all the cosmos will testify against them, for sinners cannot separate themselves or hide truth from the rest of creation. While they may have lived in honor and safety, free of violence and oppression, with lives completed with respect from their society, nevertheless "their souls will be made to descend into Sheol" (103:7). There they will find wretchedness and tribulation: "Woe

---

*Enoch Seminar Webinar, June 28, 2023.

unto you, for ye shall have no peace" (v.8). Conversely, those who cried for help from their oppressors, who hoped for alleviation of miseries, who suffered the yoke and who were hated, unpitied, homeless, without means of support or change of circumstance; who were robbed, murdered, tortured, and apparently forgotten, they, and their names, "are written before the glory of the Great One" (104:1). They will shine as the lights in heaven. The cry of judgment will be fulfilled; the portals of heaven will be opened to them. There will be no need to hide from the judgment. How this will be is known by Enoch as a "mystery" (105:10) and this mystery he is passing to the time when it will be understood.

Enoch foresees a time when his book will be translated into many languages so that miscreants will not be able to pervert the words he's spoken. "Then I know another mystery, that books will be given to the righteous and the wise to become a cause of joy and uprightness and much wisdom" (104:12).

The last chapter (105) has two verses that are a proclamation from God, a divine imprimatur for Enoch's "book" that it be respected as a guide. Charles's translation saw reference to the Son of God, or a messiah in the last words of the Epistle of Enoch. "For I and My Son will be united with them for ever in the paths of uprightness in their lives; and ye shall have peace: rejoice, ye children of uprightness. Amen." Nickelsburg's translation suggests the intended "son" of 105:2 is Methuselah: "For I and my son will join ourselves with them forever in the paths of truth in their life. And you will have peace. Rejoice, O children of truth. Amen" (Nickelsburg, *1 Enoch 1*, 531).

Fragment from a Book of Noah (chapters 106–107)

Enoch in this fragment, or what appears to be one, possibly added after the first half of the second century and before the last third of the first century BCE,[9] is consulted by Methuselah at the "ends of the earth" where he is among angels. The reason is that Methuselah's son Lamech and Lamech's wife have been blessed with a son so beautiful and otherworldly in appearance that his father thinks he may have come from the angels. He fears he has been born for a "wonder," and not a pleasant one: something terrible. Enoch hears from his son that Lamech's son has a body as white as snow and red as a rose, and eyes that are like the sun and light up the whole house. Enoch explains that in the days of his father Jared, angels transgressed. He then repeats a story Methuselah should know well enough by now! Enoch has something new to say about Methuselah's grandson. He and his three sons will survive the deluge. Enoch tells Methuselah that the boy should be called Noah. He then tells Methuselah he has seen the "mysteries of the holy ones" on the heavenly tablets, so Methuselah can take his warning as authoritative. Noah receives his name which means he will comfort the earth after the destruction.

An Addition: Chapter 108

The chapter, possibly composed in the first century BCE,[10] announces itself as "another book which Enoch wrote for his son Methuselah." It is also for a future time, for the attention of those "who keep the law in the last days." The phrase "keep the law" marks it out as distinct from other parts of 1 Enoch, which talk of righteousness, not law directly. Enoch has a vision of a kind of cloud imbued with a fire. Angels tell him it signifies the punishment of the "spirits of sinners and blasphemers" whose names will be expunged along with their seed forever. Those tried in experience and found faithful will be recompensed for they esteemed heaven more than life in the world, regarding earthly life as a passing phase, choosing not to build their destiny upon this earth. Despite being trodden underfoot by the wicked, they continued to bless God, and God heard them. "And now I will summon the spirits of the good who belong to the generation of light, and I will transform those who were born in darkness, who in the flesh were not recompensed with such honour as their faithfulness deserved" (108:11). Those who have loved God's holy name will be brought forth "in shining light" and each will be sat by God "on the throne of his honour" (v.12). And these shall see those born in darkness led into darkness (v.14). The contrast between light, including a generation of light, and the darkness is striking and suggestive, as we shall see.

FOUR

The Book of Enoch 2

The Similitudes or Parables of Enoch
(chapters 37–71)

Considered the latest components of the Ethiopic Enoch (*Mäṣṣäfä Henok Nabiy*), the so-called Parables have proved even more controversial than the grisly giants and lustful angels of the Book of the Watchers. The reason should soon be obvious, for unless I mistake, most readers will find something curiously familiar amid the Parables' contents.

While reminding us that our oldest source for the Parables is still a fifteenth-century version in Ge'ez, George Nickelsburg and James VanderKam surmise an original text composed in Aramaic rather than Hebrew since Parables shares similar tropes to the Book of the Watchers, fragments of the latter now known in Aramaic. From Aramaic it was most likely translated into Greek and from Greek to Ge'ez, if, that is, it wasn't written in Greek to start with.[1] For persons who'd inherited and shared enthusiasm for Enochic wisdom, this was likely a hot book around the time Jesus was born and in his youth.

It will have been observed that in all preceding accounts of God's final judgment of the righteous and the sinners, the key role in salvation and destruction was held exclusively by the "Great King." The Parables open with a now familiar account of the dividing of the righteous from the sinners at the end of long periods of corruption, all kicked off by the angels' descent to "join their seed" with human women—presented in Parables as a "principle" rather than historic drama.

A new salvific figure now appears when Enoch declares "mine eyes saw the Elect One of righteousness and of faith, And I saw his dwelling-place under the wings of the Lord of Spirits" (39:6). The divine title "Lord of Spirits" occurs 104 times in Parables and is peculiar to it, though 39:12–13's "Holy, holy, holy, is the Lord of Spirits: He filleth the earth with spirits" clearly evokes Isaiah 6:3: "Holy, holy, holy, is the Lord of hosts: the whole earth is full of his glory,"[2] while the famous Papyrus of Ani's Hymn to Osiris (ca. 1250 BCE) praises the judge of all spirits in the judgment hall as "governor of Spirit-Bodies," hinting remotely, just perhaps, at cross-cultural Egyptian influence on Parables.

Enoch yearns to share the dwelling place of the "Elect One of righteousness," and to join his voice to the thousands blessing the "Lord of Spirits." A "multitude beyond number" is envisioned by Enoch before the Lord of Spirits (40:1). Enoch sees four archangels at the four sides of the Lord: Michael (merciful and long-suffering), Raphael (the healer), Gabriel (master of "all powers"), and the fourth, Phanuel, administering the "repentance unto hope of those who inherit eternal life" (40:9). The note of *repentance* here is very significant, and is amplified later.*

Enoch is shown "all the secrets of the heavens" including the "mansions of the elect and the mansions of the holy,"† in contrast to the sight of sinners who are being dragged off for denying the Lord of Spirits (41:2).

Chapter 41 seems to recapitulate some of the contents of the Astronomical Book, outlining heavenly secrets, but a dualist emphasis in the eighth verse links the heavenly facts to their spiritual significance: "And the course of the path of the moon is light to the righteous, And darkness to the sinners in the name of the Lord, Who made a separation between light and the darkness, and divided the spirits of

---

*cf. Luke 2:36, where Anna, a prophetess in the temple, is the "daughter of Phanuel," prophesying Israel's redemption has come in the person of Jesus (see page 333).

†cf. John 14:2–3: "In my Father's house are many mansions: if it were not so, I would have told you. I go to prepare a place for you. And if I go and prepare a place for you, I will come again, and receive you unto myself; that where I am, there ye may be also."

men" (41:8). The "division" of men's spirits may simply mean the divide between the good and the wicked, or it may imply that each man's spirit is itself divided into a light and a dark side, but if so, whether men have the freedom to choose between these antitheses is unstated. If it were, we could better tell whether or not the author was a determinist, believing the righteous were righteous for all time, and sinners always sinners, or not. The earlier reference—though rare in the Enochic corpus—to repentance, suggests some way back might exist from an evil course, but then one could argue the repentance itself was also predetermined, with free will to choose likewise predetermined.

Chapter 42 embarks on a different setting. We find a kind of hymn to Lady Wisdom, reminiscent of Jewish wisdom literature, such as Proverbs and the first century BCE Wisdom of Solomon, the latter, especially in its fourth chapter, showing approval of Enoch's significance, including conceptions either shared with, or taken from Enochic books.

"Wisdom," we are told in the Parables, "found no place where she might dwell; Then a dwelling-place was assigned her in the heavens" (42:1). The next verse might be a parallelism (a different way of saying the same thing), or it may be intended as sequential. Wisdom seeks home among the children of men, but finds nowhere to stay (cf. Matthew 8:20). She returns to her place and takes her seat among the angels. Verse 3 is ambiguous: "And unrighteousness went forth from her chambers: Whom she sought not she found, And dwelt with them, As rain in a desert, And dew on a thirsty land." Does it mean unrighteousness fled from her chambers when she was restored to heaven? I cannot say, but the dénouement, though like a riddle, seems positive. Some persons appreciated what she offered: those who hungered and thirsted for God's wisdom.*

The next chapter has more astronomical visions; Enoch sees the functioning of lightning, the length of days, the stellar revolutions, but these things, he hears, have parabolic meaning. The powers of the universe are angels who "dwell on the earth and believe in the name of the

---

*cf. Matthew 5:6.

Lord of Spirits for ever and ever" (44:4). A "second parable" follows this one, concerning judgment on those "who deny the dwelling of the holy ones and the Lord of Spirits" (45:1). The sinners will be tried on the "day of suffering and tribulation" when "Mine Elect One shall sit on the throne of glory." "Then will I cause Mine Elect One to dwell among them. And I will transform the heaven and make it an eternal blessing and light, And I will transform the earth and make it a blessing: And I will cause Mine elect ones to dwell upon it: But the sinners and evil-doers shall not set foot thereon" (45:4–5).

Chapter 46 (vv.1–8) introduces us to another key figure of the judgment, apparently identified with the aforementioned "Elect One."

And there I saw One who had a head of days, And His head was like white wool, And with Him was another, whose face was like the appearance of a man, and his face was full of graciousness like one of the holy angels. And I asked the angel of peace who went with me and showed me all the hidden things, about that son of man, who he was, and whence he was, why he went with the Head of Days.* And he answered me and said unto me, "This is the son of man who hath righteousness, and righteousness dwells with him, and all the treasuries of what is hidden he will reveal; For the Lord of Spirits has chosen him, and his lot has prevailed through truth in the presence of the Lord of Spirits forever.

And this son of man whom you have seen—he will raise the kings and the mighty from their couches, and the strong from their thrones. He will loosen the reins of the strong, and he will crush the teeth of the sinners. He will overturn the kings from their thrones and from their kingdoms, because they do not exalt him or praise him, or humbly acknowledge whence the kingdom was given to them. The face of the strong he will turn aside, and he will fill them with shame. Darkness shall be their dwelling, and worms will be their couch. And they will have no hope to rise from their couches, because they do not exalt the name of the Lord of Spirits. These

---

*cf. Daniel 7:13–28.

are they who [text corrupt; "judge"? Nickelsburg and VanderKam also suggest "condemn"] the stars of heaven, and raise their hands against the Most High, and tread upon the earth and dwell on it. All their deeds manifest unrighteousness, and their power [rests] upon their wealth. Their faith is in the [gods?] they have made with their hands, and they deny the name of the Lord of Spirits. And they persecute the houses of his congregation, and the faithful who depend on the name of the Lord of Spirits.
(Translation by George Nickelsburg and James VanderKam[3])

Enoch is shown a place where stands the "fountain of righteousness," which is inexhaustible (48:1), around which are many fountains of wisdom, from which the thirsty drink, and are satisfied, filled with wisdom. At "that hour"—recall the importance of the wisdom of the *times*—"the son of man" is named in the presence of the Lord of Spirits, also called the "Head of Days," which title suggests either his being Lord of Time, or eternal and ageless (like Daniel's "Ancient of Days"), and wise beyond imagining. As for being "named," the implication is that he has been anointed, bearing the powerful impress of the holy, divine Name.

Crucially we now hear that the son of man is *pre-existent*: "Yea, before the sun and the signs were created, before the stars of the heaven were made, His name was named before the Lord of Spirits" (48:3). "And for this reason hath he been chosen and hidden before Him, Before the creation of the world and for evermore" (48:6).

Now, *this* is fascinating, for whatever Daniel's second-century BCE prophecy had intended by "one like the [or 'a'] son of man" coming with the "clouds of heaven" before the "Ancient of Days" (Daniel 7:13–14), Daniel's author did not apparently envision this human*like* figure as being pre-existent companion to the Lord, and it may well be that we here witness the root of the doctrine of Christ's pre-existence promulgated forcefully by St. Paul in the mid-first century CE, in, for example, Colossians 1:1–15. It barely goes without saying that the gospel Jesus's identification with the "son of man" may also partly owe its inspiration to Enoch's Parables.

• • •

A recent special session of the Enoch Seminar Webinar (June 26–29, 2023) concerned "Enoch Studies in the 2020s: 1 Enoch and the New Testament: New Trends and Most Recent Contributions." Contributions included article and book presentations relating to Parables (or Similitudes), such as Logan Williams of Exeter University's "Debating Daniel's Dream: The Synoptic Gospels and the Similitudes of Enoch on the Son of Man" (2020) which counseled reserve regarding whether Parables was the synoptic gospels' son of man's origin: *similarities do not equal dependence*. Does understanding origin mean we understand the gospels' son of man? The Son of Man's role in Parables is different from that in, say, Luke. Note also that the majority of Greek New Testament manuscripts do not capitalize the "S" of "son"—*huios anthrōpou* = the son of man—though the King James or "Authorized" English translation does, probably following the Latin Vulgate which capitalizes "Son" in, for example, John 1:51: *Filium hominis*, and John 5:27: *Filius hominis*, doubtless intended to honour Jesus as Son of God, although in honor of *God*, "man" is not capitalized by Latin translator Jerome (ca. 400 CE). The oldest near complete text of John (*Papyrus 66*; Bodmer Collection; ca. 200 CE) abbreviates and capitalizes all letters of Greek "SON" and "OF MAN," as it does the name of Jesus, for honorific purposes, that is, as a divine name. The *Codex Vaticanus* Greek rendering (fourth century) shows no interest in capitalization (the text is a mixture of upper- and lowercase Greek letters anyway, as was common form), and neither does the Greek *Codex Sinaiticus* (fourth century). The phrase "Son of Man" is sometimes capitalized in theological studies to denote it as a specific title with particular meaning, frequently seen as being a title on a par with "Son of God." If the Greek term in the gospels was a translation of a Hebrew or Aramaic title, we can but speculate as to the title's original form since the "son of man" figure is understood in the gospels in quite specific ways, primarily as a designation for Jesus himself, distinct from the phrase "son of Adam" (meaning human) in the Hebrew scriptures. We have no Aramaic version of 1 Enoch's Parables in which "son of man" (or "Son of Man") appears, and Ge'ez versions of 1 Enoch do not distinguish upper- and lowercase letters. R. H. Charles gave his translation of the Ge'ez for "son of man" capitals as a pious honorific, but he was not consistent, perhaps doubting the possibility of certainty as to a technically correct English form. I shall tend to capitalize when referring to the title "Son of Man" in 1 Enoch (except where Nickelsburg and VanderKam's translations prefer the lower case), and use lower case in gospel passages, for their characteristics, while intriguingly close, are not identical.

Examining the son of man's role in Matthew, Elekosi F. Lafitaga (Kanana Fou Theological Seminary, American Samoa) noted that Matthew's son of man end-of-the-world imagery (coming with clouds of power) derived mainly from Daniel 7:9-13 (as is likely of the son of man reference in 1 Enoch 46:1-4).* Unlike Paul, Matthew's Jesus is son of man plus Son of God, suggesting Paul's being raised outside scribal traditions favoring Parables. Nevertheless, whilst raised a Pharisee, bound to the law, Paul would join an apocalyptically inspired movement.

Matthew 12 describes aspects of the son of man without parallel in 1 Enoch. He is "lord of the sabbath," for example (12:8), and will be three days and nights in "the heart of the earth" (12:40). Lafitaga reckoned the following chapter (13) correlated Matthew's son of man to the parable of the man sowing seeds, which evokes a question from disciples about parabolic preaching, to which Jesus curiously answers it's so people will fulfill Isaiah's prophecy of sinners seeing but not perceiving: "their eyes they have closed; lest at any time they should see with their eyes, and hear with their ears, and should understand with their heart, and should be converted, and I should heal them" (13:15). This closing of eyes is reminiscent of 1 Enoch 89:41 (the Animal Apocalypse in Dream Visions; see pages 50, 51) where some of the sheep's eyes were opened but at other times closed. When open, they heeded the lord of the sheep.

A sheep motif appears in Matthew when Lafitaga notes the return of the sower motif in Jesus's parable of the wicked servant who ignored

---

*Lafitaga was presenting his book *Apocalyptic Sheep and Goats in Matthew and 1 Enoch* (2022).

the truth that the master reaped *where he sowed not** (leaving work for others to bear fruit), followed by announcement of the son of man coming in glory with his angels and sitting on his throne of glory (25:31), whence he judges "as a shepherd divideth his sheep from the goats" (v.32). Jesus is son of man (here the coming one), shepherd and king demanding obedience from his sheep, or servants. However, while in 1 Enoch the "sheep" are Israelites, the identity of the sheep and goats is ambiguous, for Matthew says "all nations" gather before the son of man for judgment. In 1 Enoch, other animals are predators on the (often blind) sheep. So, are the goats Gentiles, sinners, or both; and are the sheep *all* Israelites? The sheep on the son of man's "right hand" inherit the promise of the kingdom (v.34) for *practicing loving kindness* (hesed), while the goats on his "left hand" are cursed, *not* for what they have done to the "Lord," but for failing to care for "the least of my brethren," earning them "everlasting fire," "prepared for the devil and his angels" (v.41)—which carries unmistakable resonance with 1 Enoch's condemnation of the Watchers.

Lafitaga believes judgment in Matthew 25 represents the "renewal of humanity," indeed all creation, while the parable of separating sheep from stubborn goats is "intrinsically a form of Jewish rhetoric."

Charles A. Gieschen (Concordia Theological Seminary, Fort Wayne, Indiana), in his article "The Importance of the Parables of '1 Enoch' for Understanding the Son of Man in the Four Gospels" (2020) expressed dismay where New Testament scholars "simply don't engage with Parables." Why, he asked, is Parables not used in "Son of Man" eschatological studies? A few have gone against the grain, such as Crispin Fletcher-Louis, and Daniel Boyarin in "How Can Enoch Teach Us about Jesus?"[†]

Gieschen sees the Son of Man in Parables not only as an important development of Daniel 7, but as precursor to the gospel presentation of the son of man. He listed seven key factors about the Son of Man in Parables:

---

*cf. 1 Enoch 42:3.
[†]In *Early Christianity* 2 (2011): 51–76.

1. "One like the son of man" has become a title: "Son of Man."
2. The Son of Man is eschatological judge.
3. The Son of Man is seated on God's Throne.
4. The Son of Man is pre-existent.
5. The Son of Man shares the divine name with the Lord of Spirits, suggesting the figure of man as divine.
6. The Son of Man is worshipped.
7. The Son of Man is ultimately identified with a human (or, arguably, formerly human), Enoch.

Gieschen sees the gospels presenting a radical interpretation of Daniel 7, in presenting the Christ idea as the commencement of the son of man's eschatological enthronement and reign. He also regards it as significant that the identity of the son of man in the gospels is not explained, but presumed, concluding that if the Enochic Son of Man had not existed, it would be necessary to invent him.

Returning to the Parables narrative, it is difficult not to feel resonance with epithets later applied to Jesus in the gospels. The Son of Man in 1 Enoch 48:4–10 is a "staff to the righteous" and "the light of the Gentiles [Nickelsburg has "nations"],"* the "hope of all those who are troubled of heart." All who dwell on earth shall fall down and worship before him, praising and blessing and celebrating "with song"† the Lord of Spirits. The Son of Man has been revealed to the holy and righteous for the Son of Man has protected them because "they have hated and despised this world of unrighteousness, And have hated all its works and ways in the name of the Lord of Spirits" (v.7).

The "downcast in countenance" shall become the kings of the earth (cf. Psalm 37:11) whereas the unrighteous will sink before the face of the righteous "like lead in the water" for they have denied the Lord of Spirits "and His Anointed" (48:10). The word *Anointed* here is highly significant, for it is the meaning of "Messiah" (Greek: *Christos*), and in the context of the Parables identifies that dignity with the Son of Man.

---

*cf. Luke 2:32; Isaiah 42:6.
†cf. Psalm 100.

The next chapter uses an equivalent term, the "Elect One," and the Elect One is one who stands before the Lord of Spirits (cf. Malachi 3:1–2 for the messianic implication of the one who "stands"). The Elect One is the chosen one, and it may be noted that the Greek word for "the elect one" (*eklelegmenos*; perfect passive participle, nominative singular masculine, from *eklegomai* = to select) has been translated as "chosen one" when Jesus is "named" as beloved Son, and declared *the elect one*, in Luke 9:35's account of Jesus's baptism. While "chosen" is a valid translation, we miss thereby the link to God's formal announcing of the "Elect One," which, note, has *already taken place*, and is a *specific messianic title* with a background that includes 1 Enoch, as opposed to "the chosen one" where in English the emphasis is on *one* (nonspecific) who has been chosen.[*]

According to 1 Enoch 49, as wisdom is "poured out like water," whose glory fails not, the Elect One who participates in the glory of God is "mighty in all the secrets of righteousness," which entails having command over the elements.

Chapter 50 brings a real possibility of repentance. In days to come, when light and glory and length of days shine upon the righteous, their enemies "may repent and forgo the works of their hands" (v.2). While they have no honor "through the name of the Lord of Spirits," yet they will be saved for He is merciful and compassionate. The *unrepentant* will perish without mercy.[†]

The climactic events of God's judgment are referred to with the phrase "in those days," oft repeated in chapter 51. In those days the

---

[*]Had this link been properly understood in the patristic period, it might have served to counter the "heresy" of Adoptionism, whereby Jesus was held to be God's son only at the point of baptism when the Holy Spirit supposedly entered him, denying the elect one's pre-existence.

[†]cf. John the Baptist's "Repent!"—before it's too late (Luke 3:8–9). See also Gabriele Boccaccini, "Forgiveness of Sins: An Enochic Problem, a Synoptic Answer," in Stuckenbruck and Boccaccini, *Enoch and the Synoptic Gospels*, 14–15: Boccaccini argues that the presence in Parables (at 1 Enoch 51:1–5) of those who are neither among the righteous nor the sinners, but who repent and receive mercy, "helps unlock the background of Jesus's message of repentance before the final judgment." Without claiming literary dependence, Boccaccini sees Jesus presented as carrying out something Enochic tradition envisions for the period just before end.

earth and Sheol, the underworld of souls awaiting judgment, will give up what is owed, and "in those days" the Elect One will "arise" and separate holy from righteous. Salvation's day is dawning. The Lord of Spirits says the Elect One will sit on the Lord's throne to pour forth wisdom, and the earth will dance as angels rejoice. The Lord of Spirits will have "glorified" the Elect One and the elect will walk the earth.

Enoch is carried off in a whirlwind to the Seven Mountains of Metal: iron, copper, silver, gold, soft metal, and lead (52:1–2). If this were a reference to astrological planetary-metal attributions, then the "soft metal" might either be tin (Jupiter) or mercury (Mercury), but the text only mentions six metals for seven mountains. An angel tells Enoch the mountains will be in the Elect One's presence "as wax before the fire, And like the water which streams down from above, And they shall become powerless before his feet" (52:6). In those days no one will be able to buy salvation with silver or gold. A prohibition follows on the instruments of war the wicked Watchers introduced to humans after descending to earth: no iron for war, no breastplates; bronze will avail nothing, tin will be valueless, none will desire lead. All those things will be removed from the earth. One presumes that with the instruments will go the arts of metallurgy and chemistry, which the author relates to human downfall, their source being the fallen Watchers.

Verse 3 of chapter 3 refers to "the angels of punishment" preparing the "instruments of Satan" to vanquish forever the kings and the mighty of the earth. Satan's precise role is not clear. In the Book of Job, the Satan is the "Adversary," the name "Satan" meaning the *role*, not necessarily a proper name. God's prosecuting counsel in the heavenly court, the Satan may dispense evils as tests of loyalty to God. This figure has undergone a development. The idea of "Satan's legions" may derive from the notion that Satan was permitted to use evil spirits (resulting from the destruction of the giants' bodies) as adversarial equipment. It would be a short step to present Satan as their leader, and—conflated with Azaz'el—Satan himself as the evil that evil spirits serve.

Once the mighty are eliminated, "the Righteous and Elect One shall cause the house of his congregation to appear" (53:6), an interesting image, suggesting a particular group identity or community.

Enoch next envisions the making of enormous chains, prepared for the hosts of Azaz'el, after which they'll be plunged into an abyss and covered with rough stones, until the day when Michael, Gabriel, Raphael, and Phanuel cast them into the burning furnace, the Lord of Spirits taking vengeance thereby "for their unrighteousness in becoming subject to Satan and leading astray those who dwell on earth" (53:6).

The theme of punishment is repeated in a fragment from a Noachic work inserted as chapter 54 and running to 55, verse 2. Punishment this time is of course the Great Flood, at the end of which the "Head of Days" repents for destroying the dwellers of earth, making a pledge with a sign in heaven: the rainbow, which pledge will last so long as heaven is above the earth.

We then shift back to Azaz'el's punishment, and that of the Watchers, judged by the Lord of Spirits' Elect One. Their valley of doom will soon be filled with their loved ones.

Chapter 56 shifts again to a scene where "in those days the angels shall return And hurl themselves to the east upon the Parthians and Medes: they shall stir up the kings"—a reference that may help us date the text (see page 326).

The next chapter appears to describe what may be the return from exile in Babylon, but is more likely the nations converging on Jerusalem to worship God at the time of prophetic consummation (see Micah 4:2–3).[4] Enoch sees a host of wagons, "and men riding thereon, and coming on winds from the east, and from the west to the south. And the noise of their wagons was heard" (57:1–2). The turmoil surprises the heavenly holy ones; the pillars of the earth are moved from their place: the sound echoing from one end of heaven to the other. The last verse (v.3) suggests a gathering to worship: "And they shall all fall down and worship the Lord of Spirits." Thus ends the second parable, on triumphant note.

The third parable (chapters 58–71) first guarantees the righteous "shall be in the light of the sun, And the elect in the light of everlasting life," which rather sound like promises to be taken up by gnostic movements which, to varying degrees, saw resurrection as awakening to the light in this life. Darkness will have been destroyed by the "light of uprightness established forever" (58:6).

Chapter 61 sees angels measuring the depth of the earth with ropes to bring the righteous forth, for however they might have died, they will not be forgotten, or left behind. "And the Lord of Spirits placed the Elect One on the throne of glory. And he shall judge all the works of the holy above in the heaven, And in the balance shall their deeds be weighed" (v.8). In the presence of all the hosts of heaven, Cherubin, Seraphin, Ophanin and all the angels of power and of principalities, the kings and the mighty and all exalted in the world will be judged. In the presence of righteousness, they feel pain like a woman in labor: "And pain shall seize them, When they see that Son of Man sitting on the throne of his glory" (62:5; Nickelsburg & VanderKam translation, with, *note*, capitalization, 2012).

Nickelsburg notes that the connection between 1 Enoch 62–63 and Mark 8:38 "is especially close; both portray the Son of Man as the heavenly vindicator of the persecuted righteous."[5] In Daniel 7:13–14, "one like the son of man" arrives *after* the Ancient of Days's judgment, whereas Mark has the son of man coming to judge, suggesting familiarity with Parables: "If anyone is ashamed of me and my words in this adulterous and sinful generation, the son of man will be ashamed of them when he comes in his Father's glory with the holy angels" (Mark 8:38). In Parables, as Nickelsburg and VanderKam observe, judicial functions of the archangels are transferred to the anointed one.[6]

The son of man, we are told, was hidden from the beginning, preserved, revealed only to the elect. "And the congregation of the elect and holy shall be sown [note!]," and this community, a plant of righteousness, will stand to see the kings and mighty fall down and beg for mercy from the Son of Man. As their faces fill with shame, they realize the darkness is upon them, and they are delivered to the "vengeance" reserved for those who oppress the children of the Lord of Spirits: "His sword is drunk with their blood" (62:12). The righteous and elect, clothed in garments of glory, the "garments of life," will eat and lie down and "rise up for ever and ever" (v.14).

The kings and mighty make a great plea for mercy, telling how they worship and honor the Lord of Spirits. Now that only darkness is before them, they confess placing hope in their scepters, their kingly glory. They accept the Lord of Spirits has no respect of persons, His judgment true. Nevertheless, shamed before the Son of Man, they are "driven from his presence." Such is the fate of the mighty, the kings, the exalted, and "those who possess the earth" (63:12). Nickelsburg and VanderKam note that unlike the Book of the Watchers, the righteous are above all oppressed by "kings and the mighty," though one might also infer that *behind them* operate evil spiritual forces; in 54:5–6, the word "Satan" is used once for Azaz'el.[7]

In chapter 65 we are with Noah, who cries to Enoch bitterly with tears, seeing the earth's descent toward destruction. Noah is aware of a command from the Lord's presence that ruin is coming upon all who learnt the Watchers' secrets, "and all the violence of the Satans [note!], and all their powers," and those who practice witchcraft and sorcery, and the makers of molten images, and the workers of metals. Enoch reassures Noah his name will be among the holy, and he and his seed will be preserved to become a fountain of innumerable righteous forever.

These accounts in chapters 65–67, as well as chapter 60, seem to come from a separate book devoted primarily to Noah, perhaps inserted in the Parables because in them Noah appears reliant on Enoch for spiritual reassurance and vision of what's coming. Noah writes in the first person, in for example 67:1: "And in those days the word of the Lord came unto me, and He said unto me: 'Noah. . . .'" In this chapter (67) the Lord informs Noah of His intention to imprison the unrighteous angels in the burning valley Enoch showed him in the west among the mountains of gold and silver and iron and soft metal and tin. A somewhat complicated explanation follows for the use of the waters associated with the Flood in the final judgment of kings and the mighty, and unrighteous angels. Subterranean waters, formerly associated with healing of kings and their bodily lust, will change in temperature to torture the spirits and bodies of the angels: from freezing to trap them, to burning fire to consume them. The passage may serve to date the passage insofar as historian Josephus tells of King Herod the Great's journey to thermal springs by the Dead Sea that proved vain to heal him of agonizing skin afflictions (see page 330), frustrating his promiscuity.

Chapter 69 gives a variant list of the rebellious angels' chiefs' names and, notably, "Satans [Adversaries]." They command fifties, hundreds, and tens. According to v.4, the first was Jeqon who led the "sons of God" astray ("sons of God" is the expression for the lustful angels in Genesis 6). The second: Asbe'el; the third: Gadre'el, who showed men the instruments of war, and (note) tempted Eve; the fourth: Penemue, who taught men the "bitter and the sweet" and all the secrets of their wisdom, including writing with ink on paper, which has led many to sin "to this day" (v.9). Men were not made to confirm faith in pen and ink. This might seem an awkward inclusion if we consider writing's importance to the authors of 1 Enoch and to "scribe of righteousness" Enoch himself!* The context here may be signing oaths and possibly magic letters of protection. "For men were created exactly like the angels, to the intent that they should continue pure and righteous, and death, which destroys everything, could not have taken hold of them; but through this their knowledge they are perishing."

The fifth angel was Kasdeja, who showed magic spells involving demons that harm babies in wombs, and serpent bites, "and the smitings which befall through the noontide heat, the son of the serpent named Taba'et." Kasbe'el looked after the oath Michael had shown him, with its "hidden name" (perhaps the name of God, Jahveh). This secret power of the oath he revealed to the holy ones in heaven, then to

---

*On June 28, 2023, Fiodar Litvinau, (Ludwig-Maximilians-University of Munich, Germany) delivered his paper to the Enoch Seminar: "Reception of Hellenistic Traditions in Jewish Pseudepigrapha: Examples from 1 Enoch 69:8 and Apocalypse of Abraham 5." Litvinau located a possible origin of the Enochic criticism of writing as imparted by Watcher Penemue, in Plato's *Phaedrus* 274c–275b. There, Socrates relates how Egyptian "Theuth"—a variant of "Thoth," interestingly—declared the weakness of writing. While writing served as a reminder, it didn't possess the *essential fact* conveyed directly to the understanding by oral teaching. That is, people would claim *knowledge* merely by what they'd *read*. Reading is not true *knowing*. The likely phenomenon of transfigured Hellenistic influence rendered Jewish (the writing jibe was not Litvinau's only example) might suggest a composition environment where Greek literature had active currency among Jews.

the children of men. The oath was strong, central to the upholding of the earth and the stars (v.17–21, 25). The subtext here seems to be an implied prohibition of oaths and written declarations involving binding oaths. Binding themselves to come upon the daughters of men, the Watchers showed the danger within the oath and abuse of the hidden name.

The third parable closure (vv. 26–29) brings us back to the judgment of the sinners and the unrighteous angels: "And from then on there will be nothing that is corruptible; for that Son of Man has appeared. And has sat down on the throne of his glory, and all evil shall vanish from his presence. And the word of that Son of Man will go forth and will prevail in the presence of the Lord of Spirits" (v.29; Nickelsburg and VanderKam translation").[8]

Finale

Chapter 70 describes Enoch's parting from the world. He is "raised aloft" to the Son of Man and the Lord of Spirits during his lifetime "on the chariots of the spirit," and his name is no longer numbered among the dwellers of earth. He is set between the two winds between the north and the west where angels had measured the cords out for a place for the righteous. Enoch sees there "the first fathers" and those righteous who have dwelled there from the beginning (v.4).

In the next chapter, having ascended to the heavens, Enoch sees beings stepping on flames in white garments, with faces shining like snow. Falling on his face before the Lord of Spirits, Michael takes him by the hand and reveals all the secrets of heaven. Enoch's spirit is then translated by Michael into the "heaven of heavens" (v.5) where a structure "built of hailstones" is permeated by tongues of fire girding its four sides. And all the angels and heavenly beings surround the house, and from it pass the angels that are above the heavens, Michael, Gabriel, Raphael, and Phanuel, and innumerable holy angels. They are with the "Head of Days, with a head white and pure as wool, and his raiment indescribable" (71:10).

Something then happens to Enoch—in Nickelsburg and

VanderKam's translation: "And I fell on my face, and all my flesh melted, and my spirit was transformed [R. H. Charles had "transfigured"]. And I cried out with a loud voice, with a spirit of power, and I blessed and praised and exalted." His ecstatic utterances, suggesting union with the angelic state, are "acceptable" to the Head of Days who emerges with the four archangels and innumerable hosts. This coming out of the house, and the Head of Days's approaching Enoch with the archangels and thousands of angels, is "in the context of tradition"—as Nickelsburg and VanderKam note—"astonishing."[9]

"And he [the Head of Days? Variant texts read 'the angel'] came to me and greeted me with his voice and said to me, You (are) that Son of Man who was born* for righteousness, and righteousness dwells on you, and the righteousness of the Head of Days will not forsake you." And he said to me, "He proclaims peace to you in the name of the age that is to be, for from there peace has proceeded from the creation of the age, and thus you will have it forever and forever and ever. And all will walk on your path since righteousness will never forsake you; with you will be their dwellings and with you, their lot, and from you they will not be separated forever and forever and ever. And thus there will be length of days with that Son of Man, and there will be peace for the righteous, and the path of truth for the righteous, in the name of the Lord of Spirits forever and ever" (71:14–17; VanderKam and Nickelsburg translation).

Assumption of Enoch into the being and office of Son of Man marks chapter 71 apart from the rest of Parables. Nickelsburg and VanderKam regard it as "an appendix to the Book of Parables the function of which is to identify the patriarch Enoch as the Son of Man who has dominated the action throughout the book."[10] The twentieth century's dominant English translator of 1 Enoch, R. H. Charles,† could not imagine, as Nickelsburg and VanderKam point out, that the Parables' author would identify the Son of Man with Enoch, as such would violate the distance between the figures elsewhere observed.

---

*1 Enoch's sole passage referring to the Son of Man being "born."
†I have excluded from R. H. Charles's translation what he considered uncertain or corrupt words, Greek textual variants, and interpolations.

Charles presumed a passage had been dropped from the text, one repeating an earlier scene where Enoch inquires of an angel the identity of the one accompanying the Head of Days (the Son of Man).

Charles supposed verses 14b–17 constituted what remained of the angel's description of the Son of Man's function, mistakenly ascribed to Enoch by "some scribe" and transposed into the second person. So Charles changed the second person pronoun in verse 14b and all the second person pronominal prefixes in verses 14c–16 into the third person. "Charles's tour de force, however, has no foundation in the manuscripts, and has been universally rejected by scholars. The language here is that of an installation formula, as for example, in Psalm 2:7, and this fits well with a commissioning scene." As we shall see, this identification of Enoch as the Son of Man "can be read as a first step toward the angelification of the seer in 2 Enoch 22 and of his identity with Metatron in 3 Enoch."[11]*

And those are the narratives preserved in the Ethiopic 1 Enoch whose first English translation appeared in 1821, which, while significant, was but one more event in the amazing adventures of an amazing work.

---

*Nickelsburg and VanderKam note an alternative textual reading that reads the Ethiopian *we'etu* neither as demonstrative adjective ("*that* son of man") nor as indicating the definite article ("*the* son of man") but as a copula: "You are a son of man born for righteousness." This they consider unlikely for two reasons: the "Ezekiel-like" use of "son of man" occurs but once in 1 Enoch, in a Noachic interpolation at 60:10. The second juxtaposition of the Head of Days and Son of Man and other allusions to the Danielic context make it logical to assume the technical term occurring fifteen times in the Parables, "albeit with different Ethiopic formulations."[12]

FIVE

Further Adventures of 1 Enoch

In 1883, a new edition of Richard Laurence's translation appeared, issued by someone anxious to communicate Enoch's usefulness to criticizing belief in Christian scripture's uniqueness and providential inspiration. *The Book of Enoch the Prophet* (London: Kegan Paul & Trench, 1883) declared on its title page that its introduction was by the author of *The Evolution of Christianity* (Williams and Norgate, 1883), a work issued anonymously, like the introduction. Intelligent and educated, the anonymous writer questioned whether modern people could accept a Christianity reliant on supernatural belief. His choosing the word *Evolution* for his title doubtless alluded to aware-ness that Darwin's theory rendered Genesis's creation account scientifi-cally untenable. Hoping to avoid the slander aimed at Darwin, Charles Gill (writing anonymously*) attempted to show how Christian dog-mas were formed from unexpected sources. Chapter 5 of Gill's book, entitled "The Gnostic Gospel," for example, argued that the Gospel of John was an attempt to pass off the theology of heresiarch Valentinus (ca. 100–180 CE). In Gill's view, John's gospel's famous Prologue ("In the beginning was the *Logos* . . ."), was a condensed version of Valentinus's

---

*Possibly Sir Charles Frederick Gill (1851–1923), Irish barrister, trained at the Middle Temple, London; Recorder of Chichester (1890–1921); son of Charles Gill of Dublin.

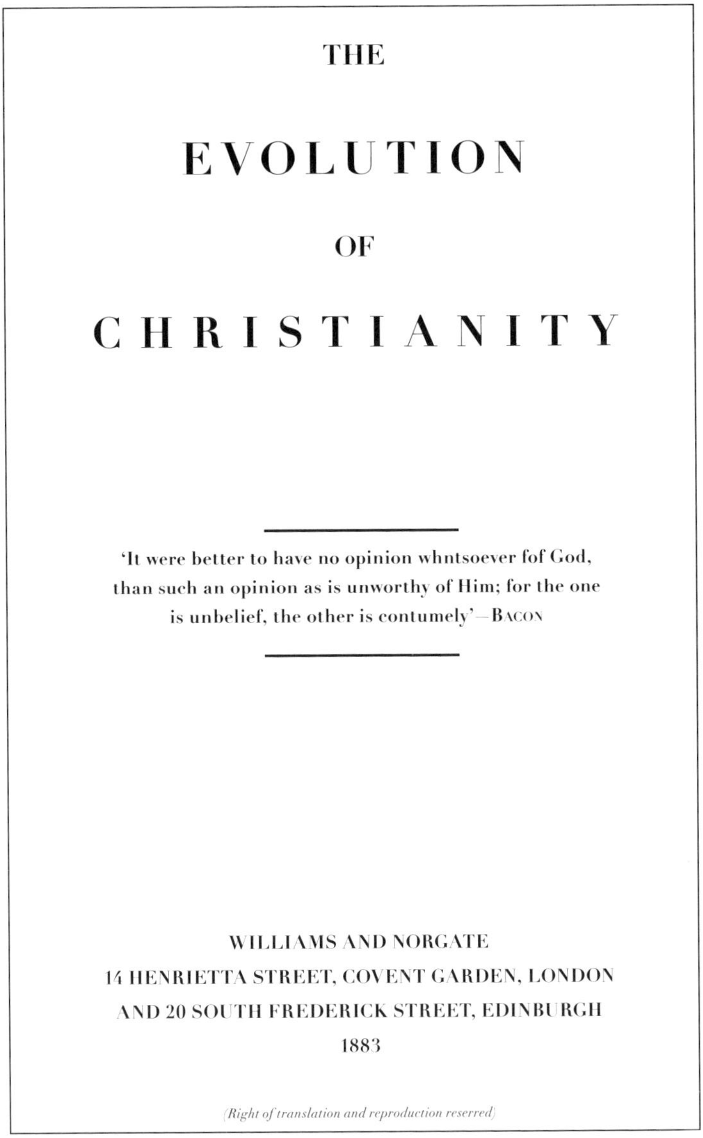

THE

EVOLUTION

OF

CHRISTIANITY

'It were better to have no opinion whntsoever fof God,
than such an opinion as is unworthy of Him; for the one
is unbelief, the other is contumely'—BACON

WILLIAMS AND NORGATE
14 HENRIETTA STREET, COVENT GARDEN, LONDON
AND 20 SOUTH FREDERICK STREET, EDINBURGH
1883

(Right of translation and reproduction reserved)

Fig. 5.1. *The Evolution of Christianity* (1883);
possibly by Sir Charles Gill.

divine Pleroma—a supposition scholars would dismiss today. Gill concluded that since Judaism and Christianity were of human origin, we
should seek truth from human experience only.

Our anonymous reissuer of Laurence's translation (Laurence had died in Dublin in 1838) appears unique in his period for seeing the Book of Enoch as providing keys to unlock Christian origins, furnishing what he regarded as proof of Christianity's derivative, human source. In a somewhat prescient introduction, Gill wrote:

> The attention of theologians has been concentrated on the passage from the Epistle of Jude because the author specifically names the prophet [Enoch]; but the cumulative incidence of language and ideas in Enoch and the authors of New Testament Scripture, as disclosed in the parallel passages which we have collated, clearly indicates that the work of the Semitic Milton [1 Enoch's "author"] was the inexhaustible source from which Evangelists and Apostles, or the men who wrote in their names, borrowed their conceptions of the resurrection, judgment, immortality, perdition, and of the universal reign of righteousness under the eternal dominion of the Son of man. This evangelical plagiarism culminates in the Revelation of John, which adapts the visions of Enoch to Christianity with modifications in which we miss the sublime simplicity of the great master of apocalyptic prediction, who prophesied in the name of the antediluvian patriarch [Enoch].
>
> It is important to observe that it was not the practice of early Christian writers to name the authors whose language and ideas they borrowed. . . . [W]hat candid and impartial enquirer can doubt the Enochian origin of the "Son of man sitting upon the throne of his glory"—the "new heaven" and the "new earth," the "many habitations" of the elect, and "the everlasting fire prepared for the devil and his angels"?[1]

Gill was quite earnest in his appeal for churches to recognize Enoch's profound implications: "Protestants, who adhere to the principles of the Reformation, and whose tenure of Christianity is therefore contingent on the appeal to reason, must inevitably enrol Enoch among the prophets, or reconsider the supernatural in Christianity."[2] Gill believed the book's existence supported his view that theological dogmas such as everlasting punishments and torture regarded as revelations from above should be considered of human origin. He believed "inevitable modifications of faith" were required by an honest response to the evidence, for 1 Enoch showed "that the language and ideas of alleged revelation are found in a pre-existent work, accepted by Evangelists and Apostles as inspired, but classed by modern theologians among apocryphal productions."[3]

Gill bolstered his opinion by an extensive series of parallel texts from 1 Enoch and the New Testament. Highlighting numerous striking links, Gill believed the new perspective could render even hitherto mysterious passages comprehensible, such as the parable in John 10:7–8 wherein the "sheep" are rescued by the "good shepherd" from hireling guardians and ferocious wolves. The reference to the shepherd's predecessors as "thieves and robbers" in the passage: "Verily, verily, I say unto you, I am the door of the sheep. All that ever came before me are thieves and robbers: but the sheep did not hear them"—was to Gill obviously borrowed from 1 Enoch 89 (from the Animal Apocalypse), where Enoch envisions rapacious shepherds killing and destroying the sheep (faithful Jews) before their lord's advent, as in v.65: "And I saw till these shepherds pastured in their season, and they began to slay and to destroy more than they were bidden, and they delivered those sheep into the hand of the lions." The chapter describes in metaphorical terms progressive enslavement of Jews at the hands of Egyptians, Assyro-Babylonians, and Persians, while all the time the "sheep and lambs" cry to the "lord of the sheep" for salvation from oppression and persecution.

Other notable parallels in Gill's inventory include the following:

1 Enoch 5:7a: "But for the elect there shall be light and joy and peace, And they shall inherit the earth."

Cf. Matthew 5:5: "Blessed are the meek: for they shall inherit the earth."

1 Enoch 94:7–8: "Woe to those who build their houses with sin; For from all their foundations shall they be overthrown, And by the sword shall they fall. And those who acquire gold and silver in

judgement suddenly shall perish. Woe to you, ye rich, for ye have trusted in your riches, And from your riches shall ye depart, Because ye have not remembered the Most High in the days of your riches."

Cf. James 5:1: "Go to now, ye rich men, weep and howl for your miseries that shall come upon you."

Luke 6:24: "Woe unto you that are rich! For ye have received your consolation."

1 Enoch 97:8–9: "Woe to you who acquire silver and gold in unrighteousness and say: 'We have become rich with riches and have possessions; And have acquired everything we have desired. And now let us do what we purposed: For we have gathered silver, And many are the husbandmen in our houses.' And our granaries are (brim) full as with water, Yea and like water your lies shall flow away; For your riches shall not abide But speedily ascend from you;"

Cf. Luke 12:16–19: "And he spake a parable unto them, saying, The ground of a certain rich man brought forth plentifully: And he thought within himself, saying, What shall I do, because I have no room where to bestow my fruits? And he said, This will I do: I will pull down my barns, and build greater; and there will I bestow all my fruits and my goods. And I will say to my soul, Soul, thou hast much goods laid up for many years, take thine ease, eat, drink, and be merry. But God said unto him, Thou fool, this night thy soul shall be required of thee."

1 Enoch 108:12: "And I will bring forth in shining light those who have loved My holy name, and I will seat each on the throne of his honour."

Cf. Matthew 19:28: "Ye also shall sit upon twelve thrones, judging the twelve tribes of Israel."

1 Enoch 63:8b: "And his judgments have no respect of persons."

Cf. Romans 2:11: "For there is no respect of persons with God."

1 Enoch 38:2c: "And where the resting-place of those who have

denied the Lord of Spirits? It had been good for them if they had not been born."

Cf. Jude v.4: "Denying our only Master and Lord Jesus Christ."

Matthew 26:24: "Woe unto that man through whom the Son of man is betrayed! It would be good for that man if he had not been born."

1 Enoch 19:2: "Here shall stand the angels who have connected themselves with women, and their spirits assuming many different forms are defiling mankind and shall lead them astray into sacrificing to demons as gods."

Cf. 1 Corinthians 10:20: "The things which the Gentiles sacrifice, they sacrifice to devils, and not to God."

1 Enoch: 39:3, 4, 7: "And in those days a whirlwind carried me off from the earth,

And set me down at the end of the heavens.

And there I saw another vision, the dwelling-places of the holy, And the resting-places of the righteous.

And I saw his dwelling-place under the wings of the Lord of Spirits. And all the righteous and elect before Him shall be as fiery lights, And their mouth shall be full of blessing, And their lips extol the name of the Lord of Spirits."

Cf. 2 Corinthians 12:1b, 2, 4: "I will come to visions and revelations of the Lord. I knew a man in Christ . . . caught up to the third heaven, . . . whether in the body or out of the body I cannot tell: God knoweth. How that he was caught up into paradise, and heard unspeakable words, which it is not lawful for a man to utter."

1 Enoch 46:3: "This is the son of Man who hath righteousness, . . . And who revealeth all the treasures of that which is hidden."

Cf. Colossians 2:3: "In whom are hid all the treasures of wisdom and knowledge."

1 Enoch 9:3–5: "And they said to the Lord of the ages: 'Lord of lords, God of gods, King of kings, and God of the ages, the throne of Thy glory unto all the generations of the ages, and Thy name holy and glorious and blessed unto all the ages! Thou hast made all things, and power over all things hast Thou: and all things are naked and open in Thy sight, and Thou seest all things, and nothing can hide itself from Thee.'"

Cf' Revelation 4:11: "Thou art worthy O Lord, to receive glory, and honour, and power; for thou hast created all things, and for thy pleasure they are, and were created."

Hebrews 4:13: "Neither is there any creature that is not manifest in his sight; but all things are naked and open unto the eyes of him with whom we have to do."

1 Enoch 25:6–7: "Then shall they rejoice with joy and be glad, And into the holy place shall they enter; And its fragrance shall be in their bones, And they shall live a long life on earth, such as thy fathers lived: And in their days shall no sorrow or plague Or torment or calamity touch them. Then blessed I the God of Glory, the Eternal King, who hath prepared such things for the righteous, and hath created them and promised to give to them."

Cf. Revelation 22:2: "On either side of the river was a tree of life, which bare twelve manner of fruits, and yielded its fruit every month; and the leaves of the tree were for the healing of the nations."

Rev. 2:7: "To him that overcometh will I give to eat of the tree of life, which is in the midst of the paradise of God."

Rev. 22:14: "Blessed are they that do his commandments, that they may have the right to the tree of life."

1 Enoch 86:1: "And again I saw with mine eyes as I slept, and I saw the heaven above, and behold a star fell from heaven."

Cf. Revelation 9:1: "I saw a star fall from heaven unto the earth."

1 Enoch 21:7–10: "I saw a horrible thing: a great fire there which

burnt and blazed, and the place was cleft as far as the abyss, being full of great descending columns of fire: neither its extent or magnitude could I see, nor could I conjecture. . . . And he [Uriel] said unto me: 'This place is the prison of the angels, and here they will be imprisoned for ever.'"

Cf. Revelation 20:1–3: "And I saw an angel come down from heaven, having the key of the bottomless pit (abyss) and a great chain in his hand. And he laid hold on the devil and . . . cast him into the bottomless pit, and shut it, and sealed it over him."

1 Enoch 80:2–7: "And in the days of the sinners the years shall be shortened, And their seed shall be tardy on their lands and fields, And all things on the earth shall alter, And shall not appear in their time: And the rain shall be kept back And the heaven shall withhold (it). And in those times the fruits of the earth shall be backward, And shall not grow in their time, And the fruits of the trees shall be withheld in their time. And the moon shall alter her order, And not appear at her time.

And shall shine more brightly than accords with the order of light. And many chiefs of the stars shall transgress the order (prescribed). And these shall alter their orbits and tasks, And not appear at the seasons prescribed to them. And the whole order of the stars shall be concealed from the sinners."

1 Enoch 45:3: "On that day Mine Elect One shall sit on the throne of glory And shall [try] their works."

Cf. Matthew 24:22, 29–30: "And except those days should be shortened, there should no flesh be saved: but for the elect's sake those days shall be shortened. . . . Immediately after the tribulation of those days shall the sun be darkened, and the moon shall not give her light, and the stars shall fall from heaven, and the powers of the heavens shall be shaken: And then shall appear the sign of the Son of man in heaven: and then shall all the tribes of the earth mourn, and they shall see the Son of man coming in the clouds of heaven with power and great glory."

1 Enoch 47:3: "In those days I saw the Head of Days when He seated himself upon the throne of His glory, And the books of the living were opened before Him: And all His host which is in heaven above and His counsellors stood before Him."

Cf. Revelation 20:11–12: "And I saw a great white throne, and him that sat on it, from whose face the earth and the heaven fled away; and there was found no place for them. And I saw the dead, small and great, stand before God; and the books were opened: and another book was opened, which is the book of life: and the dead were judged out of those things which were written in the books, according to their works."

1 Enoch 91:16: "And the first heaven shall depart and pass away, And a new heaven shall appear."

Cf. 2 Peter 3:13: "Nevertheless, we, according to his promise, look for new heavens and a new earth, wherein dwelleth righteousness."

Revelation 22:1: "I saw a new heaven and a new earth, for the first heaven and the first earth were passed away."

1 Enoch 62:2, 4: "And the word of his mouth slays all the sinners, And all the unrighteous are destroyed from before his face. . . . Then shall pain come upon them as on a woman in travail,

When her child enters the mouth of the womb, And she has pain in bringing forth. And one portion of them shall look on the other, And they shall be terrified, And they shall be downcast of countenance, And pain shall seize them, When they see that Son of Man Sitting on the throne of his glory."

Cf. 2 Thessalonians 2:8: "That wicked whom the Lord shall consume with the Spirit of his mouth."

1 Thessalonians 5:3: "For when they shall say, Peace and safety; then sudden destruction cometh upon them, as travail upon a woman with child; and they shall not escape."

Matthew 25:31: "When the Son of man shall come in his glory, then shall he sit upon the throne of his glory."

It will be noted that the canonical gospel that Gill saw as drawing most from 1 Enoch was Matthew—indeed, Matthew is traditionally held to have been written to emphasize Jesus's convincing fulfillment of Jewish prophecy pointing to the coming one, the elect of God. The original movement of "Nazarenes" was a movement within the heart of Middle Judaism.

Enter R. H. Charles

As the nineteenth century approached its end and scholars obtained variant manuscripts of the Ethiopic Enoch—developments reflected notably by German orientalist and theologian C. F. August Dillmann (1823–1894), whose Ethiopic edition of 1 Enoch appeared in Germany in 1851—the time had come for a more accurate English translation. To his great credit, the task fell to Irish Anglican Robert Henry Charles D.D., F.B.A. (1855–1931), of Trinity College, Dublin, afterward Fellow of Merton College, Oxford (1910). Oxford's Clarendon Press published R. H. Charles's *The Book of Enoch, Translated from Professor Dillmann's Ethiopic Text* in 1893. Charles's first attempt at definitive translation, including recent discoveries of Greek fragments, was followed in 1906 by his fully annotated Ge'ez text, and in 1912 with a revised translation, with introduction, notes, appendices, and indexes recast and rewritten. Published in a more popular edition in 1917 without extensive critical apparatus,[4] this edition first immersed me into waters Enochic in 1994.

R. H. Charles had interesting things to declare about 1 Enoch: "the influence of 1 Enoch on the New Testament," he wrote, "has been greater than that of all the other apocryphal and pseudepigraphical books put together." A mighty claim! Like Gill (but without referring to Gill's comparisons) Charles provided his 1912 edition with a powerful inventory of over twenty-six New Testament parallels with 1 Enoch in his chapter "The Influence of 1 Enoch on the New Testament"[5]— passages, he believed, that "either in phraseology or idea directly depend on, or are illustrative of, passages in 1 Enoch."[6] Charles further asserted that certain doctrines in 1 Enoch had "an undoubted share in moulding the corresponding New Testament doctrines,"—near explosive testimony to Enoch's importance viewable as either belated recognition, or as prescient of developments to come.

In the introduction to R. H. Charles's 1917 edition, W. O. E. Oesterley enhanced Charles's view with words from Burkitt's *Jewish and Christian Apocalypses*: "It is when you study Matthew, Mark, and Luke against the background of the Books of Enoch that you see them [the gospels] in their true perspective. In saying this I have no intention of detracting from the importance of what the Gospels report to us. On the contrary, it puts familiar words into their proper setting. Indeed, it seems to me that some of the best-known Sayings of Jesus only appear in their true light if regarded as *Midrash* [interpretation] upon words and concepts that were familiar to those who heard the prophet of Galilee, though now they have been forgotten by Jew and Christian alike."[7]

If such were the case, then the peculiar emphases of Enochic testimony must already have been resonating with people in Galilee and elsewhere for some time.

Recent scholarship, however, warns against what Leslie Baynes has dubbed "parallelomania" in comparing phrases from 1 Enoch with the New Testament.[8] Reflecting on the seventh "Enoch Seminar" at Camaldoli in July 2013, organizers Gabriele Boccaccini and Loren T. Stuckenbruck fully recognized that while R. H. Charles's powerful statement regarding 1 Enoch's influence on the New Testament "took debate to a new level," it was necessary to define the meaning of "influence." Some, they wrote, have preferred "intertextuality" or "echoes": words avoiding the inference of direct influence or of copying.[9] Another approach is simply to say knowledge of the setting of one source is enhanced by knowledge of another. The book of Revelation, for example, obviously draws by allusion, not by quotation, on declarations in Ezekiel, Daniel, Zechariah, Isaiah, and Exodus. Indeed, there "is nothing lost when saying that some traditions found in 1 Enoch contributed to the world of thought within which the convictions and ideas found in the New Testament took shape."[10] Boccaccini and Stuckenbruck reckoned it can be helpful to put infra-resonant texts "in conversation" with one another, without bending either's meaning to suit another

Fig. 5.2. R. H. Charles, D.D., F.B.A. (1855–1931).

text. In the case of the Son of Man, for example, if a late-first-century-BCE or early-first-century-CE date is correct, it is "hard not to think of a connection" between the Parables and Matthew. "In both cases, the Son of Man denotes a heavenly figure who executes divine judgment on behalf of God as the present age comes to a close." Besides, both appeal to Daniel 7:13–14, so "a connection, it seems [!], is certain."[11]

Of R. H. Charles's new commentary of 1912, Nickelsburg writes "its detailed introduction, often intelligent conjectures, and mass of informative notes make it a resource still to be consulted." It became the standard work for two generations of Enoch scholarship. Nevertheless, argues Nickelsburg (whose commentary and translations with James VanderKam have superseded Charles's), "although Charles's edition of 1912/13 is still useful in many ways, it is outdated by new textual resources, a larger corpus of related primary literature, and not least, new methodologies that clarify how Charles's rational western mind, with its desire for consistency and its aversion to symbolic narrative, sometimes hindered his understanding of the ancient apocalyptic texts that he was otherwise so well informed and gifted to interpret."[12]

It is nonetheless poignant that Charles's passionate utterance over 1 Enoch's significance to Christian origins fell mostly upon deaf ears in his own time, a ringing deafness increased by two adjectives constantly applied to 1 Enoch: *apocryphal*, and *pseudepigraphical*. When not consigned to footnotes, Enoch, despite Charles's exemplary work, was simply sidelined in mainstream theology. That *would* start to change, though it would take almost another century. Sadly, Charles did not see fulfillment of the promise he left us.

One obstruction to seeing 1 Enoch's importance was that until the fact of the Holocaust began to sink into the minds of Western academics and church people, 1 Enoch was seen primarily as *Jewish* pseudepigrapha, not even Christian apocrypha. It was taken for granted that Christianity had long been rejected by the majority of Jews because its doctrines were believed inimical, even hostile, to Jewish religious interests. Indeed, the rabbinic movement that followed the temple's destruction in 70 CE, and which moved toward a stricter canon of scripture than hitherto, rejected Enoch, though Tertullian was minded to attribute this to Jewish annoyance at Enoch's utility to Christian prophecy! So Enoch was shoved into a kind of ecclesiastical no-man's land. In the end, and with some irony, rabbinic hostility to the Enochic corpus became another reason for orthodox Christian authorities from the fourth century onward to exclude it.

R. H. Charles expressed the significance of the change that overtook Middle Judaism after the fall of the Temple: "The books, or sections, of Enoch were written by orthodox Jews, who belonged to the apocalyptic or prophetic side of Judaism, and by Judaism is here meant, not the one-sided legalistic Judaism that posed as the sole and orthodox Judaism after the fall of Jerusalem in 70 AD, but the larger and more comprehensive Judaism that preceded it. This larger Judaism embraced both the prophetic and the legalistic elements. No religion can make progress without both elements, and, if progress in spiritual development is to be realized, the prophetic element is absolutely indispensable."[13]

Interestingly, in this same chapter on the "Theology" of 1 Enoch (assuming it expresses a consistent theology), Charles observed that as far as he knew, "most Jewish writers have ascribed the Book of Enoch and kindred literature to the Essenes"[14]—a rather surprising snippet that brings us closer to the next critical revelation in Enochic studies.

R. H. Charles's 1912 publication seems to have done more than any other translation of 1 Enoch to bring Enoch studies into the open. Nevertheless, though these studies lumbered into slightly higher gear as scholars tentatively grasped what Charles had found about Enoch's significance to Christian origins, there was as yet no epiphany. Such might have come closer had not World War I's catastrophic dislocation of culture occurred. Still, Enoch had his modern scholars.

One of them was Gershom Scholem (1897–1982). Scholem's breakthrough masterpiece *Major Trends in Jewish Mysticism* first appeared in Jerusalem and New York at the time of Japan's unprovoked attack on Pearl Harbor. Having become Jerusalem's Hebrew University's first professor of Jewish mysticism in 1933, Scholem's 1941 argument that kabbalah, with its "gnostical elements,"[15] was a vital strength of the Jewish faith rather than a mistaken heresy as many rabbis thought and think, led him to delve into, at that time, still largely unanalyzed traditions.

Fig. 5.3. Gershom Scholem reading the *Zohar* during
the Sukkot Festival, 1925.

"One fact remains certain," Scholem wrote in *Major Trends*, "the main subjects of the later Merkabah mysticism already occupy a central position in this oldest esoteric literature, best represented by the Book of Enoch."[16] In that study he recognized the Book of Enoch as the pioneer work of the mystical movement whose importance and value had been underestimated.

Academically speaking, the Book of Enoch had arrived. It would take but one more spark to light the blue touchpaper.

Around November 1947, John C. Trever of the American Schools of Oriental Research, operating in the then–British Mandate of Palestine, was alerted to the selling of ancient scrolls extracted by Bedouin shepherds from a Jordanian cave near the Dead Sea between December 1946 and February 1947. Their discovery would change the shape of Enoch studies forever.

Like a jinn from a jar, the Book of Enoch was poised to return again, but this time in a form and context utterly unexpected.

PART TWO

The Qumran
Explosion

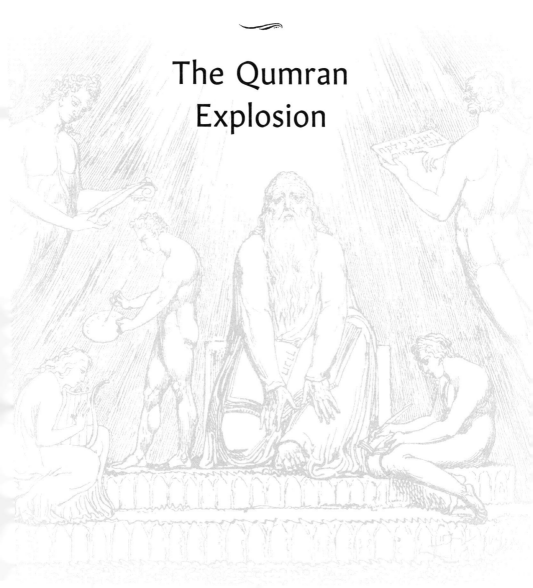

SIX

Amazing Discoveries

A *wadi* is a channel or chasm formed over millennia by brief but heavy rains eroding desert rock. The Wadi Qumran runs west into the far northwestern edge of the Dead Sea, some ten miles south of Jericho. While scholar Émile Puech reckoned Joshua 15:61's "Sokokah" (or Sakakah), near En Gedi in the Judean wilderness, was ancient Judea's name for the location,[1] Puech's supposition is uncertain since Qumran's nearby ruins (Arabic: *khirbet*) lack house foundations, suggesting neither town nor village. Numerous hypotheses account for the ruins' original function.

Some three-quarters of a mile inland from the shore rises a sandy-gold escarpment, whose bulbous steepness secretes seven significant caves. Following the cliffs northward for a mile, two more caves become visible, while a further two pock the cliffs over the next three-quarters of a mile. Ta'amireh Bedouin shepherds discovered the first Dead Sea Scrolls here in 1946 and 1947; archaeologists and biblical scholars soon followed—among them, Polish priest Józef Tadeusz Milik (1922–2006).

In September 1952, Milik was thrilled to identify the first leather fragment of an Aramaic Book of Enoch in newly excavated Cave 4 hollowed from the marl bank at the foot of Wadi Qumran. Milik dug out further fragments, and over the following years identified fragments of seven manuscripts corresponding to Ethiopic Enoch's first, fourth, and fifth sections, while four other manuscripts corresponded to its third section, the Astronomical Book, which revealed the Ethiopic version inferior to the "new" Aramaic material. Even late antiquity's church fathers had never seen such ancient copies. In April 1970, Milik identified nine fragments discovered in caves 4, 1, 2, and 6 with an Enochic Book of Giants, dated from the first half of the first century BCE to the early first century CE, absent from Ethiopic Enoch but favored by Persian prophet Mani (216–274 or 277 CE). So far, however, no fragment has been identified with 1 Enoch's controversial second section, the Book of Parables, whose remarkable descriptions of the heavenly Son of Man appear redolent, and arguably formative, of Jesus's title in the gospels.*

Also relevant to our story, eight copies of the related book of Jubilees have been uncovered, along with a pesher (interpretation) on the Watchers story (4Q 180–81), and eight copies of the crucially important Damascus Document that knows the Watchers tradition and in its account of the beginning of a "new covenant" in "the land of Damascus," appeals to the authority of the Enochic-influenced book of Jubilees.

Fragments recovered give us an Aramaic text for 50 percent of the Ethiopic Book of the Watchers, 30 percent of the Astronomical Book, 26 percent of the Book of Dreams, and 18 percent of the Epistle of Enoch.[2] As to dates—subject to a wide margin of error—manuscripts from Cave 4 have been dated to the first half, the middle, and third quarter of the second century BCE, and to the first half, middle, last third, and last quarter of the first century BCE. The four copies of the Astronomical Book may date from the end of the third or beginning of the second century BCE, from the middle and second half of the first century BCE, with one manuscript written in classical Herodian style and dated to the early first century CE.[3]

According to Jean-Baptiste Humbert and Jodi Magness's surveys of archaeological evidence, the site's initial establishment occurred ca. 100–50 BCE,[4] so the Enoch dates suggest some of the Enochic texts

---

*It's estimated that barely a quarter of manuscripts originally stored here have survived.

at least were not produced at the site, and such may be true of most or all scrolls discovered to date.

In context, Enochic texts are among approximately 800 known manuscripts. According to Devorah Dimant, 223 Dead Sea manuscripts contain biblical texts (30 percent); 192 texts employ terminology scholars have dubbed "sectarian" or pertinent to particular theological and party tendencies (25 percent); 249 texts do not employ such terminology (33 percent); while 96 texts remain unidentified (12 percent).[5] One may therefore deduce that asserting the surviving collection was owned by one group would require significant supportive evidence. Despite this, common ownership has been repeatedly deduced or assumed—and this is not the only assumption to have shaped scholars' approaches to the scrolls, a situation we owe partly to a protracted academic scandal wherein access was restricted to a coterie of scholars disposed to see Jewish sectarianism as predominant: a desert monastery with an identity—Essene—culled from works by Josephus, Philo of Alexandria, Pliny and Dio Chrysostom (early and late first century CE). Restrictive monopolizing persisted till the early 1990s when protests succeeded in opening up all pertinent photographic plates to scholars worldwide. Scholarship has since exposed the scrolls to diverse peer-reviewed interpretations as well as sensation-sensitive stories that have penetrated public awareness for half a century. However, it is arguable that the finding of Enochic books among the Dead Sea Scrolls has almost overwhelmed perception of their value and origin, as they now, unsurprisingly, tend to be viewed through a Qumran-centered lens.

The Enoch Seminar

Great strides in Enochic studies have been afforded by Professor Gabriele Boccaccini's establishment in the late 1990s of the Enoch Seminar whose first meeting graced Florence in 2001. Sharing and challenging insights and discoveries, dedicated international associates, working on contrasting, sometimes contradictory interpretations of evidence, have contributed to exemplary models of academic cooperation in seminar publications. In the process, the concept of "Enochic Judaism" has

Fig. 6.1. Wadi Qumran, with the Dead Sea above center. (Photo: Hoshvilim)

emerged to denote more a distinct variety of Judaism than a literary tradition.* Readers may examine the seminar's website (4enoch.org) to see how analysis of Enoch's influence on Christian origins, for example, has moved from interest in the Son of Man to many other issues, including forgiveness of sins, ideas of judgment and repentance, demonology, eschatology, and the origin of evil.

The June 2023 online seminar featured papers on subjects as diverse as the nature of transmission of early Enochic texts; new dating hypotheses; the myth of the Watchers compared to narratives of Phoenician historian, Philo of Byblos; the Watchers myth in relation to the Achaemenid Empire's decline; the narrator's role in 1 Enoch; royal court sociology in relation to the Enochic heaven; astral magic in the myth of the Watchers; Enochic tradition in Mesopotamian incantation bowls; the Astronomical Book's role in spreading the idea of the zodiac; the absence of covenantal theology in Enochic texts; Hellenistic myths in Jewish pseudepigrapha; repentance in Parables; John the Baptist; the gospels; Christian commentary on 1 Enoch in Ethiopia; Enoch's ascent in Islamic tradition; contemporary reception of Richard Laurence's

*Professor Boccaccini attributes the rediscovery of Enochic Judaism to George Nickelsburg and Paolo Sacchi, who founded the journal *Henoch* in 1979.

translation; and the use of 1 Enoch for apocalyptic prognosis in today's Christian fundamentalist-tending internet traffic.

The seminar continues to devote much work to tracing reception of Enochic traditions over the past two millennia. Contrary to supposition, Enoch has never been completely lost. The setting of 1 Enoch in the Ethiopic church, for example, has come increasingly under the scholarly spotlight. New assessments of text composition emerge as fresh issues are highlighted; hypotheses are modified or abandoned as perspectives become refined.

While the first summer 2001 Enoch Seminar marked a turning point, the fall of that year also saw George Nickelsburg's Hermeneia Series commentary on 1 Enoch published, its 618 pages constituting a new standard commentary on the Book of the Watchers, Dream Visions, and the Epistle of Enoch. As Nickelsburg remarked: "The discovery of the Qumran scrolls profoundly changed the study of 1 Enoch and the interpretation of early Judaism in both Jewish and Christian circles."[6]

Regarding origin and transmission of Enochic texts, Nickelsburg considered it reasonable to infer an "Enochic community," identified as possessors of Enoch's wisdom. Proponents likely included scribes, deviating perhaps from the emphatic pro-Torah tradition of priest and "scribe of the law of the God of heaven" Ezra (Ezra 7:12, ca. 450 BCE), while probably respecting Ezra's condemnation of marriage twixt Jewish men and Gentile women.

Enoch—"scribe of righteousness"—speaks much of righteousness but very little of the Mosaic Torah: a significant issue. Nickelsburg posited a link to the *maskilim*—"wise discerning ones"—of Daniel 11:33–35 and 12:3: a distinct group.[7] Nickelsburg also accepted the possibility of Enochic priorities uniting disaffected priests in Jerusalem,[8] a notion attracting much support, with many historical (including pre-Danielic) and internal textual references gathered in support. The Animal Apocalypse, for example, criticizes Jerusalem's dominant priesthood, comparing it adversely to the heavenly sanctuary. Enochic insistence on the solar calendar's reflection of heavenly itineraries may well reflect priestly efforts to resist the Hellenistic lunar year imposed by

Antiochus IV in ca. 175 BCE and still observed when Jonathan ben Mattathias became high priest in 161 BCE. Nickelsburg has also speculated that the "lambs" in that apocalypse may indicate the hasidim—meaning the pious or divinely virtuous "devoted unto the law"—who joined Mattathias and son Judas against Antiochus in 1 Maccabees 2:42–43, with a supposed exclusive community of the scrolls descended from them.[9] Such references may infer dating probabilities, but in the absence of direct positive evidence, they are still interpretive, as is so much in the field.

That Enochic texts were favorites, for a time at least, among scroll depositors has fostered numerous hypotheses around a Qumran *yahad* (Hebrew for "union") as "latterday derivative" or successor to a community or communities that wrote and transmitted Enochic texts.[10] Giving the question of origins a different emphasis, the Book of the Watchers' familiarity with Galilean geography (especially about Dan) has suggested Galilean provenance: a rich vein of research, as we shall see.

The Essene Hypothesis

In 1948, Israeli archaeologist Eleazar L. Sukenik first related the Dead Sea Scrolls to Essenism. Something had to explain why texts were appearing that did not cohere with familiar categories of Second Temple Jewish thought. While the Damascus Document (commonly called "CD" for "Covenant of Damascus") was already known from a manuscript discovered in a Cairo synagogue storeroom in 1896, previously unknown, erudite writings also emerged. The Temple Scroll, War Scroll, Community Rule, purity rules, numerous hymns, prayers, and *pesherim* (interpretative commentaries) on certain prophets appeared with common viewpoints, terminology, and elevated styles redolent of familiar sacred texts. Particular texts seemed to evince a defined community of righteous, called men, looking to the world's end and judgment of the wicked, with parts to play in a final conflict. While some apparently sectarian texts seemed more exclusive than others, all reflected disdain for corruption in temple and priesthood, with itineraries for renewal.

Josephus described four Jewish sects, and "sectarian" texts didn't fit three of them: Sadducees, Pharisees, and armed Zealots (unless Zealots fostered an unknown literary wing). That left the fourth sect: Essenes, famed for spiritual pursuits, religious discipline, and separated communal life. Furthermore, Josephus's contemporaries, Gentiles Pliny and Dio of Prusa, reported a peculiarly ancient "Essene" center near En Gedi by the Dead Sea's western shore. On the Dead's Sea's western side, Qumran's caves overlook the vicinity of long-ruined stone structures.

Enter Dominican priest Roland Guérin de Vaux (1903–1971), director of the École Biblique, a French Catholic Theological School in East Jerusalem. Inured to monastic order, and dominating the Scrolls team for over two decades, de Vaux saw sacred texts-plus-ruins, and deduced: monastery. In that arguably anachronistic frame, he interpreted the site's archaeology. To this day, Israeli tourist materials echo his conclusion: Qumran was an Essene monastery. One might have thought the absence of the word Essene from any of the scrolls might have inhibited

Fig. 6.2. Pliny the Elder.

Fig. 6.3. Roland de Vaux, 1954.

enthusiasm. Moreover, there's a notable disparity between important elements of the scrolls and Josephus's accounts of Essene beliefs.

Josephus and the Essenes

After initially defending Galilee from Roman attack during the Jewish Revolt that began in 63 CE, Jewish aristocrat and priest's son Yosef ben Matityahu (ca. 37 CE–ca. 100 CE) fell into Roman hands. Enslaved to conqueror Vespasian, the captured commander declared *Vespasian* the East's prophesied redeemer. Granted freedom and Roman citizenship, Yosef took the latter's family name and became Titus Flavius Josephus. Two enormous works, one from the late 70s (*The History of the Jewish War against the Romans*), the other from the late 80s and early 90s (*Antiquities of the Jews*) would earn the collaborator eminence as premier historian of the Second Temple period and its aftermath.

In the course of listing some of the Essene sect's demands on proselytes in *Jewish War*, Josephus mentions books valued by the sect in connection with the "names of the angels." Proselytes had to swear "to communicate their doctrines to no one any otherwise than as he received them himself; that he will abstain from robbery, and will

Fig. 6.4. Bust of Emperor Vespasian, from Naples, ca. 70 CE; Ny Carlsberg Glyptotek, Copenhagen. (Photo: Carole Raddato)

equally preserve the books belonging to their sect, and the names of the angels" (*War* 2.8.7).

It's possible that Josephus's note about preserving books and names of angels might indicate respect among Essenes for Enochic literature, since 1 Enoch contains several lists of angels, with names and functions performed by archangels in running of the universe—the latter being a topic of interest to Essenes, according to Philo of Alexandria.[11] It is certainly a book a Jew might consult—perhaps the first—in this period, to find angels' names.

In the preceding section of chapter 8, Josephus had already asserted how "They [Essenes] also take great pains in studying the works of the ancients, and choose out of them what is most for the advantage of their soul and body" (*War* 2.8.6); Josephus's "ancients" might well include Enoch. As for the body, Josephus mentions books on natural plant remedies valued by Essenes; as for the soul, there's surely meat for a soul's welfare in Enochic literature.

However, even if we conjecture Enoch's prophecies were dear to Essenes in the first century CE, there's no indication, from Josephus at any rate, that Essenes had at any time *authored* such works. Nevertheless, there is much in the Enochic books to support disciplines of personal charity and righteousness imposed on proselytes, as well as other tenets of the sect such as—for full members—*not* making oaths, restraint from passionate attachments to women, eschewing ostentatious clothing, or resorting to weapons of war, anger, or violence. These proscriptions could hypothetically have been inspired by a wish to avoid specific sins instituted by the Watchers following the Mount Hermon pact to pursue passion and vanities without restraint.

In 1912, R. H. Charles dismissed as "indefensible" the notion that 1 Enoch was penned by Essenes, citing Josephus's *War* 2.8.2 and *Antiquities* 18.1.5, along with Philo of Alexandria (*Hypothetica*: "*Essaiōn gar oudeis agetai gunaika*" = "for no Essene takes a wife"[12]), Roman historian Pliny (*Natural History* 5.15.17), and Hippolytus, *Refutatio omnium Haereses* (9.13–23). All of them, according to Charles, asserted that Essenes condemned marriage, whereas condemnation of human marriage *per se* is nowhere found in 1 Enoch.

Against this now old objection, it is recognized that Josephus's position on Essenes and marriage is nuanced. Josephus understood that Essenes regarded conquest of passion a virtue, with pleasure rejected "as an evil." According to *War* 2.8.2, Essenes "neglect wedlock, but choose out other persons' children while they are pliable, and fit for learning, and esteem them to be of their kindred, and form them according to their own manners. They do not absolutely deny the fitness of marriage, and the succession of mankind thereby continued; but they guard against the lascivious behaviour of women, and are persuaded that none of them preserve their fidelity to one man."

In *War* 2.8.13 we learn of Essenes who differ in this: "Moreover, there is another order of Essenes, who agree with the rest as to their way of living, and customs, and laws, but differ from them in the point of marriage, as thinking that by not marrying they cut off the principal part of human life, which is the prospect of succession; nay rather, that if all men should be of the same opinion, the whole race of mankind would fail. However, they try their spouses for three years, and if they find that they have their natural purgations thrice, as trials that they are likely to be fruitful, they then actually marry them. But they do not use to accompany with their wives when they are with child, as a demonstration that they do not marry out of regard to pleasure, but for the sake of posterity. Now the women go into the baths with some of their garments on, as the men do with somewhat girded about them. And these are the customs of this order of Essenes." In Josephus's later *Antiquities* 18.1.5 the view is more emphatic: "There are about four thousand men that live in this way: and neither marry wives, nor are desirous to keep servants: as thinking the latter tempts men to be unjust; and the former gives the handle to domestic quarrels. But as they live by themselves, they minister one to another."

According to Jewish philosopher, and contemporary of Jesus, Philo of Alexandria's *Hypothetica*, Essenes "eschew marriage because they clearly discern it to be the sole or the principal danger to the maintenance of the communal life, as well as because they particularly practise continence. For no Essene takes a wife, because a wife is a selfish creature, excessively jealous and an adept at beguiling the morals of her husband and seducing him by her continued impostures."[13]

Pliny's *Natural History* (5.15.17) only seems to know of Essenes living to the north of Engedi on the Dead Sea's west side, whereas Josephus puts Essene communities in cities and villages throughout the country, but Philo only in villages. The Roman Pliny doesn't say whether members might have been, or were still married, only, like Josephus, that they'd renounced passionate desire:

> On the west side of the Dead Sea, but out of range of the noxious exhalations of the coast, is the solitary tribe of the Essenes which is remarkable beyond all the other tribes of the whole world as it has no women and has renounced all sexual desire, has no money, and has only palm trees for company. Day by day the throng of refugees is recruited to an equal number by numerous accessions of persons tired of life and driven there by the waves of fortune to adopt their

Fig. 6.5. Ein Gedi, Judean desert today; botanical garden at the kibbutz. (Photo: Ester Inbar)

manners. Thus, through thousands of ages (incredible to relate) a race in which no one is born lives on forever—so prolific for their advantage is other men's weariness of life![14]

Taking these accounts on balance, one may conclude suppression of bodily desire was the root of marital issues for Essenes, so there's room for supposing some members may already have performed marital duties before becoming Essenes, rather like Hindu men who renounce social for religious obligations to become *sanyasis*, often to familial annoyance. Marriage was, if Josephus is accurate, not something most Essenes would contemplate *after* joining, though he makes clear a minority were prepared to, so long as they married for duty, not pleasure.

Objections to an Essene-penned Enochic tradition, or an Enochic tradition fostered and transmitted by Essenes, persist. Eyal Regev (Bar Ilan University, Israel) for example, emphasizes absence of celibacy in the Damascus Document, the Community Rule, and "yahad" documents, writing: "I find it impossible to argue that the Qumran sects and the Essenes are the same or that the yahad and the Damascus Covenant are groups within the large (and ultimately, celibate) Essene movement. But

. . . it is hard to deny that there is a certain, more complex relationship between them."[15*]

Tying the issue of Essenes and Enoch to the notion of Enochic Judaism, John C. Reeves (University of North Carolina) has argued the latter term is simply an abstraction of the contents of 1 Enoch.[16] A skeptic, Reeves is no more pleased with the word *Essene*, perceiving an "uncritical acceptance of the word Essene as a meaningful label for actual religious behaviour."[17] Reeves has questioned that were it true Enochic myths go back to the First Temple, then one might presume them held by Zadokites (dominant priests) as well as dissident priests. He notes absence of evidence that Zadokites were against Enochic literature. As for Philo and Josephus's evidence, Reeves has opined it "extremely improbable" they had intimate knowledge of Essenes, which Reeves considers "an ethnological trope" to be compared with that of druids, magi, and Indian gymnosophists.[18]

Less sweeping are reservations espoused by John C. Collins (Yale University) who, while having been willing to consider the Damascus Document (CD) and Community Rule identifiable with Essenes on the basis of organization—despite discrepancies with Josephus and Philo over celibacy— believes the idea of *Enochic* literary tradition-deliverers ("tradents") as Essenes "sows confusion."[19] There is no real talk of separatist communities or proscription on families in Enochic literature. CD 7 talks of people in camps living off the land with families and others walking "in perfect holiness," and CD encompasses both:[20]

> And if they live in camps according to the rule of the Land [MS B: as it was from ancient times], marrying [MS B: according to the custom of the Law] and begetting children, they shall walk according to the Law and according to the statute concerning binding vows, according to the rule of the Law which says, Between a man and

---

*Hilary Evans Kapfer's article "The Relationship between the Damascus Document and the Community Rule: Attitudes toward the Temple as a Test Case" (*Dead Sea Discoveries* 14, no. 2 [2007]: 152–77), argues against Eyal Regev's proposition in "The Yahad and the Damascus Covenant" (*Revue de Qumran* 21 [2003]: 233–36) that the Community Rule preceded the Damascus Document, possibly belonging to a rival community.

his wife and between a father and his son [Numbers 30:16]. (CD 7:5–20)

Had an Essene sought support in 1 Enoch for rejecting marriage when committing to the order, he would have found nothing, other perhaps than the idea that if you wished your soul to rise after death to angelic heaven, then you would have to accept what was *denied* to angels: the story of the Watchers being then a kind of object lesson in penalties for backsliding. Enochic texts certainly abhorred fornication, but not marriage, whereas the Essene point of view seems to have equated lust in marriage with fornication, suggesting a principle that attachment to ordinary marital emotions entailed a suffering soul, unable to embrace freedom from earth's ties. As for marriage in 1 Enoch, Enoch didn't become "seventh from Adam" through his forebears' continence!

Regarding Essene identification with Enochic texts, Collins has counted CD's centrality of covenant Torah sufficient to divide it from Enochic literature, though both texts may have been appreciated by people of differing views for other reasons. CD's Watchers story comes from Jubilees (where Moses is central), and in Collins's view is insufficient to identify the originators of CD and the Book of the Watchers. Collins has envisaged a Dead Sea sect drawing inspiration from various quarters, one being Enoch, but not to the degree that "their" originators were Enochians.[21]

Back in 1912, R. H. Charles further observed that animal sacrifices are not condemned in Enochic prophecy, whereas Essenes notably abstained from temple sacrifices, thus excluding themselves from the temple's common court. Charles also pointed out: "Not a word is said on behalf of certain characteristic beliefs of Essenism—such as the necessity of bathing before meals and at other times, the duty of having all things in common and of having common meals, the rejection of anointing the body with oil, the claim that all were free and that none should be slaves."[22]

That there was much in 1 Enoch to support Essene standards of truth, mercy, charity, rejection of the profit motive, suspicion of riches, hypocrisy, and all arts taught by the Watchers, is also true. It also might be significant in terms of dating that Josephus only mentions the Essenes' existence from the Maccabean period, while the Book of the Watchers is widely held to precede it.

Reading between the lines of known accounts of Essene beliefs and practices, one might sense the Essene life was one of preparation for an angelic existence: resurrection into a new heaven, having left earth behind with relative ease, since most attachments to earth had been trained out, an aspiration chiming with 1 Enoch's idealism. Enoch may well have exemplified one who, through righteousness, had become an angel, and as such, marriage would necessarily have become a thing of the past. Still, we see Enoch returning to son Methuselah's world to instruct from the heavenly tablets how to live to the benefit of a long posterity, at no point advising his son to abstain from furthering that posterity. Of course, we might then ask whether Josephus's Essenes *expected* much posterity. Had they at some point chosen to espouse celibacy in anticipation of the eschaton, as St. Paul would recommend (1 Corinthians 7:29–31)? Ah! Then we simply create another hypothesis!

As one may grasp, the tangled web over the question of Essene involvement in Enochic literature is a direct consequence of accepting the theory of an Essene community-plus-scrolls at Qumran; the issue practically evaporates without it.

Nevertheless, an Essene community-plus-scrolls at Qumran is still the dominant paradigm, despite its fecundity for generating interesting but unproven (some later modified) hypotheses, of which I shall mention only those with a direct bearing on 1 Enoch, for the light they shine on the history of the period whence 1 Enoch's elements derive.

The Enochic-Essene Hypothesis

Some of the so-called sectarian documents involved an aggressive, military role in a final messianic conflict between light and darkness, as well as doctrines of election to salvation exclusive to members, intolerant to outsiders. Unique in Second Temple Judaism, the combination of such doctrines could not be squared with Josephus and Philo's pacific Essenes. In 1988, Groningen University theology professor Florentino García Martínez advanced a hypothesis to explain the discrepancy. The Groningen Hypothesis posited a "parting of the ways" between a parent Essene movement and a dissident extreme movement at Qumran during the high priesthood of John Hyrcanus I (134–104 BCE) that subsequently vanished as an insignificant phenomenon in anti-Roman Zealot holocausts. Archaeology added some support. One hundred and eleven male graves were found at Qumran, strictly oriented southward, whereas Josephus numbers Judean Essenes in the thousands.* However, the projected dating for a schismatic Qumran settlement is too early for the archaeology as a whole, dated 100 BCE–50 BCE. Martínez's hypothesis, it should be noted, was only necessitated by problems within the prevalent Essene-Qumran-scrolls hypothesis.

A decade later, Gabriele Boccaccini developed the schism idea by tracing a hypothetical progress of Enochic or Enochic-influenced documents matched to known historical developments from the third century BCE to the first century CE. *Beyond the Essene Hypothesis: The Parting of the Ways between Qumran and Enochic Judaism* (1998) advanced "Enochic Judaism" as defining factor of a larger Essene movement from which Qumran may have diverted.

At the time of its publication, Boccaccini perceived 1 Enoch as the "core of an ancient and distinct variety of Second Temple Judaism" whose "generative idea . . . can be identified in a particular conception of evil, understood as an autonomous reality antecedent to humanity's ability to choose," the result of a "contamination" that has spoiled nature, produced "before the beginning of human

---

*Strict disposition of male graves is the best archaeological justification for supposing sectarian occupation at some point. A smaller number of women's graves were found at the periphery, arguably consistent with recorded Essene beliefs that sex equalled distraction from holiness. Sectarian scroll documents equate sex with impurity, and more radically, impurity directly with evil. Unique to Qumran, orientation of heads to the south may, I suggest, honor the sun at its meridian. Essene practices and Enochic texts emphatically assert a solar calendar.

history."[23] A key text here is 1 Enoch 6:8 where it is written of Azaz'el: "to him ascribe all sin." Boccaccini took Enochic Judaism as the "modern name for the mainstream body of the Essene party," an influential grouping first recognized as "Essenes" ca. 161 BCE in Josephus's *Antiquities* 13.5.9.

While this picture of politically active religious creatives may not quite tally with Philo's *Essaioi*—"full grown and already verging on old age," living by manual labor like colonists in villages and cities (*Hypothetica* 11.3)*—Josephus does suggest diversity of engagement by mentioning "Essenes" who enjoyed King Herod's ear, while another commanded a Jewish force in the anti-Roman revolt of 63 CE.

For Boccaccini, Enochic literature proved the existence of a previously unrecognized nonconformist priestly tradition. The problem remains of identifying such nonconformity with historical events. Boccaccini's 1998 hypothesis envisaged a possible development from long before the Greek conquest, with a piety and righteousness faction devoted to Ezekiel's commission to "the priests, the Levites, the sons of Zadok" (44:15–31) to approach God in a new, second temple, and to maintain purity. Zadokite history after return from exile is vague until the second century BCE when struggles over Jerusalem's high priesthood intensified, and Zadokite leadership split over issues of Seleucid Hellenization, the calendar, and foreign policy.

A peculiarity of Qumran's sectarian documents is the description of their favored priests as "Zadokites." The Essene-Enochic hypothesis posited an ancient split in Zadokite leadership (possibly over the status of the Mosaic covenant) and a dissident opposition to Zadokite priests before the Maccabean Revolt. This can be very confusing, so let's clarify that Zadok was a tenth-century BCE descendant of Aaron, who was of Levi's tribe. Levites were priests; Zadok's descendants (also of Levi's tribe) were, until the Maccabean period, *high* priests. In 175 BCE, Antiochus IV Epiphanes forced Zadokite Onias III out of

---

*In *Every Good Man Is Free* (12.75), Philo derives "Essaioi" from an inexact reference to the Greek *hosiotēs* (the holy, or pious), while contradicting himself on another matter by insisting "Essaioi" *avoided* cities as contaminating to blessedness of mind (76).

high priesthood in favor of Onias's pro-Greek brother Jason, whereafter non-Zadokite Menelaus (a Benjamite) held the dignity. Triumphant in Jerusalem in 164 BCE, Levite Judas Maccabeus, a non-Zadokite priest, assumed high priesthood. Boccaccini distinguished a "strictly Zadokite party" that "fled to Egypt" after Onias III's ejection, from "remainer" Zadokites who tolerated pro-Seleucid Menelaus and subsequent Hasmonean high priests after Judas Maccabeus.[24]

It is difficult to trace in these events disputes over arguable Enochic attitudes regarding the origin of evil or the status of the Mosaic law. The solar calendar versus the Seleucid's lunar calendar *was* an issue, especially as the alien lunar calendar persisted in Jerusalem under the Hasmoneans (descendants of Judas's family).* Boccaccini suggested a softening of "Enochic" (or Essene) attitudes toward the Mosaic Torah when pro-Hellenist Zadokites lost the high priesthood. That is, the Hasmoneans broke the link between law, temple and the Zadokite priesthood, which Enochians, hypothetically at least, opposed. After that, Enochic-influenced books (such as Jubilees) accepted Mosaic law within a specially nuanced perspective (see pages 132-35).

Boccaccini hypothesized an ideological rift among Zadokites, with the Enochic-minded seeing evil as a spiritual power constantly overwhelming human choices: a cosmic fatalism conquerable only by superhuman intervention. For humans, the less they were attached to the present world, the better their chances for deliverance from evil. The corruptions the Watchers inculcated gave clear indication of what to avoid: oaths, vanity, sexual lust, wealth, war, unnatural profiteering. Applied to Jerusalem's priesthood, this call for purity was ideal, serving to condemn Levite priests who, in the words of Ezekiel 44:13: "shall not come near unto me, to do the office of a priest unto me, nor to

---

*Henry W. Morisada Rietz (Grinnell College) has observed how the solar year acquired additional holiness since to divide 364 by sacred number 7 produces the annual number of weeks: 52 (*nun* [fourteenth letter = 50] + *bet* [second letter = 2]; 5+2=7), so that holy festivals fall on the same day each year. Jubilees reflects Enochic attitudes to the solar year as divine commandment, with the lunar year violating vital links with heaven (solar = *universal* time, operated by angels). Heliocentric time remained an outsider position to the temple's, reinforcing suspicion.[25]

come near to any of my holy things, in the most holy place: but they shall bear their shame, and their abominations which they have committed." Ezekiel wanted a Zadokite high priesthood.

Speaking of an Enochian party versus Zadokites is difficult if we assume supporters of Zadok's descendants had split into pro-Jason and pro-Onias factions by 175 BCE. Were supposed Enochians pro-Onias because they were anti-Seleucid? The Damascus Document explicitly says "the sons of Zadok are the elect of Israel" (4:5) and the Aaronic priesthood is central to its legislating the honoring of the "Covenant of Abraham" (12:10), the Covenant and "Law of Moses" (15:5), and the "New Covenant" (2:10) or "Pact," called by a figure dubbed the "Teacher of Righteousness" in "the land of Damascus."

Specifying party adherence through relating Enochic texts to Qumran's sectarian texts such as the Temple Scroll (11QT) remains an uncertain business. Josephus, if we trust him, has Sadducees competing with sects of Pharisees and Essenes in Jonathan Maccabeus's time (153–143 BCE). Whoever wrote them, it's fair to suppose Enochic works appealed to numerous spiritual idealists awaiting the "Day of the Lord" throughout this period. Speculation would be mute without the Essene hypothesis's persistence, and the fact that Enochic fragments emerged at Qumran. What if copies were found at Heliopolis, or in the land of Damascus, as well? Well, they haven't been, but accident of place may have overinfluenced interpretation. There is arguably a mismatch between the idea of issue-based party opposition and mentalities required to write Enochic works, which are predominantly apocalyptic *visions*. Enoch specialist Patrick Tiller is skeptical about "Enochic Judaism" indicating a group.[26] Comparing Daniel's apocalyptic symbolism (chapters 7 and 8 particularly) with 1 Enoch's Animal Apocalypse, Armin Lange (Tübingen University) noted similarities, but divergencies indicated they couldn't be from the same group. Lange concluded that Enochic and Danielic authors were part of a "wider apocalyptic milieu," influenced and interpreted by wisdom sages.[27]

Should we not consider *techniques* for writing revelations of a holy patriarch? Did sages achieve a specie of "astral identity" with the trans-

Fig. 6.6. Fragment of the Damascus Document 4Q271 (frag. 4QD);
Library of Congress.

figured? Did they hear voices, or experience dictation by a projected (?) discarnate entity? Or were they written as one might a novel? Not everyone can write a holy book, regardless of commitment to cause; ordinary intelligence might be a handicap. Apocalypses were not written by historians of ideas.

There are, nonetheless, indications of a specific group in the Epistle of Enoch's "Apocalypse of Weeks," where at the seventh week's end, an "apostate generation" will be challenged by "the elect righteous of the eternal plant of righteousness" who will "receive sevenfold instruction" concerning all God's creation (93:10). That instruction might be interpreted as Enoch's prophecies *themselves*. The plant image may come from Isaiah 5:7's reference to the "men of Judah" as God's "pleasant plant." Enoch's epistle probably dates to the Maccabean period, a period possibly referenced in the eighth week when the righteous receive a "sword" (93:12). It is naturally tempting to link the "instruction" to the Damascus Document's opening exhortation, which contains language that parallels Enoch's apocalypse:

> And in the age of wrath, three hundred and ninety years after He had given them into the hand of King Nebuchadnezzar of Babylon, He visited them, and He caused a plant root to spring from Israel and Aaron to inherit His Land and to prosper on the good things of His earth. And they perceived their iniquity and recognized that they were guilty men, yet for twenty years they were like blind men groping for the way.
>
> And God observed their deeds, that they sought Him with a whole heart, and He raised for them a Teacher of Righteousness to guide them in the way of His heart. And he made known to the latter generations that which God had done to the latter generation, the congregation of traitors, to those who departed from the way. (CD 4Q 265–73; 1:5–15)[28]

Taking Jerusalem's destruction in 587 BCE for Nebuchadnezzar's conquest brings us to 197 BCE for the springing of the plant root when Israel's "remnant" accepts responsibility but can't respond for twenty years, until a "Teacher of Righteousness" reveals God's intentions toward the treacherous "latter generation"—reminiscent of the Epistle of Enoch's delivery to "future generations" (1 Enoch 92:1). One might imagine the Epistle of Enoch *itself* constituting the "Teacher of Righteousness," or that its meaning was revealed by one shown its value. The Teacher's confronting "traitors" would be 177 BCE, a not insignificant date, as we shall see.

Apart from enigmas, one thing the scrolls offer is subtler, if frustrating, insight into post-exilic priestly disputes. Opposition parties become visible. Boccaccini wondered if Hasmonean consolidation and Enochian realization of minority status encouraged separation from "apostate" Israel.[29] Separation may be reflected in the Damascus Document. It seems to describe a "separated" but not isolated association "living in the city of the temple" (CD 12:1–2); Jerusalem is the "camp" (10:23), specifically the Sinai camp where Israel receives the Law, erected in the "wilderness" of apostasy and unbelief—a possible sub-meaning of "the land of Damascus."

The temple is the "tent of meeting" or "tabernacle of the congregation" (Exodus 33:7–10), outside the camp, as was Moses when he conversed with God. The "camp" might be Jerusalem envisioned under ideal jurisdiction. Alternatively, if this is all figurative language, I should suggest imagining a sectarian camp *being* the holy city, for sectarian documents see the righteous congregation itself as the "temple," wandering until a truly restored temple comes at the end, when the righteous will be exiled in the world no longer, and the wicked exiled from the righteous forever. This camp could be a literal, potentially mobile camp in a metaphorical or real wilderness, or, like Josephus's Essenes, it could be a house of holy spirits in a town, making a "way" in the (spiritual) "wilderness" outside (see 1QS 8, 10–15, The Community Rule); God's angels accompany the camp because its purity makes it accessible to the source of Law. The original document may have been a call to Israel to re-enter the ancient covenant by embracing the promised "new," and the "camp" a metaphor for Jerusalem, calling her back to the purification enacted by Moses in Sinai's wilderness.

Andreas Bedenbender (Humboldt University) has wondered if Antiochus IV's assault on Jewish religion, with Menelaus's connivance, had surrounded the authors of the Apocalypse of Weeks and the Animal Apocalypse with perceived apostates: people who, under threat of death, had "given up on Torah," lost trust in a Jewish unity with "an inseparable connection to God," leaving to themselves identity as eternity's chosen (*hasidim*?), grown from the root of truth.[30]

Interestingly, Josephus recounts a *camp of tents* erected within Herod's new temple by young Torah enthusiasts demonstrating immediately after Herod's death in 4 BCE. Their martyr-heroes were teachers of righteousness Matthias and Judas, burnt to death by Herod for inciting deposition from his temple of a Roman eagle: a sacrilegious living form that preyed on "lambs."

Boccaccini and Florentino García Martínez saw a separated "we" against a "you" and "they" in Cave 4's "Halakhic letter" (MMT: *Miqsat Ma'ase Ha-Torah*, 4Q394–99) called by translator Geza Vermes "Some Observances of the Law."[31] Vermes suggests it might originally have been the Teacher of Righteousness's work, and its eventual recipient: Jonathan Maccabeus (high priest 152–143/2 BCE), a candidate for "Wicked Priest" of the Habakkuk pesher scroll (palaeographically and carbon-dated to the second half of the first century BCE). In the Psalm 37 pesher (4Q171, 4:5–10), the "Wicked Priest" seeks the Teacher's death.

Boccaccini ascribed the Halakhic letter to "dissident Zadokites" respectful of "you" (Jonathan?) and hopeful of reconciliation, despite Aaronic priests having defiled their seed with fornication (4QMMT, 81–85).[32] If the Wicked Priest was Jonathan, and the Teacher *was* Onias III, the letter's contents must have been penned long before, for Onias was probably dead by Jonathan's heyday.

According to Vermes, the "we" party was trying to persuade the leader of the "you" party to dismiss the errors of the "they" party.[33] "They," Vermes hypothesizes, could be Pharisees, while the "we's" views suggest early or proto-Sadducees. The priests in the letter are never called sons of Zadok or Sadducees, but sons of Aaron, a familiar title in the Community Rule manuscripts from Caves 1 and 4, dated approximately to the early to mid-first century BCE. Here is the Halakhic letter's Exhortation (4Q397, 14–21):

[And you know that] we have separated from the mass of the peo[ple] . . . and from mingling with them in these matters and from being in contact with them in these (matters). And you k[now that no] treachery or lie or evil is found in our hands for we give for [these] th[e . . .

And furthermore] we [have written] to you (sing.) that you should understand {the Book of Moses} (4Q398 14–17 i) and the Book[s of the Pr]ophets and Davi[d and all the events] of every age. And in {the Book is written} (40398 14–17 i) . . . not [for] (you) {and the days of old} (40398 14–17 i).

And furthermore it is written that [you will depart] from the w[a]y and that evil will befall you (cf. Deuteronomy 31:29).*

Note the likely reference to "all the events of every age." Numerous sections of 1 Enoch (minus the Parables), including the Apocalypse of Weeks, fit that bill.

The separated but not isolated congregation of the Damascus Document then may be adherents of a group instructed by the priestly Teacher of Righteousness 390 (+ 20) years after the Babylonian exile: *177 BCE*.[34] In that year, Onias III was high priest. Supplanted by Hellenizer brother Jason (Greek form of "Yeshua") three years later, Jason was expelled in favor of extreme Hellenizer Menelaus in 172 BCE, who according to 2 Maccabees instigated Onias's murder, dated at 171 by Vermes. Needless to say, we have here candidates for Teacher of Righteousness and Wicked Priest. The story of Onias's murder by Andronicus is, however, disputed (see pages 215–16).

A New Age at Dan?

Returning to the Damascus Document's dating of the "springing of the plant root from Israel and Aaron," we're told something important had *begun* with this "plant root" (cf. the "plant of righteousness" in 1 Enoch 10:15-21) that involved priestly, possibly messianic, deliverance ("Israel and Aaron"). Nevertheless, "for twenty years" "guilty"—if repentant—men lacked interpretative guidance.

What was happening before those twenty years elapsed, namely in 197 BCE?

The year 197 BCE marked a culmination in Jerusalem of events stemming from the latest battles between Antiochus the Great of Syria and the army of young Ptolemy V Epiphanes of Egypt over 201–198 BCE. Penetrating studies by Eugen Täubler (1879–1953), published in 1946–47, revealed how their conflict precipitated what

---

*Text between {} is supplied from other manuscripts (indicated). Text between [] are hypothetical but likely reconstructions, and text in ( ) are glosses for necessary information.

he called a "messianic movement" in autumn–winter 201 BCE, projected as advance prophecy in Daniel 11:14–15:[35]

> And in those times many shall rise up against the king of the south, and the sons of the pestilent ones [*loimōn*] of your people shall be lifted up to establish the vision and they shall weaken. And the king of the north shall enter and shall discharge a mound, and shall seize fortified cities. And the arms of the king of the south shall not stand, and his picked ones [*eklektoi* = selected] shall rise up and there will not be strength to stand.
> (Septuagint translation)

"Pestilent ones" may be translated "destructive" or "disorderly" ones. Täubler suspected a reference to optimistic Judean Zealots, or bandits, fomenting sedition by preaching the day of deliverance from Egypt ("the south") had come—Ptolemy I Soter had conquered Judea in 301 BCE. In the event, having taken Gaza, Antiochus returned to Syria, while in winter 201–200 BCE, Ptolemaic commander Scopas of Aetolia, avenging Judean assistance to Antiochus, sacked Jerusalem, suppressing the uprising. Täubler saw this suppression reflected in Psalm 79: "O god, the heathen are come into thine inheritance; thy holy temple have they defiled; they have laid Jerusalem on heaps. The dead bodies of thy servants have they given to be meat unto the fowls of the heaven, the flesh of thy saints unto the beasts of the earth" (vv.1–2). Psalm 74:9 specifically cries for a *prophet* to guide them: "We see not our signs: there is no more any prophet: neither is there among us any that knoweth how long."[36]

One could imagine, therefore, Jewish astonishment at Antiochus's voluntary, unexpected return to Judea in 200 BCE. Like Assyrian Sennacherib breaking off his campaign against Jerusalem in 701 BCE, it could have seemed a miraculous sign. Antiochus did more than return. He led an army from Damascus to victory against Scopas's Ptolemaic forces.* Fought at the Paneas stream by the Damascus

---

Encyclopaedia Britannica, vol. 24 entry for the "Seleucid Dynasty" (1911, p. 605) dates the battle of Paneum to 198 BCE with Antiochus leaving to conquer Ptolemy's Asia Minor coast towns in 197 BCE, with loyal Judea practically governing itself. Most sources favor 200 BCE.

road—the biblical Dan by whose waters southwest of Hermon Enoch dreams of the Watchers' ultimate fate (1 Enoch 12:7–8)—victory was ensured by Antiochus's heir seizing a foothill of Mount Hermon the night before.

Now, it is generally believed of Jerusalem politics in this period that one party favored the Ptolemies and another the Seleucids, but as Täubler asks, is it likely that a Jerusalem party would incur Ptolemaic

Fig. 6.7. Greek coin of Antiochus III the Great.
(Photo: Antik Sikkeler)

Fig. 6.8. Four drachma coin of Ptolemy V Epiphanes,
minted in Tyre, Phoenicia, ca. 200–199 BCE.

wrath by favoring the Seleucids? The "pestilent" or "destructive ones" or zealots who wished to "establish the vision" may not have come from priestly parties but been encouraged by one. Tax-farmers the Tobiads, at odds with the Zadokites, favored the Ptolemies, though later switched to the Seleucids. What made the difference later, Täubler concluded, was Scopas's return in 201–200 BCE to punish and desecrate the temple. This, not expediency, he believed, made some join Antiochus,[37] rewarded by Antiochus at the campaign's end in 198 BCE with a letter of privileges sent via governor of Coele-Syria, Ptolemaios, son of Thraseas (*Antiquities* 12.138–44). Antiochus acknowledged Jerusalem's welcoming his forces with provisions and assistance in ejecting the Ptolemaic garrison by force. The letter indicates the strength of resistance endured against Scopas's attack. For the sacrifices incurred, Jerusalem's rulers received three-years tax exemption, a reduced tax afterward, redemption from slavery of fighters captured by Scopas, and compensation for punishments endured by "propertied persons connected with the uprising."[38]

By 197 BCE, the Ptolemies were out, Onias III was high priest, and for a staggering moment it may have seemed God had demonstrated historically his saving will, bringing ultimate deliverance closer, as the Seleucid king, who ruled distantly, respected Jewish leadership and traditions—giving monies to the temple (*Antiquities* 12.3). Prophecy incited hope: "For I have laid upon thee the years of their iniquity, according to the number of the days, three hundred and ninety days: so shalt thou bear the iniquity of the house of Israel." Thus had Ezekiel 4:5 declared God's wrath would last 390 years; with punishment expired, the new root could sprout.

Damascus

The occasion behooves us to investigate why the Damascus Document sees "the land of Damascus" as locus for the "Pact" or "New Covenant" made by the "remnant" (see Jeremiah 23:3–8; Ezekiel 6:8). Given the coincidence of the battle of Paneum (Paneas = Dan) with Enoch's vision of the Watchers' fate, and references in the Damascus Document to the "fount of living waters" (symbolic of the Law in B1:1*) from which New Covenanters must not depart—a cave of gushing water at Paneas was considered the River Jordan's source (Josephus, *War* 1.21.3)—it is tempting to see the Mt. Hermon vicinity as that part of the land of Damascus where the pact was made: a curious inversion perhaps of the wicked Watchers' pact on that mountain (1 Enoch 6:4–6).† Paneas-Dan is some twenty-two miles west of Damascus.

The Damascus Document's most intriguing "Damascus" reference occurs in what Geza Vermes calls a "most unexpected" commentary on Amos 5:26–7.[39] Amos's prophecy reads: "But ye have borne the tabernacle of your Moloch [or Sakkuth] and Chiun [or Kiwan] your images, the star of your god [Saturn], which ye made to yourselves. Therefore will I cause you to go into captivity beyond Damascus, saith the Lord, whose name is The God of hosts." The Damascus Document's take on the text *reverses* the sense. Damascus becomes *refuge*, not punishment, for those resisting apostasy: "When the two houses of Israel were divided, Ephraim departed from Judah. And all the apostates were given up to the sword, but those who held fast escaped to the land of the north; as God said, I will exile the tabernacle of your king and the bases of your statues from my tent to Damascus" [CD 7:10–20].

The writer employs a characteristic esoteric verbal symbolism, where the word *tabernacle* stands for the "Books of the Law"; *king* means "congregation"; and *bases of statues* means "Books of the Prophets": "The Books of the Law are the tabernacle of the king; as God said, I will raise up the tabernacle of David which is fallen [Amos 9:11]. The king is the congregation; and the bases of the statues are the Books of the Prophets whose sayings Israel despised." *Damascus* apparently requires no interpretation, but instead of the star-god reference, the writer startlingly

---

*The *B* here refers to the second of two medieval versions of CD found in the Cairo synagogue storeroom by Solomon Schechter in 1896. B is closest to the incomplete Qumran fragments.

†A speculation: Could the Watchers story have originated in an allegory of the descent upon the north/Dan of foreigners upon the daughters of Israel, set in antediluvian time to prefigure future redemption (Watchers = gods of the nations?)? Enoch says to Methuselah the prophecies he saw in heaven were intended for later generations, when the wise would *know how to interpret them.*

introduces the famous messianic star prophecy of Numbers 24:17: "The star is the Interpreter of the Law who shall come to Damascus; as it is written, A star shall come forth out of Jacob and a sceptre shall rise out of Israel. The sceptre is the Prince of the whole congregation, and when he comes he shall smite all the children of Seth."*

The Interpreter of the Law comes to *Damascus* . . .

The Damascus Document (6:5–10) operates similarly with Numbers 21:18 wherein "The princes dug the well, the nobles of the people dug it, by the direction of the lawgiver, with their staves" is interpreted thus: "The Well is the Law, and those who dug it were the converts of Israel who went out of the land of Judah to sojourn in the land of Damascus. God called them all princes because they sought Him, and their renown was disputed by no man. The Stave is the Interpreter of the Law of whom Isaiah said, He makes a tool for His work [Isaiah 54:16]; and the nobles of the people are those who come to dig the Well with the staves with which the Stave ordained that they should walk in all the age of wickedness—and without them they shall find nothing—until he comes who shall teach righteousness at the end of days." Messianic, eschatological notes are pronounced here, as they are in CD 8:20, B1:1, B2:1–5:

> None of the men who enter the New Covenant in the land of Damascus, [B1] and who again betray it and depart from the fountain of living waters, shall be reckoned with the Council of the people or inscribed in its Book from the day of the gathering in [B2] of the Teacher of the Community until the coming of the Messiah out of Aaron and Israel.

In the end, indifference to the New Covenant incurs judgment: "They shall be judged in the same manner as their companions were judged who deserted to the Scoffer. For they have spoken wrongly against the precepts of righteousness, and have despised the Covenant

---

*Interpreting "Seth" (or "Sheth") as Adam's third son, as many commentators do, makes little sense. It may refer to Egyptian god of victory Set, or Seth (the Greek name *Sēth* is identical to that of Adam's son): a prophecy of *Egyptian* downfall.

and the Pact—the New Covenant—which they made in the land of Damascus. Neither they nor their kin shall have any part in the house of the Law" (B2:10–15).

Several purely speculative possibilities for "Damascus" spring to mind:

1. At the exile, a group of sages and priests found refuge in Damascus from the slavery experienced by some of their countrymen. Established, they maintained a tradition of keeping from apostate Israel until prophecy/events indicated ripe time to re-establish their lineage in Jerusalem. Antiochus III's victory over the Egyptians signalled a return. Such a Damascene group may have been alerted to the "390 day" prophecy's significance after entry into the land of Damascus (Coele-Syria).

2. A group permitted to return from Babylonia by Persian Cyrus the Great's edict of 538 BCE to rebuild Jerusalem's temple, suffering outrage and/or rejection in Judea (from other returning priests, or indigenous Jews who'd escaped deportation), retired to the far north: Damascus, or Paneas-Dan, to foster enthusiasm for a New Covenant, drawing pious Jews to their base.

3. Antiochus III settled several thousand Jewish families from Babylonia in Lydia and Phrygia.[40] In this movement, or something akin, it's possible a group cherishing the "new covenant" prophecies of Jeremiah (31:31–34) and Ezekiel (36:24–28; 11:18–20) journeyed from Babylonia, eschewing Asia Minor for Damascus, where negotiation with Antiochus III or a visit by Onias III, high priest, were possible.

Such possibilities are probably too speculative. Nevertheless, their hypothetical character seems preferable to me to being satisfied that "Damascus" was code for "Babylonian exile" as some scholars suppose, or anachronistically suggesting the "land of Damascus" indicated Qumran. CD's prophecies concerning Damascus all indicate a move *out* of Judea to a place that transpired to be a refuge from divine wrath. Neither Jeremiah nor Ezekiel stumbled over "Damascus" or obscured it.

Why resist taking "Damascus" at face value? I suspect because it detracts from Qumran-centricity. Damascus could have been a significant dissident hub. We should perhaps be intrigued that according to Acts of the Apostles (9:1–25), Galatians (1:17), and 2 Corinthians (11:32–33), to "waste" the "church of God" Saul chose to march on *Damascus*, where Ananias found him blind in the house of "Judas" (identity presumed; was he Jesus's brother, an Enoch reader? Let's not guess! We lack facts).

Regarding the new covenant, it was possibly an enthusiasm that coalesced in Damascus out of absorbing Ezekiel and Jeremiah's explicit prophecies on the subject.

If we imagine a return to Jerusalem of New Covenanters with a fondness for Enochic literature (or linked to its authors), excited by the destruction of Ptolemaic Egyptian power over Judea effected by Antiochus III, enthusiasm likely waned after Antiochus III's death in 187 BCE. According to 2 Maccabees 3, all was initially well: laws were kept "because of the godliness of Onias the high priest and his hatred of wickedness" (2 Macc. 3:1) and even the late king's son Seleucus IV Philopator is reported to have borne costs for temple sacrifices. Dispute over city disorder between Onias and temple administrator Simon the Benjamite, however, led to outright treachery.

Simon informed Syrian governor Apollonius that Jerusalem's treasury held "infinite sums." Informed, Seleucus sent treasurer Heliodorus to Jerusalem. Welcomed by Onias, Heliodorus enquired concerning the money. Onias denied Simon's aspersions: monies were for widows and orphans, with some belonging to dignitary Hyrcanus. Despoiling such sums violated temple sanctity. Heliodorus demanded monies be kept in the *king's* treasury, whereupon tumult ensued among priests and population. According to Maccabees (using a divine honorific otherwise peculiar to 1 Enoch's Parables: "lord of spirits") a miracle intervened: "Now as he was there present himself with his guard about the treasury, the *Lord of spirits*, and the Prince of all power, caused a great apparition, so that all that presumed to come in with him were astonished at the power of God, and fainted, and were sore afraid" (2 Macc. 3:24; my italics).

The upshot saw Heliodorus return, after nearly dying, to tell Seleucus

God protected the temple miraculously. Simon, however, scoffed that Onias, a "traitor," caused the evil that befell Heliodorus. Realizing the stakes, Onias went to the king to avert Seleucid rage on his people. The result is not recorded, but clearly damage done was reflected in the conduct of Seleucus's successor as king, his brother Antiochus IV, with whom Onias's brother Jason conspired to effect a now distrusted Onias's deposition in 175 BCE. High Priest Jason introduced Greek games and habits to the temple's vicinity, undoing Onias's zealous work while temple morale plummeted (2 Macc. 4:14). After Menelaus ousted Jason in 171 BCE, Judea's fortunes dove precipitously when Antiochus condemned the Jewish religion in 167 BCE, resulting in the Maccabean revolt, during and after which period we may suppose the Book of the Watchers' apocalyptic content was considerably elaborated (Dream Visions; Epistle of Enoch) as priestly loyalties in Jerusalem bifurcated into factions.

Josephus indicates Essenes appeared in this period, and there remains a correlation between Josephus and Philo's accounts of Essene priorities and the Book of the Watchers. Josephus associates Essenes with healing, names of angels, and prophecy—primarily *prediction*, seldom erring in the latter (*War* 2.159). When the Watchers teach how to make poisons from roots, angel Raphael ("God has healed") is sent with the antidote. Raphael works to "heal the earth which the Watchers have corrupted" (1 Enoch 10:7). As discussed earlier, Essene postulants must carefully preserve their sect's books and the angel names (*War* 2.142); 1 Enoch 69 is devoted to a list of fallen angels' names. As for predestination—Enoch learns the destiny of everyone and everything in heaven—Josephus says Essenes maintained that fate ruled all things (*Antiquities* 13.172), but he asserted this of Pharisees too.

Sectarian documents from Qumran indicate belief that those called to the congregation were called from eternity, salvation assured. That human history was decaying because the Watchers' sin left humans powerless to change the process was, according to Boccaccini, "exactly what makes Enochic Judaism different from every other variety of Second Temple Judaism."[41] It makes apocalyptic intervention vital. Essenes described by Philo and Josephus did not see God as source of evil.

The Watchers' evils arguably dictated Essenic virtues: the Watchers swore a pact on Hermon; Essenes eschew oaths, at least according to Philo (*Every Good Man Is Free* 12.84)—but Hippolytus's *Refutatio* (9.18) is emphatic that Essene postulants were bound by "fearful oaths"—and what of oaths to the covenant in CD? According to 1 Enoch, the universe is sustained by oath: angelic operators' mutual loyalty must never risk change.

Azaz'el taught the mechanics of war, including "breastplates" (a *Greek* invention, note); "breastplates," arrows, javelins, swords, helmets, shields, and military engines are avoided by Essenes (Philo, 12.78). It is declared in 1 Enoch 52:8 that in the eschatological era, "there shall be no iron for war, nor shall anyone wear a breastplate."

The Watchers defiled human women and taught arts of seduction. The Damascus Document lists the "three nets of Belial" entangling Israel as fornication, wealth, and defilement of the Temple (4:15–17). Essenes, according to Philo and Josephus, regarded women as too great a distraction from the holy path. One might deduce from the Watchers myth that a woman could even drag an angel from his appointed station! Little wonder communities described were predominantly men tending to old age.

Essenes, like the Pharisees, but unlike the Sadducees (according to Josephus) believed in the immortal soul. In 1 Enoch 22:3–5, Enoch is shown where the spirits of the righteous dead live, separated from the wicked. Unlike the Sadducees and Sirach (Ecclesiasticus), 1 Enoch 51:1–2 accepts ideas of resurrection and a messiah, characteristics of Qumran's more sectarian documents, though Josephus's account of Essenes does not suggest a resurrection for *judgment* so much as the righteous soul rising to blissful heaven automatically after death, which is not the general expectation of 1 Enoch (though Josephus says *bad souls* go to a "dark and tempestuous den, full of unending punishments"), nor do Josephus or Philo ascribe messianism to their Essenes. This belief in a savior Josephus ascribes to his fourth sect, those, as he puts it, "addicted to liberty" (i.e., Zealots). According to Hippolytus's *Refutatio* 22: "the doctrine of the resurrection has also derived support among these [Essenes]; for they acknowledge both that the flesh will rise again, and that it will be immortal, in the same manner as the soul is already imperishable. And they maintain that the soul, when separated in the present life, [departs] into one place, which is well ventilated and lightsome, where, they say, it rests until judgment. And this locality the Greeks were acquainted with by hearsay, and called it 'Isles of the Blessed.'"

Refutatio (21) states significantly:

> The Essenes have, however, in the lapse of time, undergone divisions, and they do not preserve their system of training after a similar manner, inasmuch as they have been split up into four parties. For some of them discipline themselves above the requisite rules of the order, so that even they would not handle a current coin of the country, saying that they ought not either to carry, or behold, or fashion an image: wherefore no one of those goes into a city, lest (by so doing) he should enter through a gate at which statues are erected, regarding it a violation of law to pass beneath images.
>
> But the adherents of another party, if they happen to hear any one maintaining a discussion concerning God and His laws—supposing such to be an uncircumcised person, they will closely watch him and when they meet a person of this description in any place alone, they will threaten to slay him if he refuses to undergo the rite of circumcision. Now, if the latter does not wish to comply with this request, an Essene spares not, but even slaughters. And it is from this occurrence that they have received their appellation, being denominated (by some) Zelotae, but by others Sicarii.

Church father Hippolytus (ca. 170–235 CE) was very late in his assessments, and may have been confused by Josephus's remarks about a "fourth" sect of Zealots additional to Sadducees, Pharisees, and Essenes.

Laying up treasure in heaven, so to speak, Essenes avoided profiteering and covetousness, adopting lives of subsistence on the land God gave. It is striking that when, according to Eusebius, the Lord's brother Judas's grandsons were interrogated by emperor Domitian, they held a smallholding, eschewing wealth (see page 144). Wealth, like women, distracted from holiness, corrupting the soul's integrity. The arguably Enochic Testament of Judah (18:1–2) referenced "books of Enoch" to assert children required guarding from love of money as well as fornication. The Testament of Issachar is succinct: "I shared my bread with the poor; I did not eat alone." Wealth is particularly targeted in 1 Enoch's Parables.

Twenty-five years ago, Gabriele Boccaccini's hypothesis eminently served its purpose in initiating creative debate on the significance of "Enochic Judaism," a debate that proceeds creatively to this day and will continue. There is still no certainty regarding, for example, Essene involvement in creating or instrumentally transmitting the components of 1 Enoch, but the "conversation" between them, so to speak, in the context of Qumran manuscripts, has enlightened understanding of both, even when more questions are raised than answers.

Champion of Enoch studies at Princeton Theological Seminary James H. Charlesworth remarked in 2005 that during the 1970s, theology didn't take Enoch seriously, denigrating 1 Enoch's Parables, for example, as Christian, or Jewish-rendered-Christian. Much theological prejudice resulted from the arbitrary distinction of the Jewish and Christian canon.[42] No Hebrew canon existed pre-70 CE, and Qumran discoveries prove the Book of the Watchers, at least, was authoritative text for educated Jews well before the Christian era: the work perhaps of a wisdom figure or figures near Mount Hermon who venerated or raised antediluvian Enoch above Moses, some time after Alexander's conquest, in the late fourth or third century (the Diadochi period).[43] Enoch Seminar scholars accept neither the canon, nor categories of "pseudepigraphical" or "apocryphal" as defining forces,[44] neither do they take Josephus's division of Judaism into sects of Pharisees, Sadducees, Essenes, and Zealots at face value.

Today, theology takes 1 Enoch seriously; Charlesworth regards its contents as the Second Temple period's most important collection. Evidence for its endurance is revealed when we trace the extraordinary story of how Enoch has been received from the second century BCE to our own time. This task we now commence.

PART THREE

Enoch's Reception in History

SEVEN

Enoch Received 1

The Book of Jubilees

Discovered in its complete Ethiopic version in the mid-nineteenth century*—just over a quarter of it already available in Latin fragments—the Book of Jubilees, sometimes called the "little Genesis" or the "Apocalypse" or "Testament of Moses," was written in Hebrew. Qumran has yielded fourteen manuscripts. Estimates for composition date include the lifetime of Judas Maccabeus's nephew John Hyrcanus (164–104 BCE), king (from 134 BCE) and high priest of Judea, following father Simon Thassi. Other estimates include late Hasmonean, early Herodian (after 40 BCE), late Herodian, and first century CE. The earliest mention of Jubilees comes in Hebrew form in the Damascus Document (16:2–4), which has also proved impossible to date with certainty, beyond a fairly probable range of late second century BCE to early first century BCE.†

---

*Nearly thirty Ethiopic manuscript copies are extant.[1] Dillman published the first German translation and critical edition of the Ethiopic Jubilees in 1851 and 1859.

†Jubilees shows no acquaintance with 1 Enoch's Parables (or Similitudes) with its Son of Man in judgment. In *The Book of Jubilees, or The little Genesis* (1902) (xliv), R. H. Charles reckoned Jubilees relied on 1 Enoch 6–16; 23–36; 72–90. He also believed 1 Enoch 91–104 were *post*-Jubilees, supposing these additions acquainted with Jubilees, thus written after it (Charles, *Jubilees*, xlix). For example, 1 Enoch 103:7, 8 is compared with Jubilees 7:29 and 22:22, with a shared metaphor noted in Jubilees 1:16 when Israel is promised "they will be the head not the tail," while in 1 Enoch 103:11: "they hoped to be the head and have become the tail."

Evidently based on the Book of the Watchers and the Astronomical Book, Enoch appears in Jubilees' genealogy of antediluvian patriarchs (4:17–25):

And he was the first among men that are born on earth who learnt writing* and knowledge and wisdom and who wrote down the signs of heaven according to the order of their months in a book that men might know the seasons of the years according to the order of their separate months. And he was the first to write a testimony, and he testified to the sons of men among the generations of the earth, and recounted the weeks of the jubilees, and made known to them the days of the years, and set in order the months and recounted the Sabbaths of the years as we made known to him. And what was and what will be he saw in a vision of his sleep, as it will happen to the children of men through their generations until the day of judgment; he saw and understood everything, and wrote his testimony, and placed the testimony on earth for all the children of men and for their generations.

And in the twelfth jubilee, in the seventh week thereof, he took to himself a wife, and her name was Ednî, the daughter of Dânêl, the daughter of his father's brother, and in the sixth year in this week she bare him a son and he called his name Methuselah. And he was moreover with the angels of God these six jubilees of years, and they showed him everything which is on earth and in the heavens, the rule of the sun, and he wrote down everything. And he testified to the Watchers, who had sinned with the daughters of men; for these had begun to unite themselves, so as to be defiled, with the daughters of men, and Enoch testified against all. And he was taken from amongst the children of men, and we conducted him into the Garden of Eden in majesty and honour, and behold there he writeth down the condemnation and judgment of the world, and all the wickedness of the children of men. And on account of it (God)

---

*Note that in Parables (69:8), writing is revealed by Watcher Penemue, suggesting Jubilees was prior to Parables.

brought the waters of the flood upon all the land of Eden; for there he was set as a sign and that he should testify against all the children of men, that he should recount all the deeds of the generations until the day of condemnation. And he burnt the incense of the sanctuary, sweet spices, acceptable before the Lord on the Mount. For the Lord hath four places on the earth, the Garden of Eden, and the Mount of the East, and this mountain on which thou art this day, Mount Sinai, and Mount Zion will be sanctified in the new creation for a sanctification of the earth; through it will the earth be sanctified from all guilt and its uncleanness throughout the generations of the world.

As Professor Boccaccini has observed, early Enochic literature does not refer to the Mosaic law or emphasize its importance for Israel, whereas Jubilees gives Mosaic and Enochic traditions "within the Sinaitic revelatory framework."[2] The book opens on Sinai in a scene reminiscent of Enoch's revelations to Methuselah. Moses is shown heavenly tables by the "angel of the presence." The tables indicate sabbaths and "jubilees." A jubilee represents seven "weeks," with a "week" meaning seven years. History is thereby divided into successions of 49 years. Enoch was born in the fourth jubilee. God commands the angel of the presence to write details down for Moses.* As in 1 Enoch, we see angelology at an advanced stage—indeed, we first hear of a "guardian" angel specifically over individuals in Jubilees 35:17 (cf. Matthew 18:10), while God is not only attended by angels but delegates specific tasks to them, like acquainting Moses with secrets written in heaven.

Calendrical knowledge in relation to the universe is attributed to Enoch. Jubilees seems to take from 1 Enoch the idea that evil demons are derived from discorporated giants, with only nine-tenths of them angelically bound. The unbound are governed by a Satan-like figure called "the prince of the Mastema" (10:9), sometimes called "Satan," or just "Mastema," whose task is to afflict humans with evil. The demons can corrupt, lead people astray, or destroy the wicked; they have their

---

*Is this the background to Paul's reference to the law "ordained by angels in the hand of a mediator" in Galatians 3:19? (See page 56.)

uses. In Jubilees, an angel saves Moses from the predations of Mastema, and in the book, Mastema and "Belial"—a kind of negativing conglomerate of unrighteousness, lord of lies and impurity—seem practically identified. "Belial" is a ubiquitous bête-noir of Qumran sectarian texts (he appears in the much later Christian, or Christianized, Ascension of Isaiah).

The book of Jubilees shows signs of emanating from an optimistic period of Maccabean rule as Judea struggled, often effectively, with Seleucid rulers to the north and Ptolemaic royalty in Egypt to the southwest, with religious parties in Jerusalem favoring opposing alliances amid military and territorial gains with sudden setbacks for all sides

While trying to delineate parties and ideologies at any particular moment in this period is fraught, clues for establishing context can be intriguing. For example, to counter priestly collaboration with Greek rule, the Hasmoneans (Judas Maccabeus was descended from one Hasmon) switched temple authority from Zadokites—priests descended from Moses's brother Aaron's elder son Eleazar, which line included Zadok, high priest of Solomon's temple—to themselves and supporters who were also Levites descended from Aaron's younger son, Ithamar.

When Hyrcanus followed murdered father Simon Thassi as high priest in 135 BCE, he took the title "priest of the Most High God," honorific of *Melchizedek* (meaning "my prince is righteousness"), king of Salem, who appears mysteriously in Genesis 14:18–20 (see also Psalm 110 and 1 Maccabees 14:41). The Hasmoneans apparently assumed they'd revived an ancient priestly order of Melchizedek that *preceded* Levi, Aaron, Eleazar, and Zadok. Jubilees 32:1 calls Levi "a priest of the Most High God." The only priests bearing this title were Maccabean. The title roused indignation, especially when John Hyrcanus, for political reasons, switched approval from Pharisees to wealthy, Greek-accommodating Sadducees (*Tzedokim*—probably from "Zadok") late in his reign.

Another possible clue to pro-Maccabean authorship is that Jubilees omits Genesis chapter 49 (vv.4–7), where Levi—and afterward Judah—are denounced by father Jacob. The author appears to invest in a Levitical-Maccabean rather than Levitical-Zadokite priesthood.

The tribe of Levi is indicated in Jubilees 45:16 as having special responsibilities for guarding knowledge: Israel (Jacob), before his death "gave all his books and the books of his fathers to Levi his son that he might preserve them and renew them for his children until this day" (cf. 4 Ezra 14:6). Jubilees stands then as a kind of supplement to the Pentateuch. Enoch may have been considered a renewed tradition of books passed by Jacob to Levi, guardian of written tradition. This literary provision allows for the development of esoteric commentary and interpretation: the roots of kabbalah.

That Levite Maccabees displayed exemplary zeal in resisting Hellenistic contamination of the faith was a factor R. H. Charles believed ensured them Pharisee support, justifying his view that Jubilees was written by a Pharisee no later than 96 BCE, because in that year John Hyrcanus's son Alexander Janneus (127–76 BCE) fell out with Pharisees and established Sadducean control over Jerusalem's temple.[3] Charles believed Jubilees' priorities echo what little we know of Pharisees in this period: defense of the faith from Hellenism, glorification of the law (hence its opening on Sinai with Moses receiving the tablets of the law), and interest in customs derived from biblical events, such as the proscription on nudity—a shocking feature of Greek games—deriving from shame leading to covering of privates after expulsion from Eden, and Ham's seeing father Noah's nakedness (Genesis 9:22–25). Advocacy of strict sabbath law (which Antiochus IV had forbidden) reinforces the centrality Jubilees gives to divine communication of eternal law from heaven.

The Greek *Pharisaios* (Pharisee) comes from the Hebrew and Aramaic *parush* or *parushi*, meaning someone "separated." This could imply a purity distinction; a religious separation through taking a vow or joining an order; a separation from a ruling élite (such as Zadokites); separation to some degree from the Second Temple administration; separation from Jews considered godless or impure; separation from Gentiles (Hellenism in particular); or separation for a path of holiness by strict Torah observance; or, indeed, all or a combination of any of these. *Pharisee* doesn't in fact occur in extant writings until the gospels and shortly after; Josephus first mentions them in connection with Jonathan Apphus, brother and successor (161–143 BCE) to Judas Maccabeus. The name "Pharisee" may once have been a nickname for numerous kinds of separated groups, with room for confusion over past lineage.

Anyhow, the notion of Pharisaic authorship has garnered little enthusiasm. Rabbi Adolf Jellinek (1821–1893) considered Jubilees' author Essene (1855); Chanokh Albeck (1890–1972) attributed it to Enochic circles (1930).[4] Today, Enoch Seminar members may typify adherence to the Torah covenant and Pentateuch a Zadokite emphasis, with some scholars seeing Zadokite Judaism in rivalry with Enochic Judaism—with Enochic Judaism's supporters institutional losers—despite having allegedly compromised over Mosaic law—long before the Herodian period.

The fourth Enoch Seminar, held at Camaldoli, Italy, in July 2007, found views about Jubilees' relation to Enochic Judaism could be grouped into four tendencies:

1. Jubilees came directly from an Enochic source, with some Mosaic influence subordinated to Enochic ideology.
2. Jubilees was a conscious synthesis of Enochic and Mosaic tradition, yet autonomous from both.
3. Jubilees was Mosaic with some Enochic influence.
4. There was no gulf between competing "Judaisms" (such as "Enochic Judaism" and "Zadokite Judaism") at the time of composition.[5]

While Gabriele Boccaccini had to conclude that "Camaldoli has not solved the enigmas of Jubilees,"[6] one thing is clear: Jubilees' author regarded his Enochic sources as authoritative as Genesis, and while both 1 Enoch and Jubilees had long been classified, or dismissed, as pseudepigrapha, meaning of false or uncertain authorship and origin, we needn't conclude they were so regarded by learned Jews in general until perhaps the late first or second century CE.

Camaldoli may not have solved the enigmas of Jubilees but it did occasion the publication in 2009 of fascinating papers on the subject. In "The Heavenly Counterpart of Moses in the Book of Jubilees,"

Andrei A. Orlov focused on the role of angels in Jubilees, following James VanderKam's observation that the "angel of the presence" writes the Pentateuch, not, as in Leviticus and Numbers, as direct revelation to Moses. That the celestial scribe arrogates Moses's role promotes Orlov's question: *Is the angel the "heavenly counterpart" of Moses*?[7] The idea appears in several Targums (Aramaic, originally spoken, translations of the Hebrew Bible with sermon-like additions): Pseudo-Jonathan, Targum Neofiti, and the Fragmentary (of the Pentateuch) Targum, where Jacob's heavenly identity is an image engraved on the Throne of Glory.[8] Orlov relates the idea to the idea of the Son of Man being the heavenly double of the seer in Parables (1 Enoch 71). Human beings could not stand proximity to God. When the visionary is identified with his heavenly double, the seer must be installed into the status of the angel or prince of the presence. According to Orlov: "both Jacob and Enoch traditions identify the heavenly counterparts of the seers as angelic servants of the presence."[9] In the case of Enoch, the angel of the presence who instructs Enoch is named Phanuel or Uriel or Sariel.[10]

The notion seems akin to the relatively modern idea of the "Holy Guardian Angel" with whom the spiritual magician may obtain "knowledge and conversation" in *The Book of Abramelin* (MS Wolfenbüttel Library, Codex Guelfibus 10.1, ca. 1608). This brings Orlov to a question I asked earlier regarding the technique or "mechanics" for composing holy books, such as 1 Enoch.[11] He too sees a link with the idea of a tutelary spirit in communication with the scribe that "allows authors to unveil new revelations in the name of some prominent authority in the past." Orlov suspects identifying the celestial scribe in the form of the angel of the presence might advance understanding of the "enigmatic process of mystical and literary emulation of the exemplary figure, the cryptic mechanics of which often remain beyond the grasp of our postmodern sensibilities."

Could, he asks, "the tradition of unification of the biblical hero with his angelic counterpart be part of this process of emulation if an exemplar by an adept?" Does the angel of the presence offer intermediate authority and "safe haven of the author's identity?" Could this angel allow "an adept to enter the assembly of immortal beings consisting of the heroes of both the celestial and the literary world?"[12] Orlov sees no coincidence in the fact that "these transformational accounts dealing with the heavenly doubles of their adepts are permeated with the aesthetics of penmanship and the imagery of the literary enterprise. In the course of these mystical and literary metamorphoses, the heavenly figure surrenders his scribal seat, the library of the celestial books, and even personal writing tools to the other, earthly identity who now becomes the new guardian of the literary tradition."[13] Such mechanics might help explain, with some plausibility, the origin of such documents as *Liber AL vel Legis* (1904), which scribe Aleister Crowley attributed to an angel from "Mezla,"* whom his wife Rose named "Aiwass."

In "From a Movement of Dissent to a Distinct Form of Judaism: The Heavenly Tablets in Jubilees as the Foundation of a Competing Halakah," Gabriele Boccaccini examined, among other issues, how the status of the oral Torah appeared relegated by Jubilees' emphasis on *heavenly* tablets as source.[14] Jubilees' Sinaitic setting might imply authoritative interpretation of the Mosaic revelation required more than the familiar tablets of the law, rather the angel of the presence with access to heaven. What Boccaccini called the "Zadokite Torah" was thus only "the book of the first Torah" (6:22). Heavenly tablets trumped the Torah. Thus, Moses was arguably co-opted as an authority for a perspective beyond the Zadokite Torah, while that authority was already preceded by that of Enoch and Noah. Boccaccini thus saw Jubilees subtly undermining Mosaic-Aaronic authority.

Summing up this line of insight, Boccaccini asserted that Jubilees' author wished "neither to strengthen the Pentateuch nor to replace it,"[15]—a perspective bolstering the perception of Jubilees as an Enochic or Enochic-influenced work.

---

*cf. *Kabbalah Denudata* (from the *Zohar*), translated by S. L. Macgregor Mathers (1912); ch. 18, "On the Beard of Microprosopus (= creator of the microcosm)," verse 666: "For whensoever the universe hath need of mercy, the Influence, Mezla, of the Ancient one is uncovered; and all those conformations which exist in the most adorned beard of Microprosopus are found to be entirely mercies, yet so that they can exercise vengeance against the haters of the Israelites, and against those who afflict them."

While earlier commentators had tended to see Jubilees as a kind of midrash or commentary on Jewish scriptural history, the emphasis moved to the idea of the law's reliance on an angelic revelation, thereby containing Zadokite tradition as well as anti-Zadokite Enochic tradition, with Moses receiving Jubilees in addition to the Pentateuch. The chapter suggests a group point of view was behind Jubilees, one that believed, in line with the Book of the Watchers, in a universe and history subject to demonic forces, rebelling against God, predestined to decline until God was vindicated. This represented an apocalyptic "counterstory" extraneous to the "master narrative" of the Mosaic Torah, dramatically altering "its theological outlook."[16] However, Boccaccini was now hesitant to label Jubilees as a work of Enochic Judaism. He perceived too many elements of discontinuity, especially in the direction of enhancing human responsibility—rather than attributing all evil to the Watchers—and in Jubilees' "safeguarding the eternal validity of God's covenant with Israel."[17] Enochic Judaism's "counterstory" was rather "a paradigm of disruption that challenged the Mosaic 'master narrative,' and denied the Zadokite paradigm of order."[18]

John J. Collins (Yale Divinity School) agreed with Boccaccini that Enochic literature did reflect a distinctive form of Judaism in the late third/early second centuries BCE, but held it incorrect to say it was a "Judaism without the Torah." The problem for Enochic supporters perhaps was the sense of being victimized, or marginalized within the priesthood. Did they believe it impossible to follow laws in a world corrupted by evil?[19] It's possible their inherited wisdom prevented the creation of laws, ordinances, and observances (halakah) that competed with the Zadokites'. According to this model, the Maccabean period confirmed for Enochians a world flawed by evil, rather than a world ordered by Mosaic law. At the same time, Zadokite Torah was extended from priests to become Israel's national law, pivot of Jewish identity. According to the argument, 1 Enoch's Dream Visions represents a somewhat uneasy rapprochement enabling Enochians to be pro-Mosaic without being pro-Zadokite. According to Paolo Sacchi, this synthesis enabled a tiny group of disenfranchised priests to form a new form of Judaism *between* Enochic and Zadokite poles, leaving the problem of maintaining blamelessness in a corrupt world.[20] Sacchi regarded this as the "genius" of Jubilees: a firm covenant despite the universe's corruption, valid for Jews unless individuals opened themselves to the ways of Gentiles dominated by evil forces. The security of the covenant depended on its reliance on heavenly tablets, beyond the reach of this world.

Following this line, we may imagine a reform movement that against intentions was driven by logic of separation from evil to become sectarian. Boccaccini was inclined to believe Essenes most likely candidates for transmitting Jubilees,[21] typified as a group of anti-Zadokite priests who believed the heavenly tablets enabled them to make the best of Enochic and Mosaic traditions, with the covenant requiring them to separate from evil. While after the Maccabean revolt they'd dreamed of leading a new order, the dream proved vain. Refusing to surrender, they looked forward to a time when their righteousness and faith in God would be vindicated by God—a time, as Boccaccini poignantly adds, "they never saw."[22]

The Testaments of the Twelve Patriarchs

For a long time disregarded as a pseudepigraphal Christian forgery, R. H. Charles, back in 1908, was in no doubt the Testaments of the Twelve Patriarchs was essentially a pre-Christian work that influenced Jesus's ethics in the gospels and Pauline letters.[23] While not finding fullest form in Greek until the second century CE, before which time it was likely adapted to Christian usage, it shows acquaintance with Jubilees, and in chapters 14 to 18 of the Testament of Levi (the book is divided into twelve books of parting words from Jacob/Israel's sons), a reference to a "book of Enoch" details Enoch's descendants' sins in a manner reminiscent of the Apocalypse of Weeks. Chapters 2–8 of the Testament of Levi were perhaps inspired by Enochic imagery, for in those chapters, Levi is taken to heaven to be endowed with the promise of priesthood forever, and though the Levite priesthood would suffer debasement, it would be restored to its dignity by a divinely sanctioned priest. The messiah is "from Levi and Judah," and is the "unique prophet" (Levi 19:1).

The interest in the problems of Levite priesthood seem most relevant to the Hasmonean period discussed above, though its author or authors may have taken its Enochic account of the Watchers from Jubilees rather than the Book of the Watchers; the Watchers story is adapted to its own priorities.

According to Gabriele Boccaccini's reading (1998), human beings are not subject to the Watchers' sin, but are jointly responsible. Indeed, "blame shifts from the angels to women."[24] According to the Testament of Reuben (5:1–7): "They charmed the Watchers, who were before the flood. As they continued looking at the women, they were filled with desire for them. . . . Since the women's minds were filled with desire for their apparitions, they gave birth to giants." According to Enoch specialist Loren T. Stuckenbruck: "On seven occasions the Testaments appeal to the authority of 'the writing (or words) of Enoch' (T. Simeon 5:4; T. Levi 10:5, 14:1; T. Judah 18:1; T. Dan 5:6; T. Naphtali 4:1; T. Benjamin 9:1) and once, in a textually contested place, to 'the writing of the law of Enoch' (T. Zebulun 3:4)."[25]

The Testaments apparently take some ideas from Jubilees and Enochian prophecy but present them in a more dualist direction akin to the Gospel of John, emphasizing human responsibility for sin. The Testament of Levi (19:1) contrasts God and Belial as "light and darkness," and as the "spirit of truth and the spirit of error." As Boccaccini observed, Belial *will* suffer a final defeat, but until then is an aggressive challenge to God, with the human soul the battlefield. Belial placed seven spirits of deceit in humans.*

Belief in human responsibility prevents assumption of Azaz'el and his ilk's full guilt for sin—such a marked doctrine of the Book of the Watchers, *taken in isolation*. While 1 Enoch, or components of it, is to Testaments and Jubilees a source of *history*, and to an extent, prophecy, it is not the last word in doctrine. In the Testament of Judah (20:1–2), man can choose between two opposing spirits: truth and error. Evil is an inner temptation fostered by the devil, a conception consistent with

---

*Might we compare them to the seven spheres (planets) representing sins to be divested as the soul rises toward the fixed stars in the Hermetic *Poimandrēs*? (See pages 206-07.)

the paternoster of Matthew 6:9–13. Belial can be resisted by developing inner integrity of heart, a quality Belial is utterly without. Love God and your neighbor, and Belial "will flee from you."[26] That is not advice the angels give to sufferers from the Watchers' and giant offspring's wickedness in 1 Enoch, where only heavenly intervention can save them from evil.

EIGHT

The Epistle of Jude

By far the most significant early reference to Enoch's prophecy appears in the canonical Epistle of Jude. Its author, believing Jesus's followers would soon be saved from a plague of moral corruption and persecution, reinforced the message by citing Enoch's prophecy:

> And the angels which kept not their first estate, but left their own habitation [the wicked Watchers], he hath reserved in everlasting chains under darkness unto the judgment of the great day. . . .
>
> And Enoch also, the seventh from Adam,* prophesied of these, saying [Enoch 1:9], Behold, the Lord cometh with myriads of his holy ones, to execute judgment upon all, and to convince all that are ungodly among them of all their ungodly deeds which they have ungodly committed, and of all their hard speeches which ungodly sinners have spoken against him. (Jude vv.6, 14–15)

Jude's quotation from a presumably Greek copy of Enoch (1 Enoch 1:9) makes Jude unique. It contains the only Jewish prophecy quoted in the Christian Bible whose source is not *in* the Bible—excepting of course the Ethiopian Orthodox Church's unique canon.

---

*The designation "seventh from Adam" occurs, significantly, in 1 Enoch 60:1, in the Parables. This may indicate the author's familiarity with that component of 1 Enoch, which includes the detailed account of the heavenly Son of Man.

Who is this "Jude"?

The author calls himself the "slave"—meaning he *belongs to the house of*—"Jesus Messiah." The Greek epistle has *Iēsous Christos* where *Christ* means "anointed one." Jude shared the Enochic vision of God saving Israel from evil by sending His anointed one to rule an eternal kingdom. Prophecies in Isaiah, 2 Samuel, and Micah indicated the leader would be of the tribe of Judah, a descendant of King David (Isaiah 11:10; 2 Samuel 7:12–16; Micah 5:2).

"Jude" is an English form of the writer's Jewish name "Judah." In Greek that's *Ioudas*; in English: Judas. Judas states in his letter that he is "brother of James." Mark 6:3 tells us plainly that Jesus had sisters (unnamed), and brothers named (in English) James (Jacob), Joses (Joseph or Yosef), Juda (Judah or Judas), and Simon (Shimon or Simeon). According to Matthew 1:25, Joseph "knew her not [= did not sleep with Mary] till she had brought forth her firstborn son . . . Jesus." Siblings could have followed.

Judas's brother James was one of three "Nazarene" leaders in Jerusalem until high priest Ananus ordered James stoned to death in 62 CE, some twenty-five years after his brother Jesus's crucifixion. Traditionally, authorship of Judas's letter has been ascribed to James's brother Judas, who believed his brother Jesus (Yeshua) God's anointed (in Hebrew: *Mashiah ha-Zedek*, the messiah of righteousness) and would return. Catholic tradition prefers "half brother," assuming Jesus's mother was perpetually virginal: an assumption implying Joseph had children from a previous marriage.

I see no compelling reason to be overly skeptical about the traditional ascription to Judas because neither it nor the letter of James, to which it is similar, have invoked their names as props to authorize special polemics or doctrines. Neither epistle claims uniquely superior insight or special revelation, or speaks, as far as one can tell, for a "party." Like James, Judas speaks in the mode of a non-Pauline, Jewish messianic belief-world entirely consistent with a wholly Jewish "Nazarene" (*Natzarim*; see page 341) movement, as we should expect in the mid-to late first century. That it is markedly different in tone and style to Pauline epistles lends additional credibility in my judgment; this letter appears as an authentically Jewish message independent of Paul's distinctively pro-Gentile doctrinal coloring.

Furthermore, evidence survives that Jesus's brother Judas's Enochic vision crossed two generations, *through his own descendants*. We find it in second-century Jewish-Christian historian Hegesippus's *Commentaries on the Acts of the Church* (ca. 170 CE) paraphrased in Eusebius's *Ecclesiastical History* 2.23, where Judas's family descendants are referred to directly and unselfconsciously. In doing so, Hegesippus demonstrated that descent from the House of David was no free ticket.

Roman emperor Domitian (81–96 CE) saw the House of David's existence as directly subversive to Roman rule, because many Jewish rebels against Rome believed a Davidic messiah would lead them. According to Hegesippus, when Emperor Domitian received intelligence that Judas's *grandsons* were members of that house, and believed in a messiah, Domitian interrogated them as political suspects. Judas's grandsons' defense was that they paid taxes to Rome—something rebels abhorred—while their beliefs threatened no one, since Jesus's kingdom was spiritual, and did not seek earthly power; judgment would come at the end of time. Their inherited belief that Jesus ruled spiritually from heaven is reminiscent of numerous passages concerning the Son of Man in Parables. When the famously avaricious Domitian saw Judas's grandsons' open hands, revealing calluses from manual labor on a quarter-acre smallholding, Domitian deemed them too poor to finance rebellion or much else. Thinking them unworthy of attention, he uncharacteristically let them live. Jesus's great nephews lived on as church leaders until emperor Trajan (98–117 CE) started persecuting Christians. They apparently suffered martyrdom along with grandfather Judas's—and Jesus's—cousin Simeon. Simeon, described as son of Clopas—Clopas being Jesus's supposed paternal uncle—was accused as a descendant of David before Roman consul Atticus Herodes. Having survived days of torture, 120-year-old Simeon was crucified by consular order. Aged Simeon had served as Nazarene (or "Nazorean") leader after Judas's brother James the *Zaddik* (righteous, translated "the Just") was killed on Jerusalem's temple steps.

Fig. 8.1. Bust of Emperor Domitian, found in 1898 close to Via Principe Amedeo on the Esquiline; Musei Capitolini, Rome.

While Judas's letter is similar in style and content to James's letter, Judas, uniquely, envisions Jesus's return to establish God's righteousness by quoting Enoch, evidently attributing evils afflicting brethren to the wicked Watchers' persistent influence, and deliverance as fulfillment of Enoch's prophecies. Judas sees Enoch's vision as substantiating, or incorporating, Jesus's message, a message that Judas saw close to fruition; its itinerary is Enochic.

According to church father Clement of Alexandria (ca. 150–215 CE), Jude was authoritative scripture, as reported in Eusebius's *Ecclesiastical History* (6.14.1): "To sum up briefly, he [Clement] has given in the *Hypotyposes* abridged accounts of all canonical Scripture, not omitting the disputed books—I refer to Jude and the other Catholic epistles [1–2 Peter, James, 1–3 John], and Barnabas and the so-called Apocalypse of Peter." Only the latter two works are now excluded from the canon. Interestingly, the only known reason why some Christians disputed the authority of Jude's epistle was due to its use of Enoch, which some (but not all) considered pseudepigraphical, and because of Jude's allusion to

Fig. 8.2. Colophon at the end of the Epistle of Jude; *Codex Alexandrinus*, late fourth to early fifth century. (British Library)

the *Assumption of Moses* (pre-30 CE),[1] whose first-person testament of Moses to Joshua was considered falsely attributed.

When church father Tertullian (155–ca. 220) addressed the authenticity of Enoch in his *de cultu feminarum* (*On female fashion* 1.2–3), he not only attributed ostentatious feminine adornments to the wicked Watchers, but, in defending Enoch's prophecy as his source, asserted that its use by "Jude the Apostle" was sufficient justification for its genuineness:

> For they, withal, who instituted them are assigned, under condemnation, to the penalty of death, those angels, to wit, who rushed from heaven on the daughters of men; so that this ignominy also attaches to woman. For when to an age much more ignorant [than ours] they had disclosed certain well-concealed material substances, and several not well-revealed scientific arts—if it is true that they had laid bare the operations of metallurgy, and had divulged the natural properties of herbs, and had promulgated the powers of enchantments, and

had traced out every curious art, even to the interpretation of the stars—they conferred properly and as it were peculiarly upon women that instrumental mean of womanly ostentation, the radiances of jewels wherewith necklaces are variegated, and the circlets of gold wherewith the arms are compressed, and the medicaments of orchil with which wools are coloured, and that black powder itself wherewith the eyelids and eyelashes are made prominent. [from chapter 2]

I am aware that the Scripture of Enoch, which has assigned this order to angels, is not received by some, because it is not admitted into the Jewish canon either. I suppose they did not think that, having been published before the deluge, it could have safely survived that world-wide calamity, the abolisher of all things. If that is the reason, let them recall to their memory that Noah, the survivor of the deluge, was the great-grandson of Enoch himself; and he, of course, had heard and remembered, from domestic renown and hereditary tradition, concerning his own great-grandfather's "grace in the sight of God," and concerning all his preachings; since Enoch had given no other charge to Methuselah than that he should hand on the knowledge of them to his posterity. Noah therefore, no doubt, might have succeeded in the trusteeship of preaching; or, had the case been otherwise, he would not have been silent alike concerning the disposition [of things] made by God, his Preserver, and concerning the particular glory of his own house.

If [Noah] had not had this [conserving power] by so short a route, there would be this [consideration] to warrant our assertion about this Scripture: he could equally have renewed it, under the Spirit's inspiration, after it had been destroyed by the violence of the deluge, as, after the destruction of Jerusalem by the Babylonian storming of it, every document of the Jewish literature is generally agreed to have been restored through Ezra.

But since Enoch in the same Scripture has preached likewise concerning the Lord, nothing at all must be rejected by us which pertains to us; and we read that "every Scripture suitable for edification is divinely inspired." By the Jews it may now seem to have been rejected for that reason, just like all the other (portions) nearly which tell of Christ. Nor, of course, is this fact wonderful, that they did not receive some Scriptures which spake of Him whom even in person, speaking in their presence, they were not to receive. To these considerations is added the fact that Enoch possesses a testimony in the Apostle Jude.

[from chapter 3, *de cultu feminarum*]

Bishop of Alexandria Athanasius's thirty-ninth festal letter of 367 CE included Jude in his canon for Christians in Egypt—and it was in Egypt, some 7.5 miles east of Nag Hammadi, near Dishna, that a large cache of papyrus manuscripts was discovered in a jar in 1952. The jar held Papyrus 72 (P^{72} or Papyrus Bodmer VII and VIII), a codex of early Christian works that included the earliest known complete versions of Jude and 1–2 Peter, probably copied in Greek by monks living in Upper Egypt between about 275 and 325 CE.* Dishna is close to monastery ruins by Jabal Abū Mannā overlooking Faw al-Qibli (Coptic: *Pbow*), established by St. Pachom, founder of Christian monasticism.

Most of the papyri are now held in the Bodmer Library of World Literature, Cologny, Switzerland, having been bought from a Cairo antiquities dealer in 1956 by banker Martin Bodmer. Bodmer gave the papyrus leaves of 1–2 Peter (Bodmer VIII) to the Vatican Library. The original codex—containing seven other works, including a third apocryphal epistle of Paul to the Corinthians and the Nativity of

---

*Some four or five probably Coptic scribes copied the texts in Greek (the original codex held at least 190 pages), though there is a marginal note to 2 Peter 2:22 in Coptic. The scribe of Jude 5 has used the expression *theos christos* (God Christ) in the sentence "God Christ saved the people from Egypt," whereas most manuscripts say the "Lord" or "Jesus," suggesting the scribe upheld complete doctrinal identification of God and Jesus Christ—also evident in 1 Peter 5:1 where most texts say "The sufferings of Christ," the scribe has "the sufferings of God."[2] According to Brent Nongbri, 1–2 Peter and Jude were originally copied in different codices. Jude was originally accompanied by the Nativity of Mary, the apocryphal letter of Paul to the Corinthians, and Ode of Solomon; the four works are still paginated in order, from pages 1–68.[3] Bodmer VIII had a different codicological construction, that is, 1 and 2 Peter were copied separate from Jude, so that "the degree to which P.Bodmer VII and P.Bodmer VIII could be said to constitute a single papyrus continuous-text 'manuscript of the New Testament' is open to some question in light of these findings."[4] Nongbri concedes that P^{72} was probably copied by the same scribe, but at different times.

Fig. 8.3. Bodmer Papyrus VIII; End of I Peter (left); start of 2 Peter (right);
Biblioteca Apostolica Vaticana.

Mary from the apocryphal Protoevangelium of James—says something about how some religious literature was gathered and circulated in Upper Egypt in the period. There was apparently no interest in compiling what we think of as a Bible. The papyri seem to have been regarded as sacred literature because they dealt with sacred subjects in a sacred manner. We may imagine copies of Enoch were regarded similarly, indeed, it might possibly have been the practice of miscellaneous gathering that, at least in part, motivated Athanasius's festal letter of 367 CE condemning unauthorized books, a stricture aimed at books regarded by the orthodox as heretical, such as the contents of the world-famous Nag Hammadi library, also allegedly found in a jar not far from Faw al-Qibli. One possible result of Athanasius's canonical clampdown might have included production of the first known Christian Bibles combining old and new testaments and some then-acceptable apocryphal works, such as can be found in the celebrated Codex Alexandrinus and Codex Sinaiticus, both found in Egypt and dated broadly to the mid-fourth century, though it's possible they were more or less contemporaneous with Athanasius's Egyptian strictures on recognized scripture.

It is also arguable that the appearance of Jude and 1–2 Peter among some apocryphal and other respectable homiletic works was because their compilers considered them *supplementary* to canonical works. This notion is complicated by the evident fact that in the absence of any definitive episcopal ruling, views differed over precisely which texts were marginal or disputed. Certainly, Athanasius did not exclude Jude or 1–2 Peter. The earliest fragments of canonical gospels discovered, from ca. 100–200 CE (there are eleven that probably fit that period), tell us nothing about what traveling companions they may once have journeyed with, if any.

What is a little uncanny about P^{72}—though it may still be mere coincidence—is to find the two allegedly Petrine letters so close to Jude, since not only was there some dispute about their authenticity (especially 2 Peter), but also because 1–2 Peter show traces of acquaintance with the Book of the Watchers and possibly other Enochic material. As Peter Strickland notes in his article on P^{72}: "the literary relationship between 2 Peter and Jude has been well commented upon by scholars, and most believe that Jude must have been a source for 2 Peter since 90% of the content of Jude appears again in some way throughout 2 Peter. The two minority positions in scholarship that challenge the majority view are: (1) that Jude instead borrowed from 2 Peter; and (2) that 2 Peter and Jude simply drew from a common source. The first possibility seems especially unlikely as it raises more questions than it answers."[5]

It is possible that P^{72} demonstrates a community's special interest in St. Peter since the codex also contained psalms 33 and 34, which were used in 1 Peter. Prof. James Robinson, supervising editor of *The Nag Hammadi Library in English*, thought the community from which P^{72} came was an orthodox one, perhaps distinguishing itself from a gnostic community nearby.[6] Gnostic writings using Peter's name in the Nag Hammadi library are strictly unorthodox, and that collection eschewed the Petrine epistles as clearly as the arguably orthodox possessor of P^{72} excluded gnostic texts. Jude and 1 and 2 Peter all share an interest in condemning false, corrupting teachers in the church (for example 2 Peter 2:1). If this is so, then we can say that in this hypothetical orthodox or proto-orthodox community at least, Enochic material may to some degree have been accepted as scripture, if only via Jude and its impress on the Petrine letters. Their usefulness in ideological conflict with gnostic theology may also in part account for the final acceptance of both Petrine letters in the orthodox canon.

I Peter, 2 Peter, and I Enoch

Let us look more closely at what looks like the impress of 1 Enoch on the Petrine epistles. A fairly obvious parallel is that between Jude v.6 and 2 Peter 2:4:

> And the angels which kept not their first estate, but left their own habitation, he hath reserved in everlasting chains under darkness unto the judgment of the great day. (Jude v.6)

> For if God spared not the angels that sinned, but cast them down to Tartaros, and delivered them into chains of darkness, to be reserved unto judgment; (2 Peter 2:4)

The use of the place-name Tartaros (which the King James Version translates as "hell") in 2 Peter even finds an echo in 1 Enoch 20:2. In Plato's *Gorgias*, Tartaros is an underground pit where souls are judged and, if transgressive, punished: a rationalization of traditional Greek mythology wherein Tartaros was imagined as a remote underground pit-prison for challengers to the will of Olympian gods, whereas in 1 Enoch 20:2 Tartaros is ruled over by archangel Uriel, and reserved for final judgment of the Watchers and the unrighteous.

In 1 Peter 3:18–20, Christ's work *exactly* parallels Enoch's mission when Enoch is sent to confront the Watchers with God's judgment on their misdeeds (1 Enoch 12:4–5; 13:3). Thanks to the resurrection, according to 1 Peter, Christ is able to preach to the disobedient "spirits in prison," incarcerated since the Flood. In doing so, his role and actions are practically identified with Enoch's; namely, what Enoch did before the Flood, Jesus now does before the final judgment:

> For Christ also hath once suffered for sins, the just for the unjust, that he might bring us to God, being put to death in the flesh, but quickened by the Spirit: in which also having gone he preached unto the spirits in prison; Which sometime were disobedient, when once the long-suffering of God waited in the days of Noah, while the ark was a preparing, wherein few, that is, eight souls were saved by water. (1 Peter 3:18–20; cf. 2 Peter 2:5)

In 2 Peter 2:5 Noah's providential deliverance from the Flood is placed immediately after the reference to the angels' imprisonment, showing that the author of 2 Peter certainly read Jesus's preaching to the spirits in prison in 1 Peter referring to the Watchers' condemnation:

> For if God spared not the angels that sinned, but cast them down to hell, and delivered them into chains of darkness, to be reserved unto judgment; And spared not the old world, but saved Noah the eighth person, a preacher of righteousness, bringing in the flood upon the world of the ungodly.

It's worth noting that Jude does not link its angels who "kept not their first estate" to the Flood-judgment, suggesting 1 Peter and 2 Peter accessed Enoch's prophecy directly or indirectly from elsewhere, possibly the book of Jubilees.

Freelance biblical commentator Paul Davidson has drawn attention to what might once have been a direct reference to Enoch himself, *by name*, in 1 Peter 3:18–20.[7] The phrase "in which also having gone he preached to the spirits in prison" (*en hō kai tois en phylakē pneumasin poreutheis ekēryxen*) is rather awkward. If we add the Greek letter chi (χ) to the Greek for "in which also" (ἐν ᾧ καὶ), we get ἐν ᾧ χ καὶ (*enhōch kai*): enhoch. Taking the omega (ᾧ) without the aspirate and iota subscript (ω), *enōch kai* simply means "and enoch," and the sentence could read: "and Enoch having gone he preached to the spirits in prison." We would then have a set of homiletic associations linking Christ's resurrection in the spirit to Enoch's underworld adventure, subsequent Flood or cleansing of the world, expressed as a "figure" for Christian baptism (v.21) where the conscience is washed clean thanks to Christ's resurrection. In fact, this arguably remote possibility has been followed in "An American Translation" (AAT, 1939) and the Moffatt New Translation (MNT, 1922), where the former has: "In it Enoch went and preached even to those spirits that were in prison, who had once been disobedient, when in Noah's time God in his patience waited for the ark to be made ready," while the Moffatt has: "It was in the Spirit that Enoch also went and preached to the imprisoned spirits who had disobeyed at the time when God's patience held out during the construction of the ark in the days of Noah." Christ's passion and resurrection bring Christians through baptism to salvation from spiritual error.

In Jude v.7 the sins for which Sodom and Gomorrah were obliterated are compared directly to those of the wicked Watchers in lusting after what to them was "strange flesh": "Even as Sodom and Gomorrah, and the cities about them in like manner, giving themselves over to fornication, and going after strange flesh, are set forth for an example, suffering the vengeance of eternal fire" (cf. 2 Peter 2:6). Genesis 19:4–5 makes it plain "strange flesh" implies illicit sex (with respect to Sodomites, sodomy).

Jude compares sinners afflicting his community to a disorder in the governing essence of nature. Whereas 1 Enoch 2 points to the wonder of divine order in the stars, the provision of dew, the fruitfulness of trees, and providential winds and seas, Jude vv.12–13 shows this order reversed among corrupters of Christian love-feasts: "clouds they are without water, carried about of winds; trees whose fruit withereth, without fruit, twice dead, plucked up by the roots; Raging waves of the sea, foaming out their own shame; wandering stars, to whom is reserved the blackness of darkness for ever." And note the last line, that "blackness of darkness" seems to echo 1 Enoch 10:4 when the Lord tells Raphael to bind Azaz'el hand and foot and "cast him into the darkness." 2 Peter 2:17 simply compresses Jude's account: "These are wells without water, clouds that are carried with a tempest; to whom the mist of darkness is reserved for ever."

Direct parallels between 1 Peter and 1 Enoch indicate a strong likelihood the author was familiar with the Parables of 1 Enoch where the redemptive and judging functions of the Son of Man are adumbrated:

Who verily was foreordained before the foundation of the world, but was manifest in these last times for you. (1 Peter 1:20)

And for this reason hath he been chosen and hidden before Him, before the creation of the world and for ever more. He was chosen and hidden in his presence, before the world was created and forever. And the wisdom of the Lord of Spirits hath revealed him to the holy and righteous; For he hath preserved the lot of the righteous. (1 Enoch 48:6–7a)

Who shall give account to him that is ready to judge the quick and the dead. (1 Peter 4:5)

And he sat on the throne of his glory, And the sum of judgment was given unto the Son of Man, And he caused the sinners to pass away and be destroyed from off the face of the earth. (1 Enoch 69:27)

There remains a question of whether there was any specific thematic intention in the association of Jude and the Petrine epistles in the Bodmer Codex; could the Enochic element have been significant? An interesting article by Brice C. Jones of McGill University, Montreal, has examined the issue with regard to the Bodmer Codex and its relation to another composite or "miscellaneous" collection, the Coptic Crosby-Schøyen Codex MS 193. Having examined some leading hypotheses, Jones tends to favor the view that "miscellaneous" means what it says, and that arguments for finding common themes, such as suffering, or material suitable for Easter homilies, tend to lose what force they had because it's unclear whether texts belonged to prior collections before being reassembled in known codices. Nevertheless, some texts may have been together for a reason now lost to us through later amalgamation. Jones writes: "It is quite likely that scribes found certain texts (like 1–2 Peter and Jude) already joined in their exemplars, and that this original textual bond was preserved. Furthermore, it may well be the case that 1–2 Peter were joined early on because they were considered authored by the same person, and that Jude was also attached because of its close textual affinities to 2 Peter. In any case, we will never know with any real certainty why particular texts were chosen over others; the question is really unimportant."[8]

The very size of the Bodmer Codex is a strong suggestion that it was quantity of new translations that was uppermost in the minds of those who required them, and it is reasonable to suppose translations were added "as texts came to hand." Of course, had a copy of 1 Enoch been included in the codex, such would constitute sufficient cause to look further into the possibility of theological collusion. The discovery of a Greek codex containing material from 1 Enoch came from another source, as we shall see.

NINE

2 Enoch

In 1892 a German review mentioned a version of the Ethiopic Enoch written in Church Slavonic.[1] While investigation proved first identification erroneous, the effort revealed that in Russia and other Slavic countries numerous versions of an entirely unanticipated work, one sometimes entitled the "Book of the Secrets of Enoch," existed. Manuscripts pointed to there having been longer and shorter versions, with extracts from both bound into compendia of other noncanonical works for Slavonic-speaking churchmen. The version Charles arranged to be translated into English by William Morfill, Oxford's first professor of Slavonic languages, was known as manuscript "P," containing a two-part text that ended at chapter 68, verse 7. The first part (1–38) relates Enoch's angel-guided, revelatory ascent through ten heavens to God's throne. God explains His creation and how death was made punishment for sin (30:16). Archangel "Satanail" (31:4) was hurled toward the abyss "with his angels" for trying to make himself equal to God (29:4). The second part (39–67) relates Enoch's thirty-day return to earth to deliver celestial secrets, knowledge of God's judgment on the world, and spiritual and sacerdotal guidance to his sons. Enoch then reascends.

From what he learned in heaven, Enoch knew *everything*. Privileged to sit before God to compose 366 books, God insisted Enoch pass knowledge to his sons as a guide for their time and

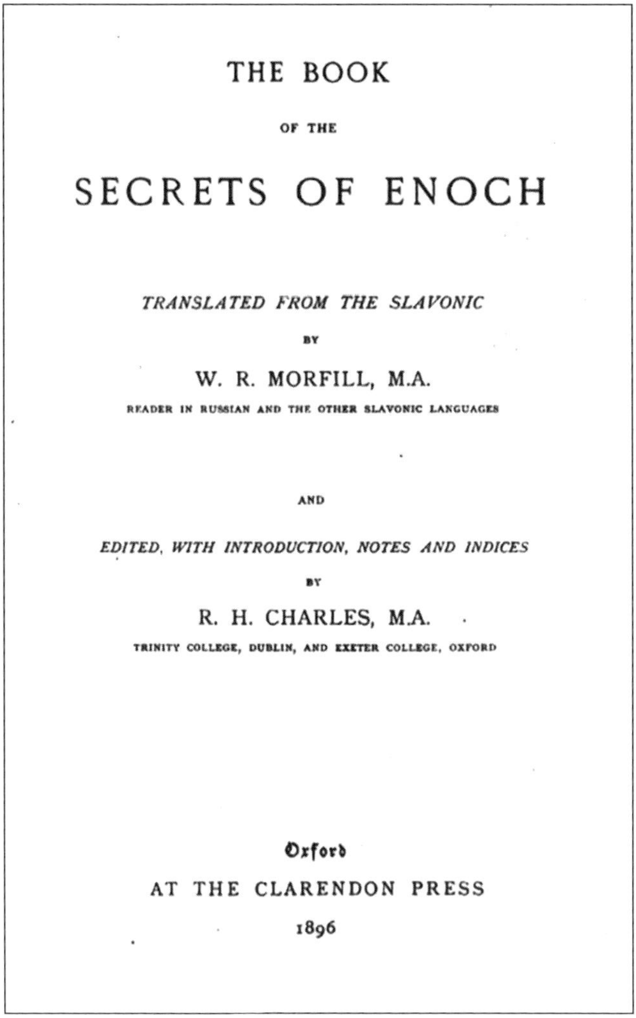

THE BOOK

OF THE

SECRETS OF ENOCH

TRANSLATED FROM THE SLAVONIC

BY

W. R. MORFILL, M.A.

READER IN RUSSIAN AND THE OTHER SLAVONIC LANGUAGES

AND

EDITED, WITH INTRODUCTION, NOTES AND INDICES

BY

R. H. CHARLES, M.A.

TRINITY COLLEGE, DUBLIN, AND EXETER COLLEGE, OXFORD

Oxford

AT THE CLARENDON PRESS

1896

Fig. 9.1. R. H. Charles, *The Book of the Secrets of Enoch translated from the Slavonic*, translated by W. R. Morfill, Oxford, 1896.

times to come, lest anyone doubt God's intentions for sinners who oppressed and hurt the innocent, and for the righteous who suffered them (23:6; 33:8–9).

Manuscripts A, U, and B extended the narrative to 72:10, with manuscript R including material about Noah's Flood up to chapter 73:9. Chapters 68 to 73 described duties performed by Enoch's family as priests making sacrifices on the Lord's altar, with an account of Melchizedek's miraculous virgin birth—redolent of Noah's remarkable birth in 1 Enoch—leading up to the Flood. Numerous fragments of the book also existed, though none included a seventy-third chapter. Charles published the "third part" (68–72) as an appendix.

The book advocates a high ethical standard:

> When a man clothes the naked and feeds the hungry, he gets a recompense from God. If his heart murmurs, he works for himself a double evil: he works destruction to that which he gives and there shall be no reward for it: And the poor man, when his heart is satisfied or his flesh is clothed and he acts contemptuously, he destroys the effect of all his endurance of poverty and shall not gain the blessing of a recompense. For the Lord hates every contemptuous and proud-speaking man: and likewise every lying word: and that which is covered with unrighteousness. And it is cut with the sharpness of a deadly sword, and thrown into the fire, and burns for ever. (63:1–4)

R. H. Charles had little doubt the work post-dated 1 Enoch, constituting an elaboration upon it. He felt confident dating much of it to about 1–50 CE due to numerous references to Jerusalem's temple, and the attention given, especially in chapter 59, to the legal or halakhic (purity-oriented) performance of animal sacrifices at the altar. The sacrificer's state of heart matters as much as the state of heart of the doer of charity to his fellow. Most scholars today favor a pre-70 CE date.

Ethical demands are consistent with Matthew 22:37–39, that the righteous must love God and neighbor as one loves oneself. A rationale for this is found in 2 Enoch 44:1–4 based on the principle that man was made in God's image, which belief is here extended to the image or *face*—meaning that which we show—and see, of others. The reflection of God to ourselves we should recognize in others:

> God made man with His own hands, in the likeness of His countenance, both small and great the Lord created him. He who reviles the countenance of man, reviles the countenance of the Lord. He who shows wrath against another without injury, the great wrath of the Lord shall consume him. If a man spits at the face of another

insultingly, he shall be consumed in the great judgment of the Lord. Blessed is the man who does not direct his heart with malice against any man, and who assists the man who is injured, and under judgment, and raises up the oppressed, and accomplishes the prayer of him who asks! [cf. Matthew 25:31–40]

As animal sacrifices are performed at the temple's altar,* and since there's no allusion whatever to the temple system's destruction, the view that 2 Enoch was originally written before 70 CE is reasonable. The difficulty in establishing confidence in such a date had been that there was no manuscript or fragment of the book in Church Slavonic before the fourteenth century, and while Charles, for example, believed the book translated from Greek—perhaps based on Hebrew components of earlier provenance—no Greek fragment of it had come to light. That situation has now changed radically (see Orlov, Boccaccini, and Zurawski, *New Perspectives on 2 Enoch: No Longer Slavonic Only*; see pages 165–67).

Apparent awareness in 2 Enoch of the Wisdom of Solomon (circa mid-first century BCE), thought composed by an Alexandrian Jew, and its interest in an Adamic tradition associated with Alexandria, disposed Charles to favor Alexandria as 2 Enoch's birthplace, its influence extending to other pseudepigraphical works of the first century CE and patristic period, including the Book of Adam and Eve, the Apocalypse of Zephaniah (in Clement of Alexandria's *Stromateis* 5.11.77), the Ascension of Isaiah, and the Apocalypse of Baruch. Possible influence on the New Testament, especially St. Matthew, is more difficult to

---

*This is at a place called Akhuzan, a cryptic name for Jerusalem's temple mountain. Its altar is erected by Methuselah and his brothers at the place where Enoch is taken up (68:6; it later appears as the place where Adam was created). That place becomes the center of the earth from the priestly point of view, suitable for blood sacrifice. According to scholar Andrei Orlov, *Akhuzan* is an enigmatic Slavonic word traced by scholars to the Hebrew word אחזה, "special property of God," which in Ezekiel 48:20–21 is applied to Jerusalem and the temple. According to Orlov: "Enoch's eschatological role is tied to the idea of the earthly counterpart of the [heavenly] Throne, the earthly temple. The vertical axis of throne and temple is thus explicitly reaffirmed in the text, as is the horizontal line connecting the protological and eschatological events."[2]

establish as numerous texts with similar phrases or ideas to Matthew and other gospels are shared in essence with 1 Enoch.[3]

Apocalyptic portions of the Testaments of the Twelve Patriarchs (possibly early first century CE) appear to draw on what Enoch saw ascending through the heavens in 2 Enoch. From this, Charles deduces original Hebrew components of 2 Enoch predate the first century CE, but perhaps no earlier than 30 BCE.[4] Hellenistic influence may also be discernible in 23:4–5 where Enoch is informed by angel Vereveil of the Platonic doctrine visible in the Wisdom of Solomon that "every soul was born eternally before the foundation of the world." The latter phrase may be linked to the pre-existence of the Son of Man in 1 Enoch's Parables, and the co-creative status of the divine Wisdom in Wisdom of Solomon.

Charles believed we owe to 2 Enoch 33:1–2 the first articulation of the idea of the Millennium,[5] an account used by church father Irenaeus in the second century (*Adversus Haereses* 5.28), namely, as God made the world in six days, resting on the seventh, so history would last 6,000 years, with a 1,000 year sabbatical following, since our thousand years are to God but a day (e.g.: 2 Peter 3:8; Psalm 90:4)—with the eighth "day" of judgment following.

Andrei Orlov sees a tendency in 2 Enoch to take the figure of Enoch a stage beyond that of 1 Enoch where he is a human being who becomes angelic, to a point where he seems to assume supercelestial status above the angelic world.[6] In 24:1, for example, God instructs Enoch to sit on his left hand with Gabriel, while chapter 37 has an angel come to "freeze" Enoch's face before coming to earth lest it prove unbearable to earthlings. In 24:3 God says to Enoch: "Not even to My angels have I told My secrets, nor have I informed them of their origin, nor have they understood My infinite creation which I tell thee of today." God then tells the story of the creation from His *own* point of view, delivered as an intimate confidence to Enoch that might even have been taken as an account that trumped Genesis, attributed to Moses. In the end, Enoch is raised to his "eternal habitation" before God's very face, a scribe eternally, involved intimately with running earth and the heavens, even as an instrument in His final judgment.

The text, however, seems determined to avoid communicating such an elevation to the reader more directly: enough indeed is it for Enoch to be so chosen. He's certainly no longer mortal, telling his sons there is no *food* in him; how could there be? He is nourished on God's presence. However, the placing of Enoch personally at two points—the throne in heaven, and the center of the earth, with a role in antediluvian and final judgment—could much later have inspired explicit elevation to archangel-hood, or beyond, even to very divinity, evident in the much later 3 Enoch, akin to Merkabah ("Throne") and Hekhalot ("Palaces") mysticism that encouraged later Jewish mystics to attempt inner, contemplative ascents through the heavens in search of divine secrets (gnosis), with expanded consciousness a means to spiritual transformation, for which efforts the figure of Enoch became a dominant type or archetype among Jewish mystics or "gnostics." Enoch, you could say, pioneers the idea of channeling through ascent to more purified modes of consciousness and being, the effort linked intimately and directly to the notion of *science*, knowledge of truth both physical and spiritual.

Ten Heavens

Perhaps 2 Enoch's most influential aspect comes from its clear account of ten heavens above the earth, ascent through which Enoch is angelically guided to face God. It shaped the cosmology of the heretical Bulgarian Bogomils, presumed precursors of the Cathars. The journey forms the mechanics of countless future ascent itineraries prefigured to canonical readers by St. Paul's account of ascent to the third heaven in 2 Corinthians 12:2–4 where Paul himself, he implies, heard things not lawful to utter: a notion reinforced by 2 Enoch's account of the third heaven.

First Heaven

Two men with golden wings, faces like the sun, eyes like lamps, with fire from their lips summon Enoch from his bed. On their wings he flies through the clouds, then the ether to the first heaven (2-3:2).

Here the earth's atmosphere is controlled by "elders and rulers" and two hundred angels who rule the order of the stars and fly around them with their wings. Enoch sees treasuries of rain and dew like "oil for anointing" (6:1), and treasuries of clouds into which snow and ice enter.

Second Heaven

Here amid gloom is a prison for rebellious angels. Having apostatized from God, they and their prince are perpetually tortured (Watchers are not here mentioned as such). Enoch pities them, but when they ask him to plead their case before God he asks what need have angels of a mere mortal like himself? (7:5).

Third Heaven

The Garden of Eden with an astoundingly beautiful "tree of life," is found here, guarded by three hundred angels whose voices never cease in "blessed singing," as St. Paul described: a place for the righteous; to the north, by contrast, is one of utter horror where every kind of sinner and worker of sodomy and black magic and profiteering and godlessness is consigned eternally.

Fourth Heaven

Here are the controlling entities for the movements of sun and moon, including "phoenixes" and other flying creatures called "chalkadri" (12:1), purple and rainbow-like, with feet and tails of lions, and heads of crocodiles: they move the sun over and beneath the earth. Movements of the sun and moon are described in detail, like in 1 Enoch's Astronomical Book. A choir's heavenly singing is utterly beautiful.

Fifth Heaven

Here are found "Grigori" (Watchers), soldiers of Satan resembling mortals but who were giants. They await judgment; Enoch recommends repentance.

Sixth Heaven

Archangels govern life on earth here, including the time scheme and the seasons, and every living thing that derives life from the earth. Records are kept of all deeds and states of soul of all men, which they relate to the Lord.

Seventh Heaven

Guided now by Gabriel, Enoch is told: "Be of good cheer, do not be afraid," as Gabriel directs Enoch's gaze far above, where the Lord's throne and face are visible. A heavenly light illuminates: "all the fiery hosts of great archangels, and incorporeal powers and lordships, and principalities, and powers; cherubim and seraphim, thrones, and the watchfulness of many eyes. There were ten troops, a station of brightness, and I [Enoch] was afraid, and trembled with a great terror" (20:1).

Eighth Heaven

This heaven, called "Muzaloth" in Hebrew, is just below the upper firmament in which are sited the zodiacal constellations.

Ninth Heaven

This heaven is called "Kukhavim," home of the zodiacal signs.

Tenth Heaven

Called "Aravoth," God is here enthroned, and Enoch sees him face to face, closely. Enoch says the glory of God's face is unspeakable. Who is Enoch to speak of the divine knowledge and "various utterances" he hears (22:2)?

In 2 Enoch the way is pointed to a realm where secrets of wisdom were born. To an extent then, it hints at a new state of being beyond the world, and may have provided an exit door for some mystically minded souls from the partial, or arguably total, failure of time-tuned apocalyptic promises to relieve the Jews from political oppression in the first and second centuries.

The legacy of Enochic projections, both projected in time and beyond it, within the world and beyond that too, had two major effects on the minds of those receiving them, whether directly or indirectly.

First, 1 Enoch *relativized human history* and human civilization. What mattered primarily was not what men were doing, but what *God* was going to do; all human achievement, other than the spirit of endurance to witness it, would be swept away and be as nothing. What kings, princes, generals, or glamorous persons did was ultimately and intrinsically vain: acquisition of salvation was all. Recognizing the world's vanity was the triumph of wisdom. All history and life was precomposed and predestined to eventual end; there would be nothing truly new under the sun. Thus, the activity of relatively unknown Galilean fishermen and their adventures in following a relatively unknown rabbi would stand as infinitely more meaningful and real than the building and demolition works of Emperor Nero in Rome, while Vespasian's conquests were simply instruments of God's overarching will. Imperial grandeur and the passing invader and slaughterhouse could elicit less than a shrug of contempt from one "in the know" of God's ultimate scheme. When death itself was seen as incidental or even a passage *out*, then martyrdom became a life achievement and sign par excellence of the true believer: the badge of honor to belittle any imperial decoration or civic gift. This could be a truly liberating consciousness, and a near-visceral hope to the desperate and the enslaved. As Gibbon* pointed out, however, there could be a serious downside: a lack of interest and commitment to the world one wished to leave behind, or that, psychologically, one *had* left behind. As the Gospel of Thomas (42) has it: "Become passers-by." Born of a Buddhistic indifference, resignation can be ruinous to a company—and, arguably worse; what happens when the belief falters or dies? Result: nihilism, or moral negation. Gibbon attributed the fall of the Roman Empire and ensuing Dark Ages to such detachments from the world; they can be as dangerous as mass

---

*William Gibbon (historian), author of the classic *The History of the Decline and Fall of the Roman Empire*, 6 vols., 1776–1778.

alcoholism. Should one care about the time-scheme? The Enochic synthesis says: leave all *that* to God, who has time in the palm of His hand—but be sure to do good while time lasts, or you will go down with it!

Second, the notion of a personal ascent, while alive, as Enoch had been led to, was now discernible as a viable "way out" on an interior level, from a world denuded of any but its ultimately transcendental meaning and value, opening the door both to an intense monasticism, encratism (hatred of the body), and numerous types of gnostic experience, both world-accommodating (Hermetism) and world-denying (radical "gnostics").

Furthermore, can we separate entirely 1 Enoch's conviction that the fault and source of human corruption and misery lies with rebellious angels from the radical gnostic assessment of harmless "pneumatics" (spiritual Christians) imprisoned in an ultimately finite world, made and governed by ignorant angels (archons)? In Gnostic mythology, we even find what appears to be a transposed theme of inferior angelic lust for the sexually alluring female figure, for in numerous Gnostic myths the lower world is itself generated when the divine, feminine Wisdom figure (Sophia) yearns sexually for gnosis of the ultimate Father, which illegitimate desire opens herself to be subjected to the lust and jealousy of the archons among whom she tragically falls. Indeed, it is hard to imagine a Christian gnostic movement without the daring, provocative stimulus of Enochic literature among other, more familiar, factors.

2 Enoch Bounces Back—in Coptic!

New discoveries are still illuminating our vista of the amazing books of Enoch.

Excavations by the Egypt Exploration Society at Nubia's Qasr Ibrim's fortress site—now a small island in Lake Nasser thanks to the Aswan High Dam's construction—have revealed previously unknown texts, recorded in director of excavations (1963–1976) Coptologist Prof. J. M. Plumley's notebooks. Examining these in Cambridge, "probably in April 2006," doctoral student Joost L. Hagen noticed a fragment in Coptic from a 1972 excavation:[7]

> "The circle of the moon I have measured . . . and the . . . (?) of its light," "great heat," "one of the angels," "and the appearance . . . was like snow, and . . . were like ice," ". . . spoke to me all these words," "I have come to know everything," "and their chambers," "my descendants . . ."
> (no. 72.3.3.; Plumley notebook 3, 11–17)

It was not until March 2009 that checking a phrase with Google Books, Hagen was alerted to 2 Enoch as the fragment's source. Recalling an old lecture on Slavonic apocrypha given by Christfried Böttrich of Griefswald, an email sent to him with news of a non-Slavonic version led to not only discovering the lecturer was a 2 Enoch expert, but also an invitation to the fifth Enoch Seminar of June 2009, held in Naples, devoted serendipitously, to 2 Enoch.

Fragments 1 and 2, revealed by Hagen, settled old disputes, such as a sequence of disputed chapters 36–40, where the Coptic, omitting chapter 38, matched the *short* recension of the Slavonic work. The Coptic also included material from the end of chapter 36 (vv.3–4) present only in the oldest Slavonic manuscript ("U") and in sixteenth-century manuscript "A."[8]

As for dating the Coptic fragments, they were found in a pit before the altar's southern side in a small church by the ninth-century Qasr Ibrim cathedral's south wall (Qasr Ibrim became a Christian center in the early eighth century). Plumley reckoned the pit predated the church. Fragments of St. Mark's gospel in Greek found there have been palaeographically dated to the fifth century, possibly brought to Nubia in the sixth century when it was first part-Christianized. The 2 Enoch fragments are not that old, with a date spectrum of eighth to ninth, maybe tenth century, that is, *before* the supposed translation date into Slavonic (tenth or eleventh century).

Other Coptic fragments found in 1972 were kept in Cairo's Coptic Museum's library, but Hagen has not yet found the 2 Enoch fragments there.

Christfried Böttrich has since pointed to the milieu from which 2 Enoch emerged in his article, "The 'Book of the Secrets of Enoch' (2 Enoch): Between Jewish Origin and Christian Transmission,"[9] where he notes that the text betrays some eighteen instances indicating kinship to popular religious ideas familiar to Hellenistic Egypt.[10] The intellectual level is not that of a Philo, though the likely metropolis is Philo's Alexandria. A definite clue is the presence of the four-feet-fetter custom of sacrificing animals peculiar to Egypt. As Böttrich observes: "So the custom is not a proof of a sectarian milieu, but of some openness towards the surrounding society in ordinary day life. At least, we must be content with the picture of an open-minded form of Judaism in an urban context, with some wealth and some education, living in accordance with its own tradition and looking for cautious accommodation to the Hellenistic world. Here we can find the best legitimization for the Torah when we realize that the antediluvian patriarchs had already kept it long before it was given to Moses."[11]*

---

*These insights may be a clue to a connection with the Jewish temple founded by high priests Onias III or Onias IV in the Heliopolitan nome after Onias III was deposed by brother Jason and Antiochus IV. See pages 219-225 graves about the archaeological site indicate a level of diaspora integration with Graeco-Egyptian norms, with an abiding pride in Jewish tradition. A disposition to Enochic works there would make sense if we see Onias as a "teacher of righteousness" committed to a new covenant. This is pure speculation, however.

TEN

Testimony to Enoch
from Church Fathers, or
. . . *Enoch Gets Around*

We've already mentioned what some church fathers—notably Tertullian and Clement of Alexandria—thought about Enoch's prophecies, but those testimonies, generally positive, hardly exhaust the seam.

The fascinating Epistle of Barnabas, dated by Loren T. Stuckenbruck to the late 130s, argues that Jewish scriptures were *always* Christian, but Jews, misled by an evil angel, had misinterpreted their full import and taken the legal aspects too literally, ignoring the salient message of their being essentially prophecies of Jesus. Despite doubt over the epistle's authenticity—Paul's assistant Barnabas was claimed as author—numerous church fathers nonetheless regarded Barnabas as scripture, and it was included in the fourth-century Codex Sinaiticus with the rest of the Christian Old and New Testament canon, kept at Sinai's St. Catherine's monastery until removed to Russia by Constantin Tischendorf in the 1850s, thence sold to the British Museum in 1933.

Stuckenbruck notes how the Epistle of Barnabas "cites the patriarch Enoch as 'scripture' twice beginning in 16:5ff. when reviewing material from the Animal Apocalypse (1 Enoch 89:56, 60, and 66ff.) and the Apocalypse of Weeks (1 Enoch 91:13—taken as a prediction of an eschatological temple)."[1] Barnabas's citing of Enochic prophecy is prefaced by the words "it is written," denoting its authority. Stuckenbruck notes another passage attributed by Barnabas to Enoch, which while corresponding generally to 1 Enoch 100:1–3, has no direct counterpart in 1 Enoch, though similar to an account of difficult times preceding the last judgment in Testaments of the Twelve Patriarchs.[2]

Christian writers clearly found Enoch more useful to them, to say the least, than did non-Christian Jewish writers post 70 CE—hardly surprising since Christians saw the temple's destruction as fulfillment of Christ-vindicating prophecy, closely linked to Enochic apocalyptic promises. We may perceive a dynamic here that Enochic works *anticipated*, doubtless unconsciously, core structures of the Jesus movement's original message (as far as we can ascertain it), namely, the Jesus movement may be seen as a *development* of an Enochic Judaism, as numerous scholars have suggested (see pages 323–328).

Another vital point to note is that if we consider Jesus's immediate disciples were on average aged as much as thirty at the time of the crucifixion (in my analysis dated 37 CE; see *The Mysteries of John the Baptist*), then even at the temple's destruction in 70 CE, their average age would have been only about sixty-three, with good years yet to give eyewitness accounts, and to trumpet the apposite value of Enoch's prophecies. It becomes evident that Enoch's prophecies, regarded as scripture, were inherent to the first stratum of Nazarene witness, and this adequately accounts for their presence among very early patristic writings.

Judean born, but from a Greek family, Justin "Martyr" would certainly have assented to the idea of pre-Christian "Christianity." For him, the mind of Christianity existed in seed form before Jesus's birth, being the perennial fruit of providential wisdom, or the divine word (*logos*) scattered, waiting for fulfillment. Wisdom seekers, be they pagan philosophers or others, inevitably found elements of spermatic "Christian" truth. Others, Justin believed, were misled by demons. Justin is familiar with the Enochic idea of demons derived from bodies of otherwise vanquished giants mothered by violated human women, with the giants' wandering spirits worshipped as gods by nations who abandoned God after the Flood. Justin employs this notion in chapters 5 and 5 respectively of his *First* and *Second Apologies* where he appeals to the highest Roman authority to acquire true understanding of the faith, and having done so, act favorably toward it instead of persecuting Christians for nonexistent crimes.

> For the truth shall be spoken; since of old these evil demons, effecting apparitions of themselves, both defiled women and corrupted boys, and showed such fearful sights to men, that those who did not use their reason in judging of the actions that were done, were struck with terror; and being carried away by fear, and not knowing that these were demons, they called them gods, and gave to each the name which each of the demons chose for himself.
> (*First Apology* 5)

> God, when He had made the whole world . . . committed the care of men and of all things under heaven to angels whom He appointed over them. But the angels transgressed this appointment, and were captivated by love of women, and begot children who are those that are called demons; and besides, they afterwards subdued the human race to themselves, partly by magical writings, and partly by fears and the punishments they occasioned, and partly by teaching them to offer sacrifices, and incense, and libations, of which things they stood in need after they were enslaved by lustful passions; and among men they sowed murders, wars, adulteries, intemperate deeds, and all wickedness.
> (*Second Apology* 5)

Stuckenbruck observes that the reference to angels transgressing their appointed task (cf. 1 Enoch 12:4; 15:3) suggests Justin's reliance on Jubilees 4:15 and 5:6 where the angels were originally sent to instruct humanity but were distracted by female beauty: a pitfall not unknown to many teachers of humanity, though none since have generated giants in the process.

• • •

Self-styled "Athenian," philosopher Athenagoras (ca. 130–190 CE) started reading Christian scripture to expose its errors but instead became a convert, writing a *Legatio pro Christianis* or "Embassy for the Christians" addressed "To the Emperors Marcus Aurelius Antoninus and Lucius Aurelius Commodus, conquerors of Armenia and Sarmatia, and more than all, philosophers," to demonstrate how provincial authorities persecution of Christians was unworthy, by contrasting the faith's philosophical eminence with the persecutors' moral baseness. This motive dates the work to ca. 176–177 when a persecution raged in Lyon in which Pothinus, Irenaeus's episcopal predecessor, was martyred. Campaigning in Asia Minor at the time, balance of evidence suggests philosopher-emperor Marcus Aurelius did not authorize the persecution, and may have tried to prevent it. Athenagoras furnished him with reasons for preventative measures.*

Arguing about free will to choose virtue or vice, Athenagoras refers to rebellious angels in chapter 24 of the *Legatio*: "Some, free agents, you will observe, such as they were created by God, . . . (you know that we say nothing without witnesses, *but state the things which have been declared by the prophets*); these fell into impure love of virgins . . . Of these lovers of virgins, therefore, were begotten those who are called giants" (my italics).

This suggests Athenagoras's source was a prophet, a point already iterated in chapter 7: "But we have for witnesses of the things we apprehend and believe, prophets, men who have pronounced concerning God and the things of God, guided by the Spirit of God." While Genesis 6 could have provided bones for Athenagoras's account of angels and giants, chapter 25 relies on Enochic testimony (cf. 1 Enoch 15:11 to 16:2) for its account of wandering demons: "These angels, then, who have fallen from heaven, and haunt the air and the earth, and are no longer able to rise to heavenly things, and the souls [*psychai*] of the giants, which are the demons who wander about the world, perform actions similar, the one

---

*Paul Keresztes, "Marcus Aurelius a Persecutor?" *Harvard Theological Review* 61, no. 3 (1968): 321–41.

[that is, the demons] to the natures they have received, the other [that is, the angels] to the appetites they have indulged." Most interestingly, Athenagoras holds a being he calls "the prince of matter" responsible, contrary to God's good will, suggesting a mild, gnostic-like dualism.

While Athenagoras defended the faith in Alexandria, Irenaeus picked up the pieces while writing a massive work to refute heresies he believed misrepresented the faith, mostly of gnostic types. In his *Adversus Haereses* (4.16.2) he refers to Enoch's commission to denounce the Watchers, which, while mentioned in Jubilees 4:2, owes, in Stuckenbruck's view, more to 1 Enoch 12:4–5, 13:4–7 and 15:2.³ Elsewhere, Irenaeus insists angelic rebellion was "announced through the prophets" by the Holy Spirit (*Adversus Haereses* 1.10.1).

Christian poet Commodianus (ca. 240 CE) was also familiar with Enochic prophecy, as was Clement of Alexandria (ca. 150–215 CE). Clement's *Prophetic Eclogues* (2.1) state that Enoch and Daniel were harmonized on divine blessings for the faithful. ("Blessed art Thou, who lookest on the abysses as Thou sittest on the cherubim," says Daniel, in agreement with Enoch, who said, "And I saw all sorts of matter.") Clement also attributes to Enoch the belief that humans acquired astronomical and harmful arts from the fallen angels (53:6–7: "And already Enoch had said, that the angels who transgressed taught men astronomy and divination, and the rest of the arts").

Another Alexandrian theologian, Origen (185–254 CE), when explaining prophetic vision in *de Principiis* (4.35), was happy to quote Enoch with regard to the prophet's special vision of "matter": "Enoch also, in his book, speaks as follows: I have walked on even to imperfection; which expression I consider may be understood in a similar manner, viz., that the mind of the prophet proceeded in its scrutiny and investigation of all visible things, until it arrived at that first beginning in which it beheld imperfect matter (existing) without qualities. For it is written in the same Book of Enoch, I beheld the whole of matter; which is so understood as if he had said: I have clearly seen all the divisions of matter which are broken up from one into each individual species either of men or animals, or of the sky, or of the sun, or of all other things in this world."

In *de Principiis*, chapter 8, Origen refers to archangels assigned specific tasks, an idea almost certainly carried from Enoch's prophecies: "We are not," Origen writes, "to suppose that a special office has been assigned by mere accident to a particular angel: as to Raphael, the work of curing and healing; to Gabriel, the direction of wars; to Michael, the duty of hearing the prayers and supplications of men."

Despite employing Enoch to make a point, however, Origen's polemical defense of Christianity against pagan Celsus's attack (*Contra Celsus* chapters 54–55), adds a caveat to his—and Celsus's—reliance on Enoch:

> And in a most confused manner, moreover, does he [Celsus] adduce, when examining the subject of the visits of angels to men, what he has derived, without seeing its meaning, from the contents of the book of Enoch; for he does not appear to have read the passages in question, nor to have been aware that the books which bear the name Enoch do not at all circulate in the Churches as divine, although it is from this source that he might be supposed to have obtained the statement, that "sixty or seventy angels descended at the same time, who fell into a state of wickedness."
> (chapter 55)

Then, mixing up and confusing whatever he had at any time heard, or had anywhere found written—whether held to be of divine origin among Christians or not—he adds: "The sixty or seventy who descended together were cast under the earth, and were punished with chains." And he quotes (as from the Book of Enoch, but without naming it) the following: "And hence it is that the tears of these angels are warm springs,"—a thing neither mentioned nor heard of in the Churches of God!

Evidently, Celsus was acquainted with Book of Enoch, and while it was perhaps only in opposition to Celsus that Origen noted its circulation confined to churches where its divine source was recognized, Origen himself is loath to discount Enoch his prophetic dignity.

Criticism of Enoch's authenticity—or was it lack of doctrinal usefulness?—had apparently increased by St. Augustine's time (354–430).

Bishop of Hippo Regius in North Africa, famous for his massive literary response to the Gothic pillage of Rome of 410, *The City of God* (*de Civitas Dei*), Augustine insisted, despite Jude's quoting Enoch, that though Enoch might have left some "divine writings," his prophecies were nevertheless uncanonical as they contained "false statements" contrary to Christian doctrine. The prophecies' assumption of extreme antiquity was, Augustine asserted, untenable.

In *The City of God* (15.23), for example, though aware of the Petrine epistle's reference to angels chained for transgression, Augustine says he cannot believe this referred to God's "holy angels," because Genesis 6's reference to "sons of God" lusting after beautiful women couldn't have meant *angels*, but Seth's descendants, besotted with Cain's female descendants (Cainites being rogues, and Sethites, to that point, uncorrupted):

> From these assertions [that spirits have violated human women in guise of creatures], indeed, I dare not determine whether there be some spirits embodied in an aerial substance (for this element, even when agitated by a fan, is sensibly felt by the body), and who are capable of lust and of mingling sensibly with women; but certainly I could by no means believe that God's holy angels could at that time have so fallen, nor can I think that it is of them the Apostle Peter said, "For if God spared not the angels that sinned, but cast them down to hell, and delivered them into chains of darkness, to be reserved unto judgment." I think he rather speaks of these who first apostatized from God, along with their chief the devil, who enviously deceived the first man under the form of a serpent. But the same holy Scripture affords the most ample testimony that even godly men have been called angels; for of John it is written: "Behold, I send my messenger (angel) before Thy face, who shall prepare Thy way." And the prophet Malachi, by a peculiar grace specially communicated to him, was called an angel.

Ridiculing the notion of giants issuing from unions of women and angels, Augustine asserts that giants were familiar accidents, citing a

Fig. 10.1. *St. Augustine*: earliest known portrait (sixth century); fresco, Archbasilica of St. John Lateran, Rome.

recent appearance in Rome of a giant daughter of less than ordinary-sized parents. Giants could have appeared "before the sons of Seth formed a connection with the daughters of Cain. For thus speaks even the canonical Scripture itself in the book in which we read of this; [he quotes from Genesis 6]." Enoch's "fables" are "apocryphal," "because their obscure origin was unknown to the fathers from whom the authority of the true Scriptures has been transmitted to us by a most certain and well-ascertained succession." He accepts "there is some truth in these apocryphal writings" but their "many false statements" lacking canonical authority disqualifies them. "We cannot deny that Enoch, the seventh from Adam, left some divine writings," but Jewish authorities were unconvinced of their antiquity, along with other "prudent men." He compares Enoch to writings "produced by heretics under the names both of other prophets, and more recently, under the names of the apostles, all of which, after careful examination, have been set apart from canonical authority under the title of Apocrypha." Scripture admits the existence of giants but "these were citizens of the earthly society of men, and that the sons of God, who were according to the flesh the sons of Seth, sunk into this community when they forsook righteousness. Nor need we wonder that giants should be born even from these. For all of their children were not giants; but there were more then than in the remaining periods since the deluge." God allowed giants. They show "that neither beauty, nor yet size and strength, are of much moment to the wise man, whose blessedness lies in spiritual and immortal blessings," a belief confirmed by quoting Baruch 3:26: "These were the giants, famous from the beginning, that were of so great stature, and so expert in war. Those did not the Lord choose, neither gave He the way of knowledge unto them; but they were destroyed because they had no wisdom, and perished through their own foolishness." In fact, Jews regarded Baruch as apocryphal, as do protestant churches today!

While accepting Jude's declaration that Enoch "prophesied," Augustine insists in *City of God* 18.38 that neither "Jews" nor "us" accept books of Enoch or Noah because "their too great antiquity" invites suspicion. People who quote them "loosely believe what they please. But the purity of the canon has not admitted these writings, not because the authority of these men who pleased God is rejected, but because they are not believed to be theirs." Authority belonged to those directly inspired by God's Holy Spirit, not writings of "historical diligence," where lack of trust discounts them. Enoch's prophecies deviated from Genesis so were "contrary to the truth" and outside the canon.

Augustine's approach became the concreted orthodox position regarding Enoch thereafter (outside Ethiopia anyway). His main sticking point was profound unwillingness to accept the idea of angels, once holy, falling to earth out of lust (a human failing), and consorting with flesh. In this regard, it's significant that before Augustine converted to the faith—by pondering what he considered the unique doctrine of the incarnation—Augustine had been a Manichean "hearer," following gnostic teachings of Persian prophet Mani (216–274/277 CE). Mani's doctrine was pivoted on absolute dualism, a separation between matter, including flesh, and divine spirit. While Augustine continued as a Christian to site his faith in spiritual eternity, he couldn't abide the idea of holy spirit enslaved to earthly temptation; such made the *divine* passible. Sin meant death, and heavenly angels could not die, and so, presumably, could not sin. *Christ*, on the other hand, *could* be man because *his* was human nature fully redeemed in uniquely perfect conformity to God's will and very nature.

Furthermore, by Augustine's time, the doctrinal matrix of the Christian churches had changed from the early second century when the presence of Jewish Christianity, in which Enoch's prophecies were significant, was still felt in many churches. Increased Hellenization and Romanization of the faith, in line with Pauline emphases, as against "Nazarene" ones, had pushed Enoch out of the mainstream. In his antiheretic books called *The Medicine Chest*, Augustine's considerably older contemporary Epiphanius, bishop of Salamis (ca. 310–403) dismissed Jewish Christians (*Ebionites* = the poor) who did not accept Jesus the man as being fully God, as contemptible heretics (*Panarion* 30.18.5–6). The Book of Enoch was arguably a victim of a gradual de-Judaizing of the faith. That *rabbinic* Judaism had also rejected Enoch constituted more of an additional excuse than valid motive, for if the church did not hold itself obliged to consider the rabbinic view of Jesus, why should it attend to rabbinic views of Enoch's prophecies? Like the Catholic communion's relations to the pre-Pauline Jesus or *Natzarim* movement in Augustine's time, rabbinic Judaism represented a distinction from more pluralistic Middle Judaism.

That is to say, after Augustine, Enoch, from the standpoint of the Catholic church, was *out*.

"Out," yes, but not gone completely. As Annette Yoshiko Reed has recently asserted,[4] it would be erroneous to imagine the establishment of an enforceable canon meant knowledge of the Book of Enoch was lost because it was deprived of Catholic authority.

Proof of Enoch's longevity in certain circles comes from Jacob, learned bishop of the Syrian Orthodox Church's see of Edessa (ca. 640–708). Interpreter of the scriptures, revered figure of Syriac Christianity, Jacob wrote to Syrian Orthodox monk John the Stylite (or John of Litharb; died 737/38), an intellectual "pillar saint"— living and preaching on a pillar—attached to Ataraib monastery, west of Aleppo. In letter thirteen of sixteen from Jacob to John, Jacob addressed John's question: *Was it true that letters and books were unknown before Moses?* Such, replied Jacob, was Athanasius's view. Athanasius, however, was arguing a particular case—wishing to rid the church of apocrypha, he sacrificed the Book of Enoch along with dispensable works. Athanasius's logic was wrong. Were it right, Jacob asserted, one would agree with Basil that wine was unknown before the Flood! Writing was prerequisite to prosperity and development before Moses. Jewish traditions maintained Amram taught Moses Hebrew, as well as Egyptian letters, in pharaoh's house. Pre-Mosaic books obviously existed—the Book of Enoch being prime example. While Athanasius denied writing existed before the Flood, Athanasius was not all-knowing. Were the Book of Enoch not genuine, the apostle Jude would not have cited it—or in Jacob's words:

Now many acted foolishly and spoke nonsensically during the time of that holy saint [Athanasius], each [doing] as he pleased. They were displaying a large number of different secret books and bringing arguments from them which provided support for the deviance of [their] thought. Among all those secret books which they exhibited was also the secret Book of Enoch. . . . Due to their attraction toward and attachment to the secret books, some of which were spurious but others of which were authentic, he forbade and passed sentence on all of them collectively. Among all these books was the Book of Enoch, which is authentic. Athanasius says in one of his epistles, "How can they have a book of Enoch? Literature and writings did not exist prior to the Flood!" . . . But recognize well and accept as true, O man, that humanity had developed the technology of wine-making then, and they also used letters and produced a book. The Book of Enoch is quoted during the time of the apostles, for Jude the apostle cited it as a proof-text in his catholic epistle [Jude 14–15]. The Book was in existence before the time of Moses: written narratives quoted by the Jews declare this clearly, and there are no deceptions in it![5]

Scholar of Jewish pseudepigrapha William Adler believes Jacob's letter shows Enochic tradition was not lost after the fourth century. When pseudepigrapha fell under ecclesiastical judgment, the debate was usually about the works' status. Were they privileged insights into high matters, or spurious productions encouraging heresy? As Adler puts it: "Paradoxically, the sharpening of the distinction between 'canonical' and 'apocryphal' in the fourth century may actually have enhanced the standing of certain Jewish pseudepigrapha at the centre of this controversy. This is in fact what Jacob suggests in his defence of Enoch."[6] When Athanasius wrote his critique, heresy was so threatening that he felt compelled to proscribe *all* secret books from which heretics sought support, despite Jacob's insistence that though some were not genuine, others, like the Book of Enoch, definitely were. Danger of heresy having passed, Jacob believed Enoch's book deserved serious attention, for, as Adler asserts, it "had once enjoyed a high standing in the early Church."[7]

ELEVEN

Panopolis

······················

Zosimos, Enoch, and
Hermes Trismegistos

Readers may recall James Bruce, traveling home up the Nile in late 1773, with copies of the Ethiopic Book of Enoch in his baggage, meeting a friendly tax-collecting Copt at textile center Akhmim in the Thebaid. One hundred and thirteen years later, during the winter of 1886–87, recently resigned curator of Cairo's Bulaq Museum, Urbain Bouriant (1849–1903)—the Egyptologist who discovered the famous Hymn to the Aten at Amarna—was excavating a grave in Cemetery A at Akhmim's desert necropolis at al-Hawawis.[1] Within the grave his team found a roughly bound codex of thirty-three leaves between two leather-covered boards, 15 centimeters tall, 12 centimeters wide, with a first page depicting a Coptic cross. From this cross, and from examining the codex's contents, Bouriant assumed it was a *monk's* grave without confirmatory evidence.

Transcribed in Greek, the remarkable codex contained the majority of the Book of the Watchers, along with part of the apocryphal Gospel of Peter, and about a third of the Greek Apocalypse of Peter (bound upside down). Now called Codex Panopolitanus, after "Panopolis," Akhmim's ancient name, it is now kept at Alexandria's Bibliotheca Alexandrina Antiquities Museum. This version of the Book of the

Fig. 11.1. *Shores of the Nile at Akhmim*, painted by Karl Werner (1821–1888) for *Egypt* by Georg Moritz Ebers (Barcelona: Espasa y Compañía, 1882).

Watchers is the oldest known Greek version of the text, and since the Ethiopic 1 Enoch is believed to have been translated into Ge'ez from Coptic, after the Greek, it is widely regarded as an earlier version than the Ethiopic Enoch, though scholars observe parts of it are significantly different.

As Harvard-based Elena Dugan notes, 1 Enoch 19:3 to 21:9 appears twice. One "duplication" opens the codex's Enoch section, leading directly and without interruption into the "beginning" of the work—what we now call 1 Enoch 1.[2] The second duplication appears after 1 Enoch 18 and before 1 Enoch 22. Ms. Dugan believes deliberate reordering of a prior Enoch text was to create a Genesis-style Enoch biography, a process involving two scribes (evident from the script); a different scribe making each duplication. Dugan's analysis suggests that while formerly regarded as a hurried, or corrupt transmission, its intention was to structure Enoch's life according to Genesis, starting with his angelic tour, followed by proclamations on earth and translation to heaven, with the tour corresponding to Genesis's "Enoch walked with God" (Genesis 5:22), his earthly life and proclamations to Genesis 5:23, and the ascent to Genesis 5:24: "for God took him."

It appears, however, that two scribes worked independently, so that duplicates only appear so when reading the two scribal contributions together.[3] One scribe in particular seems to have "made the running" as far as biographical logic goes.

By closely analyzing the ordering, Dugan has gone some way to showing certain jumps in the text were made to concentrate attention on particular aspects of the story, such as the role of angelic guidance.[4] Dugan finds a precedent in the Ethiopic *Ascension of Isaiah* becoming the eleventh- or twelfth-century Greek Legend of Isaiah where reordering presents Isaiah's death by being sawn in half as biographical conclusion. Interestingly, Dugan speculates that 1 Enoch's Parables—sometimes considered a later addendum to a pre-existing Book of Enoch—could represent "a parallel example of the textual development of Enochic works better to reflect Enochic biography, with special interest in capturing a final ascent."[5]

Dugan's analysis shows a text's important aspects can become invisible when emphasis is placed on textual variation alone, rather than investigation as individual artifacts.[6] It also shows that while "variants" may derive from intentional design, it's unwise to presume too much too quickly about new discoveries. Another point is that while we should like scribes to copy faithfully one version of a narrative into a duplicate, the copying process itself may involve deliberate creativity. We shouldn't discount the idea of a copyist being inspired by a text to turn it in his own style, or be inspired to add to it, or even compose additional text. Is that not how epics grow, by temporal accretion?

Fiodar Litvinau's article "A Note on the Greek and Ethiopic Text of 1 Enoch 5:8"[7] has challenged other assumptions about the Codex Panopolitanus, such as the view that the Greek text necessarily represents an older reading than the Ethiopic. Litvinau observes that the Greek and Ethiopic versions of 1 Enoch 5:8 preserve different texts at the passage's end. He believes the Ethiopic text of 1 Enoch 5:8 is superior to Codex Panopolitanus's because the Greek is likely a scribal addition influenced by Gnostic terminology: a gloss "inspired by the notion of 'light' as a reward for the righteous in previous verse (5:7), and by the reference to wisdom in the first part of 1 Enoch 5:8. What sounded like a moral maxim was intellectualized by a copyist, who shifted its sense from the notion of humility toward the concept of spiritual knowledge. Not only the Enochic writings made their impact on the Gnostic thought, but the reverse influence was also possible during the course of transmission of the text. . . . One should not assume that the more ancient textual witness preserves a more original tradition."[8]

On palaeographic grounds, the Greek Book of the Watchers can be roughly dated to the late sixth or early seventh century CE, so the codex's discovery at least testifies to Enoch's currency in Upper Egypt over a century and a half after Augustine's death in 430. Whether that means currency among Christian monks in the period before the Islamic invasion (639) is uncertain. If the codex did belong to a monk, it would show Enoch's accommodation among obviously Christian (if apocryphal) works, though whether a hypothetical monk considered it and its accompanying apocalypse and gospel as apocryphal is unanswerable, but given the codex was chosen as a *grave* enclosure, one might suspect not. There are reasons, as we shall now see, for questioning the assumption that monks had "first call" on such a codex.

In a fascinating 2013 article, Professor Nicola Denzey Lewis reiterated a hypothesis that the Codex Panopolitanus is a kind of Christian "Book of the Dead" funeral deposit, redolent of ancient Egyptian internment practices. The texts' shared "preoccupation with death, resurrection and the topography of the heavens"[9] was of great interest to the dead and the dying. Likewise, much Gnostic literature is concerned with the soul's ascent, so depositing Gnostic books and other "heaven-oriented" works—especially in jars, like the Nag Hammadi library—could function as postmortem soul-guides or literary *talismans* to ensure smooth passage to heaven, providing reassuring keys to recognizing and verbally saluting or dismissing beings that help or hinder passage of soul or spirit to its destination (I am using *soul* and *spirit* to

denote an immortal identity-essence loosed at death, akin to the traditional Egyptian *khu*).* The books would serve as lodestones to the fearful or apprehensive, while perhaps serving as offerings to powers above
of sincere intent.

Prof. Lewis followed Coptologist Birger Pearson's lead in seeing how such a function would find a natural home in late antique
Egypt where such concerns had been instituted over millennia, and
around which much religious devotion was oriented. The practice
would then appear as a persistent traditional Egyptian practice—the
placing of postmortem documents, such as the *Opening of the Mouth*
ritual, at the top of a mummy's head, for example—being effectively
"Christianized."

In Egypt, written words were powerful for magic spells and prayer-
ful communication with deity. Irenaeus (*Adversus Haereses* 1.25.5)
tells of Gnostic "Marcosians," followers of magus Marcus, being given
verbal passports to rise unhindered after death, while words to that
purpose were spoken into the ears of the dying. The words stated
who one was in relation to where one *belonged*, such as with the "pre-
existing Father." One thus declared oneself property of the Father's
house with expectation of being delivered there as one expects a postal
service to respect the address and name on a letter. None being equal
or superior to the Father, no inferior should hinder His will.

Along with Coptologist Martin Krause,[10] Prof. Lewis would thus
see the Nag Hammadi codices as personal grave goods rather than
extracted volumes from a monastic library. The Jabal al-Ṭārif where
local Muhammad Ali al-Sammān claimed he and his brothers discovered the famous "Gnostic Gospels" was an ancient burial area, not a
monastic site, and Prof. Lewis suspects a grave-exploring, or robbing,
exercise was covered by a "discovered-while-digging-for-birdlime" story.

It is significant that Thebes was where production of traditional
Egyptian funerary documents continued until the second century CE.
"It seems to me," writes Prof. Lewis, "that there was a concerted effort

---

*Another example of such a thanatology (anthology of works for death) would be the
Berlin Codex that appeared on the antiquities market in 1896, containing the Gospel of
Mary, the Apocryphon of John, the Sophia of Jesus Christ, and the Acts of Peter.

at some unknown point from the second to the fourth century to draw on only some of the elements of Egyptian afterworld texts and teaching, while repressing or rejecting explicitly other elements in favour of Jewish or Greek themes."[11]

Another interesting suggestion made by Prof. Lewis concerns the texts' authorship. She speculates they would have been learned intellectuals of the fourth century, associating them with people who may have commissioned the Dishna papyri and Theban magical papyri (see my *The First Alchemists* [2023] pages 14–43), that is, lay persons with independent incomes and spiritual interests.

There is merit in Prof. Lewis's overall hypothesis that may force us to see other late antique literary collections from the Thebaid in a different light—and that light may illuminate Upper Egyptian interest in 1 Enoch, which contains bounteous information about heavenly topographies, and salvific promises to the righteous and repentant, as well as showing an ideal prototype of one who made the heavenly ascent in the most successful manner.

Apart from the Codex Panopolitanus's late possessor, we know of one other person with access to the Book of the Watchers from Roman Panopolis. That person was the remarkable Zosimos of Panopolis (fl. ca. 300 CE), practicing alchemist, and almost certainly an independent, lay intellectual with pronounced spiritual interests.*

Zosimos of Panopolis: Scourge of Demons

Zosimos's name means "Survivor," appropriately enough. Possessing encyclopedic, practical knowledge of chemical dyeing techniques and furnace work, Zosimos enjoyed insight into a symbolic interpretation of chemical processes. In chemistry's concern for purification and release of formerly hidden energy, he saw its processes epitomizing not only God's means of cosmic transformation, but of personal transcendence

---

*While some scholars consider Zosimos an Egyptian temple priest, or accessory to a temple, my assessment in *The First Alchemists* (2023) should convince that such an occupation makes no sense in the light of Zosimos's repeated condemnation of non-Christian or non-Jewish Egyptian temple beliefs, practices, and personnel.

of matter as well. For Zosimos, the chemical art was justified only if it brought profound respect for God's laws of nature, and the infinite power of His creative imagination, along with purification of soul and motive: simple truth was all. Otherwise the "holy and noble art," as he called it, simply wouldn't fulfill its potential. Seeing how priestcraft and idol worship had manipulated believers for millennia, he suspected "mysteries." Pure knowledge ultimately came from God, cosmic worker of truth. Behind twisting of divine truths by priests and numerous chemical charlatans, he saw the invisible work of recalcitrant demons, enemies of the true God, of truth, and her sister, utility.

In one respect, however, Zosimos was in a slight intellectual bind. Acquainted with "holy scriptures" concerning angels overwhelmed by passion, he believed knowledge of *chēmeia*, that is, chemistry (*alchemy* is derived from the considerably later Arabic translation of this word), came to earth illicitly, a conviction made plain in a letter to lady friend Theosebeia, whose name means "God-fearer." Possibly a Jewish or Christian convert, she may have run a business employing others for chemical work. Concerned she was slipping back to unsound magical supplications to demons who, like their forebears the Watchers, tempted women with "secrets," Zosimos criticized Theosebeia's requiring associates to swear oaths to keep these secrets while taking advice from an Egyptian priest called "Neilos" and "virgin" alchemist Paphnutia, whom Zosimos dismissed as useless amateurs tainted with powers vainly summoned to grant success in the art.

Zosimos recommends Theosebeia obtain her "secrets" from the source, the true source: God, whose will in the matter Zosimos discerns in at least two respectable sources, one being Enoch's prophecy, the other, interestingly, in Hermes Trismegistos.

Zosimos's letter is extant in two forms, one copied some five hundred years after composition in the *Chronographia* (History) of eighth-century Byzantine clergyman George Syncellus (or Synkellos; died 810), the other from a collection of Zosimos's alchemical writings preserved in Syriac.

Syncellus says the letter came from Zosimos's "ninth book of Imouth." Imouth or Imouthes, god of medicine, worshipped at

Memphis, was known to Greeks as Asklēpios, a figure presented in second- and third-century CE "Hermetic" tracts as pupil of Hermes Trismegistos, and to whom the *Perfect Discourse* (excerpted in Nag Hammadi library Codex 6), and familiar to Latin readers as *Asclepius*, is addressed. Zosimos writes:

> The Holy Scriptures, that is the books, say, my lady [Theosebeia], that there is a race of demons [*daimōnes*] who avail themselves of women. Hermes also mentioned this in his *Physika*, and nearly every treatise, both public and esoteric, made mention of this. Thus the ancient and divine scriptures said this, that certain angels lusted after women, and having descended taught them all the works of nature. Having stumbled because of these women, he says, they remained outside heaven, because they taught mankind everything wicked and nothing benefiting the soul. The same scriptures say that from them the giants were born. So theirs is the first teaching concerning these arts. They called this the Book of Chēmeu, whence also the art is called chēmeia.[12]

The reference to "holy scriptures" *might* include Genesis, but Zosimos also refers to Hermes's writings as such, and since the story he tells is not that told in Genesis—where there is nothing about "sons of God" teaching secrets of nature, for example—we may assume Zosimos's acquaintance either with the Book of the Watchers in Greek, the book of Jubilees, or a work attributed to Hermes Trismegistos with the story taken from an Enochic source, or possibly all of them, plus perhaps the Genesis 6 passage—where the "sons of God's" lust is *not* joined to teaching dangerous arts.

The Syriac version of Zosimos's reproof to Theosebeia reads as follows:

> Book Eight on the work of tin; letter *η* [hē: seventh letter of Greek alphabet]
>
> Book on tin that Zosimos presents. To Theosebeia, the queen, hail! [possibly sarcastic]

The holy Scriptures, O woman! Say that there's a race of demons who have commerce with women and direct them. Hermes also mentions this in his book on natural sciences; his entire book offering a sense manifest, and a sense hidden. He puts it there in these terms: the ancient and divine books say that certain angels were taken by passion for women. They descended to earth and taught there all the operations of nature. It's concerning them that our Book has said that, filled with pride, these were they who were driven out of heaven, because they'd taught to men all the bad things, which do not serve the soul. These are they who composed the [chemical] works, and from whom comes the first tradition of these arts. Their book's called Chema [*koumou*], and it's from there that chemistry [*koumia*] received its name. The Book consists of twenty-four sections; each of these has its proper name, or letter, or treatise. They are explained by the voice of priests. One of them is called Imos; another Imout; another has for title *surface*: this is how we translate it. One section is called *key*; another *seal* or *sealed*; another *manual* [or *guide*]; another *epoch* [or *age*]. As I said, each its own name. One finds in the book the arts set out in thousands of words.

Those who came after composed as many, in order to comment on them themselves. But these commentators wrote nothing good. Not only did they spoil the *koumia* books, but they wrote mysteries. The Philosopher [Democritus] says they drowned the books of natural science in a great ocean. Doubtless they wished to instruct you; or if they instruct souls, then they're philosophers. If you're a philosopher, don't lie; because you know what education is, that it's body and soul, and always accomplishes its duty. The word of wisdom says that everything is meditation. Isidos ["gift of Isis" = Egyptian alchemist Petesis] also says that meditation accomplishes the work.

I know that that doesn't escape you; to you [woman]; you know it, because you are of those who would like to secrete the art, if one had not written it. That's why you have formed an assembly and established oaths between one and another. But you [woman], you have put your disciples apart from the multitude, you gather them in little groups, where you instruct them openly. Meanwhile you say this book can only be acquired in secret. If mysteries *are* necessary, then it makes it even more necessary that each possess a book of *koumi* that is not held in secret.[13]

Among other things, Zosimos is saying to his female friend, or pupil, that chemistry has been dosed with corruption and deceit ever since its appearance, and that *women*—like Theosebeia, addressed perhaps sarcastically, as "queen"—are perilously susceptible to such demonic predations. She'd better watch out and listen to him. Zosimos is also saying that original writings were at least sound in knowledge, but the deposit was ruined by successive commentators. It is not clear what the "Book" is that they "share" with regard to the matter. While the Bible says nothing about demonic pride ensuring expulsion from heaven, we can be confident the story's source and lesson is Enochic.

Much of Zosimos's strictures to Theosebeia are based on the problem of a demonic role in chemistry. He grants that demons (properly *daimonēs*, with a sense of angels—he uses *both* words for the same miscreants[*]) had authentic knowledge of the art, but Zosimos was incensed to hear Egyptian priests, and their pupils, insisted daimons were essential to chemical success, believing all operations in the cosmos required their participation (rather as Enoch saw angels turning the cosmic taps and wheels). According to Theosebeia's misguided advisors, daimons demanded propitiation through ritual prayers and sacrifices, and operations at precise times when daimon-administered astrology was favorable. To Zosimos, all this was just *old world* magic: impostures complicating natural knowledge that followed God's uniform, beneficent laws, which could be practiced without such paraphernalia, so long as the practitioner respected God, and refrained from abusing it as had the lustful daimons/angels of "holy scripture."[†]

---

[*]In Greek a *daimōn* is a minor god or spirit, equivalent to an ordinary angel, hence the distinction of earthly and heavenly "demons."

[†]Detailed treatment of Zosimos's approach to daimons and chemical tinctures and propitious times is given in my book *The First Alchemists* (2023), with all relevant quotations from Zosimos's works.

In this, Zosimos went against a tide of third-century fascination with revived arcane Egyptianism. Zosimos also opposed widespread responses to belief that daimons were everywhere to be feared, controlling the very seconds of the day, seasonal courses, and powers of the zodiac, dwelling in temple statues and other cultic objects. All this is quite ironic: for centuries alchemy has been dismissed as magic, yet here we find one of its greatest exponents doing his utmost to cleanse what was for him highborn *science*.

The daimons' corrupting activity in chemistry (or alchemy), was a major theme of Zosimos's polemics to Theosebeia, and one senses the story of the fallen Watchers behind or enhancing much of it. Zosimos's *The Final Account*, for example, specifically warns against producing dyes at allegedly propitious times since it involves appeal to daimons. Apparently alluding to the Watchers condemned by God in 1 Enoch to exile from heaven, Zosimos describes daimons as *hoi kata topon ephoroi* which means "overseers," operating in specific locales, watching over perceived inferiors. Overseers command *slaves*. Confined, ephoroi operate in particular places. The allusion seems both to be to Watchers condemned to subterranean enclaves in 1 Enoch, and to spirits of wandering giants attaching themselves to places that they haunt. Another word Zosimos uses for these daimons is *perigeioi*, which means "near the earth," which might mean dwelling in the earth (as the condemned Watchers) or just above it, scouting the firmament or the air. Contact with them is, for Zosimos, an impurity. He says tinctures produced by will of overseers are given to the *priests* in return for nourishing statues where the daimon is worshipped. Against the tainted tincture, Zosimos's treatise's seventh section advocates the "natural" (*physikos*) tincture. Knowledge of them has, however, become obscured because *ephoroi*, begrudging the natural tinctures, hid them, replacing knowledge of them with non-natural tinctures. The allusion here seems to be both to the Watchers, and to priests hiding secrets in the temples' dark recesses. It also refers to spurious books on the art referred to in the letter above to Theosebeia, regarding which he also condemns their obsession with making silver and gold dyes, when the art was intended to produce *all the colors of the rainbow*.

Fig. 11.2. First page of the Stockholm Papyrus, ca. 300 CE, one of the two oldest recipe texts of Graeco-Egyptian alchemy, discovered in the Thebaid in the 1820s (Stockholm, Royal Library, Dep. 45).

The title of Zosimos's work *The Final Account* (or "Quittance") may allude to the Book of the Watchers' end-time when "Azael" (in the Greek version) and his fellows will be disposed of eternally after long haunting obscure places. Indeed, Zosimos uses the example of the tinctures to plead a universal case for religious corruption in Egyptian temples. He's clearly absorbed the spiritual import of Jewish, Jewish-Christian, or Gentile Christian viewpoints on pagan gods as fallen daimons lording it over the gullible.

Those who brought the colours made by non-natural means, being thus set aside, advised considerable numbers of people to act against us all, the savants, operating by natural actions. They [the daimons] did not want to be set aside by men, but to be supplicated and adjured to yield what they had made, in return for offerings and sacrifices. They therefore kept hidden all the natural processes, those that give results without artifice. It was not only out of jealousy against us, but because they were concerned about their existence and did not want to expose themselves to being beaten with rods, driven away, to starvation, censuring the offerings of sacrifices. They hid the natural processes and put forward their own, which were of an unnatural order; they exposed to their priests that the mass of the people would neglect their sacrifices, if they no longer had recourse to the unnatural (or supernatural) processes, to address those who possessed this supposed knowledge of vulgar alloys, this art of making water and washing. Thus, by the effect of custom, law, and fear, their sacrifices were greatly followed. They did not even respond to their false advertisements. When their sanctuaries were deserted and their sacrifices neglected, they still obtained men who remained (with them), and they devoted themselves to the sacrifices, flattering them with dreams [oneiromancy] and other deceptions, as well as with certain councils. They kept going back to these false and supernumerary promises, to please men who were friends of pleasure, miserable and ignorant. You too, O woman, they want to win you over, through their false prophet [Neilos?]; they flatter you; being hungry, (they covet) not only sacrifices, but also your soul.[14]

As I make clear in *The First Alchemists*, this passage represents nothing less than a plea for pure science within the epoch's terms. Thus, it is absurd to imagine Zosimos a pious member of Egyptian temple priesthood, as some scholars have speculated. Zosimos had been inspired by a vision of a new freedom—quite possibly gnostic in character—liberated from slavery to daimonic interference and oppression.

TWELVE

Hermes Trismegistos and Enoch

I f there was a brand of gnosis that spoke to Zosimos, it's clear he found its most dynamic expression in the philosophy-melding, natural and divine science of tracts attributed to Hermes Trismegistos, where the cosmos is revealed as divine *Mind* projected, whose human correspondent is *nous* or higher, spiritual mind: primary and dimensionally superior to mechanical reason. Union of nous with enlightened will makes man a "great miracle," as the Hermetic *Asclepius* famously has it.

Zosimos refers to Hermes's *Physika* as an authority for the story of fallen demons, or angels, seducing women—a reference that leads us to a thorny problem, but before we get pricked, let's examine the identity of the "Thrice Greatest."

According to Athenagoras's *Legatio pro Christianis*, chapter 28 (ca. 177 CE), Hermes was a *man*:

> But as Alexander [the Great] and Hermes surnamed Trismegistos, who shares with them in the attribute of eternity, and innumerable others, not to name them individually, [declare the same], no room is left even for doubt that they, being kings, were esteemed gods. That they were men, the most learned of the Egyptians also testify, who, while saying that ether, earth, sun, moon, are gods, regard the rest as mortal men, and the temples as their sepulchres.

Athenagoras explained to emperor Marcus Aurelius that apart from sun, moon, and planets, pagan "gods" were originally men, and subsequently called, or rather were mistaken for, gods. Athenagoras knew the Greek Hermes was identified with Egyptian god of magic, writing, and wisdom, Thoth, to whom a notable sanctuary was dedicated in Heliopolis, just north of today's Cairo, where worshippers deposited mummified ibises, the animal sacred to Thoth. Some eighteen miles southwest, at Saqqara, an ostraca was found in the 1960s in priest Hor of Temenesi's archive. Dedicated to "great and great the great god Hermes," it was dated to 172 BCE, shortly after Egypt ceded Judea to the Seleucids. The inscription is the earliest known instance of the three-times-great title. *This* figure may likely be identified with the tracts' supposed author. However, not until the second century CE did tracts appear under the moniker offering spiritual rebirth and liberation from daimonic fate. Zosimos's contemporary Lactantius (240–320), theologian and religious advisor to emperor Constantine I, considered Trismegistos an ancient Egyptian patriarch. Discussing pagan prophecies in *Divine Institutes* 1.6, Lactantius wrote:

> Let us now pass to divine testimonies; but, first of all, I will bring into court testimony which is like divine [witness], both on account of its exceeding great age, and *because he whom I shall name was carried back again from men unto the gods.* [my italics]
>
> In Cicero, Caius Cotta, the Pontifex [high priest of Rome] . . . declares that there were five Hermeses; and after enumerating four of them in succession, [he adds] that the fifth was he by whom Argus was slain, and for that cause he fled into Egypt, and initiated the Egyptians into laws and letters.
>
> The Egyptians call him Thoyth, and from him the first month of their year (that is, September) has received its name. He also founded a city which even unto this day is called Hermopolis. The people of Phenëus [in Arcadia], indeed, worship him as a god; but, although he was [really] a man, still he was of such high antiquity, and so deeply versed in every kind of science, that his knowledge of [so] many things and of the arts gained him the title of "Thrice-greatest."

He wrote books, indeed many [of them], treating of the Gnosis of things divine, in which he asserts the greatness of the Highest and One and Only God, and calls Him by the same names as we [do]—God and Father. And [yet], so that no one should seek after His name, he has declared that He cannot be named, in that He doth not need to have a name, owing, indeed, unto the very [nature of His] unity. His words are these: But God [is] one; and He who's one needs not a name, for He [as one] is The-beyond-all-names. [A logion unknown to extant Hermetic texts.]

In fact, Cicero, writing his *de natura deorum* ("concerning the nature of gods," 3.22) a year before Julius Caesar's assassination (44 BCE), did not specify *his* "Mercurius" (Roman form of Hermes) as being either "Trismegistos" or a writer of many books:

One Mercury has the Sky for father and the Day for mother; he is represented in a state of sexual excitation traditionally due to passion inspired by the sight of Proserpine. Another is the son of Valens and Phoronis; this is the subterranean Mercury identified with Trophonius. The third, the son of the third Jove and of Maia, the legends make the father of Pan by Penelope. The fourth has Nile for father; the Egyptians deem it sinful to pronounce his name. The fifth, worshipped by the people of Pheneus, is said to have killed Argus and consequently to have fled in exile to Egypt, where he gave the Egyptians their laws and letters. His Egyptian name is Theuth, which is also the name in the Egyptian calendar for the first month of the year.

Trismegistos's absence is significant because had Cicero dubbed his Latin Mercurius "Thrice Greatest" and attributed books to him, as Lactantius did over three hundred years later, then we could date the Hermetic tracts to at least the first century BCE—and *this* matters because by the eighth century CE, Hermes Trismegistos was regarded by at least one scholar as the *same* figure as Enoch. An identification confusing scholars for centuries, it leads to the thorny question: *Did*

Graeco-Egyptian pseudepigraphers create their philosophical Hermes from the patriarch Enoch, or did Enochic literature draw on Graeco-Egyptian literature and "Judaize" it?

We shall return to this question soon.

In the meantime, it's remarkable how Lactantius also absorbed a message from the Book of the Watchers (*Divine Institutes* 2.15), interpreting it identically to Zosimos's polemic to Theosebeia. Even more remarkable is that Lactantius regarded *Hermes Trismegistos* as an authority for what is in fact an *Enochic* account of the wicked Watchers.

In Lactantius's account, God, having given the devil "power over the earth," sent free-willed angels to protect and improve burgeoning humanity, warning the angels not to forget their heavenly dignity through earthly contamination. Nevertheless, the devil enticed them into intercourse with women. Excluded from heaven for their sins, they "fell to the earth," becoming the devil's "satellites," their offspring a second kind of daimōn. These "authors of all evils that are done" had the devil for prince. "Whence Trismegistus [Latin spelling] calls him the ruler of the demons." I can't trace this in the extant Hermetica, but the "ruler of the demons" *can* be found in Matthew 12:24. Lactantius castigates "grammarians" for thinking them as "dœmones," gods skilled with superior knowledge. Lactantius admits they have some future knowledge, but being outside "the counsel of God," they give ambiguous answers. Affecting to be guardians of humanity, they expect worship while denying worship of God. Plato's *Symposium* tried to explain their nature, while "Socrates said that there was a demon continually about him, who had become attached to him when a boy, by whose will and direction his life was guided." They also deceive the Magi whose power derives from their influence. "These contaminated and abandoned spirits" wander the earth, finding solace in destroying men with "snares, deceits, frauds and errors," clinging to individuals and households, assuming the name "genii," while working inwardly to "corrupt the health, hasten diseases, terrify their [men's] souls with dreams, harass their minds with frenzies, that by these evils they may compel men to have recourse to their aid."

• • •

Looking further into the Hermetic corpus, we shall find teaching so akin to that in 1 Enoch and 2 Enoch, albeit expressed in a very different idiom (for a very different audience), that it becomes practically inescapable but to conclude that one body has employed the texts of another: either Hermetic tracts were turning a Jewish Enoch into Egyptian patriarch Hermes Trismegistos, or the other way around. In order to get a grip on this conundrum, our first port of call must be the first known explicit identification of Hermes with Enoch.

It comes from an astrological history, *The Thousands*, by Baghdad's Abbasid court astrologer Abu Ma'shar Ja'far ibn Muhammad ibn 'Umar al-Balkhi (787–886 CE). He identified the "title" Hermes not only with Enoch, but also with Kayumarth, the Iranian "Adam." Abu Ma'shar was perhaps aware of Cicero's account of numerous "Hermeses" before one found divine status in Egypt.

> The name Hermes is a title, like Caesar or Khusrau. Its first bearer, who lived before the Flood, was he whom the Persians call Abanjhan, the grandson of Jayumart [Kayumarth], the Persian Adam; and he whom the Hebrews call Khanukh [i.e., Enoch], whose name in Arabic is Idris.[1]

Abu Ma'shar employed Christian chronographies for his history, including fourth-century Alexandrian monk Annianus's world chronicle, completed in 412, based on the now-lost work of contemporary Egyptian monk Panodorus. Eighth to ninth century Byzantine chronicler George Syncellus was suspicious of Annianus and Panodorus because they tried to reconcile Christian with pagan histories in what Syncellus judged a forced manner. Due to the fragmentary nature of chronicle references, we cannot be confident Abu Ma'shar's identification of Enoch and Hermes came from them. Perhaps Abu Ma'shar consulted Syncellus's *Chronographia* where he would have found not only a substantial collection of quotations from the Greek Book of the Watchers but also an account of Hermes Trismegistos allegedly sourced from supposed third-century BCE Egyptian priest, "Manetho." Note the reference to Hermes's having left *books* for posterity:

It remains now [writes George Syncellus] to make brief extracts concerning the dynasties of Egypt from the works of Manetho of Sebennytus. In the time of Ptolemy Philadelphus [282–229 BCE] he was styled high priest of the pagan temples of Egypt, and [note!] wrote from *inscriptions in the Seriadic land* [my italics; the Greek is *en tēi Sēriadikēi gēi*], traced, he says, in sacred language and holy characters by Thoth, the first Hermes, and translated after the Flood . . . in hieroglyphic characters. When the work had been arranged in books by Agathodaemon, son of the second Hermes [Hermes Trismegistos] and father of Tat, in the temple shrines of Egypt, Manetho dedicated it to the above King Ptolemy II Philadelphus in his Book of Sothis, using the following words:

Letter of Manetho of Sebennytus to Ptolemy Philadelphus. To the great King Ptolemy Philadelphus Augustus. Greeting to my lord Ptolemy from Manetho, high-priest and scribe of the sacred shrines of Egypt, born at Sebennytus and dwelling at Heliopolis. It is my duty, almighty king, to reflect upon all such matters as you may desire me to investigate. So, as you are making your researches concerning the future of the universe, in obedience to your command I shall place before you the Sacred Books which I have studied, written by your forefather, Hermes Trismegistos. Farewell, I pray, my lord King. Such is his account of the translation of the books written by the second Hermes. Thereafter Manetho tells also of five Egyptian tribes which formed thirty dynasties.[2]

Now, if Syncellus's material was what it purported to be, we'd have reason to consider a date for writings by Hermes Trismegistos before— at least the bulk of—1 Enoch, and we could then wonder about relations between the two. However, while this letter is certainly a forgery (the word *Augustus* applied to Ptolemy Philadelphus is anachronistic), there is great doubt about works attributed to Manetho in general, even to whether he existed as an Egyptian historian.

It should be said that before, during, and after the first century CE there existed aggressive competition among different countries for historical primacy. *Who came first?* was a question implying authority

and dignity in philosophy and religion. Greeks were taught to vener-
ate Egypt; Romans followed—assumptions challenged by Jews whose
Pentateuch took an unbroken history back to the creation itself. As
far as Jews were concerned, *all* nations post-dated the Flood; only Jews
upheld the promises of the antediluvian patriarchs. Asserting this dignity was part of the rationale for Josephus's great *Antiquities of the Jews*,
and in another work, *Against Apion*,* Josephus took serious issue with
anti-Jewish statements attributed to a book called *Aegyptiaca* (of which
little now survives), allegedly by Manetho, as well as to "Manetho's"
historical veracity overall. It appears that if there ever was an authentic
history of Manetho, it was being added to by Egyptian polemicists. One
such spurious work was a "Book of Sothis," about Egyptian regal chronology and calendrical knowledge. It described Manetho as "high priest
and scribe of the sacred shrines of Egypt . . . dwelling at Heliopolis,"
city of Re.[3] Its dynastic entries vary markedly from texts supposedly
from an original *Aegyptiaca* attributed to the same Manetho. Manetho's
name was probably used to lend spurious authority to forgery and propaganda.

Syncellus's other references to Hermes could easily be gleaned
from tracts of Hermes Trismegistos, tracts that by Syncellus's time had
acquired an aura of antiquity from references to them in church fathers
Augustine and Athenagoras, whereas Enoch's stock had long fallen in
value—though not everywhere.

While Abu Ma'shar practiced astrology in Baghdad, an anonymous
writer was retelling events from the Bible, employing rare pseudepigraphical and para-biblical stories about characters within those events.
The original of the ninth-century *Palaea Historica* is lost, but the earliest twelfth-century text incorporates material apparently from two
Enochic works: a Book of Giants and a Book of Noah, either directly or
indirectly, part of the latter related to segment inserts in 1 Enoch. What

---

*Apion Pleistoneices (30–20 BCE to 45–48 CE), or Apion Mochthos, was a Hellenized
grammarian of Alexandria. An expert on Homer, Apion fomented anti-Jewish feelings
in Egypt and Rome, insisting Jewish history was *stolen* from Egypt's. Josephus believed
Egyptians had deviated from the one true God to worship demons; Egyptians were
descendants of Noah's progeny gone bad.

is particularly interesting is that the *Palaea Historica*'s account links Enoch directly to a story whose earliest known telling is in Josephus's *Antiquities*, but which would enter the Middle Ages linked to Enoch and to Hermes.

> Concerning Enoch. Enoch was born and became a good and devout man, who fulfilled God's will and was not influenced by the counsels of the giants. For there were giants (on earth) at that time. And Enoch was translated (to heaven) by God's command, and no one saw [how] his removal [happened]. Concerning Noah. In the days when the giants were around and did not want to glorify God, a man was born whose name was Noah, who was devout and feared God, and like Enoch he was not influenced by the giants' counsels. . . .
>
> . . . When the giants heard that the righteous Noah was building an ark for the Flood, they laughed at him. But Enoch, who was still around, was also telling the giants that the earth would either be destroyed by fire or by water. And the righteous Enoch was doing nothing else but sitting and writing on marble (tablets) and on bricks the mighty works of God which had happened from the beginning. For he used to say: "If the earth is destroyed by fire, the bricks will be preserved to be a reminder [for those who come after] of the mighty works of God which have happened from the beginning; and if the earth is destroyed by water, the marble tablets will be preserved." And Enoch used to warn the giants about many things, but they remained stubborn and impenitent, nor did they want to glorify the Creator, but instead each [of them] walked in his own will of the flesh.[4]*

Josephus's telling of the pillars story is, like the following account of the "Angels of God" becoming enamored of women in his *Antiquities* 1.3.1, very muted, cleaned-up, you might say, for civilized Gentile consumption:

---

*For a full account of the "pillars of Enoch" through history, see my *The Lost Pillars of Enoch* (2021).

For many Angels of God accompanied with women, and begat sons that proved unjust, and despisers of all that was good; on account of the confidence they had in their own strength. For the tradition is, that these men did what resembled the acts of those whom the Grecians call *Giants*. But Noah was very uneasy at what they did: and being displeased at their conduct, persuaded them to change their dispositions, and their actions for the better. But seeing they did not yield to him, but were slaves to their wicked pleasures, he was afraid they would kill him, together with his wife and children, and those they had married. So he departed out of that land.

Josephus hasn't lifted this out of Genesis, but another source, possibly a Book of Noah, or a Book of Giants. Even though he's obviously diluted the grisly impact of the giants' story, he doesn't seem to rely on the Book of the Watchers for it, which might explain why Josephus's pillars account—that by the ninth century had been linked to Enoch—does not mention Enoch at all. If Josephus was hostile to a Book of Enoch because of its apocalyptic aspect—which Josephus might have associated with rebellion against Rome—we have no evidence, other than its absence, to suggest he dismissed it, which by itself leaves no ground to speculate upon.

Josephus attributes the pillars to the virtuous "children of Seth [Enoch's forebear]."

They also were the inventors of that peculiar sort of wisdom, which is concerned with the heavenly bodies, and their order. And that their inventions might not be lost before they were sufficiently known, upon Adam's [not Enoch's!] prediction that the world was to be destroyed at one time by the force of fire, and at another time by the violence and quantity of water, they made two pillars: the one of brick, the other of stone: they inscribed their discoveries on them both: that in case the pillar of brick should be destroyed by the flood, the pillar of stone might remain, and exhibit those discoveries to mankind: and also inform them that there was another pillar of brick erected by them. Now this remains in the *Seirida land* to this day. (*Antiquities* 1.2.3)

The last line is revealing: the Greek *kata tēn gēn Seirida* means "in the Siriusite land"; that is, among worshippers of the star Sirius (Greek: *Seirios*)—Egypt and/or Kush (today's Sudan and northern Ethiopia). The Greek phrase is very close to that used by George Syncellus in his account of how Manetho allegedly took his information from the "first" Thoth's inscriptions *en tēi Sēriadikēi gēi* (in the Sēriadic land), then "translated after the Flood." Curiouser and curiouser . . .

According to Josephus, Sethite patriarchs seem to have been active in what would become Egypt. Sirius's summer rising marked the Egyptian new year, and the star was worshipped as goddess Sopdet (Greek: *Sothis*). Did Josephus take this detail from something written by "Manetho"? This might argue for an Egyptian source for his pillars story.

Where the compiler of the *Palaea Historica* found the specific link between Enoch and the pillar story told by Josephus is unknown. Obviously, there already existed vital details in Enochic tradition of Seth's descendant Enoch inventing writing, being God's scribe, and writing books from heavenly tablets and angelic dictation, warning of coming judgment, *and* his getting son Methuselah to preserve the predictive writings through all vicissitudes and pass them through generations until their fulfillment. These basic structural components were, as we have seen, applied with subtly different emphases to Hermes Trismegistos by at least the second century CE.

Is there a candidate for Josephus's surviving pillar in Sirius-worshipping land?

Well, it happens that the Heliopolis temple complex was called in Egyptian *'Iwnw*: "The Pillars"—which may have inspired the story. An area once abundant in ancient pillars, it has provided London, New York, and Rome with obelisks. Of what's left, the major remnant today is the single red granite temple obelisk to Ra-Atum erected by nineteenth-century BCE pharaoh and prolific builder Senusret I* of the Twelfth Dynasty (once *one of two* erected for Senusret's thirti-

---

*The pharaoh's name *Senusret* means "man of Wosret." Consort of Amun, Wosret was revered in the Eighteenth Dynasty. Symbolizing great power, woe betide any who transgressed her. As protector of youthful Horus, she was known as a protector of the next generation.

eth jubilee). Ancient in Josephus's time, it stands in its original position, now in Cairo's Al-Matariyyah district. Perhaps this or such a monument was conflated with a story about a pillar preserving the knowledge of Thoth. In this regard, it's worth observing that since Josephus did not believe much in Egyptian history, convinced that its gods derived from men, it's quite likely he would have attributed any antediluvian survival in Egypt to Seth's descendants, since Seth was Adam's righteous third son, and, for Josephus, there *were* no "Egyptians" until after Noah's time. If Egyptians were touting a similar story to one in Jewish lore, he would almost have certainly regarded it as a steal. Such might explain apparent reticence regarding the pillar's specific architect.

Since Josephus believed Egypt purloined *Jewish* history, he would have felt justified in attributing to, say, Jewish patriarch Seth, achievements Egyptians attributed to Thoth. Contrary to an Egyptian claim to have invented astronomy, Josephus insisted *Abraham* brought astronomy to Egypt. Conversely, Graeco-Egyptian supporters of Apion encountering Enoch could have taken him as being, or having been taken from, their own Thrice Great Hermes. Jews familiar with Enochic texts believed *Enoch* invented writing, Egyptians claimed the same for Thoth-Hermes!

The problem of *who came first* could be solved if only we could pinpoint composition dates for Enoch and Egypt's rival, or arguably, in parts, version, *Hermes Trismegistos*. While we know works of Enoch certainly existed in the first century BCE, we know of no work attributed to Hermes Trismegistos written *before* Josephus wrote his histories in the late first century. Surviving texts bearing Hermes Trismegistos's name are usually dated to the second or third century CE. While the Greek style, Platonist-cum-Stoic philosophy, *and* cursory knowledge of ancient Egyptian religion and history in the Hermetic tracts fit a Graeco-Egyptian composition date of the Roman period, some scholars (such as Jean-Pierre Mahé) think "Hermetic" works derive in part from authentic Egyptian traditions predating Josephus. There is, however, insufficient evidence to link such traditions with the distinctive *literary* identity of sage, Hermes Trismegistos.

Fig. 12.1. François de Foix Candale (translator), *Pimandras utriaque lingua restitutus* (1574); opening of the *Pymandēr* in Greek, where Poimandrēs, the sovereign nous, guides Hermes on an ascent to the highest heaven. (Photo: Rodak)

Fig. 12.2. *Hermes Trismegistus*; unknown artist's impression, seventeenth century; Museum of the Faculty of Medicine, Nancy (originally from Jesuit university of Pont à Mousson), France.

It is currently impossible to be absolutely certain who first took from whom, but we may get more than a clue that there was at least *some* lifting from Enoch by Graeco-Egyptian writers.

Normally, a philosophical or abstract interpretation of a story suggests a secondary development upon a less sophisticated, perhaps more visceral original. It seems to me that it is *psychologically* easier to take Enochian accounts and retune them to a more philosophically palatable, and above all *non-Jewish*, even cosmopolitan-style henotheist presentation, while applying a kind of cool, almost timeless embrace of an idealized, romanticized Egyptian past, than it is to take a Hermetic version and turn it into a *grand guignol* nightmare of cannibalistic giants, apocalyptic world history, and justice-seeking imperative, with a specifically Jewish prophetic time-scheme and "wisdom-trail." It is arguable that key elements of the Hermetic philosophical tractates have watered down Enochic tropes and reblended them into a heady soda pop. If you were a creative, insightful writer with a brief to make Enoch acceptable to an enlightened or would-be enlightened pagan intellectual (or even Jew or Christian), then the first thing you'd do is rebrand with a distinctive, time-honored name with cosmopolitan credentials: Hermes—*Thrice-Greatest* Hermes—fits the bill perfectly.

So, what specifically has Enochic literature got in common with Hermetic doctrine?

1. The Hermetic tracts and 1 and 2 Enoch feature revelation dialogues given to, and by, a revered ancient patriarchal figure who knows everything and has seen everything.
2. They both endeavor to contain their revelations in many books to be preserved for posterity.
3. Both revelatory figures are carried upward in an ascent narrative. In libellus 1 of the *Corpus Hermeticum*, Hermes is guided by Poimandrēs to the seventh heaven, at which point he is fully divested of the last of the "passions" or material bindings, whereafter the soul ascends to the eighth zone as "himself," where the soul hears heavenly, musical voices, and having heard them, rises further to join the "Powers." Coming to the "Father," Hermes

becomes a Power himself. Those who follow the path of righteousness, who are "holy, and good, and pure and merciful" (libellus 1:22) then "enter into God." "This is the consummation, for those who have got *gnosis*" (1:26a). "God-inspired," Hermes "attained to the abode of truth" (1:30). Having reached the height of aspiration, both Enoch and Hermes sing intense prayers of thanksgiving praise to God.

4. Both Enoch and Hermes have a specific message for the salvation of mankind.

5. Both acquire authority through visionary and self-transforming experience.

6. Both offer means of redemption from destruction and are commissioned to do so.

7. Both envision dark times ahead, before final salvation.

8. Both Enoch and Hermes teach sons to promote the doctrines in their absence.

9. Both figures reside in heaven.

10. In both Enochic and Hermetic doctrine, passion is the cause of human downfall, and bodily lust entails death and spiritual eclipse.

11. Where in Enochic books, the guides are archangels, in libellus 1, the guide is Poimandrēs, a supercelestial Being of boundless size, who calls himself "the authoritative [or 'absolute power'] *nous*." Both Enoch and Hermes are summoned by supercelestial figures from a state of sleep to make the ascent to perfect vision or divine perception. If *Poimandrēs* means "shepherd of men," it's relevant that guides for the righteous are called shepherds by Enoch.

12. Narratives in both Enoch and Hermes Trismegistos delineate disobedience in heaven, leading to a fall. For example, *Kore Kosmou* 15–16: "They [the heavenly Souls created by God in heaven] then, my son, as though they had done something grand, with over-busy daring armed themselves, and acted contrary to the commands they had received; and forthwith they began to overstep their proper limits and their reservations, and would no longer stay in the same place, but were for ever moving, and thought that being ever stationed in one place was death.

"That they would do this thing, however, O my son (as Hermes says when he speaks unto me), had not escaped the Eye of Him who is the God and Lord of universal things; and He searched out a punishment and bond, the which they now in misery endure.

"Thus was it that the Sovereign King of all resolved to fabricate with art the human frame, in order that in it the race of Souls throughout might be chastised. 'Then sending for me,' Hermes says, 'He spake: "Soul of My Soul, and holy mind of My own Mind, up to what point, the nature of the things beneath, shall it be seen in gloom? How long shall what has up to now been made remain inactive and be destitute of praise? Bring hither to Me now, My son, all of the Gods in Heaven," said God'—as Hermes saith." We see here I think the fate of both Watchers and giants become a philosophical interpretation of corporeal existence's peril for the divine soul: fallen Souls take the place of fallen Watchers, and like the giants' discorporated souls, are joined to humans, making them behave demonically.

13. Whereas in the Book of the Watchers angels transgress, enamored of feminine nature below them, leading to a fall, in libellus 1, "Man" (*Anthrōpos*) in his proto-supercelestial state is drawn down to Nature by passionate attraction to his own divine image reflected in waters below the heavens. His soul descending to unite with that vision, feminine powers of nature envelop the attractive alien soul, binding him to earth, with baleful consequences for humanity, suffering corporeal imprisonment and loss of gnosis. Only ascendants to heaven through gnosis can envision the human dilemma's solution.

Closer analysis of texts yields closer association of dynamics. Let's examine *Kore Kosmou* ("The Virgin of the World" or *The Cosmic Virgin*), preserved by John of Stobi in the fifth century CE in a collection of otherwise lost passages of Greek literature. It describes goddess Isis conveying to son Horus knowledge from remotest antiquity, according to which, those destined to find the works of Hermes "will get knowledge of all my [Hermes's] hidden writings, and discern their meaning; and some of those writings they will keep to themselves, but such of them as tend to the benefit of mortal men, they will inscribe on slabs and obelisks." *Slabs and obelisks* . . . Even more striking is the work's account of how, following heavenly ruptures, humanity came to suffer evil: a different, but analogous account to that told in the Poimandrēs narrative.

Isis tells Horus that divine souls dwelling in heaven were originally placed by God in sixty heavenly divisions based on quality, but the souls, growing unruly, transgressed allotted limits. Souls were therefore punished: sent down to earth in bodies. Body-life caused anguish: "Then were they first plunged in deep gloom, and, learning that they were condemned, began to wail. I was myself amazed at the Souls' utterances" (*Kore Kosmou* 18). Mutually disaffected, the souls filled the earth with terror (like the giants in Enoch). The four elemental spirits complained to God for relief (cf. four archangels conveying the righteous cry to heaven in 1 Enoch), so the "Father" sends Isis and Osiris to watch over and care for them by ordering the souls' lives around temples that incline them to knowledge of the good. Good men after death are freed from the body; wicked souls transmigrate into animals (a judgment). Incarnation punishes primal sin; release demands adherence to virtue.

We note how "knowledge" inscribed on primal tablets has, through a Graeco-Egyptian cultural lens, arguably become considerably less prophetic—and Jewish—and more universalist and philosophical. The Hermetic tracts still carry that universalist appeal.

Sometimes sequence-parallels between Enochic passages and Hermetic ones are striking. Compare, for example, the following from 2 Enoch with *Kore Kosmou*:

> 2 Enoch 40:1–2:
> And now, my children, I know all things! From the lips of the Lord; for my eyes have seen from the beginning to the end. I know all things and have written all things in the books, both the heavens and the end of them, and their fullness, and all the hosts, and I have measured their goings, and written down the stars and their innumerable quantity.

Kore Kosmou 3:

Such was all-knowing Hermes, who saw all things, and seeing understood, and understanding had the power both to disclose and to give explanation. For what he knew, he graved on stone; yet though he graved them onto stone he hid them mostly, keeping sure silence though in speech, that every younger age of cosmic time might seek for them. And thus, with charge unto his kinsmen of the Gods to keep sure watch, he mounted to the Stars.

2 Enoch 47:1–3:

Now, my children, put my thoughts in your hearts; pay attention to the words of your father, which have come to you from the mouth of the Lord. Take these books of the writings of your father, and read them, and in them ye shall learn all the works of the Lord. There have been many books from the beginning of creation, and shall be to the end of the world, but none shall make things known to you like my writings. But if you shall preserve my writings, you will not sin against God. For there is no other besides the Lord, neither in heaven nor in earth, nor the depths below, nor the solitary foundations.

Kore Kosmou 5:

[Hermes], ere he returned to Heaven, invoked a spell on them, and spake these words. (For 'tis not meet, my son, that I should leave this proclamation ineffectual, but [rather] should speak forth what words [our] Hermes uttered when he hid his books away.) Thus then he said: "O holy books, who have been made by my immortal hands, by incorruption's magic spells . . . free from decay throughout eternity remain and incorrupt from time! Become unseeable, unfindable, for every one whose foot shall tread the plains of this [our] land, until old Heaven doth bring forth meet instruments for you, whom the Creator shall call souls."

As Enoch instructs Methuselah to keep the books till time of fulfillment, so Hermes in *Kore Kosmou* enjoins his sons to keep the books until "the time heaven begets organisms worthy of you." Whereafter, "having spoken this prayer over the work of his hands, Hermes was received into the sanctuary of the everlasting zones."

Again, it may be stressed that in some Hermetic passages, it is nature's feminine aspect that disrupts heavenly schemes. In others, the feminine is of the essence of God's creation, intended always to cause "amazement." Thus in *Kore Kosmou*:

And Nature, O my Son, was barren until the hour in which those who are ordained to survey the heavens, advancing towards God, the King of all things, deplored the general inertia, and affirmed the necessity of setting forth the universe. No other than Himself could accomplish this work.

"We pray Thee," said they, "to consider that which already is, and that which is necessary for the future." At these words, the God smiled benignant, and commanded Nature to exist. And, issuing with His voice, the FEMININE came forth in her perfect beauty. The Gods with amazement beheld this marvel. And the great Ancestor, pouring out for Nature an elixir, commanded her to be fruitful; and forthwith, penetrating the universe with His glance, He cried, "Let heaven be the plenitude of all things, and of the air, and of the ether." God spake, and it was done. But Nature, communing with herself, understood that she might not transgress the commandment of the Father, and, uniting herself to Labour, she produced a most beautiful daughter, whom she called Invention, and to whom God accorded being.

Of course, it doesn't take long before invention leads to transgression, and the need for the unconscious sufferers of life to heed the divine call of Hermes to be baptized in a bowl of divine nous and attain "rebirth" (*palingenesia*; see *Pimander*, libellus 4).

We might now ask how to account for proximity, possibly competition, between these pools of thought: Graeco-Egyptian and Jewish Enochic. Obviously, cross-cultural currents through Alexandria, where existed a notable Jewish community, accommodated transposition of ideas. The Greek translation of scripture (the Septuagint) was of great interest, undertaken to satisfy Greek-speaking Ptolemaic rulers' curiosity after Alexander the Great's conquest.

However, there is another possible environment where religious competition—or, ultimately the *lack* of it—may have been experienced more sharply.

A Jewish Temple . . . in Egypt

Few readers will know that a functioning Jewish temple stood in Egypt between the Maccabean period and the end of the Jewish war against Rome: that's some 240 odd years. It surprised me too. It seems contrary to everything assumed about Middle Temple (singular) Judaism. But it's a fact.

Historian Josephus gave two contradictory accounts of it, the later one in *Antiquities* 13.3.1–3 being paltry. *War* 7.10.3 gives more detail, having been written shortly after a Roman army forced the temple to close in 73–74 CE following disturbances among refugee *sicarii* (Zealot "dagger-men") that made Roman commanders anxious about the Jewish community's strength around the temple in the "district of Onias." This happened shortly after the Romans famously took Masada to end the Judean war. The Romans wanted the Oniad temple's treasure and, according to Joan Taylor's fascinating article, there may have been just enough time to get "treasures and manuscripts" out before the Romans sacked it.[5] Where, we wonder, did such items go?

The temple resulted from a not unfamiliar dispute between two dominant parties in Jerusalem around the year 170 BCE, with one side favoring the Egyptian Ptolemies, the other seeking to placate the Seleucids in Syria. For a brief time, Zadokite high priest Onias III—favoring Ptolemaic dependency—gained leverage to expel the pro-Hellenist tax-farming "Tobiads," who petitioned Antiochus Epiphanes. Antiochus's Greek-Syrian army duly attacked Jerusalem, killing pro-Ptolemy Jews. The temple was subsequently sacked, sacrifices prohibited, and an "abomination" placed on the holy altar. According to Josephus, High Priest Onias fled Jerusalem for protection from Ptolemy VI Philometor (reigned 180–145 BCE) and wife Cleopatra. Onias assured Egypt's king, who hated Antiochus, that allowing a temple to God in Egypt would dispose more Jews to support Ptolemy's anti-Seleucid strategy. Ptolemy duly gave a tract of land twenty-two miles from Memphis, in the Heliopolitan nome (Egypt's administrative regions were called "nomes") where a fortress was erected (Onias had Jewish mercenaries with him to serve the Ptolemies) and a tower-temple "not like to that at Jerusalem, but such as resembled a tower. He built it of large stones, to the height of sixty cubits [about ninety feet]" with an altar like Jerusalem's, but instead of a menorah, a gold chain supported a gold lamp that emitted dazzling light. Surrounded by a baked brick wall with stone doorways, the temple enjoyed sufficient land to support the priests' revenue. Onias's case was apparently aided by Isaiah's prophecy (19:19): "In that day shall there be an altar to the Lord in the midst of the land of Egypt, and pillar [*note!*] at the border thereof to the Lord."*

While in Josephus's *War* the high priest was "son of Simon the Just" (Onias III); in *Antiquities* the temple's founder was Onias IV, son of Onias III. Some scholarly opinion currently favors Onias IV, but the attribution involves serious problems.

For example, Erich S. Gruen's skeptical analysis in "The Origins and Objectives of Onias's Temple" (*Scripta Classica Israelica* 16 [1997]: 47–70), points out that 2 Maccabees was closer to events than either Josephus or rabbis, who always regarded usurped High

---

*There may be more to the design than meets the eye. The Enoch Seminar webinar (June 26, 2023) hosted two papers investigating whether 1 Enoch 14's heavenly architecture derived (as Martha Himmelfarb and Jonathan Klawans suggested) from Jerusalem's temple, with Watchers as priests. Logan Williams (Exeter University) doubted this, a doubt supported by Philip Esler (Gloucestershire University) who hypothesized Enochic heaven's metaphorical structure derived from royal courts and courtiers of ancient Near Eastern and Hellenistic kingdoms, such as the Achaemenid capital, Pasargadae: a surrounding wall with gateway before a low building, with towering edifice behind. Esler suggested the Enochic scribal group was not temple-based. Sages could be courtiers—such could explain temple tensions: king and courtiers in conflict with temple scribes. I speculated to Esler that both temple *and* court models could fuse if the Onias temple was inspired by 1 Enoch 1–36's arguably courtly basis. Josephus's *War* description, coupled with archaeology at Tell el-Yehoudieh (mostly likely site for Onias's temple), indicates a baked brick wall with stone doorways surrounding a tower temple. The extraordinary lamp could have symbolized the dazzling impact of the glorious shekhinah of God's throne in 1 Enoch.

Fig. 12.3. Ptolemy VI
Philometor; engraved ring
(second century BCE);
Louvre Museum.
(Photo: Marie-Lan Nguyen)

Fig. 12.4. Ptolemy VI and wife Cleopatra II (right) bring gifts to the gods;
drawing (1849) from Philae Temple Pylon H. (New York Public Library)

Priest Onias III as the temple's founder. The rabbis, Gruen writes (at
p. 50), "had no access to historical records and no interest in historical
research," which seems sweeping. Gruen thinks the temple's ascription
to Onias IV carries "greater plausibility, and it has drawn the endorse-
ment of most scholars." Yet Gruen admits the *Antiquities* story is also
riddled with serious difficulties: "A blunder occurs right at the outset,"

he writes, "with regard to the relationship of high priests. Josephus has Menelaus as brother of Onias III and Jason, all sons of Simon. Menelaus, however, was not a Zadokite, as 2 Maccabees informs us, but of a different priestly clan. The fact is significant, for it means that Menelaus, not Alcimus, broke the Oniad hold on the high priesthood, thus undermining Josephus's explanation for the flight of Onias IV to Egypt. The muddle gets worse. Onias IV was a mere child, even an infant, upon his father's death, so Josephus reports more than once. Yet, after arrival in Egypt, he obtains high honors from Ptolemy VI Philometor, and, according to his letter, which Josephus quotes, he gave substantial military aid to the king for his war in Coele-Syria and Phoenicia. On that version, Onias would have had to reach a swift maturity, establish credentials as a military leader, and round up a significant force to make a difference in Ptolemy's war—most unlikely. And what war was it anyway? Surely not that between Ptolemy and Antiochus IV which occurred between 170 and 168 when Onias was a boy—and well before he went to Egypt on Josephus's own account. Ptolemy VI did, to be sure, engage in subsequent contests with brother and rival Ptolemy VIII Euergetes over the next two decades. But none of these struggles happened in Coele-Syria or Phoenicia. Josephus's reliability becomes increasingly suspect." Joan Taylor thinks that when Josephus wrote *Antiquities*, he'd acquired poor, biased source material. Gruen's criticism of Josephus only really applies to the *Antiquities* account.

Josephus's earlier account has more logic about it. Zadokite Onias III was resentful of the new priests in Jerusalem—pro-Seleucid Jason had usurped the high priesthood—with impure rites, and Onias wished to draw Jews away from perceived apostasy.

In 2 Maccabees 4:30–5 is the only source of a story that Jason's successor as high priest, Menelaus, incited Syrian official Andronicus to murder Onias III when taking refuge in Syria in the temple at Daphne near Antioch, while serving Ptolemy. This is dated three years after the death in 175 BCE of Antiochus Epiphanes's predecessor Seleucis IV Philopator, that is, before the sack of Jerusalem's temple and *War*'s account of Onias III's flight from Jerusalem. In 2 Maccabees a first sacking of Jerusalem's temple is set in 170–169 BCE and in 1 Maccabees 1:29, a second sacking occurs in 167. Meanwhile, Josephus's *War* and 2 Maccabees are at variance—and Antiochus's second sack of the temple that fails to mention Onias also doesn't fit, while in *Antiquities* (12.237) Onias dies without Andronicus's involvement. Joan Taylor suspects 2 Maccabees of a propaganda spin whereby good high priest Onias is murdered by bad usurper Menelaus, thus clearing the way for victorious Maccabees (Hasmoneans) to become high priests.

In the later *Antiquities*, Josephus seems to have absorbed similar propaganda and has Onias IV founding the temple in Egypt around 162 BCE *after* Jerusalem's temple was cleansed and rededicated by Judas Maccabeus. Onias IV would have been only fifteen at the time! Jerusalem was besieged again by Antiochus Eupator, after which Menelaus was killed by the Syrians. Onias IV should have been high priest but the Syrians chose Alcimus, who was not a Zadokite (*Antiquities* 12.386–89). According to this narrative, Onias IV flees in a state of alleged resentment at being pipped to the high priesthood, while Josephus judges his alleged founding of the temple in the Heliopolitan nome as consequence of lust for fame and glory, and not because of a reaction to the savagery and desecration of Antiochus Epiphanes and pro-Seleucid Jews. Onias IV's claims are then dashed when after Alcimus's death, Levite Judas Maccabeus became high priest with popular approbation. The Egyptian temple becomes a victim of Hasmonean triumphalism, which politically and historically speaking, is understandable.

In order to support his revised account, Josephus cites an alleged correspondence between Onias and Ptolemy and Cleopatra (*Antiquities* 13.62–73). Onias writes of how he came "with Jews to Leontopolis in the Heliopolis nome and other places where our nation is settled" and found a suitable place in a fortress named after Bubastis-of-the-Fields, by a ruined temple to cat goddess Bast, surrounded by a variety of trees and sacred animals. He begs permission to cleanse it, so that Jews in his hosts' country could come and "serve your interests." The temple would have the dimensions of Jerusalem's temple (contradicting *War*'s account). Then comes the quote from Isaiah that there shall be an altar in Egypt to the Lord God. The Ptolemies' reply expresses surprise that a pagan temple could be suitable but they wouldn't offend the Lord God and His prophet, Isaiah.

I favor Joan Taylor's view that this letter in its simplistic manner betrays itself as anti-Oniad hinting at bad motives from Onias with hints of possible blasphemy, while in every way exonerating the Ptolemies, even making them acquiescent to Jewish prophetic judgments. Furthermore, *Antiquities* 13.72 even casts aspersions on its construction, calling it "smaller and poorer" than Jerusalem's temple. Tinged with criticism of Onias's motives, and quite unlike *War*'s "relatively impartial" account, it is hard to defer from Joan Taylor's judgment that it's "difficult not to feel highly skeptical about its historicity as a whole."[6] We have seen such a simplistic letter before in the alleged dedication of Manetho's history to the Ptolemies; it was typical of propagandists of the time to use pseudepigraphical letters. Such could have been the work of pro-Jerusalem Alexandrian Jews. That Onias IV had never been Jerusalem's high priest would also lower esteem for the Heliopolitan temple.

The letter also refers to Onias's help with the Ptolemies' war, and this can only mean the war against Antiochus Epiphanes, and that means the figure behind the story was Onias III, as his son was a child when Jerusalem was sacked. There's no supportive evidence that Onias IV was embittered at Jerusalem's Maccabean priesthood. According to *Antiquities* 13.353–64, Onias IV's son Ananias argued for peace with Judea's king and high priest Alexander Jannaeus (also known as King Jonathan, 103–76 BCE). It is also notable that while the *third-century CE* rabbinic Mishnah reported that Oniad temple priests were regarded as unfit for service in Jerusalem (m. Menaḥot 13:10), the records still maintain high priest Onias III was the temple's founder.

It seems the case that the temple and land were granted to Onias III for leading the war for Ptolemy VI Philometor against Antiochus Epiphanes, the temple being a "nucleus of a prominent pro-Ptolemaic Jewish military colony, led by Zadokite high priests."[7] The temple provided a legitimate cult against Hellenist Jason.

There may be a residuum of symbolism in Josephus's account that until its destruction, the Heliopolitan temple had stood for 343 years. It seems in the "city of the sun" (Heliopolis), the solar calendar was a vital part of the Jews' temple calendar, and Taylor has speculated that

Fig. 12.5. *Antiochus IV Epiphanes*, ca. 175 BCE, Altes Museum, Berlin. (Photo: Richard Mortel)

its great golden lamp that shone so brightly symbolized the sun's centrality (a significant Hermetic theme) based perhaps on Isaiah 30:26 where the sun will shine seven times brighter, like seven days in one, when Jahveh dresses the wound of his oppressed people. The *Targum* of Isaiah in this regard refers to seven times seven times sevenfold increase in light that will shine on the people of God on the day he brings back his exiled people ($7 \times 7 \times 7 = 343$). Readers will of course recognize the importance of the solar year to the Enochic tradition and its opposition to the lunar year of Hellenists in Jerusalem.

Heliopolis was capital to the thirteenth nome, situated on the Nile's Pelusiac branch near the road to Judea. Supposedly home to Joseph's wife, it was one of three cities rebuilt by Israelites (Exodus 1:11 in the Septuagint). Josephus in *Contra Apion* (2.2) reports Apion saying that Moses prayed in the direction of the sun to suit the people of Heliopolis and built a kind of gnomon-pillar devised so it cast a shadow into a dip that showed the sun going round its base; Josephus dismissed the whole story, but it's suggestive.

Even in the second century CE, Claudius Ptolemy called the region around Heliopolis "Oniou," and "Pillars." Locating the original temple site has proved difficult and the location is still disputed. In alleged letters between Onias and the Ptolemies, it says he chose Leontopolis, but only in those suspect letters is that identification made. The reference to Bubastis may have been intended to denigrate the site. Leontopolis is today Tell-Muqdam, and the city of Bubastis is now Tell Basta; neither are in the Heliopolitan nome.

Southwest of Bubastis is Tell el-Yehoudieh (the "Mound of the Jews"), once a Jewish town, that today can be found about 2 kilometers from the village of Shibin al-Qanatir between the Cairo to Ismaliya road and Kafr Hamza St., some 13 kilometers north of Heliopolis.[8] Archaeology currently suggests that Tell el-Yehoudieh is the most likely site yet explored. There are remains of an enclosed temple on the edge of an ancient Hyksos site. Outside the community lie remains of a red granite statue bearing the cartouche of Pharaoh Merenptah, son of Ramesses II (Nineteenth Dynasty; 1213–1203 BCE), who claimed on the Theban "Merenptah Stele" to have wiped Israel out in a campaign against Canaan (the first reference to the people of Israel recognized in Egypt).

Tell el-Yehoudieh is not only distinguished in height but was anyway a center for Jews in an area called the "land of Onias." Two ancient Hebrew inscriptions have been found there, and for his paper "Priests in Exile," Meron M. Piotrkowski studied the evidence closely to gain understanding of the Onias Jewish community. What he has discerned may have a bearing on the origin of the Hermetic tracts under discussion.

A cemetery, "explicitly connected to the temple" has yielded several burial epitaphs. "JIGRE 38" for example, reads: "The stele bears witness—'Who are you that lie in the dark tomb? Tell me your country and your father.'" "Arsinoe [the name of the famous Cleopatra's younger sister], daughter of Aline and Theodosious, and the land which nourished us is called the Land of Onias."[9] As Piotrkowski notes, the phrase implies a substantial territory, so Tell el-Yahoudieh appears to have been located within it. Roman ballista balls have also been found at the site,

Fig. 12.6. Tell el-Yehoudiyeh.
(*Diarna*; Digital Heritage Mapping)

which would chime with Josephus's account of an order going out for the temple's destruction in 73–74 CE since it attracted refugee Zealots (sicarii). Piotrkowski also notes cemetery names showing adoption of Greek names popular among non-Jews, suggesting assimilation, supported by a lack of Hasmonean names popular in Judea in the period (Jesus's brother Judas was probably named after Judas Maccabeus; Simon possibly after "Simon the Just," for example). Piotrkowski speculates that this may evince a tradition of tension between the Hasmonean and Oniad priesthoods, though some passages in Josephus suggest relations may gradually have improved during and after the time of Alexander Jannaeus (see *Antiquities* 13.353–55), such as when Oniad Jews assisted Julius Caesar's relief force from Judea under command of Idumean ruler of Judea Antipater, and Hyrcanus II (*War* 1.190 and

Antiquities 14.131–32).* According to *Antiquities*: "Antipater persuaded them to come over to their party; because he was of the same people with them; and that chiefly by shewing them the epistles of Hyrcanus the High Priest; wherein he exhorted them to cultivate friendship with Caesar, and to supply his army with money, and all sorts of provisions which they wanted. And accordingly when they saw Antipater and the High Priest of the same sentiments, they did as they were desired." As Gruen also has observed, this rather argues against too much emphasis being put on alleged conflicts between the Oniad community and the Hasmoneans. However, why Josephus amplified his story from that in *War* to show such harmony is obscure.

Piotrkowski draws attention to a reference in 3 Maccabees (1:3) to a Dositheus, son of Drimylos, "a Jew by race who later on abandoned the Jewish way of life and became estranged from his ancestral tradition." Dositheus was also the name of a high-ranking Ptolemaic official, identified as a priest of Alexander and the deified Ptolemies, the senior (pagan) priests in Hellenist Egypt, who appears in documentary papyri, though they say nothing of Jewish race.[10]

---

*This assistance to forces of Julius Caesar, Parthian King Mithridates, and Idumean Antipater (father of Herod the Great) in 47 BCE is interesting. They cooperated against Cleopatra VII's brother Ptolemy XIII. After taking Pelusium in the Nile Delta, Antipater was stopped, Josephus tells us, by "Egyptian Jews" in the Oniad patrimony. Antipater persuaded them not only to let him pass, but to give provisions to his army, which being done led Memphis's inhabitants to collaborate with Mithridates, who advanced round the Delta to defeat Ptolemy's men at a place called "the Jews' Camp" (*War* 1.9.4). Caesar subsequently made Antipater procurator of Judea with son Herod as ruler of Galilee. Well over a century before, Onias had been able to settle near Heliopolis with his mercenaries because they supported the Ptolemies. Their descendants must have faced a conflict of loyalties, for the 47 BCE campaign was also a civil war: brother against sister, with sister now supported by Caesar. When Roman commander Octavian conquered Egypt in 30 BCE and Cleopatra VII committed suicide (after Mark Antony), what then became of past loyalty to the Ptolemaic regime? Unfortunately we don't know how the Oniad community's priests responded either to this or to Herod's subsequent obliteration of the Hasmonean dynasty, and pro-Roman domination of Jerusalem's ruling priests. We may also ask why, as Josephus reports, sicarii refugees from their anti-Roman revolt headed for the Oniad temple 73–74 CE when Egypt was a *Roman* province. Did they expect reinforcements? Had they been invited? We don't know.

Perhaps Jewish authorship of the henotheist Hermetic tracts should be considered, written by persons acquainted with Enochic writings. Tracts speak of one Father of all, but tacitly accept respect for some traditional gods. The attracting of "demons" into statues by priests in *Asclepius*, for example, is not condemned, but seen, if subtly, as an achievement; the bets are hedged as to whether the "gods" were men made divine or something else. There are gods that God the maker of all makes, and gods that men have made. In *Asclepius* 37–38, for example, Hermes says: "What we have said of mankind is wondrous, but less wondrous than this: it exceeds the wonderment of all wonders that humans have been able to discover the divine nature and how to make it. Our ancestors erred gravely on the theory of divinity; they were unbelieving and inattentive to worship and reverence for God. But then they discovered the art of making gods. To their discovery they added a conformable power arising from the nature of matter. Because they could not make souls, they mixed this power in and called up the souls of demons or angels and implanted them in likenesses through holy and divine mysteries, whence the idols could have the power to do good and evil. . . . Anger comes easily to earthly and material gods because humans have made and assembled them from both natures [cf. the "giants"]." This could come from a person raised a monotheist but who'd acquired affinity with cosmopolitan tolerance, while yet aware of the first commandment's condemnation of *worshipping* intermediaries. Hermes makes it plain that God needs no propitiatory sacrifices but honest thanks, that is, do not go to gods but, through gnosis, direct to the Father, who having made all, has no need of things. Piotrkowski again: "Oniad Judaism was unique, blending two major aspects of both Diasporan and Judean Judaism: the universalistic aspect and the assimilatory aspect usually associated with the former on the one hand, and the priestly Judaism usually characteristic of the latter, based on a holy place, holy seed, and sacrifices on the other hand."[11]

In Egypt, Jews would be introduced to alternative approaches to religious life. Philo of Alexandria's *De Vita Contemplativa* (para. 28) talks about a "race" of "Therapeutae," found about the world but particularly in Egypt: men and women dedicated to God, that is, to a "medicine" of the soul, and like Hermetic tracts' approved practice, to contemplation, hymnody, and reflection. Therapeutae enjoyed six days of solitude, when they might fast, pray, study scriptures in their cells by solitary, enclosed sanctuaries, to emerge on the seventh for teaching and hymns. According to Philo, spiritual exercises included drawing out "in thought and allegory their ancestral philosophy, since they regard the literal meanings as symbols of an inner and hidden nature revealing itself in covert ideas": plainly referring to esoteric interpretation. According to paragraphs 29–30: "They have also writings of ancient men, who having been the founders of one sect or another have left behind them many memorials of the allegorical system of writing and explanation, whom they take as a kind of model, and imitate the general fashion of their sect; so that they do not occupy themselves solely in contemplation, but they likewise compose psalms and hymns to God in every kind of metre and melody imaginable, which they of necessity arrange in more dignified rhythm. Therefore, during six days, each of these individuals, retiring into solitude by himself, philosophizes by himself in one of the places called monasteries, never going outside the threshold of the outer court, and indeed never even looking out." Such an approach could be matched to transmitting Enochic themes into a philosophically universalist setting.

In paragraph 70, Philo writes of how Therapeutae (deemed as admirable as Essenes), meet to hear discourses on the seventh day in a house with men on one side, women on the other. Every seven weeks, a night-long vigil followed a banquet, where they served one another, slavery being held, quite remarkably, as "contrary to nature." "For she [nature] has begotten all men alike free." Antiphonal hymns were sung till dawn. One wonders if Zosimos and Theosebeia had attended such a body at some point.

Back at Tell el-Yahoudieh's cemetery, Piotrkowski notes the absence of Jewish motifs or identity markers such as have been found in other Diaspora burial sites, a feature of other Egyptian sites where Jews were buried.[12] According to Piotrkowski, "it is clear that the overall Greek/ Hellenistic form and notions inherent in these epitaphs reveal a striking degree of acculturation and 'openness towards the other' or, to use another more radical term, 'universalism.' Jewish universalism, in its extreme form, implies a complete detachment from traditional norms and customs. The example of the Oniad community, however, is far less extreme and far more complicated."[13]

A mixture of Jewish biblical names with Greek names prevails in the surviving epitaphs, even within the same family, for example in "JIGRE 34": "I am Jesus, my father was Phameis, passer-by; and at the age of sixty I went down to Hades . . . And you, Dositheus, bewail me . . . You are my child."[14] The reference to "passer-by" recalls logion 42 of the Nag Hammadi Gospel of Thomas: "Become passers-by," or alternatively: "Be wanderers," meaning, don't build your spiritual house in this world.

Piotrkowski notes a tendency in Jewish-Hellenistic literature to diminish the importance of being a priest or of priestly lineage in favor of emphasizing moral virtue. For example, in 2 Maccabees 6:18, priest Eleazar is praised as a "man (ανηρ) advanced in age and of noble presence," rather than as a pious Jew or priest. Also in 2 Maccabees, Onias III receives praise as a "noble and good man (ανηρ)" who hates wickedness (2 Macc. 3:1, 33; 4:35; 15:12) rather than as a high priest.[15]

On the other hand, priestly pedigree is proudly emphasized in Marin's epitaph, ("JIGRE 84"): "Marin, of priestly family, excellent woman, friend of all, and who caused pain to none, and a friend of your neighbours, farewell. About 50 years old. In the third year of Caesar, Payni [tenth Egyptian month] 13 [June 7, 28 BCE]." According to Piotrkowski, "no other known Jewish inscription from Egypt preserves such a reference," and it is "significant that the only known epigraphic source for the emphasis of one's priestly pedigree comes from a site associated with the Temple of Onias. In my opinion, this is no mere chance, and it is not necessarily connected to the privileged social status that priests enjoyed within Jewish society. Rather, it reflects the fact that the community was founded by a scion of the Jerusalem priesthood and maintained a sanctuary where priestly status, or priestly heritage, was crucial for the cult's upkeep. Thus, it is the existence of a Jewish temple that accounts for the reference to the priesthood on Marin's tombstone."[16]

Piotrkowski's conclusion is worth repeating verbatim:

The observations presented in this paper reflect a very distinct and unique religious identity of a community of Jews in Egypt at whose core was a group of Judean exiles-turned-mercenaries. The main marker for the uniqueness of the Oniad community vis-à-vis other Jewish communities of the Diaspora, is that they had brought their holy place to their place of exile in the Egyptian Diaspora and it was here that they maintained their form of priestly Judaism. Nonetheless, the forces and temptations of assimilation posed by the Greco-Egyptian Diaspora setting and by, especially, the non-Jewish mercenaries with whom they lived and served, certainly impacted the community. From this new situation, a somewhat dichotomous orientation emerged that comes to light particularly in the contents and form of the funerary epitaphs from the cemetery of Tell el-Yahoudieh. It is interesting to observe both identities operating coevally within the same community.[17]

Now, I strongly dislike bare speculation, but we are in our search faced with much evidence, some few certain facts, and connections between these that vary on a scale from conceivable to not improbable, to possible, to arguable, to likely, to probable, but only rarely to *certain*. We *know* very little, and considerably less about our subject the more we investigate it. The only value in a speculative hypothesis lies in its usefulness in getting us to look at evidence in a fresh way that draws out patterns and significant factors formerly obscure, or missed altogether. It is not vain in itself to speculate; what is vain is the populist tendency to speculate as a means of telling a surprising or sensational narrative, whose only excuse covering its naked vacuity is the statement: "Well, it might have happened like that; and it's a good story." The best story for our purposes is the true one, and that is where we try to direct our efforts, elusive as the goal so often is.

Anyhow, I flag up here two speculative questions for pondering, both devoid of confirmatory evidence, and just wonder if there might be a connection. First, is it possible that Enochic literature found a particular home among priests of the Oniad temple, being regarded simply as scripture among other scripture? Second, according to Matthew 2:13, an angel alerted Joseph in a dream (before 4 BCE) that Herod the Great intended to kill Jesus, and that Joseph should take the child to safety in Egypt. Could his family's place of refuge have been the Oniad community near the road from Judea?

THIRTEEN

Ethiopia

We began our investigation with James Bruce returning from Ethiopia. Now it's time to return to see how or when the Book of Enoch might have found its way into the canon of that country's Tewahedo Orthodox Church as *Mäṣṣäfä Henok*.

Due to lack of earlier manuscripts, our only certainty is that it was included as scripture in the fifteenth century CE. Before that time it may have been acceptable as apocrypha, or it may have been fully accepted following translation from Greek into Ge'ez between the fourth and sixth centuries.[1] It might have "got in," so to speak, *before* serious criticism by church figures in the Roman Empire dampened enthusiasm, or such reservations and criticisms may have had little or no impact, as seems to have been the case in Upper Egypt in the early fourth century, at least.

Midway into that century, Alexandria's Bishop Athanasius (died 373 CE) appointed Frumentius (died 380 CE) as bishop to Ethiopia. Today Ethiopia's patron, Syrian Frumentius is thought to have converted Emperor Ezana of the Axumite kingdom to the faith. Stuckenbruck thinks it's possible the appointment coincided with or followed Ethiopian reception of Egyptian-manufactured scriptures in Greek, though Athanasius himself regarded Enoch as uncanonical.[2] Enoch may have arrived in the kind of mixed scriptural codex we looked at in chapter 8. Such might also account for the inclusion of the book of Jubilees (*Kufale*) in Ethiopian scripture.

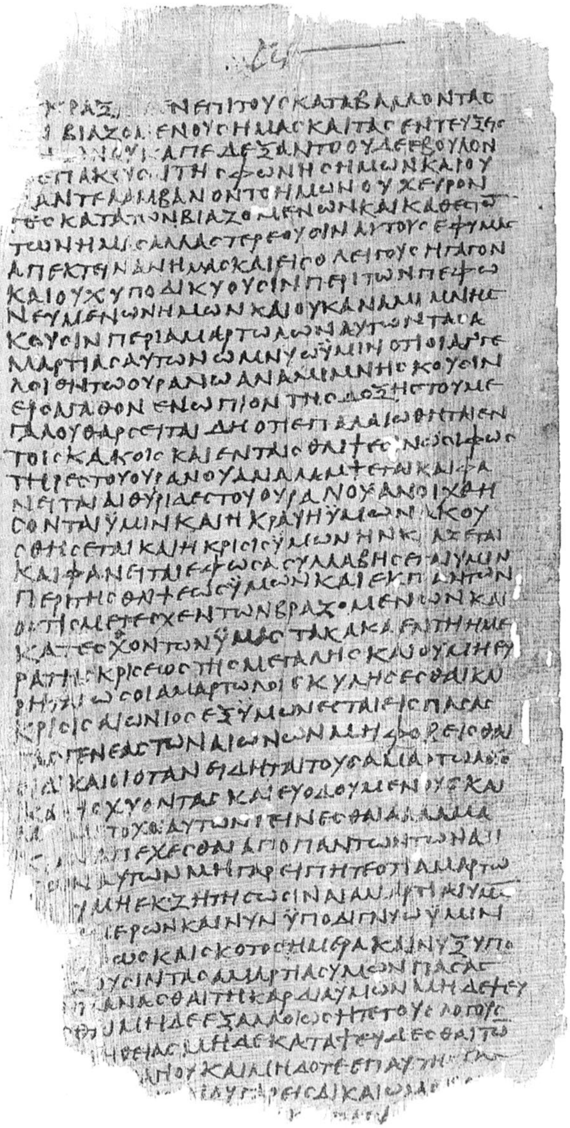

Fig. 13.1. Last chapters of the Book of Enoch (97:6–104; 106–107:3); fourth century CE; Leaf 5 of a Greek codex also containing Melito of Sardis's *Homily on the Pascha*; P. Mich. Inv. 5552 verso. (University of Michigan Library, Ann Arbor, part of the Chester Beatty Papyri; acquired in Fayum, Egypt, by Mr. Peterson in 1930)

The Axumite empire was unstable, especially in the seventh century when threatened by Islamic expansion. In the mid-tenth century a foreign queen called variously Yodit (or Judith), Gudit, and Esato, invaded, wasting the church while attempting to extinguish Christianity and the ruling House of David. Disruption may account for variant text-versions in Ge'ez, where books were possibly copied in isolation, or new versions obtained and translated.

Ambiguous evidence exists for Enoch and Jubilees' presence in the *Mäshafä Senodos*, a collection of canons sometime connected with liturgy, allegedly drawn from apostles and early church councils, dating from the formative period of the Tuwahedo Orthodox Church in the fourteenth and fifteenth centuries. Its "Apostolic Canons" contain four canon lists. Two contain Jubilees, none contains Enoch. *Kufale* (Jubilees) was important at the time for supporting a Saturday sabbath in addition to Sunday's day of rest, and for suggesting the trinity in the Old Testament (Jubilees 2:18's "Angel of the Presence" was taken for Christ and the "Angel of Sanctification," the Holy Spirit). Reference to Enoch in Jubilees 4:25 has apparently inspired three mentions of him in three "Anaphoras," or liturgical services, of the church's fourteen, namely those of Mary, St. Cyril, and the 300.

Stuckenbruck refers to liturgical use of the *Mäshafä Henok* in a manuscript from Daga Estifanos on Lake Tana, considered on palaeographic grounds to be from ca. 1400.[3] On the manuscript are notations added later to mark above the Book of the Watchers (title plus Enoch 1:1); the Book of Parables (37:1); the Book of the Heavenly Luminaries (72:1); above a description of the chiefs of the seasons in the latter book (82:12); and above the Epistle of Enoch (92:1) their use as "liturgical" readings for the second, third, fourth, fifth, and sixth days of the week—perhaps to be read for a specific festival.

Enoch also appears in thirteenth-century translations of commemoration readings referring to Enoch's ascension, as well as citations from the above mentioned Enochic books and the Animal Apocalypse.[4] Aspects of 1 Enoch also appear in fourteenth- and fifteenth-century theological texts whose names in English read: *The Book of Mystery* (by Giyorgis of Sägla, 1424); the *Book of the Nativity*; the *Book of the Mystery of Heaven and Earth* (four treatises, possibly late fourteenth century, given to mentor Bäsälotä Mika'l by a monk named Yshaq). The latter work only came to light because French collector Nicholas-Claude Fabri de Peiresc (1580–1637) thought it was the Book of Enoch, which he'd requested. Peiresc never knew the identity of the work mistaken for Enoch (see page 18). The *Book of the Mystery of Heaven and Earth* contains revelations of Bäsälotä Mika'l inspired or related to Enoch, including a list of thirty-eight rebel angel names, of which none compare to the familiar text.[5] Enoch is presented as first prophet of the revelations attributed to him, as well as revealer of secrets not revealed by prophets and apostles. According to Enoch Seminar scholar Ralph Lee, the author seems to recognize the "Apocalypse of Weeks" as a distinct unit of the text and makes his own interpretation of it. For example, in the sixth week, he interprets the man who ascends as Christ, and the ascent being one to the cross; the dispersed are the Jewish people after the crucifixion. Week seven marks the belief of those coming to the Lord while the double doctrine is Old plus New Testament.[6] Week eight is the age of the 318 Orthodox faithful; the sword is the Word of God; the palace is the churches built in Constantine's age. Week nine is the week of the heretics, while week ten is the age of the false messiah, the world's end, and all fulfilled as Daniel prophesied. The angels who fell in week two did so because they glorified themselves; therefore humans should not glorify themselves.

The sixteenth-century Gundä Gunde commentary from Gundä Gunde in Tigray follows broadly the Christian interpretation of the Apocalypse of Weeks found in the *Book of the Mystery of Heaven and Earth*. There is no mention of the "many weeks" when sin will vanish in an eternal kingdom of heaven. Several seventeenth-century commentaries on *Mäshafä Henok* also interpret the weeks in a Christian manner, with slightly different emphases.[7] The Amharic *Andəmta* commentary, for example, sees the "many weeks" after week ten as the period following the Lord's birth when many generations without number will know truth and goodness, while the judgment of Satan and his angels becomes the judgment of the children of Seth because *they* were the Watchers. Seth's descendants are also identified with monks who abandon their vocation (presumably through abandonment of celibacy: the Watchers' sin).

The fifteenth-century *Book of the Nativity* (*Mäshafä Milad*), attributed to Emperor Zär'a Ya'qob himself, contains the most citations from *Mäshafä Henok*, with twenty-six appeals to the Book of Parables on account of the Christological value of its presentation of the Son of Man

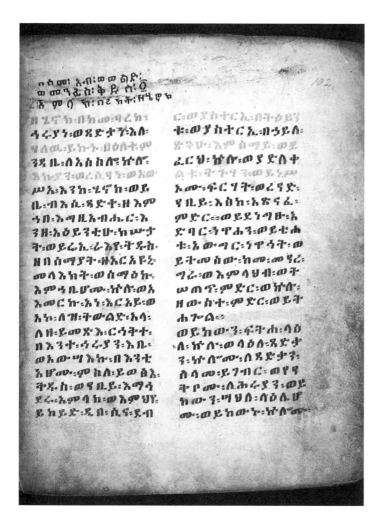

Fig. 13.2. Opening to Ethiopic Book of Enoch (*Mäshafä Henok*), sixteenth century. (British Library, Or. 485, folio 102r.)

in heaven and his place in God's scheme of judgment. The author also names Enoch as the first to prophesy the coming of Christ, described as the "birth of God" and identified with the Son of Man in 1 Enoch 46:4. The author takes it that this prophecy trounces Jewish denials of Jesus's divinity. The description of the "head of days" serves similarly, for His appearance is human, so, it is implied, the humanity of Christ is no less divine, and Jews are wrong to deny it when their own most vital prophet tells them, the prophet who also gave them dates for their passover, and knowledge of months, feasts, years, weeks, and the heavenly bodies. All this the author uses as a polemic against deniers of Enoch's canonical status, a significant factor in assessing that status in Ethiopia at the time.[8] Another claim for Enoch is that the book was employed by Jubilees, itself writ by the Angel of the Presence. For the author of the book, whose work established Enoch firmly in the Ethiopian canon and stimulated further gathering of respect in the seventeenth and eighteenth centuries, the Book of Enoch was, he writes, like the sun, and without it, the path is darkness. Enoch's prayer protects the believer for ever and ever; his instruction and prophecy are the way to stay in the light of salvation. Enoch is prophet and scribe, master of the calendar, predictor of the future.

Ralph Lee believes it was the ease by which the Apocalypse of Weeks could be interpreted as an unfolding of God's foreknowledge leading to the coming of Christ and his eternal kingdom that made it the most extensively referenced part of Enoch's prophecies in the Ethiopian tradition.[9] The tradition as a whole shows great interest in the number seven's messianic significance, so that in some commentaries the birth of Christ appears in week seven rather than week ten. This may have originally been inspired by the *Book of Mysteries of Heaven and Earth*.

As to our original question—when did Enoch enter the Ethiopian Church—it's likely it arrived in the fourth century, and there's no compelling reason to think it didn't come as a complete work, judging by the use made of it in that state from at least the late fourteenth century.

FOURTEEN

3 Enoch

....

Enoch-Metatron,
Hero of Jewish Mysticism

Rabbi Ishmael said:

Metatron, the Prince of the Presence, said to me: All these things the Holy One, blessed be He, made for me: He made me a Throne, similar to the Throne of Glory. And He spread over me a curtain of splendour and brilliant appearance, of beauty, grace and mercy, similar to the curtain of the Throne of Glory; and on it were fixed all kinds of lights in the universe. And he placed it at the door of the Seventh Hall and seated me on it. And the herald went forth into every heaven, saying: "This is Metatron, my servant. I have made him into a prince and a ruler over all the princes of my kingdoms and over all the children of heaven, except the eight great princes, the honoured and revered ones who are called YHWH [probably meaning they have the tetragrammaton as part of their names], by the name of their King." (*Sefer ha-Hekhalot* 10:1–3)

And He called me THE LESSER YHWH in the presence of all His heavenly household; as it is written [Exodus 23:21]: "For my name is in him." (*Sefer ha-Hekhalot* 12:5)

According to the *Sefer ha-Hekhalot* ("Book of the Palaces"), this Metatron, Prince of the Presence, introduces himself to Rabbi Ishmael ben Elisha as having been known among men as Enoch, and informs the rabbi of what happened to him after being brought to the heavenly *merkaba* [chariot] and Throne of Glory. Having committed cosmic governance to Enoch-Metatron, and service to the Throne of Glory, and to the "wheels" (*Galgallim*) of the merkaba, and the needs of *Shekhinah* (the divine presence, dwelling), Enoch's flesh is transformed by the Holy One into flames, his sinews into flaming fire, his bones into coals of burning juniper, his eyelids into splendor of lightnings, his eyeballs into firebrands, his hair into hot flames and the whole of his body into glowing fire. Around him are flames, firebrands, storm and tempest blowing while before and behind the roar of thunder and earthquake (15:1–2).

This transformation seems nothing less than an apotheosis, representing a kind of *ne plus ultra* for our patriarch: you don't get higher than this. The curious thing perhaps in the light of 1 Enoch's Parables, and of 2 Enoch, is that while Enoch here becomes the Angel of the Presence, and Metatron, Enoch in the *Sefer ha-Hekhalot* is not identified with the Son of Man (a title unmentioned), and this tells us something about this intriguing text's background, something that prevents us from seeing it as simply another logical stage of Enochic enthusiasm, as its frequently used title *3 Enoch* might suggest, that is, that it was produced by the same kind of persons—in the sense of a continuity-group—responsible for 1 Enoch, or 2 Enoch.

Indeed, there's a bit of mystery about the work scholar Hugo Odeberg dubbed "3 Enoch." Odeberg's first critical edition of 1928 is based on the earliest extant complete manuscript, dated 1656, now in Oxford's Bodleian Library.* *Sefer Hekhalot* is an eclectic fusing of

---

*Bodleian MS OPP. 556, foll. 314 seqq. (Neubauer, 1656: "Written in German Hebrew cursive characters by Yiṣḥak, about A.D. 1511?") containing chapters 1–48 and entitled "Book of Enoch by R[abbi]. Ishmael ben Elisha, High Priest." Odeburg considered it based on an earlier manuscript in "very good textual condition" but which had suffered through the copyist's carelessness, though his corruptions were easily amended. Odeberg considered the text provided the "very best" readings of all the manuscripts and printed fragments.[1]

different sources, sometimes carelessly. Unlike other hekhalot compositions, it gives no instruction as to preparing for mystical ascent, no theurgical prayers to ward off hostile obstructions to ascending, and is devoid of hekhalot hymns, but as Gruenwald has observed, it offers fascinating insight into the esoteric thoughts of its time of composition, which Gruenwald puts probably in the fifth century, in post-Talmudic times (Gruenwald, *Apocalyptic and Merkavah Mysticism*, 193).

Aspects of an Enoch-Metatron narrative appeared in Jewish mystical literature throughout Middle Ages, notably in the *Zohar*, and while some early scholars saw it as post-800 CE, the scholarly dating range today varies between 200–800 CE. If the text's own author statement at its start were genuine, there'd be no problem with dating, for Rabbi Ishmael (or Yishmael) ben Elisha was a rabbi born of a priestly family in upper Galilee in the late first century CE. Distinguishing himself as third generation "Tannaim," his thoughts on biblical and legal exegesis (Ishmael specialized in "aggadah") contributed to the Mishnah, redacted in the early third century CE to preserve oral traditions of Second Temple Pharisaism, which would otherwise have been lost after the catastrophe of 70 CE. The Tannaim contributed to eventual production in the fourth century of over sixty rabbinic tractates of the "Land of Israel" (Galilean) and Babylonian Talmuds (*Talmud* means learning or instruction): collections of oral teachings, remembered stories of thousands of rabbis, interpretation of the Torah (*halakha*), guides to customs, folklore, and wisdom, comprised of the Mishnah and the "Gemara": explanatory works on the Mishnah combined with other Tannaitic writings. The Babylonian Talmud expanded with further additions after 500 CE, becoming, with the Tanakh (scriptural canon), the basis of Jewish life into the Middle Ages and well beyond.

Unfortunately, titling Rabbi Ishmael as "High Priest" in 3 Enoch seems oblivious to the fact that the role ceased (as far as we know) with the temple's destruction in 70 CE. Either the ascription was a simple error, or wishful thinking, or indicated another kind of high priest, such as the priestly title given to Christ in the epistle to the Hebrews where it's said that Jesus was priest "after the order of Melchizedek" (Hebrews 7:21; Psalm 110:4). Melchizedek was of great interest to

Jewish mystics. No evidence survives of a continuity high priesthood. On the other hand, the status given to Ishmael in the text—to ascend to the heavenly court itself and discuss with Metatron matters of high divinity—would certainly merit a priesthood higher than any other!

Nevertheless, there are other aspects of the text that are difficult to dismiss, and that make one seek a later date, while providing a reason why the text makes Rabbi Ishmael's alleged experience with Enoch its narrative spine.

Merkaba and Hekhalot Mysticism

The majority of manuscripts call Odeberg's 3 Enoch a "book of the Hekhalot," and its disparate contents justify the description. The "palaces," "mansions," or "heavenly halls" represent the abodes of power, or anachronistically speaking, heaven's God-powered "hard drive." Rabbi Ishmael goes to the seventh *Hekhal* (palace) in typical hekhalot manner, except that he associates it with escaping from the angel Qefziel, who Ishmael feared might throw him down from heaven: a unique threat from a gatekeeper in the hekhalot corpus. In *Hekhalot Rabbati* (18), Qefziel is gatekeeper of the *sixth Hekhal*. God hears Ishmael's prayer for deliverance and sends Metatron to save him. This favor excites resentment and envy from other angels (a hint of humanlike emotions that overcame the Watchers in 1 Enoch?). Defending Ishmael, Metatron says that Ishmael is of the tribe of Levi, and a priest, and the angels seem satisfied that that gives him access to a vision of the Merkaba. There was a tradition that the high priest in the temple's Holy of Holies could experience visions, and with logic reversed, it seems that having visions makes Ishmael a priest, which he was not. One wonders if this transposition of the priestly role reflects the demise of the old priesthood following 70 CE. The "new" priest attends on the holy vision directly in heaven, and the merkaba and court of God become the mystic's new temple. Was this some kind of fulfillment of the Enochic apocalyptic promise of a new spiritual temple, one wonders?

Such intense interest in heavenly topography and systems grew out of Merkaba or "Chariot" mysticism, founded on contemplation of

Ezekiel (1, 8, and 10), Daniel 2, Isaiah 6, and presumably, elements of 1 Enoch. The reference in Ezekiel to a vision of "wheels" (galgalim) was not taken as a reference to the chakras (= wheels) as we might do today, but to wheels of a divine chariot, possible envisioned as whirlwinds or spheres. Elijah's ascent to heaven in a fiery chariot evinced such a vehicle might be a heavenly feature. It seemed fitting to associate it with the Throne of Glory, but its meaning inspired spiritual reflection, serving as a communication device with a chosen saint of earth.

As Don Karr and other scholars have observed, scattered references to the merkaba and hekhalot appear in the Mishnah, "Land of Israel" Talmud, and the Babylonian Talmud, reflecting Jewish scholarship in Galilean Caesarea, Sepphoris, and Tiberias, and in Babylon and other Babylonian academic centers, such as Nisibis.* The name Metatron also appears in some rabbinic sources, but in these rabbinic sources the prophet Enoch's name was not linked to the title. Enoch, as we have seen, did not represent a valid literary source for post-70 CE rabbis attached to traditional Pharisaism. Such might explain then a polemical or mischievous motive in ascribing the encounter with Enoch-Metatron with respected Tannaim member, Ishmael.

Obviously, some person or persons concerned with mystical ascent to the hekhalot was inspired to associate Enoch with an exercise in educating a literary "Rabbi Ishmael." The provenance was probably Babylonia. Hugo Odeberg observed a passage in 3 Enoch where the spiritual accusers of Israel are named as coming from Persia and Rome: from Dubbiel, "prince" of Persia, and Sammael, "prince" of Rome (3 Enoch 26:12). This suggested to Odeberg Jewish colonies in Babylonia during the third and fourth centuries when Jews enjoyed toleration from Sassanid rulers.[3] Most scholars today would regard Odeberg's dating of the text to the second half of the third century as too early, partly on the grounds that in other Babylonian hekhalot texts, Enoch is not identified with Metatron, with the implication that Enoch-as-Metatron was a late arrival.

There is always the possibility, though vague, that rabbinic sources

---

*For example, in the Mishnah: *Megillah* 4:10, *Hagigah* 2:7, *Tosefta Hagigah* 2:1–7, Land of Israel Talmud (also called "Jerusalem Talmud") 77 a-d, Babylonian Talmud 11b–16a.[2]

had long since excised Enoch from the Metatron role and established a dogma to that effect followed by mystics, who already operated under rabbinic suspicion, on account of an implicit claim to privileged insight. Rabbi Ishmael, for example, had been emphatic that the Torah should be read in its plain sense since it was intended for ordinary men. Since no extant pre-Mishnaic text identifies Enoch with Metatron, however, the idea of active rabbinic censorship of hekhalot texts is speculative. However, Odeberg did identify a reference in the Babylonian Talmud, *Hagigah* 15a where it's said that Metatron had been permitted to sit down in the heavenly court to write down the merits of Israel: "Metatron's function of Scribe here is most naturally explained from the assumption that he has already been identified with Enoch, 'the scribe of righteousness" (Odeburg, introduction, 36). Indeed, contributors to the Babylonian Talmud occasionally let forth some uncredited acquaintance with the Book of the Watchers. For example, the names of two Watchers (1 Enoch 6–16), Shemhazai and Azael, appear in *b. Niddah* 61a, and *b. Yoma* 67b, as well as Aramaic magical incantation bowls of the same period.

Gershom Scholem, who first introduced Jewish mysticism to that wider scholarly interest it now enjoys, dated 3 Enoch to the fifth to sixth centuries, long after a decidedly unsympathetic Heinrich Graetz, referenced by Odeberg, insisted on a tenth–eleventh century composition date. Odeberg rejected this, and the rejection stands. The acceptable range is still very wide: 200 to 800 BCE, with the latter date marking the most intense period of hekhalot composition among Babylonian mystics or would-be mystics.

Much scholarly interest tends to focus on whether 3 Enoch was reliant on 1 Enoch or 2 Enoch. In this regard, Jonas Greenfield considers "3 Enoch" a hazardous misnomer. Only one Oxford manuscript adds the title "Sefer Ḥanok." Greenfield considers Enoch's involvement a mere assimilation to Metatron; it is hekhalot material that's delivered to Rabbi Ishmael.[4] In 1 Enoch and 2 Enoch, Enoch is still accessible to humans. Able to visit his son on earth, he does not become the Prince of the Presence (*Sar ha-Panim*), whereas in 3 Enoch (so-called), Enoch has no human fellowship after absorption into hekhalot circles.

Parallels between 3 Enoch and earlier Enochic works are few, differences numerous. For example, in 3 Enoch 5, angels Aza and Azael are angels who merely strayed, objecting to Enoch's presence among exalted heavenly company for which they dismiss him as unfit (a polemic against anti-Enoch rabbis?), implying a prior rejection of the original Watchers narrative. In 3 Enoch, humans cause evil; the viewpoint you'd expect from a rabbi. Indeed, 3 Enoch comes over as an angelic merkaba text whose descriptions of angelic functions are to support the merkaba, similar to the *Sefer ha-Razim* or "Book of Mysteries," with no interest in astronomical science.[5]

A description of God's chariots, Ophanim (another word for wheels), Seraphim, and archangels occurs in 3 Enoch 24–26. There's no multiplication of chariots in Enochic tradition prior to this text. In 3 Enoch 26, the Seraphim destroy Satan's written indictments against Israel, the work of the spiritual princes of Rome and Persia, because the Seraphim know God protects Israel. This is a far cry from 1 Enoch's regular intercession of the angels on behalf of suffering humanity, even though there might be a slight dependency here on 1 Enoch 40:3–7's account where a single archangel intercedes to forfend against "Satans"; 3 Enoch is working on its own imaginative territory. While in 1 Enoch a single divine recorder reads his own records (1 Enoch 89:61–64; 70–76), in 3 Enoch 27 there are numerous heavenly libraries. In 3 Enoch, there is reciting of qedushah by camps of angels typical of other hekhalot texts.[6] While 3 Enoch 42 describes storehouses of lightning, thunder, snow, hail, and rain, the details are different to 1 Enoch 60:11–21. Angels in 1 Enoch receive punishment for numerous sins, such as interest in women or the stars coming out at the wrong time; in 3 Enoch punishment is for praising God at the wrong time. The sense is rather that whoever wrote 3 Enoch had heard something of earlier material but had no scribal respect for it as authoritative revelation when it came to details—any sense of lineage is absent. According to Lawrence Schiffman, earlier assumptions of relations between the texts are greatly exaggerated, with no evidence of direct influence from 1 Enoch.[7]

Metatron

Odeberg saw an indirect parallel with 1 Enoch 45:3 where an "elect one" (*baḥir*) will sit on a "throne of glory." Despite philological objections, Odeberg was convinced Metatron derived from the Greek *meta thronos*, "along with the throne," which numerous scholars today doubt or reject outright.

Odeberg did recognize that 3 Enoch owed much to 2 Enoch, and it can be argued it took 2 Enoch a stage further, but whether that's a logical, theological progression is questionable; 3 Enoch simply places some aspects of 2 Enoch in the context of personal ascent mysticism, stimulating the imagination of would-be practitioners of transcendent, or transcending, trance.

Common areas with hekhalot texts lie in the developed angelology from 2 to 3 Enoch, though the old list of rebel angels has been ignored in the main. Obviously, in 3 Enoch, Enoch has been promoted. In 2 Enoch, he becomes a celestial being, having received the "ointment of glory" (2 Enoch 22:9; 56) but is still below Michael. Schiffman considers Odeberg's linear theory from one to three redundant, mainly because 3 Enoch is framed by rabbinic priorities. It has its cake and eats it: mysticism sanctioned in a rabbinic framework, but it's the mysticism that matters. Arguably it's a plea for rabbinic tolerance.

The distinctive factor that remains is the identity of Metatron, the one who will "stand in front of the face of the Lord forever," and who is "wise in the secrets and Master of the mysteries" (3 Enoch 2:30 and the hekhalotic *Shi'ur Qomah*)[8] and in 3 Enoch is called by "my King" *Na'ar* ("Youth" or "Lad*").

The *Shi'ur Qomah* ("the Measurement of the Body") is a controversial Merkaba text based on the Song of Songs 7:8, wherein God's "limbs" are numbered. It may also reflect 2 Enoch 39:6 on the measureless form of the Lord. The book begins with the now familiar Rabbi Yishma'el announcing he is seeing the "King" sitting on high. Metatron

---

*A title also given to Enoch by an angel in 2 Enoch 9, encouraging Orlov in the view that the Metatron identity is deliberately foreshadowed in 2 Enoch.[9]

appears and shows him the measurement of God's form. Metatron is busy organizing the heavenly *Qedushah* (= angelic prayers of sanctification of God from Isaiah 6:3; Ezekiel 3:12) (see Gruenwald, *Apocalyptic and Merkavah Mysticism*, 213–14).

As Odeberg noted, the derivation of *Metatron* seems to have been forgotten shortly after its appearance,[10] before devoting many pages to interpretations and attempted philological explanations of the intriguing word; quite enough anyway to deter anyone from adding to the speculations. Was Metatron of Greek, Latin, Hebrew, or even Persian derivation? Odeberg considered whether it was related to the Persian *Mithra*, which might explain the cognate title "Youth," a feature of popular views of Persian redeemer and solar deity, Mithra. Odeberg prefers a Greek origin: *meta thronos*, since in 3 Enoch, Enoch is not called Metatron until enthroned, and Metatron references consistently feature proximity to the divine throne, and his being worthy of his own distinct throne. Odeberg also considered the origin of the idea of Metatron was related to Greek pseudepigraphical interest in the angelic world, where angels were sometimes called *thronoi* or "throned ones" (as in Testament of Levi 3:8). The name would conceivably have distinguished itself from the Throne of Glory, being the "next best thing."

Józef Tadeusz Milik in his much challenged study of Enoch relates how the name Metatron appears in Judaeo-Babylonian Aramaic on magical bowls of the seventh to eighth and even ninth centuries as a mighty prince, not alone in heaven, but in the company of other named angels, including Azael and Aza, and on one magical bowl appearing as "Hermes-Metatron."[11] It is typical of magical spells to throw in as many holy or spiritually powerful names as possible, but it does show how prevalent in Babylonian Jewish circles the name Metatron was.

Milik completely rejects Odeberg's etymology of the name, emphatically stressing its breaking transcription rules, requiring invention of a Greek compound substantive. Milik holds the only sensible derivation was one known to medieval kabbalists: mem, yod, tet, tet, resh, vav, nun ("mittrun") a Hebrew derivative, with elative "-on" from Latin *metator*, through Greek *mētatōr, mitatōr*. In original Latin, the sense was one who sets bounds to a field, and in later use, a quartermaster arranger of lodgings for an army or prince, with here perhaps the inference of one preparing a place in heaven.[12] Perhaps there's also a sense of the herald, or one like the Arabic *wazir*. Gruenwald openly ridicules Milik's views with regard to kabbalist references: "J. T. Milik's attribution of the book [*Sefer Hekhalot*] to the Kabbalistic literature of the twelfth or thirteenth centuries only shows how little Milik knows of both the Hekhalot literature and of the Cabbalah [*sic*]."[13]

The link in the magical bowl inscriptions with the god Hermes, as spokesman for the gods, is suggestive and might even account in part for a Hermes-Enoch conflation behind Enoch's acquiring identity as Metatron (this Hermes-Metatron link also occurred to Gruenwald [*Apocalyptic and Merkavah Mysticism*, 196]). The god Hermes also has the possibility of leaving the abode of the gods for the lower realms of human action (though *Sefer Hekhalot's* Enoch is apparently heaven-bound). The name of Youth being given to Enoch-Metatron is also suggestive since Hermes was often depicted as a good-looking, super-fit beardless youth. This youthfulness might also be reflected in Metatron's extraordinary title in *Sefer Hekhalot*: *Yahweh Ha-Qatan* (Smaller or Lesser Yahweh). The herald idea here is also strong, and one naturally thinks of a symbolic identity of John the Baptist (cf. *Corpus Hermeticum* 4 where Hermes Trismegistos tells of a herald sent by God who calls mankind to be baptized in a bowl of nous, with those dipped acquiring gnosis). Milik observes also that the term *metator* was unlikely in his opinion to have been adopted into Mishnaic Hebrew and Judaeo-Aramaic before the Byzantine period (in this case fifth–sixth centuries) when Latin borrowings began to enter written Greek, particularly in military and administrative terminology.[14]

Milik makes the additional point that while identification of Metatron and Hermes features in the magical texts, there is no comparable identification of Metatron with Enoch in those texts. To these Jewish magi, Enoch was not a power-name to call upon. Nevertheless, medieval Germany's Ashkenazi Hasidim included *Sefer Hekhalot* in their collections of pre-kabbalistic Jewish mysticism. Indeed, Jewish kabbalistic interest in Enoch-Metatron had to precede the quiet, golden age of Enoch-Metatron when Christian scholars got their teeth into

Fig. 14.1. In Islamic tradition Metatron is Mītatārūn, angel of the veil, depicted here carrying a spear and magic table or tablet in the *Daqa'iq al-Haqa'iq* ("Degrees of Truths"), a thirteenth-century work about prognostic astrology, angelology, and talismanic magic by al-Nasiri (Nasir al-Din Muhammad b. Ibrahim b. 'Abd Allah al-Rammal al-Mu'azzim al Sa'ati al-Haykali). The section on Mercury's conjunction with the moon shows a turbaned man (Hermes?) in scribe's robe with four hands, each holding snow, fire, a reed pen, and a book.

kabbalah after European Jews showed the way to "Christian Cabalists" during and after the Renaissance. Such excitements in turn gave rise to eager interest in the whereabouts, and surviving fragments, of the by-then fabled 1 Enoch.

In the meantime, 3 Enoch stands, in Ithamar Gruenwald's words, as "a romance or grand summary of the Jewish apocalyptic and mystical traditions."[15] Its assumption that a human being could assume a position over the angels if God so wished it was tantalizing to mystical humanists like Pico della Mirandola, as we shall see. In the meantime, humanity had a representative, albeit utterly transformed, at the highest level of the divine (mystical) corporation.

FIFTEEN

Enoch in Medieval Islamic Traditions

Scholarly acquaintance with Enoch appears in Islam during the third caliphate after the prophet Muhammad: the Abbasids, named after Muhammad's uncle Abbas ibn Abdul-Muttalib (566–633 CE). The Abbasids overthrew the Ummayad caliphate in 750 CE, and in 762 Abbasid caliph Al-Mansur moved his court from Kufa to new city Baghdad, close to Babylon's flourishing Jewish intellectual community. Baghdad opened its gates to Islam's golden age characterized by broad-minded engagement with science, religious philosophy, and classical tradition. Through those gates entered talents like itinerant scholar Ibn Ishāq (704–767) who, after a difficult early life, became tutor at the caliph's court where Al-Mansur commissioned a history of the world from Adam, entitled: "In the beginning, the mission, and the expeditions." The "mission" was Muhammad's, and the history contained the *Sīrah*, an influential biography of the prophet.

Ibn Ishāq identified Enoch with Idrīs, a mysterious figure of whom the Qur'ān said: "We raised him up to a lofty place" (19:57). As in the *Sefer Hekhalot*, the key to Enoch was ascent to heaven. That's why Idrīs was not only identified with Enoch (Akhnūkh) but also with Elijah (Ilyās) and the equally mysterious Khiḍr (Khāḍir). The Qur'ān had little else to impart about Idrīs, except that he was a prophet (*nabī*), a trustworthy or righteous man (*ṣiddīk*) (19:56), and that he was counted among the patient (*min al-ṣabirīn*) and the righteous (*min al-ṣaliḥin*) (21:85–86). Ibn Isḥāq recognized Jared's son Enoch as first prophet after Adam, and first to use a pen: associations echoed by later historian Tabari (959/60–1058) who attributed thirty scriptures to Enoch, and his enslaving some of Cain's descendants. None of this reflects direct access to Enochic books.

We have already noted Abū Ma'shar al-Balkhi's identification of Enoch with Hermes Trismegistos. Following Abū Ma'shar's account, Toledo-based science chronicler Ṣā'id al-Andalūsi (1029–1070) also exhibits ideas drawn from Alexandrian monk Annianus and Byzantine scholar George Syncellus. Andalūsi noted the first Hermes living in Upper Egypt, authoring all antediluvian science. Identifying him with Enoch and Idrīs, Andalūsi also credited Enoch-Hermes-Idrīs with astronomy, celestial substances, medicine, and initiating temples to glorify God (implied by the Hermetic *Kore Kosmou*). Andalūsi further recorded how Hermes-Enoch "was the first to give advance warning of the Flood, and he thought that ruin would overtake the earth from water and fire. He feared that knowledge would pass away and that the arts would perish in the Flood, so he built the pyramids and the monumental temples in highest Upper Egypt. He portrayed in them all the arts and the instruments, indicating the features of the science by illustrations, out of desire thereby to preserve the science forever for those after him, fearing that all trace of it would perish from the world."[1]

Kameliya Atanasova has recently written of Enoch-Hermes-Idrīs, indicating that identity's reflection in the spiritual science, or mystical gnosis, if you prefer, of the Sufis, whose first "paths" (*ṭuruq*) to reunion with divine spirit appeared in the tenth century. Atanasova notes an interesting appeal to the value of prophecy (in the person of Enoch-Hermes) in a debate about human reason. Ismā'ilī sect preacher Abū Ḥātim al-Rāzi (died ca. 943) believed philosophy needed divine revelation, whereas doctor and philosopher Abū Bakr al-Rāzi (died 925) favored a philosopher's reliance on reason (*al-Rāzi* means "one from Ray," Persia).

A single prophet, asserted the preacher, straddled philosophy as well as the Qur'ān and other revealed books. Known to philosophers as

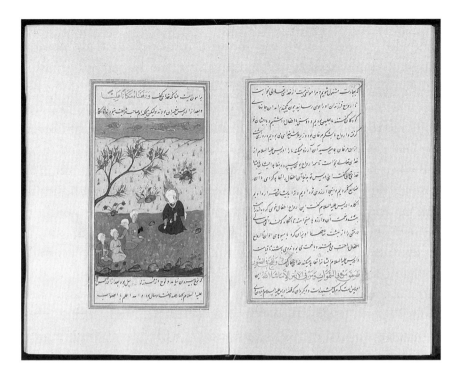

Fig. 15.1. Idrīs instructing his children, from *Qiṣaṣ al-anbiyā'* (Tales of the Prophets) by twelfth-century writer Ishaq ibn Ibrahim al-Nishapuri. Note Idrīs's face is white-veiled lest the glory acquired in heaven blind the children. Iran (probably Qazvin), 1570–80; Chester Beatty Library Per 231, f.22a.

Hermes, he was Idrīs to the Qur'ān and Enoch to other scriptures. Abū Ḥātim fortified his critique of rationalism by saying Idrīs would have known nothing of astronomy unless an angel had taught him (reminiscent of the Angel of the Presence's role in 2 Enoch).[2]

Possibly reflecting Ismāʿīlī beliefs, and curiously akin to Philo's *Therapeutae*, the secret society of philosophers called the Brethren of Purity (*Ikhwan al-Safā*) was a hierarchical group who ascended in grades through a system of progressive enlightenment, from "craftsmen" to "prophets and philosophers," the rank that came above "kings." Convening three evenings a week to discuss science and philosophy, and to sing philosophical hymns, their meetings, according to Seyyed Hossein Nasr, included a supplication for Idrīs.[3]

Commentator on the Qur'ān, al-Thaʿlabī (died 1035) considered how the etymology of Idrīs reflected the Arabic verb *d-r-s* "to study"—and concluded the name was given "because of his copious study [*dars*] of the books and scriptures of Adam and Seth, and his mother Ashuth."[4] Crediting Idrīs as pioneer astronomer, writer, and cloth sewer, al-Thaʿlabī explained the Qur'ān's raising of Idrīs "to a lofty place" (19:57): "God sent him to be the son of Cain and then raised him into the heavens. The reason God raised him into the heavens is what [Qur'ān exegete] Ibn Abbas and others say, that he walked one day until the blaze of the sun set upon him. Holding the sun on his back he cried out to God for relief, so God sent the Angel of Death to rescue him from the heat and the weight of the sun. The Angel of Death lifted him on his wing into the heavens."[5]

According to Atanasova, early and classical Muslim scholars could not agree on what happened to Idrīs once in heaven. Some said he died there, in the sixth heaven, others that he still lived there; all acquiesced in Idrīs's growing reputation as scholar, astronomer, and prophet.[6]

Atanasova attributes Idrīs's association with Sufism to his reputation as wise man, inventor, writer, diviner, and sewer of garments—the latter relevant since Sufism permeated craft guilds and *futuwwa* (fraternities),* while Idrīs's elevation fed into heavenly speculation and upwardly yearning mysticism.

Sufi Muhyī al-dīn Ibn'Arabi (died 1240) referred to Idrīs as "prophet of the philosophers," while philosophy itself he described as the "law of Idrīs."[7] Ibn'Arabi's *Bezels of Wisdom* (*Fuṣūṣ al-ḥikam*) devoted a chapter to Idrīs: "The Wisdom of Holiness in the Word of Idrīs." It discusses spiritual elevation according to the Sufic doctrine of the *axis mundi* ("the world axis").

The world's destiny apparently turns on the high status of the "Perfect Man"—reminiscent of the gnostic Valentinians's *Anthrōpos* or heavenly principle of Man, mirror of God, as well as the kabbalists' Adam Kadmon (= primordial Man)—and arguably the Son of Man figure in the Parables of 1 Enoch. So when the Qur'ān speaks of Idrīs raised to a lofty place: "The loftiest of places is that one around which the Celestial Spheres revolve, that is the Sphere of the Sun where Idrīs's spiritual sta-

---

*In this regard it may be significant that one of the greatest saints of Sufism, Duhl-Nun al-Misri (796–862), alchemical adept, was born in Akhmim, both textile center and home of alchemist Zosimos.

tion (*maqām*) dwells."[8] Ibn'Arabi further expounds that the solar sphere is the "Pole" (*quṭb*) of the celestial spheres, and while lofty in regard to *place*, loftiness of *rank* belongs to Muhammad's heirs, as is written in the Qur'ān (47:35): "You are the lofty ones and God is with you." Loftiness of rank requires *knowledge*; loftiness of place requires *action*. In the Perfect Man loftiness is attained through divine union of place *and* rank. Place and rank make him lofty; loftiness does not derive from his own essence. God is *singularly* lofty, in very essence, and ultimately, as *being (wujūd)*, God is the essence of all created beings, while being also unlike anything else. Likewise, the number one is *in* all numbers but as one remains singular and absolute. One can partake of the divine essence, yet the essence in itself is unknowable, being beyond all created things.

Such a train of thought could, I presume, also issue from profound meditation on the figure of Enoch-Metatron, insofar as there seems to be a spiritual relation between that ideal figure of vision and Ibn'Arabi's and the Sufis' Perfect Man.

According to Atanasova, Ibn'Arabi's metaphysics was not left behind in the Middle Ages, but became chief conduit for discussions about Enoch/Idrīs until as late as the seventeenth and eighteenth centuries, namely, the period of early modern Ottoman Sufism, concluding that "Sufis appear as the exclusive heirs of centuries-old Idrīsian wisdom which remains otherwise inaccessible."[9]* Ibn'Arabi's vision of the Perfect Man may also be discerned in the key philosophical shift of the Florentine Renaissance.

---

*In this regard, Atanasova has studied two representatives of Ottoman Sufism: Abdullah Bosnevi (1584–1644) and Ismail Hakki Bursevi (1653–1725), about whom one can read in her excellent article.[10]

SIXTEEN

"Holy Enoch" and the Renaissance

A great miracle, O Asclepius, is man.

HERMES TRISMEGISTUS IN THE *ASCLEPIUS*

(LATIN VERSION PRINTED 1463)

Interest among Renaissance scholars and other enthusiasts for Enoch derives primarily from a fortuitous blend of late antique spiritual esotericism—such as the Hermetic tracts, first brought to Florence from Greece in 1460—and the post-Talmudic integration of hekhalot visionary meditations into what emerged in the twelfth and thirteenth centuries as "*kabbalah*" or "received" tradition: esoteric interpretative understanding of God and the universe open to—and arguably a long extension of—Enochic influence.

The *driving force* of radical Renaissance philosophy in the Florentine quattrocento was a burgeoning awareness of human potential, freed from bond and bound of earth and flesh to explore realms above earthly powers and inhibitions; old-style churchmen felt the challenge.

Florence received its first printing press in 1471, and as with everywhere else in Europe so equipped, an influx of classical learning into the minds of educated aristocrats and gentry created a realization that the Bible was neither alone in significance nor sole source of wisdom; secrets apparently existed beyond doctrines imposed on believers by religious authorities. Whereas most patristic writers had attempted to establish Christianity's superiority to classical learning, the new "humanism" embraced classical learning, seeking its glories on its own terms. Indeed, a few daring scholars believed the Bible could be *better* understood through para-biblical lenses. Where translated Arabic writings reflected antique Neoplatonism and Sufic mysticism, they too joined an ambrosial blend the inspired hoped would transform the world into a system governing and expanding knowledge of nature in potentially unlimited directions. A growing band of scholars were prepared to absorb works by inspired Jews, Muslims, and classical pagans, from which sources a new religious harmony could be envisioned, that is, a reconstitution of formative knowledge that existed before humanity fractured. Enoch could crystallize such concerns, for Enoch enjoyed a reputation as first intellectual: scribe of God, no less, and first of earth, it was believed, to achieve heavenly identity. Most importantly, Enoch went back to the beginnings, where he and his kin preserved pristine philosophy—the "ancient theology" (*prisca theologia*)—untarnished truth of the mind of God, which, having been lovingly embraced, sliced open the skies to reveal an eternity for which providence provided a guide; Enoch had traversed, encompassed, and understood the heavens.

Many excited by such possibilities were themselves church representatives, or close to appendant holy orders; the church was still educator, theology "queen of the sciences."

Intended by his aristocratic mother for the church, that embodiment of harmonious idealism Giovanni Pico della Mirandola, conte di Concordia (1463–1494), is remembered as the "phoenix of the wits," youngest and brightest among very bright Italian philosophers. Desiring to harmonize truth from all sources, Pico abandoned canon law for immersion in philosophy. Desiring to know everything, he believed that if you reached the spiritual kernel of all thought, the divine principle of the "One" would coruscate, dissolving apparent conflicts. Through unity of understanding, division among faiths and philosophies could be overcome in an ascent beyond clouds of matter to the purest spiritual air above.

Fig. 16.1. *Giovanni Pico della Mirandola*,
by Christofano dell'Altissimo (ca. 1525–1605);
Uffizi Gallery, Florence.

In 1486, twenty-three-year-old Pico della Mirandola wrote an oration to introduce a great debate summoned to discuss his *900 Conclusiones* to inaugurate a new understanding of man's relation to God and the universe. Precise, erudite, poetic, the *Oratio de dignitatis homini* was partly a peroration on the Hermetic theme: *magnum miraculum homo est*—"a great miracle is man." Man has *freedom* to rise on the great ladder of being, or to fall; to become angelic or beastly or plantlike; the trajectory depends on his *own will*. "We shall fly up," Pico writes, "like earthly mercuries, to the embraces of our blessed mother." "Mother" is wisdom: divine, governing intelligence.

Concerned that young genius threatened the old order, Pope Innocent VIII forbade the debate while investigators declared several "conclusions" heretical. Troubles that marked Pico's short life had begun. Imprisoned by papal order, freed by patron Lorenzo dei'Medici,

Fig. 16.2. Pope Innocent VIII (1432–1492), bronze medal ca. 1480/86; Samuel H. Kress Collection, National Gallery of Art.

he was imprisoned again, and again freed, whereupon, subdued, he sacrificed his fortune, and after short retirement to a Dominican house in Florence, was poisoned by arsenic. He was thirty-one.

As Giulio Busi has demonstrated, Pico referred to Enoch as Metatron on three occasions by name.[1] The first was written a few months before his *Oration on the Dignity of Man*. Entitled *Commentary on a Canzone by Girolamo Benivieni* (1486)—Benivieni being a Florentine poet Pico had befriended—it seems reminiscent of Ibn'Arabi's view of the Perfect Man, and of Idrīs raised to a lofty place, some two and a half centuries earlier: "The loftiest of places is that one around which the Celestial Spheres revolve, that is the Sphere of the Sun where Idrīs's spiritual station (*maqām*) dwells." Pico writes:

> Since . . . the rational faculty is peculiar to man, but in his intellectual [noetic] faculty he corresponds to the angels, a man who functions only in his intellect no longer lives with a human life, but with an angelic life. He becomes dead to the sensible world, and is reborn to a more perfect life in the intelligible world. Motion and function are signs of life; the loss of them is a sign of death. Thus when no human function can be seen in a man, it is truly dead with respect

to human existence. If he passes from human existence to intellectual existence, he is by that death transformed into an angel. This is what the statement of the Cabalist wise men must mean when they say that Enoch was transformed into Metatron, the angel of divinity, or in general, that any other man is transformed into an angel.[2]

"Intellect" here stands for the *nous*, higher mind that receives light, and life, from pure spiritual truth, or heaven. Not dependent on sense perception, as ordinary human reason is, nous enables comprehension of the *meaning* of things perceived as separate. For Pico, what has made Enoch-the-man into Metatron-the-little-god is Enoch's direct absorption into noetic consciousness. *This* is the gift for those who ascend to the embraces of "our blessed mother." Metatron thus becomes a symbol of "Renaissance Man" risen free into that freedom this world cannot give, or understand.

Metatron reappears by implication in Pico's *Oration on the Dignity of Man*, where Pico compares four kinds of seeds that man may cultivate if he wills: vegetative seeds will make of him a plant; seeds of the senses make man a brute animal; seeds of reason open the door to becoming a "heavenly being" with a purview of the world; "intellectual" (noetic) seeds offer existence as "an angel and a son of God." Thereafter, the life of any other creature cannot satisfy, and he may gather himself "into the center of his own unity," a single spirit with God "in the solitary darkness of the Father," set above all things, superior to all things. "Who," Pico asks, "will admire any other being more?" Man is protean, a "chameleon"; he has a "metamorphous" nature, capable of change. Such, Pico believes, explains the "metamorphoses" celebrated by Jews and Pythagoreans. "Indeed," he writes, "even the most secret Hebrew theology at one time transforms holy Enoch into an angel of divinity, whom they call Metatron, and at other times it reshapes other men into other spirits. According to Pythagoreans, wicked men are deformed into brutes and, if Empedocles is to be believed, into plants as well."

Bologna-based scholar Giacomo Corazzol has identified one of the texts that inspired Pico: a "Commentary on the Torah" by Menahem Recanati. An Italian kabbalist, Pico had the renowned Flavius

Mithridates translate Recanati's Commentary from Hebrew to Latin, and relied heavily on it, which itself drew heavily on the Babylonian Talmud, as this passage makes plain:

> Similarly, our teachers of blessed memory have said: "In the world to come, blessed be He, make to the righteous wings with which they fly over the waters" [*b. Sanhedrin* 92b]. Interpretation of "wings": the soul is clothed with the angelic nature [cf. *Bereshit Rabbah* 50:2] in the same way as it is clothed with bodily limbs; the wings, however, do not fail with the disappearance of the elements. What they mean to say is that Enoch stripped himself of his bodily element and clothed himself with the spiritual element, and that the Lord, be He exalted and blessed, crowned him with the vigour of his procession, He who performs wonders in the camps.[3]

While Pico sees the "Cabala's" Metatron as—in Busi's expression—"the arrival station" of his interest in metamorphosis, he also, in *Conclusiones* 19:2, sees Metatron as the illuminative "active intellect" referred to by fourth-century philosopher Themistius when commenting on Aristotle's *de anima* ("concerning the soul"; 98.35 [430a, 2.5–17]).[4] Themistius's "active intellect" advances the "potential intellect," enabling perception of "forms" sensible to vision as objects perceptible to the senses. The "potential intellect" then is equivalent to Pico's rational faculty, the *ruach* of the kabbalist. The "active intellect" enables *thinking about* or intellectualizing objects. It is the mobility and freedom (winged!) of mind to get round and *into* things to understand their root in their idea, that is, what is thinkable about them in relation to all other things, ideas, and causes. The active intellect is like the light necessary for *potential* color to become visible as color; thus the active intellect is united with what it illuminates, being itself of the principle of unity, which Plato likens to the sun, source of light. We may then recall once more Ibn'Arabi's view of the Perfect Man, and of Idrīs raised to a lofty place: "The loftiest of places is that one around which the Celestial Spheres revolve, that is the Sphere of the Sun where Idrīs's spiritual station (*maqām*) dwells." This is classic

Pico, harmonizing insights from kabbalist, Sufi, and Greeks Plato and Aristotle.

So, for Pico, Metatron has become, in a sense, an attainable faculty, the highest faculty of human mind, enabling true *discrimination* in the spirit of the Good.

Having employed Flavius Mithridates to translate for him the *Sitre Torah* of Rabbi Abraham Abulafia, Pico had another Jewish source behind him. Born in Zaragoza the year Ibn'Arabi died (1240), Abulafia worked out a kabbalistic system designed to turn aspiring ordinary men into prophets. In this passage from Abulafia's *Sitre Torah*, Abulafia emphasizes the value of gematria, using numerical equivalents for Hebrew letters to highlight parallel or kindred meanings:

> For this reason, it will be necessary for me to mention that the *res* [thing], which guides our intellect from potentiality to actuality, is the intellect that is separated from any material, and which can be expressed in many ways in our language (using numerical equivalents for the letters). Indeed, it is said *hu saro shel ha-'olam*, or rather, "this is the beginning of the world," and "Metatron, prince of the countenances," in Hebrew Metatron *sar ha-panim* [Prince of the Presence]; this latter expression has the same numerical value as the former.[5]

According to Giulio Busi: "Both the angelic metamorphosis of Enoch in Metatron and the function of the latter as the active intellect, go in a direction that we might call bottom up, that is, they increase man's possibilities, making him climb the ladder that leads from corporeality to the incorporeal and luminous world of eternal knowledge."[6] For Pico, Metatron represents humanity rising from the created realm, and thus Metatron pertains to the tenth sefira (enumerated emanation) of the kabbalist's Tree of Life: Malkuth—"kingdom," meaning the realm of creation: earth, stars, planets, which Enoch knows so well, and as Metatron, rules. Wisdom is above him, and on the Tree of Life, literally so, for Wisdom (Hokma) is the second sefira. Metatron expresses human potentiality realized, and that impulse is what drove

Pico's thought, and what men long afterward called the Re-naissance, or rebirth.

Lodovico Lazzarelli and Divine Regeneration

It is a rather curious coincidence that around the time twenty-one-year-old Pico first arrived in Florence to assemble his *900 Conclusions*, another appeared in Rome already *embodying* the highest aspects of Pico's philosophy. While the story's outlines are confirmed from numerous contemporary sources, our principal knowledge relies on two rare works by poet-turned-Christian Hermetist, Lodovico Lazzarelli (1447–1500). Lazzarelli's *Epistola Enoch* ("The Letter of Enoch"), and *Crater Hermetis* ("Hermetic Bowl") were discovered in the 1930s at Viterbo's Community Library by Renaissance scholar Paul Oscar Kristeller, and it was on Kristeller's work that I relied when first writing about Lazzarelli in *The Golden Builders* (2002). Since that time, other scholars have noticed what was then plain to me, that Lazzarelli's works are probably the most astounding works of Enochic theology and Christian Hermetism ever to emerge from Renaissance shadows. In recent times, study of Lazzarelli has preoccupied Wouter Hanegraaff, Amsterdam University's professor in Western esotericism. I recommend his *Lodovico Lazzarelli and the Hermetic Christ: At the Sources of Renaissance Hermetism* (2005) to those inspired to extend their range.

Lazzarelli was turned from Mount Parnassus (mount of poets) to Mount Zion (mount of prophets), when dubbed "Enoch," spiritual son to an extraordinary individual. Initiated, his soul regenerated with divine life, the poet was not, *for God took him*. Enoch-Lazzarelli dedicated *Epistola Enoch* to "my father Ioannes *Mercurio* de Corigio [*sic*]." Despite Lazzarelli's devotion to autodidact Giovanni, it may yet be that Lazzarelli himself fully acquainted his (younger) "father" with the philosophical background to the name *Mercurio*, for it appears only after meeting the poet and scholar in 1481 did Giovanni da Correggio (born ca. 1451) identify *himself* with Hermes (or Mercurius) Trismegistus, whose sermon given by pupil Asclepius to King Ammon—a Hermetic tract missing from Ficino's *Divine Pymander* of 1471—Lazzarelli had translated as

Fig. 16.3. Viterbo's Community Library in central Viterbo
(currently closed for renovations), where Kristeller discovered
the *Epistola Enoch* and the *Crater Hermetis*.

Definitiones Asclepii, having already made the uniquely staggering assertion that Poimandrēs—supreme nous of libellus 1—was *Christ*.

Lazzarelli made this startlingly clear in his poetic masterpiece *Fasti
christianae religionis* ("Holy Days of the Christian religion") XIII, 377–400:

> Jesus is the Logos and the Word, the Mind and Wisdom,
> who first was Pimander in the mind of Hermes.
> Oh, we happy ones, children of the final age,
> if the awakening mind can grasp such very great blessings!
> The Word that was hidden to the ancients

Becomes apparent in the flesh, to turn us earthlings into gods.
We do not follow Socrates, nor Plato's ancient names;
Christ-worshippers we are called, after the name of Christ.[7]

Prophet Giovanni of Correggio believed the being who regenerated
Hermes had been incarnated in himself, rendering him able to regen-
erate spiritually those who heard him. Lazzarelli was convinced he'd
entered the most sacred confines: Hermetic rebirth's supreme mystery,
which, readers will recall, was pictured in *Pimander* libellus 4 as being
baptized by the "herald" in the Hermetic bowl of nous (*Mind*). While
we often hear *Renaissance* meant "rebirth" of classical learning, here we

Fig. 16.4. Lodovico Lazzarelli with his muse; miniature by an unknown artist from a manuscript of *Fasti christianae religionis* dedicated to King Ferrante (Ferdinand I) of Aragon, Naples, and Sicily, and his Son Alphonso, Duke of Calabria. ca. 1485 (Beinecke Library, MS 391).

have an extraordinary phenomenon enabling us to see what one aspect of reborn ancient learning actually *portended*, for with it, and from it, came Enoch and Hermes Trismegistus not only as an authentic religious message, but living, as it were, reborn in the world!

Possibly the illegitimate offspring of a Bolognese noble family, Giovanni da Correggio first appeared in Rome on November 12, 1481. According to *Epistola Enoch*, he came to the papal palace stairs during a cardinals' consistory meeting, where, holding a Bible closed with seven seals—an apocalyptic reference to Revelation 5:1—he called for repentance, speaking with a firm boldness that in Hanegraaff's words "swept him [Lazzarelli, who was present] off his feet."[8] It's noteworthy that Giovanni's prophetic demonstrations were thoroughly biblical and apocalyptic in content, executed in prophetic manner. Nevertheless, Lazzarelli identified the essence of Giovanni's understanding of repentance as being that of Hermes in the *Pimander*, a copy of which Lazzarelli sent to Giovanni as a gift. In his epistle's second preface, Lazzarelli addressed his master: "You alone have gone through the secret caves of father Hermes, by roads unknown to all, and have returned from there." Hermes taught that to be reborn one must *turn away* from body-centered consciousness and turn toward the divine identity, forgotten when Anthrōpos fell into his reflection in matter. If he but knew it, reborn man is god on earth. *Know thyself!* It would appear Lazzarelli was able to give Giovanni's apocalyptic message a new emphasis, for on Palm Sunday, April 11, 1484, Giovanni entered Rome in entirely different rig.

First, a finely clothed Giovanni entered the city on an ass accompanied by four servants, two walking in front, two at the rear on horses. Leaving the city he donned, at the river Manara, a bloody white mantle and crown of thorns, above which was a crescent moon of silver plate, thus making, with the bloody symbols of the cross, the astrological sign for mercury: transformation. On the crescent was written:

> This is my Servant Pimander, whom I have chosen. This Pimander
> is my supreme and waxing [growing, as in the moon] child, in whom

I am well pleased, to cast out demons and proclaim my judgment and truth to the heathen. Do not hinder him, but hear and obey him with all fear and veneration; thus speaks the Lord your God and Father of every talisman of all the world, Jesus of Nazareth.

Hanging an inkwell from the reins, he took a scepter or staff, made of reed, and possibly a reference to Matthew 11:7–10 where John (Giovanni) the Baptist is compared to a man dressed in "fine clothes" and a reed swaying in a wilderness wind: "What did you go out into the wilderness to see?" asks Jesus of the crowd. "A reed swayed by the wind? If not, what did you go out to see? A man dressed in fine clothes? No, those who wear fine clothes are in kings' palaces. Then what did you go out to see? A prophet? Yes, I tell you, and more than a prophet. This is the one about whom it is written: "I will send my messenger ahead of you, who will prepare your way before you." The reed may also have symbolized the scourging of Christ before crucifixion.

Another biblical reference (this time Ezekiel 9:2–4) accounts for two round, gold disks on chest and back depicting a Hebrew *tav* on a blue-and-black background. The tav would mark the righteous, separating wheat from chaff, the latter to be burned in judgment fire, as John the Baptist declared. Lazzarelli observed texts and symbols on the disks that elicited his amazement: "If I would even begin to relate what was engraved and symbolized thereon, my mind would fail me, nor would there be words capable of describing the magnitude of these sacraments. Immortal God! What secret mysteries and stupendous oracles were laid open there" (*Epistola Enoch* 6:3).

Giovanni also carried boxes black and blue with Latin text from 2 Esdras 7:25: *vacua vacuis, plena plenis*. The full text up to v.28 reveals Giovanni Mercurio's intention: "*for the empty are empty things, and for the full are the full things. Behold, the time shall come, that these tokens which I have told thee shall come to pass, and the bride shall appear, and she coming forth shall be seen, that now is withdrawn from the earth. And whosoever is delivered from the foresaid evils shall see my wonders. For my son Jesus shall be revealed with those that be with him, and they that remain shall rejoice within four hundred years.*"

Taking a human skull in a basket, the two walking servants now mounted horses, wearing sky-blue tunics embroidered with hills surmounted by a star generating lightning and thunder. One held a sheathed sword; another a book. They led Giovanni on his white ass to the gates of St. John's of the Lateran where folk leaving church were addressed with a proclamation of damnation for those not marked by the tav, culminating in three blows against the skull from the reed; men's sins would be avenged. Texts of the sermon were distributed introduced by these words: "I, Giovanni Mercurio of Correggio, the Angel of Wisdom Pimander, in the highest and greatest ecstasy of the Spirit of Jesus Christ evangelize loudly unto all this water of the kingdom for the few" (*Epistola Enoch* 8:3:1).

Given palm branches at the Mass, churchgoers followed the prophet in a scene resembling Christ's entry into Jerusalem. A further sermon at the Campo de' Fioro preceded arrival at St. Peter's. While horsemen of the guard were confused, Lazzarelli reported Giovanni's being permitted entry. He gave out papers and hit the skull again. Dismounting, his servants led the ass to the sanctuary, where Giovanni also dismounted and approached the altar, divesting himself of the bloody mantle and other symbolic attachments before praying on his knees and departing, having left a paper entitled "The Eternal Gospel" (see Revelations 14:6: "And I saw another angel fly in the midst of heaven, having the everlasting gospel to preach unto them that dwell on the earth, and to every nation, and kindred and tongue and people").

Giovanni Mercurio may have been cast into prison by church authorities after this display; Hanegraaff thinks it likely,[9] as possibly suggested by Lazzarelli's comment: "For those who in this world dedicate themselves to divine and spiritual wisdom do not like the multitude, nor does the multitude like them; they are considered insane and are laughed at; at times they may even be hated, maltreated or murdered" (*Epistola Enoch* 4:2; cf. Matthew 23:37). Lazzarelli only says that Giovanni stayed in Rome a while and met people before leaving to rejoin wife and children in Bologna.

In 1486, year of Pico's *Oratio*, Giovanni was arrested at night with two servants by order of Lorenzo dei' Medici, the Magnificent (yes, the

Fig. 16.5. *Façade of St John's of the Lateran.*
Etching by Giovanni Battista Piranesi (1720–1778).

man who secured Pico's release from papal ire, friend of Ficino who revered the Pimander he translated). According to the Este ambassador to Florence, Giovanni was tortured by the Franciscan inquisitor who then publicly humiliated the shackled Giovanni, self-recognized spiritual child of Pimander.[10] This dramatic event was the result of Mercurio's being summoned by King Ferrante (Ferdinand) of Naples, impressed by Lazzarelli's praise of the man from Bologna. Mercurio had the misfortune to stop at Florence en route for Naples. Ferrante wrote to Lorenzo that Giovanni was simply acting on his invitation; Lorenzo let Giovanni go.

In late 1492, Giovanni was in Rome again, shortly after the election of Borgia pope, Alexander VI, who took an interest in matters Hermetic. Giovanni wrote a sonnet, commented on by Carlo Sosenna of Ferrara, which Sosenna recognized as a treatise on spiritual regeneration through seeing that above is a heaven of the Good, and that in the center of the earth is a place where the enemy of humanity rules "the wandering spirits of the wind" (have we not encountered these disembodied souls of giants?). If man turns away from the vanity of competing passions, to initiate an inner ascent to the One above, he will be saved from eternal death confronting those attached to corruptible flesh, self-hallucinated by vision of superficial nature as ultimate reality, blind to their true identity. In Rome Giovanni wore sackcloth and traveled with about a dozen: wife Elena Maria, children, and servants.

The entourage entered Lyons in 1501, after Lazzarelli's death, when Giovanni called a crusade against the Turks and all infidels, seeking food for his family from King Louis XII in return for his gift to the king of promise of an heir and alchemical longevity. Giovanni, the personified spirit and wisdom of Jesus, who now understood all the mysteries and secrets of nature (as Enoch did) was now self-proclaimed alchemist with skill of transmutation, able to change men's fate by natural magic.[11] He also claimed great medical acumen, devoting time to an alchemical plague cure. The king asked two doctors to meet him. One was Lyonnese medical star, Symphorien Champier (1471–1539). According to brilliant abbot of Sponheim Johannes Trithemius (1462–1516), who was informed of the occasion, Giovanni's knowledge of medicine impressed the doctors. Another aspect of the trip was that in offering a work to the king (whom Giovanni first approached on an ass with a scimitar in his hand), he appears to have given Italy's ambassador Lazzarelli's beautiful gift to himself, the *Pimander*, *Asclepius*, and *Definitiones Asclepii*, with three prefaces that comprise the *Epistola Enoch*. The ambassador gave the manuscript to collector Pietro Aleandro, through whose hands it may have passed to become the first published version of the *Definitions* by Symphorien Champier in 1507, and through Aleandro's other contacts in Rome, the manuscript may have come to its rest in Viterbo, north of Rome, where Kristeller found it in the 1930s.[12]

His ultimate fate unknown, Giovanni's impact on Lazzarelli was profound. Lazzarelli believed Giovanni had improved and enriched what was known of the "ancient theology" by dint of divine gift. He had grounds, for Lazzarelli seems to have been impressed by kabbalah to a deep level even before Pico, usually credited as father of Christian Cabalism. Like Pico, Lazzarelli learned from Jewish rabbi and kabbalist philosopher Yohanan Alemanno (ca. 1435–after 1504) who taught Pico Hebrew and impressed him with the view that kabbalah was divine magic. Lazzarelli's kabbalist knowledge is evident in his work most influenced by Giovanni, the "Dialogue on the Supreme Dignity of Man, entitled The Way of Christ and the Mixing-Bowl of Hermes," or simply *Crater Hermetis* (1492–94), whose full title seems to represent a completion of Pico's *Oratio* of 1486. The *Crater* is an imagined dialogue, chiefly between Lazzarelli and King Ferrante of Naples.

After an introduction, Lazzarelli leads the king to encounter the following themes: what Hermes intended by "know yourself" (followed by a prayer to God); an interpretation of the trees in paradise; proverbial wisdom on women; finding spiritual meaning in myths; what Genesis meant by the "daughters of men" whom "sons of God" lusted after (Lazzarelli interpreted them as fallen angels, typifying unregenerated Man); the fall of man; knowledge of self and knowledge of God; the nature of the "true man"; a hymn of contemplation ("contemplation" was Ficino's translation of *gnosis*); divine fertility, or how to generate divine beings (followed by a hymn of divine generation); and the Mystery (of divine generation), followed by a conclusion and hymn of praise in true Hermetic style.

Lazzarelli confessed a period of confusion was alleviated from heaven when "He that was Pimander in the mind of Hermes, has deigned to take up residence within me as Christ Jesus, and has consoled me by illuminating my mind with the light of Truth, being the everlasting Consoler" (*Crater* 1.2). The supreme mystery of divine generation, or how a mind can be transformed into a divine mind involving an ecstatic liberation of the unknown god, he asserts, can only be passed to those fit to hear it; *no new wine for old wineskins*, and the mystery has been kept secret for this reason, lest it be profaned by the ignorant. Daringly he says the *Asclepius* is referring to it in the very passages singled out for condemnation as demonic idolatry by the church and even by scholars otherwise sympathetic to Hermes. The notorious idol-making passages, where Hermes describes how demons were ritually drawn into statues in Egyptian temples, were, according to Lazzarelli's reading, coded references to the static, sleeping human being being brought to rebirth by divine fire. Lazzarelli audaciously compares the same to the appearance of flames above the apostles' heads at Pentecost, when the "old" men were new made into apostles enlightened to preach and persuade; how else could the message of Christ have spread, but by such compelling power of light in darkness, and the example of men who lived what they knew? He finds the same message symbolically conveyed in the *Sefer Izira* (or Yetzirah) in a passage describing how Abraham made new men from red earth ("adam"). Enoch, Lazzarelli believed, had grasped the secret, hence Enoch's translation from bodily sense-life to divine being: "God took him."

Lazzarelli and Enoch

A man who addressed himself to Giovanni in his prefaces as "Ludovicus Enoch Lazzarelli of Sanseverino" was clearly captivated by the identity and idea of Enoch, the significance of whose ascent to heaven he saw as symbolic of the spiritual reality of rebirth. Obviously the emphasis Giovanni paid to God's words in Genesis 3:5: "ye shall be gods" and Jesus's in John 10:33–36: "For a good work we stone thee not; but for blasphemy; and because that *thou, being a man, makest thyself God. Jesus answered them, Is it not written in your law, I said, Ye are gods?* If he called them gods, unto whom the word of God came, and the scripture cannot be broken; Say ye of him, whom the Father hath sanctified, and sent into the world, Thou blasphemest; because I said, *I am the Son of God?*" (my italics)—would have inclined him, to say the least, to see Enoch as exemplar of this potential, revealed in kabbalist texts probably drawn from 3 Enoch.

Lazzarelli's "Hymn of Divine Generation" refers to Enoch in its first lines; the hymn being followed by revelation of soul-making. *Crater* 29.1, just before the *Sefer Izira* passage mentioned above, asserts how Hermes alluded to the mystery frequently, but directly in the *Asclepius*, while "the wise men of the Hebrews" refer to a book written by Enoch where he speaks of a higher and lower king, and that the one who unites them will know great joy from above: an image not found in extant Enochic literature but which probably derives from unpublished mystical texts concerning Enoch-Metatron as revelatory angel.

Lazzarelli must have had access to texts currently unknown, perhaps pseudepigraphical works going under the name of notable rabbis. For example, a passage allegedly from midrash *Berashit Rabbah* in *Crater* 27.7, probably inspired by tenth-century Narbonnese Rabbi Moshe Ha-Darshan's aggadic *Yesod*, is not found in known copies. Then again, the rabbi's writings are known only from fragments in other works; confusion of authorship is endemic to rabbinic commentaries. Attributing *Berashit Rabbah* to "Adersan" (Ha-Darshan), Lazzarelli says the rabbi describes a debate on sacred matters between Talmudists. Rabbi Jonah claims authority from Enoch for mentioning the secret (*generatio mentis*), at which Rabbi Symeon laughs *and* cries before uttering: "This is the will of God, which he does not want to be revealed to any generation until the King Messiah has come, who will give permission for these mysteries to be revealed." For Lazzarelli, this supports his contention that the secret of god-making was revealed by Jesus. For Lazzarelli, this is the number-one secret of the pre-existent Christ, imparted to Hermes, to initiates, and to Giovanni directly, and so to him: "Enoch" symbolizes it.[13]

Another fascinating Enochic reference from Lazzarelli's mind occurs on his pondering Revelation 14:3–4 in *Crater* 14.1's treatment of the "daughters of men" from Genesis 6:2. Revelation reads: "And they sung as it were a new song before the throne, and before the four beasts, and the elders: and no man could learn that song but the hundred and forty and four thousand, which were redeemed from the earth. These are they which were not defiled with women; for they are virgins. These are they which follow the Lamb whithersoever he goeth. These were redeemed from among men, being the firstfruits unto God and to the Lamb." Lazzarelli sees this as an allegorical—to the initiated—sign that followers of the Lamb have not succumbed to earth's seductive passions. These passions Moses in Genesis calls "the daughters of men" to and for whom the "sons of God" fell.

Hanegraaff observes that Lazzarelli was almost certainly cross-referencing here with *Asclepius* 25's lament for a world abandoned by the gods: "How mournful when the gods withdraw from mankind! Only the baleful angels remain to mingle with humans, seizing the wretches and driving them to every outrageous crime—war, looting, trickery and all that is contrary to the nature of souls."[14] This stands out as one of those Hermetic allusions that almost certainly draws on the Book of the Watchers. Indeed, as Hanegraaff notes, scholar Moshe Idel has taken the possibility to the level of direct assertion with his advocating: "one must go a step further and reveal the real figure who is hidden under the name of Hermes: It is Enoch."[15] Very bold, and if true, we may envisage future Enochic and Hermetic studies converging in numerous creative ways.

It's clear Lazzarelli did not have access to 3 Enoch, for had he done so he would have used it, and probably added the name Metatron to Giovanni's escutcheon. There is something distinctly Metatronic about Giovanni's later claims to hold all the secrets of nature, but the text was, for Lazzarelli, one that got away. Still, he intuited quite correctly and clearly, as well as uniquely, the import of such traditions of Enoch as entered kabbalist understanding: Enoch had the *gnosis*, and Lazzarelli got the message.

And here's the message: Man's failure was to attach himself too much to the physical; in doing so he lost extra-dimensional vision and perception of the invisible. God is only envisioned by those for whom the invisible, with infinite dimensions, has become real and perceptible. Out of his failure, Man became prey to demonic impulses that serve the physical realm. To be reborn to his proto-heavenly state, he must will to ascend to his true home; he must rise out of his darkness and the spiritual blindness of matter. He can accomplish this because he is made in the divine image. He has free will, and may, and must, rely on his knowledge of God. The beauty of the body and the created realm is good if the perception of it is focused on and directed to the divinity from which it came, whose vestiges may be discerned by the initiated within it; otherwise he will be swallowed up in materiality as in a flood. The holy spirit is the light of God within us, and to come to know this divine dignity is to be reborn into a new perceptual setting, to become fearlessly acquainted with the infinite and the eternal: the nature of divine life itself.

As one rises, the power of love becomes more evident than the presence of knowledge; the result: ecstasy of praise, music beyond words. Having arrived at the outer courts of heaven, the soul is bidden to enter God's lucid darkness, wherein lives the source of divine fertility, the ability to call forth being from nothingness. So for Lazzarelli, the critical words of Genesis are: "Be fruitful and multiply," an imperative guarding the spiritual secret that the True Man can generate new spiritual beings: an *imitatio dei* open to the cleansed and the reborn. When one "knows oneself," one perceives and experiences the divine generative character, and as Abraham created souls at Harran according to the *Sefer Izira*, so the en-graced Christian Hermetist can create spiritual beings. Thus, "ye shall be as gods," knowing good and evil (Genesis 3:5). Lazzarelli's wholesale, reverent sublimation of biblical memes to this brilliantly erudite conception is unique, and for him at least, constituted the hidden promise of Enochic revelation. For Lazzarelli, it came from the source, unmediated. It took the "fool" Mercurio da Correggio to make him see.

SEVENTEEN

John Dee, Guillaume Postel, and the Book of Enoch

In Paris, around 1600, French scholar Isaac Casaubon found a rare manuscript copy of George Syncellus's *Chronography*, transcribed in 1021 CE (now MS Bibliotheque Nationale *gr.* 1711). Casaubon's transcription of Syncellus's Greek extracts from the Book of Enoch were then published in Latin by fellow scholar Joseph Justus Scaliger (1540–1609) in his *Thesaurus Temporum* (Leiden, 1606). After that, the notion of a complete Enoch text passed out of legend into a state of frustrating fact, and while Scaliger himself dismissed the Syncellus fragments as a Jewish forgery, interest in Enoch's reputation remained very much alive.

One figure gripped by the idea of obtaining the complete book was French diplomat, linguist, and Christian Cabalist Guillaume Postel (1510–1581). Thanks to Postel, scholars would duly learn at least *where* the book might be found.

Finding books was Postel's passion. Sent to Constantinople in 1536 as the French embassy's official interpreter to Sultan Suleiman, Postel's collecting bore fruit in pioneering works on Semitic languages. His mind opened through encounters with non-Christians with similar beliefs, Postel began to promulgate the idea of a world religion uniting all peoples. The key was *language*, which, after Babel, had divided mankind. The idea of an original Adamic language known to Enoch,

Fig. 17.1. Portrait of Guillaume Postel, possibly by François Clouet (died 1572).

deviser of writing and communicator with angels, shot to the core of the problem: the root of language. Original *names* held magical power; God's *Word* made the universe, and when Adam named the animals, they obeyed.

Returning to Europe, Postel's unconventional ideas provoked dismissal from the Jesuit Order, but by 1547, Pope Paul III thought well enough of him to summon his knowledge of Chaldean and Arabic to answer letters from an extraordinarily knowledgable Portuguese woman. Postel got to know the visionary as "Mother Zuana," or Mother Johanna. Convinced the soul consisted of intellect (male) and emotion or heart (female), with their union necessary for spiritual rebirth, he believed a female messiah was vital to redeem the heart—and *he* had found her. *She* called him spiritual son, divinely commissioned to show the world the true path to restore human dignity.

In Rome Postel met the pope's former secretary, orientalist, and

Fig. 17.2. Guillaume Postel's *Histoire et Consideration de L'origine, Loy, et Coustume des Tartares, Persiens, Arabes, Turcs, & tous autres Ismaelites ou Muhamediques, dits par nous Mahometains, ou Sarrazins,* Poitiers: Enguilbert de Marnes, 1560. (Bibliothèque Nationale de France)

Copernicus advocate, Johann Albertus Widmanstadt (1506–1557), now working for a princely German cardinal. Widmanstadt ignited Postel's burgeoning interest in kabbalah, which Postel linked to his vision of the "eternal gospel." In Venice, he began translating the *Sefer Bahir*, and obtained a manuscript of the *Zohar* from Hebrew printing pioneer Daniel Bomberg, studying it with Mother Johanna. Scholars today credit kabbalist Rabbi Moses de León (ca. 1240–1305; fl. Spain) with authorship of the *Zohar*, though he claimed only to be *referring* to a work of the Tannaitic period. Annette Yoshiko Reed observes that in Moses de León's book about Eden (*Sefer Mishkan ha-'Edut* in Adolph Jellinek, *Bet ha-Midrasch: Sammlung kleiner Midraschim und vermischter Abhandlungen aus der jüdischen Literatur* [BHM], Leipzig, 1853–1877, vol. 2, xxxi), he claims he "saw . . . esoteric books of wisdom (containing) the supernal wisdom of the ancients which recount what they said was in the Book of Enoch," describing knowledge of the firmament, cosmos, angels, heaven, and the Garden of Eden. He then states that "they have said in the Book of Enoch, the one known to the ancient sages because it recounts all the features of the Garden . . . that there are three walls in the Garden, arranged concentrically . . . Enoch stated that he saw them, but did not learn who they were or what they signified. . . . And this esoteric mystery was revealed in his book for the sages: before Adam the protoplast had been introduced there, the Garden was not empty. . . . Watch and wait for the truth of the matter, for it is all to be found in the Book (of Enoch), and therein are marvellous things" (BHM, vol. 2, xxxii).[1] Also, Menahem ben Benjamin Recanati (1223–1290; fl. Italy) in *Perush Bereshit* in BHM vol. 3, 197–98 associates a "Book of Enoch" with knowledge about Eden, without any claim to have seen it: "I have seen where some of the recent kabbalistic sages have written that they have found this esoteric topic [Eden] written about together with a number of other marvellous mysteries in the Book of Enoch, the son of Yared, the one whom God took (to heaven). Our Sages of blessed memory have previously mentioned that book in the Zohar." (Jellinek, "Hebräische Quellen für das Buch Henoch," *Zeitschrift der Deutschen Morgenländischen Gesellschaft* [magazine of the German Oriental Society], no. 7, 1853, 249. Fabricius cites Recanati in *Codex pseudepigraphus Veteris Testamenti*, Hamburg, 1713, 208–9, deducing that an Enochic book "exists among the Jews" (208).[2] See John C. Reeves, Annette Yoshiko Reed, *Enoch from Antiquity to the Middle Ages*, vol. 1, Oxford, 2018.

In 1551, Postel's *De Etruriae regionis*, published in Florence, insisted the Book of Enoch's prophecies were canonical in distant Ethiopia. Two years later, Postel's thoughts regarding books of Enoch and Noah, and his search for the Edenic language through the origins of Turks, Tartars, Persians, and mysteries of the Brachmans,

De Originibus, seu, de varia et potissismum orbi Latino ad hanc diem incognita ("On the Origins, or, of various and especially regions related to Latin unknown to this day"), was published by Johannes Oporinus at Basel's relatively free press. In it, Postel described how in Rome an Ethiopian priest (*sacerdote Aethiope*) explained to him that in the Church of the Queen of Sheba the books of Enoch and of Noah shared canonical authority with Moses, having been preserved to Moses's time in Chaldean. The priest explained the substance and context of the books' argument that helped Postel understand various histories. Seeing Ethiopian script (Ge'ez), Postel thought it derived from what he understood as "Chaldean."* This all fired Postel's conviction of an original language known to Enoch and familiar to the angels that prophesied the world's destiny.

Synthesizing linguistic discoveries with his visionary faith, Postel produced *De Restitutione humane naturae* ("On the restitution of human nature"), which, though sent to Basel for publication, was seized beforehand by the Inquisition. Postel would eventually be imprisoned at Ripetta (1555–59), accused of insanity—possibly to save him from a capital heresy charge.

Before imprisonment, he spent two years in the Middle East, whence he returned to France to hear Johanna had died: painful news that in 1551 led to a mystical experience that convinced him she had possessed his body for several weeks. Calling himself the new Elijah he preached in earnest about his Mother Johanna.

Enter John Dee

Meanwhile, England's leading mathematician, John Dee (1527–1608), was nearing the end of a long educational tour of the continent. In Paris in 1551 he lectured on Euclid's *Elements* so successfully a profes-

---

*The Latin of the book's subtitle reads: *ex libris Noachi et Henochi, totiusque avitae traditionis a Moysis tempore servatae et Chaldaicis litteris conscriptae.* Postel's account of his meeting reads: "Audivi esse Romae librorum Enoch argumentum, et contextum mihi a sacerdote Aethiope (ut in Ecclesia Reginae Sabba habetur pro Canonico libro instar Moseos) expositum, ita ut sit mihi varia supellex pro Historiae varietate."

sorial appointment in mathematics was offered, which he declined, intending return to England with numerous astronomical instruments he hoped would impress King Edward VI's court. Before leaving Paris, Postel encouraged Dee's interest in kabbalah and "occult" or hidden knowledge. Dee's personal copy of Postel's *De Originibus*, with its account of the Book of Enoch, is now in London's Royal College of Physicians library, among more than one hundred books stolen from Dee's library while he was in central Europe in the 1580s. The surviving copy shows whoever stole it tried to bleach Dee's name from the title page, but retained Dee's annotations and notes on Enoch, Adam, Hebrew letters, and what he spelt as "cabala" (kabbalah).

Fig. 17.3. *John Dee*, aged 67 (ca. 1595); Ashmolean Museum, Oxford.

In England, Dee pursued his scientific interests to the limits of the known. What he sought pointed to unknown and untested regions. Enoch's reputation for knowing everything because guided by angels became for Dee a lodestone. By 1579 at least, he was praying that God show him what God showed Enoch in heaven.

Dee's fervency became public knowledge in 1659 when Isaac Casaubon's son Meric edited a collection of Dee's "angelical conferences" undertaken with "skryer" Edward Kelley, who between 1581 and 1585 progressively manipulated Dee, possibly duping himself in the process. In British Library, MS. Sloane 3188 (folio 7a; saved originally from destruction by Elias Ashmole), Dee writes: "I have often read in thy [God's] books & records, how Enoch injoyed thy favour and conversation; with Moses thou was familiar; And also that to Abraham, Isaack and Jacob, Joshua, Gideon, Esdras, Daniel, Tobias & sundry others thy good angels were sent by thy disposition, to Instruct them." In folio 5a of MS Sloane 3188, Dee states that he had prayed "from the year 1579 in approximately this manner, in Latin or English (and furthermore in another singular and particular manner around the year 1569, sometimes for Raphael and sometimes for Michael) it was most pleasing to me to pour forth prayers to God. May God grant his wonderful mercy to me Amen."[3]

The point about the scientific legitimacy of angelic guidance he had noted previously in his famous "Mathematicall Preface" to Henry Billingsley's translation of Euclid's *Elements* (1570). Since man is made in the image of God, he may, if deemed righteous, potentially enjoy intercourse with spirits and angels.

Through scryer Edward Kelley's mediumship, Dee was instructed to obtain the angelic language. That "angelicall tongue," as he called it, has since become known as "Enochian," chiefly because Kelley's angels began dictating to him via medium of a polished shew-stone a curious work Dee and Kelley began calling the "Book of Enoch," either because Dee believed it was in the language known to Enoch, or because he thought it linked to the original book.

An angel—apparently Gabriel in the record of Saturday, July 7, 1584, in Cracow, Poland—rebuked Dee and Kelley for not understanding what they were involved with:

Ave [Greetings] . . . My brother, I see thou do not understand the mystery of this Book, or work thou hast in hand. But I told thee, it was the knowledge that God *delivered unto Enoch*. I said also, that Enoch laboured 50 dayes. Notwithstanding, that they labour be not frustrate, and void of fruit, Be it unto thee, *as thou hast done*.

Fig. 17.4. Edward Kelley as depicted in Meric Casaubon's *A True & Faithful Relation of What Passed for Many Years Between Dr. John Dee and Some Spirits* (1659).

Edw: Kelly *Prophet or Seer to D.ʳ Dee.*

The angel then explains the work of the fifty days:

He made, (as thou hast done, thy book) Tables, of Serfasan [*sic*] and plain stone: as the Angel of the Lord appointed him; saying, tell me (O Lord) the number of the dayes that I shall labour in? It was answered to him 50. Then he groaned within himself, saying, Lord God the Fountain of true wisdom, thou that open up the secrets of thy own self to man, thou knowest mine imperfection, and my inward darkness: How can I (therefore) speak unto them that speak not after the voice of man; or worthily call on thy name, considering that my imagination is variable and fruitless, and unknown to my own self? Shall the sands seem to invite the Mountains: or can the small rivers entertain the wonderful and unknown waves?

Enoch's prayer continues: "Thou shalt light me, and I will become a Seer; I will see thy Creatures, and will magnify thee amongst them. . . . Then, lo the Tables* (which I have provided, and according to thy will, prepared) I offer unto thee, and unto thy holy angels, desiring them, in and through thy holy names . . . O Lord, Is there any that measure the heavens, that is mortal? How, therefore, can the heavens enter man's imagination? Thy Creatures are the glory of thy countenance . . ." (Casaubon's *A True & Faithful Relation of What Passed for Many Years Between Dr. John Dee and Some Spirits*, 196). Dee was more than ready to believe the angels would lead him to the original book *through* the book. Indeed, there are passages discerned by Kelley in the shew-stone implying acquaintance with Enochic traditions of good and evil angels; for example:

> The Lord appeared unto Enoch, and was mercifull unto him, opened his eyes, that he might see and judge the earth, which was unknown unto his Parents, by reason of their fall: for the Lord said, Let us shew unto Enoch, the use of the earth: And lo, Enoch was wise, and full of the spirit of wisdom. And he sayed unto the Lord, Let there be remembrance of thy mercy and let those that love me taste of this after me: O let not thy mercy be forgotten. And the Lord was pleased.
>
> And after 50 dayes Enoch had written: and this was the Title of his books, let those that fear God, and are worthy read.
>
> But behold, the people waxed wicked, and became unrighteous and the spirit of the Lord was far off. And gone away from them. So that those that were unworthy began to read. And the Kings of the earth said thus against the Lord, What is it that we cannot do? Or who is he, that can resist us? And the Lord was vexed, and he sent in amongst them one hundred and fifty Lions, and spirits of wickedness, error and deceit: and they appeared unto them: for the Lord had put them between those that are wicked, and his good

---

*Regarding the "Tables." While referring primarily to the "holy tables" Kelley's angels had the pair construct for interpreting the angelic language, the "Tables" may also cross-reference to the "tablets" revealed to Enoch in heaven in 1 Enoch, and, arguably, the "tablets" of knowledge inscribed by Thoth-Hermes (see page 209). The English tablet originally meant a small table, which is what Dee and Kelley used.

Angels; And they began to counterfeit the doings of God and his power, for they had power given them so to do, so that the memory of Enoch washed away: and the spirits of error began to teach them Doctrines: which from time to time unto this age, and unto this day, hath spread abroad into all parts of the world, and is the skill and cunning of the wicked.

Hereby they speak with the Devils: not because they have power over the Devils, but because they are joined unto them in the league and Discipline of their own Doctrine.

For behold, as the knowledge of the mystical figures, and the use of their presence is the gift of God delivered to Enoch, and by Enoch his request to the faithfull, that thereby they might have the true use of Gods creatures, & of the earth whereon they dwell: So hath the Devil delivered unto the wicked the signs, and tokens of his error and hatred toward God: whereby they in using them, might consent with their fall: and so become partakers with them of their reward, which is eternal damnation.

These they call Characters: a lamentable thing. For by these, many Souls have perished.

Now hath it pleased God to deliver this Doctrine again out of darkness: and to fulfill his promise with thee, for the books of Enoch: to whom he sayeth as he said to Enoch.

Let those that are worthy understand this, by thee, that it may be one witness of my promise toward thee.

Come therefore, O thou Cloud, and wretched darkness, Come forth I say out of this Table: for the Lord again hath opened the earth: and she shall become known to the worthy.
(*True Relation*, 174 [1659])

The passage is followed by long, complex instructions to fill the square line-grids of the square tables with letters to make words (?) such as: *rZilafAntlpa*; *Vastrim*; *ardza*; *aLOai*; *aozpi*; *Lexarph*; *Comanan*; *Tabitom*.

One thing Kelley was quick to get right was to allay Dee's anxiety. Kelley's angels assured Dee that their sins were forgiven because

God had a very special commission for them. They were to be prophets, God's representatives in a great change, a new age for the world. They were *sanctified*, said the angels, for the task. *God had taken them . . .*

Fig. 17.5. Dee and Kelley's holy table as recreated by 3D computer model in 2007 (Image by The .:X).

One feature of the "Liber Logaeth," as the unfolding work was called, is that the peculiar language Kelley *first* recited as angelic has been analyzed by linguistic experts as trance-glossolalia, different to the syntactical language constructed after alleged angelic instructions to build tables of letter correspondences within the "Liber Logaeth." Kelley seems to have assembled his angelical language in stages, with the result that many of the words generated from cross-referencing the holy tables' letter-grids during long séances emerged as random consonantal monstrosities, while others had an intriguing faery-like ring, with tendencies to the letter z and the vowel *a*: a lot of "zaza's." Nevertheless, Kelley and his voices created an attractively magical, pictographically arcane, and grimoire-friendly script, as well as original verbs and nouns, with a grammar structurally English, that practitioners today claim has a magical effect on the imagination when uttered respectfully. There's something to be said in magical practice for the sound effect of words that appear meaningless, as with the "barbarous words of evocation" familiar to Egyptian Gnostic magical spells.

The angels instructed their communicants to construct nineteen "Calls." Recited in the angelic language, they were believed to open thirty "Aires" or inner-plane extra-dimensional worlds that revealed visionary images and secret instruction. Each Aire was guarded by angels, akin to the storehouses of cosmic powers to which Enoch was introduced in the Dream Visions.

Dee himself would have been utterly horrified if he thought for a minute he was an accomplice to grimoire magic of the old devilish kind, but was convinced by Kelley's adoption of apocalyptic, Bible-like phrasing that the voices came whence Kelley told him they did, resulting from fervent prayer and sublime exaltation of spirit granted to unworthy but repentant sinners, though occasionally Dee—or pre-empting him, Kelley—questioned the import of matters conveyed, such as nudity characterizing the redeemed, or sharing wives. Kelley had his way with Dee's wife, but Kelley's would not physically commit to Dee.

In the end, finding continental patrons willing to keep him for the sake of his alchemical boasts, Kelley abandoned Dee. After initial success (and a knighthood) it ended badly for Kelley (see my Ashmole biography *The Magus of Freemasonry* [2007]; Elias Ashmole preserved Dee's secret papers). The prophet had turned to profit, but poor Dee, back in England with declining fortunes, never got over the excitement experienced when he first believed he was playing a pivotal role in a supra-cosmic operation to prophesy divine science, calling all souls from this "earthly scaffold," as Dee called it, to the universal light of God. Maybe there was *something* in Kelley's angels, and Kelley's Enoch, after all:

> In 40 dayes more must this boke [book] be perfyted [perfected] in his own marks to the intent that you also may be perfyted in the workmanhip of him, which hath sealed it.
>
> Oute of this shall be restored the holy bokes [books], which have perished even from the begynning, and from the first that lived
>
> And herein shalbe deciphred [deciphered] perfect truth from

imperfect falshode [falsehood], True religion from fals [false] and damnable errors, With all Artes,

which are propre [proper] to the use of man, the first and sanctified perfection: Which when it hath spread a While, THEN COMMETH THE ENDE.[4]

Dee was not alone in foreseeing a great restoration of man and knowledge of nature, an incipient millennium of revelation when God would reveal his secrets before the final judgment. How kings, queens, and their subjects responded to the prophetic good news that would enliven the minds of many scientists in the seventeenth century would decide their fate in the end. Dee earnestly wished to play his part both in the revelation of an absolute science, physical and metaphysical, that led men to God, and in the prophetic task of announcing it. There were men who followed him, if discreetly, recognizing his contribution to both missions for the well-being of fallen humanity.

EIGHTEEN

A Rosicrucian Fludd and Freemasonry

*Our Philosophia is nothing new, but is the same which
Adam received after his fall and which Moses and
Solomon applied. . . . And as he [Jesus] is the true Image
of the Father, so is she ["our Philosophia"] his Image;
Thus it should not be said: "This is true according to
philosophy but false according to theology," for everything
which Plato, Aristotle, Pythagoras, and others recognized
as true, and which was decisive for Enoch, Abraham,
Moses, and Solomon and which above all is consistent
with that wonderful book the Bible, comes together,
forming a sphere or ball in which all the parts are
equidistant from the centre, as hereof more at large and
more plain shall be spoken of in Christianly Conference.*
FAMA FRATERNITATIS ("THE FAME OF THE FRATERNITY"),
CASSELL, GERMANY, 1614[1]

I n the year 1610, a mysterious manuscript circulated in the Tyrol
signed by the "Brothers R.C." It seemed to promise a second
European reformation through the self-revelation of a hidden fraternity
possessing transformative knowledge from the East to initiate a golden
age of unheard-of spiritual and scientific advance. Pirated in 1614

for a publication printed by Wilhelm Wessell in Cassell, it appeared with an extract from Venetian satirist Trajano Boccalini's *News from Parnassus*, entitled "On the Reformation of the Whole Wide World," together with a moving account of what happened to Tyrolean doctor Adam Haslmayr when attempting to find the Brotherhood. Arrested by Jesuit inquisitor Hyppolyt Guarinoni, Haslmayr was sentenced to the galleys in 1612. The "Fame of the Fraternity" was followed in 1615 with a "Confession of the Fraternity." When Lazarus Zetzner published a third work apparently from the Brotherhood, in Strasbourg in 1616: *The Chemical Wedding of Christian Rosencreutz*, it was presumed "R.C." stood for *Rosen Creuz* ("Rose Cross"), thus the brotherhood's nickname "Rosicrucians."*

The first so-called Rosicrucian manifesto had invited all sympathizers with its aims to make contact, despite leaving no contact address. Before long, concerned persons imagined the hidden Brotherhood's apparent (or nonapparent) omniscience would "know" supporters' minds, and merely publishing a response would secure attention. A "furore" quickly ensued with booklets for or against the Brotherhood flying across an anxious continent. While reaction came chiefly from Protestant countries, France generated its own reactionary scare stories. Were not these subversive brethren infernally *invisible*?—this in an era of witch trials while Rosicrucians promised that perilous attainment: *enlightenment*.

Learned Paracelsian Dr. Robert Fludd (1574–1637) became an early English supporter in print after German doctor Andreas Libavius (1555–1616) criticized the manifestos for adhering to macrocosm-microcosm theory, and for tolerating "Magia" and "Cabala," all of which Fludd greatly favored. Libavius regarded microcosm-macrocosm theory as metaphor taken too literally, namely, that human anatomy mirrored, through correspondences, the cosmos, with health influenced by astrology, as Ficino had taught—wishful thinking to Libavius, but to

---

*For a thorough account of the Rosicrucian movement, see this author's *The True Story of the Rosicrucians* (2008), and for the movement's links with Enoch, see *The Lost Pillars of Enoch* (2021).

Fig. 18.1. *Fama Fraternitatis* (including Boccalini's "General Reformation of the whole wide World," Cassell: Wilhelm Wessell, 1614.)

Fludd, cornerstones of his practice. In his Rosicrucian defense *Apologia Compendiaria, Fraternitatem de Rosea Cruce suspicionis*, &c. (Leyden, 1616), Fludd hoped for recognition as a junior brother.

The following year, Fludd delivered his three-part *Tractatus Theologo-Philosophicus* on life, death, and resurrection to Oppenheim printer Johann Theodore de Bry, Fludd's chief authorities being the Bible, Hermes Trismegistus, Plato, and Dionysius the Areopagite.

In chapter 5, Adam is formed in a time of light when the earth was God's temple. His breath of life contained a portion of the divine trinity: light of the Father, splendor of the Son, and divine knowledge and intelligence of the Spirit, as Trismegistus, in Fludd's interpretation, taught. Chapter 6 asks what God's breath of life is. It is eternal life, which is God's son. All was well so long as Adam's mind concentrated on God and not the sphere of generation, the body. After the fall, the true light was carried by initiates lest the world scoff at it; the world

Fig. 18.2. Oil painting:
Dr Robert Fludd; Wellcome
Collection gallery.

being those for whom love of the body is irresistible. Fludd says the *light* is what the Rosicrucians mean by their promise of "treasure": more, they said, than the King of Spain brings from the Indies! Ordinary men believed the Brotherhood was incredibly wealthy, having powers of transmutation; Fludd sees the spiritual meaning. The Rosicrucian's unseen "House of the Holy Spirit" is where the spirit of wisdom finds congenial home among men. That wisdom is breath of Eden.

The book's third part examines the Resurrection. Christ's triumph explains why our minds can be raised now, bodies later. Enoch and Elijah are exemplars: born in sin and mortal, but by God's power regenerated. As fire always rises, fire is an image of divine spirit. The risen Christ's body was purified of materiality by spiritual light; such will renovate man like the bodies of Enoch and Elijah, raised to heaven. Enoch and Elijah show what can happen to men of earth if they recover wisdom, and the *love of her*, or what the *Fama* calls "our Philo*sophia*," our love of wisdom, second of the trinity, and source of the dignity of the tree of life's second sefira: Hokma. Human life is currently ruled by the Devil, prince of this world, but the new heaven and new earth are coming, and those who respond to the Brotherhood's holy call may look to the divine sun above, and raise their heads, that is their minds, toward it and become gathered into the light.

Philosophia Moysaica, published a year after Fludd's death in 1637, links the theme of the breath of life Adam first received in Eden to the figure of Metatron. The soul and intelligence that sustain the natural creation Fludd understands as the *anima mundi*, or "soul of the world." That is what Adam had to accept to become a living soul. The anima mundi Fludd identifies with the Cabalists' Metatron, into whom Enoch is transformed by the Holy One in 2 Enoch's tenth chapter. That Fludd doesn't follow this line exactly is chiefly because he wishes his readers to recognize Metatron in a more august identity. Metatron in 3 Enoch is given a throne and plenipotentiary powers. Fludd wants his readers to recognize only one figure worthy to sit at God's right hand.

> The more secret Theologians and those most expert in true Cabbala say that just as Mind has domination in the human Soul, thus does Mettatron [*sic*] in the celestial world, where he rules from the Sun, and the Soul of the Messiah in the Angelic world, and Adonai in the Archetypal. And to the degree that the active intellect of Mind is the light of the soul, even so the light of that same Mettatron or World's Soul is Sadai, and the light of the Messiah's soul is Elchai, which signifies the living God, and the light of Adonai is Ensoph, signifying the infinity of Divinity. The world's soul is therefore Mettatron, whose light is the soul of the Messiah or of the Tetragrammaton's virtue, in which is the light of the living God, in which is the light of Ensoph, beyond which there is no progression.[2]

"I will begin my relation," writes Fludd, "with the Cabalist's Great Angell, whom they call Mitattron: which by interpretation, is *Donum Dei*, the Gift of God, which as they say is the catholick intellectuall Agent, from which all peculiar forms do descend. . . . And this was that catholick angelicall Spirit, which God sent out as a Spirituall Messenger from himself, and out of himself, in the form of an emanation, to move upon the waters, and to inform and vivify them, and give life and being, not only to the great world, but also to every particular thereof, and the emanation was this Word of God, by whom all things were made, and vivified, forasmuch as in it was life: I mean that . . . By the Word of the Lord the heavens were framed and setled, and by the breath of his mouth, all the virtues thereof, namely, the life, preservation, and being."

"Mettatron is nothing else," Fludd insists, "but that universall Spirit of Wisdome which God sent out of his own mouth, as the greatest gift and token of his benignity unto each world, and the members thereof: to reduce them from deformity, and nonexistence, into act and formall being. . . . And this therefore was termed rightly in the eies [eyes] of wise men Mitattron or *Donum Dei catholicum*, which reduceth the universall Nothing into a universall Something."[3]

Remarkably, Robert Fludd interprets, and seemingly translates "Mitattron" as *donum dei*, universal "gift of God," something that had to be received and *accepted*: the gift or inner life of creation. As I explain in *The Lost Pillars of Enoch* (2021), "Donum Dei" is the expression we find in an important engraving by Henry Vaughan in Elias Ashmole's *Theatrum Chemicum Britannicum* ("British Alchemical Theatre," 1652) where the would-be adept kneels before the seated master, and kisses a holy book, promising to keep alchemical secrets secret. The master imparts a secret to initiate him, saying: *"Accipe donum Dei sub sigillo sacrato,"* that is: "Accept the gift of God under the sacred seal." The scene takes place on a (Masonically?) checkered floor before two pillars joining which is an arch, behind which is a veil illuminated by two angels and a bird with outstretched wings (dove of Holy Spirit?) whose head is illuminated by a glory of coruscating light.

It happens that Fludd's "Mosaic Philosophy" was published in 1638, coincidentally the same year that the Renter Warden's accounts of the London Company of Freemasons—the organization that governed trade among London's master masons of freestone (sculptor-architects)—show three past masters of the company, including arguably England's finest sculptor, Nicholas Stone (1586–1647), attending a special meeting in the city of London, where, as the accounting entry states, they were "taken into the Accepcon [Acception]."

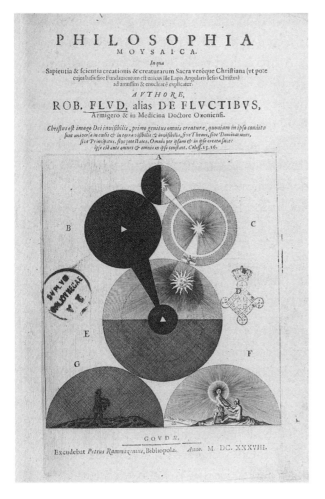

Fig. 18.3. Title page of Robert
Fludd's *Philosophia moysaica.*
In qua sapientia & scientia
creationis & creaturarum
sacra vereque Christiana . . .
ad amussim & enucleate
explicatur. . . . Goudae: Petrus
Rammazenius, 1638.

My chapter "Enoch and the Genesis of Freemasonry" (in
Rediscovering Enoch?, 2023) contains a supported hypothesis that the
occasion may have represented a symbolic acceptation of a *donum dei* to
the livery company's senior members, formally receiving a secret relating
to the creative, animating anima mundi, without which the inanimate
remains inanimate.[4] In this regard we should reflect on the nature and
mythos of sculpture, with perhaps a hint of the Hermetic *Asclepius* on
en-spiriting statues.

Evidence suggests a link between Fludd and the Company of
Freemasons—he lived round the corner from company headquar-
ters. A Mister Fludd provided a Bible for Acceptions. Elias Ashmole

(1617–1692), who commissioned Vaughan's engraving, was not only an alchemical initiate, but recorded his attending a dinner for "newly accepted masons" in 1682. Ashmole had been "made a Free-mason" in Warrington near Chester in 1646, and knew how to keep a secret.

Incidentally, Fludd fought a "paper war" with French polymath Marin Mersenne (1548–1648) over *prisca theologia* themes advocated in Florence by Ficino and Pico. Jesuit-educated Mersenne denied authority to many of Fludd's cherished sources, taking particular exception to Fludd's interpretation of tradition, such as the—to Mersenne absurd or impious—identification of Christ with "Mettatron" and anima mundi (soul of the world).

Interlude: The First Commentary on 1 Enoch by Pompeo Sarnelli (1710)

Gabriele Boccaccini has recently drawn scholarly attention to Bishop of Bisceglie, Pompeo Sarnelli's commentary on Enoch: the "first commentary specifically and exclusively devoted to the apocryphal text."[5] Appearing in 1710—six years before first suggestion of London's "Grand Lodge" of "Free and Accepted Masons"—Sarnelli (1649–1724) believed Enoch penned four books: (a) the Prophecy, (b) the Astronomy, (c) the History, and (d) the Book of the Watchers. While ancient authors referred to all four, Sarnelli believed the first three lost, excepting the quotation in Jude.

Perusing his Enoch texts, based on Scipione Sgambati's 1703 edition, quoted in Latin and translated into Italian, Sarnelli celebrated how Enoch "lives now with Elijah in the Earthly Paradise . . . and before the Last Judgment . . . he will come back to preach to his sons (that is, all humans), and will be killed . . . by the Antichrist but . . . risen from the dead after three days and half will ascend [to heaven] in glory."[6] Sarnelli dealt with the issue of sinful angels thus: "Incorporeal natures are not affected by carnal desires . . . but demons instigate men to those. . . . The purpose of the demons was to introduce so much corruption into the world that it would go to ruin; as it happened."[7] Evil has a supernatural origin, Sarnelli asserts: "we have to fight not against humans but against demons . . . until the Day of Judgment."[8] Sarnelli followed the conservative line on miscegenation: corruption was not from demons impregnating women but because "the seeds of Seth and Cain were mixed."[9] From an Enoch fragment about Uriel warning Noah about the Flood, Sarnelli concludes: "all revelations are made through the Angels, as affirms St. Dionysius the Areopagite."[10]

In Sarnelli's chapter 20—"The Fable of the Hebrews taken from the Book of the Watchers"—he asserts the fallen angels story suffers Jewish misunderstanding when "they" claim good angels Azael and "Samchazi" were permitted by God to demonstrate righteousness to men but fell into temptation of women. Sarnelli reports a story of one Esther obtaining a revelation from Samchazi that made her famous: "This is the Kabbalah of the Rabbis, which perverts all Scripture."[11] Sarnelli believed that while Azael refused repentance, Jews offered him a goat on the Day of Atonement (a reference to the scapegoat covered with the people's sin and sent out to the wilderness).

Sarnelli accuses Jews of falsity and blasphemy, echoing Augustine's incredulity regarding corruptible angels: "How many words, how many blasphemies: because the spirits do not fall in love with the flesh, and especially the good angels. . . . He who has a clear vision of God cannot sin."[12]

Sarnelli rounds off by recommending a golden cenotaph to Enoch be erected, for "while he transformed his disciples into angels, he was taken by the angels and transferred to where from the scythe of death he gathers the years and centuries in bundles. Freed from the company of the living, he survives the dead, young and old at the same time. Spectator of the Universe, he sets up the extreme spectacle for it. At the end of the world he will start his fight with the Antichrist, and killed, he will kill the killer. Know therefore, O Wanderer, that Enoch does not rest here. When he rests, everyone will rest. So cry before he rests and comes."[13]

Boccaccini notes Sarnelli's approval of Enoch, his front-page subtitle describing it as "apocryphal for too much antiquity. Very ancient work, and very new, without authority; but not without benefit to scholars." Holding it to be genuine prophecy, the bishop found its doctrine consistent with the church fathers.

Boccaccini concludes that Sarnelli's commentary, along with Manin's (see pages 19-20) "demonstrates that common claims about 1 Enoch as a book 'lost' to Judaism and Mediterranean Christianity for several centuries until its rediscovery in Ethiopia at the end of the eighteenth century [Bruce] are largely exaggerated."[14]

Enter the Grand Lodge

We should doubtless know more about the London Company of Freemasons' "Acception" were it not that London lodge organization underwent an effective takeover in the early to mid-eighteenth century when, according to uncorroborated statements in Rev. James Anderson's *New Book of Constitutions of the Free-Masons* (1738) members from four London Lodges met at the Apple Tree Tavern, Covent Garden, in 1716 and decided to call themselves a "Grand Lodge" for purposes of assembling the following year for an annual feast on St. John the Baptist Day (June 24, 1717) to elect a "Grand Master" from among themselves, that is, until a noble could be found. Whether or not this actually happened in the manner described, there was, by 1723, a functioning Grand Lodge, and their noble Grand Master was Whig aristocrat, the Duke of Montagu. Montagu and his cronies commissioned cleric and Scottish "admitted mason" Anderson (also a Whig supporter) to write novel *Constitutions* and rules that effectively severed the new Grand Lodge from any oversight by the London Company of Masons in Masons Avenue. According to Anderson, in the years preceding, valuable documents, including one by Nicholas Stone, were destroyed to prevent their getting into "strange hands."[15] One wonders whose hands the alleged destroyers were concerned about. London's Hanoverian-oriented Grand Lodge soon became the Grand Lodge of England with jurisdiction over English territories. Scottish Masons formed their own Grand Lodge in 1736 (the Acception was unknown in Scotland). The word *Accepted* was adopted by London's Grand Lodge and applied to all members, with the still-current implication that a Freemason was someone accepted by other Masons into Freemasonry. Any idea that it referred to someone who had accepted a gift of God, or anything else but a set of rules, disappeared.

We may say that something that did not disappear—all at once at any rate—was the name Enoch. Enoch apparently enjoyed an old connection to the craft. Perhaps surprisingly, given Anderson's rewriting of traditional Masonic history, it was Anderson who highlighted this. His *Constitutions of Free-Masons* (1723) included a footnoted account of "Enoch's Pillars," in line with the tradition first recorded in the *Palaea Historica* (late ninth–early tenth century), that Enoch inscribed all known science on marble and brick to survive the Flood.[16] Pre–Grand Lodge written evidence, however, indicates a belief that late medieval masons attributed civilization's partial re-constitution not to Enoch, but to "hermes the philosopher" who discovered an antediluvian pillar made by Jabal, its knowledge subsequently transmitted via Pythagoras, Euclid, and a continuum of lodges.[17]

The second-oldest masonic manuscript, the Cooke MS, declares the building of "Enock" by Cain's master mason Jabal ("Jobell"; cf. Gen. 4:17) marked first practice of "the science of Geometry, and masonry."[18] This Cainite tradition is unique to old freemasonry. Masonic traditional history was written down—though only when required—in copies of "Old Charges," which Anderson treated as dilapidated; nevertheless, all pre-1723 copies attribute the pillars to Jabal, and describe Hermes as son to Cush, son of Noah's son Shem (despite Genesis holding Cush to be Ham's son). That Hermes is shown as Cush's son renders it problematic to assume late medieval and early modern Masonry habitually identified Hermes with Enoch, as Arab traditions maintained, reflected in Roger Bacon's thirteenth-century comments on pseudo-Aristotle's *Secretum secretorum*.[19]

If "old Masons" ever were—as Anderson would maintain in his *Constitutions* of 1738—emphatic in revering "Enoch's Pillars," such reverence did not derive from the Old Charges alone. It is also significant that the Old Charges gave more attention to Josephus's antediluvian pillars than to the biblical pillars of Solomon's Temple (Jachin and Boaz) that dominated masonic pillar-symbolism after London's Grand Lodge extended itself throughout England.

Anderson possibly disregarded the Jabal tradition because it conflicted with Josephus, and while in the fifteenth and sixteenth centuries

Fig. 18.4. Frontispiece and title page: *Constitutions of the Ancient and Honourable Fraternity of Free and Accepted Masons Containing their History, Charges, Regulations, Etc. Collected and Digested by Order of the Grand Lodge from their old Records, faithful Traditions and Lodge-Books, for the Use of the Lodges,* 1723, by Rev. James Anderson.

the tradition of Hermes discovering one of the pillars would have lent authority to the Old Charges' account, such authority was now diminished thanks to French Huguenot scholar Isaac Casaubon's *De rebus sacris et ecclesiasticis exercitationes XVI* (1614), which re-dated the *Corpus Hermeticum* on philological grounds to the third or fourth century CE, undermining Hermes Trismegistus's *prisca theologia* status, though not for enthusiasts.[20]

Anderson appears slightly uncomfortable by the notion of *Cain's son* Enoch as inheritor of Adam's primal geometrical knowledge, but couldn't argue with Genesis 4:17's record that the figure who shared the name with a Sethite patriarch built the world's first city. Anderson manages a quick switch of emphasis: "Nor can we suppose that SETH was less instructed, who being the Prince of the other Half of Mankind, and also the prime Cultivator of Astronomy, would take equal Care to teach Geometry and Masonry to his Offspring, who had also the mighty Advantage of Adam's living among them."[21]

A footnote on page 3 brings *"godly* Enoch" (my italics) to the fore:

> For by some Vestiges of Antiquity we find one of 'em, godly ENOCH, (who dy'd not, but was translated alive to Heaven) prophecying of the final Conflagration at the Day of Judgment (as St. Jude tells us) and likewise of the General Deluge for the Punishment of the World: Upon which he erected his two large Pillars, (tho' some ascribe them to Seth) the one of Stone, and the other of Brick, whereon were engraven the Liberal Sciences, &c. And that the Stone Pillar remain'd in Syria until the Days of Vespasian the Emperor.[22]

Anderson's "columns" story derives in part from Josephus's account of Sethite pillars (*Antiquities* 1.69–71). In the second, revised book of *Constitutions*, Anderson perhaps attempts to reconcile discrepancies:

> ENOSH, KAINAN, MAHALALEEL and JARED, whose Son, Godly ENOCH died not, but was translated alive, Soul and Body, into Heaven, aged 365 Years.
>   A.M. ["Year of Masonry"] 987 He was expert and bright both in the Science and the Art, and being a Prophet, He foretold the Destruction of the Earth for Sin, first by Water, and afterwards by Fire: therefore ENOCH erected Two large PILLARS,* the one of Stone and the other of Brick, whereon he engraved the Abridgement of the Arts and Sciences, particularly Geometry and Masonry.[23]

---

*Some call them SETH'S Pillars, but the old Masons always call'd them ENOCH's Pillars, and firmly believ'd this Tradition: nay Josephus (Lib. i. cap. 2) affirms the Stone-Pillar still remain'd in Syria [*sic*: error from translator William Whiston's "Siriad"; the original referred to Sirius-worshipping lands, probably Egypt] to his Time.

Anderson's asterisk refers to an important sidenote:

Perhaps Anderson was aware of the old conflation of Hermes and Enoch, and having excised Hermes, partially reinstated him with a role for biblical Enoch. However, the reference to "old masons," meaning probably pre–Grand Lodge freemasons, may have been a salve to brethren disaffected by the new Grand Lodge spin, conscious of different times and perhaps stranger secrets than those Grand Lodge offered.

There has existed longstanding suspicion within the craft that Freemasons are close to a great secret, but try as one might, it remains elusive to those not easily satisfied by rituals of which the rest of the world has little or no knowledge. I suspect this suspicion goes back to the earliest days of London's Grand Lodge and may have been a concern even of its leadership, who, in the early days at least, might have been aware of a privileged level that once existed, but that no one knew, or would tell, what it was.

Early Grand Lodge Masonry seems to have been content with something like apprentice and fellow craft degrees. The appearance of a fairly elaborate *Third* "Master Mason" Degree around 1730 seemed to offer a sense of more visceral initiation with a hint of rebirth symbolism, through confrontation with mortality. After a while, even this failed to satisfy all brethren, and the symbolism of "lost secrets of a master mason," implying a quest to find them through self-knowledge, sent numerous Masons, especially in France and Germany who had initially followed the imported Grand Lodge pattern, into esoteric waters.

The first recorded appearance of something like a Royal Arch degree to reveal the "lost word" occurred in Ireland in 1743. In 1751, Irishmen in London formed a rival Grand Lodge: the "Antients." Laurence Dermott became its second grand secretary in February 1752, the year that yields first evidence of the Royal Arch in lodge minutes. Cherished among Antients, Dermott would call the Royal Arch the "Root, Heart and Marrow of Masonry."[24]

In 1757, a version of the Royal Arch was worked in Fredericksburg, Virginia. From out of the Royal Arch template, a new degree would be formulated in America. The reason for the degree's existence is unknown, but I suspect it came from looking closely at Anderson's *Constitutions* and noticing "Enoch's Pillars," then wondering a) what happened to them?; b) what did Anderson's "old masons" actually believe about them?; c) why are the pillars in Masonry now identified with Jachin and Boaz in the Jerusalem temple, not Enoch's antediluvian pillars?; and d) what can we do to return to what might be vital, lost secrets of Masonry?

In the 13th Degree of "Morin's Rite," called in England the "Royal Arch of Enoch," the task of resolving these questions was ingeniously undertaken by blending antediluvian with Solomonic mythology.

The quasi-Enochic degree that eventually emerged might have been different if its creators had been able to read in English what James Bruce returned from Ethiopia with in 1773. Bruce, after all, had the *real* lost Book of Enoch. As things transpired, Enoch's return to Masonic significance manifested in the "Ancient and Accepted" or "Scottish Rite" sometime between the late 1760s and 1783.

The so-called Scottish Rite began when Creole trader Éstienne Morin (1717–1771) took what he could from the work of Lyon-based "high-grade" Mason, Jean-Baptiste Willermoz (1730–1824). Willermoz began assembling elements for a twenty-five degree system around 1761. Two years later, authorized by Écossais Masons from the Council of the Grand and Sovereign Lodge of St. Jean de Jérusalem, Morin went to Port au Prince to promote Masonry in the Americas. In about 1766, Morin completed a constitution (backdated to 1762), a foundation document for what would eventually become the Ancient and Accepted (Scottish) Rite.[25]

Offering an additional slant on the Royal Arch, its 13th Degree would address two problems. First, how to connect Enoch with the "lost word" of the Royal Arch, and second, how to connect Enoch to the more familiar temple at Jerusalem. The solution to the first issue lay in Genesis 4:26: "And to Seth, to him also there was born a son; and he called his name Enos: then men began to call upon the name of the Lord." The *name* then was vouchsafed to Seth's progeny. It was then a small step to insist Enoch preserved the true *name* from the Flood in a (new) pillar story. The second issue was addressed through novelties in the pillar story, inspired by the Royal Arch and other sources.*

---

*See my *Lost Pillars of Enoch* for sources.

The degree legend has Enoch, seeking revelation, experiencing a vision that took him to a mountain to see God's name impressed in a triangular, golden plate. Manifest to Enoch in the vision, God forbade him pronounce the sacred name. Enoch was then carried underground perpendicularly, finding nine levels, each with an arch above it. In the ninth arch, Enoch saw the plate, again surrounded by flaming light. Filled with God's spirit, Enoch built a subterranean temple in Canaan with the nine arches he had envisioned. He had a triangular plate made, each side a cubit, and had gems set within the gold. The name inscribed, it was placed on a triangular pedestal of white and black marble, deposited in the deepest arch. Temple completed, Enoch made a stone door and put a ring of iron in it and placed it over the first arch's opening to save the temple from impending deluge.

Enoch then made two pillars, one of brass, to withstand water, the other of marble, to withstand fire, engraving on the marble pillar hieroglyphics signifying a most precious treasure concealed in the arches underground, while on the pillar of brass were inscribed principles of the liberal arts, particularly of masonry. In the degree legend, a masonic account of Lamech, Noah, and the Ark followed.

Moving on to Solomon's wish to establish a temple, potential "Knights" were informed that digging its foundations, an ancient ruin was found with many treasures, duly carried to Solomon. Fearing pagan provenance, Solomon moved the project to Mt. Moriah, where a vault beneath the Holy of Holies was constructed, supported by a large pillar called the Pillar of Beauty to support the Ark of the Covenant. Solomon later sent three craftsmen to search the ruins for more treasures. They discovered a stone door with an iron ring. Undeterred, they lowered by rope one of the three who found the ninth arch, leading to the precious treasure's retrieval and delivery to Solomon, who made them Knights of the Royal Arch. The plate was taken to the Pillar of Beauty.

By the time Charleston saw a "Lodge of Perfection" established for the Ancient and Accepted Rite in 1783, Scottish explorer—and Freemason—James Bruce, Laird of Kinnaird (1730–1794), had been back in Great Britain for a decade, so there is just a chance that members of the new rite knew about Bruce's discovery, though too late for it to impact upon the 13th Degree. Besides, no translation existed. Extant book fragments would not have served Masonic purposes anyway. Removed from their Masonic context, degree legends (sometimes erroneously called "histories") have confused untutored investigators who have accepted as fact that precious relics have been discovered beneath Jerusalem's Temple Mount, unaware of the contrived root of such fables.

NINETEEN

Prophets
and Magic Galore

Readers may recall how Rabbi Abraham Abulafia worked out a kabbalistic system designed to *turn aspiring ordinary men into prophets*. Perhaps we now see just what a double-edged sword such an ability may be.

What is it about the Enochic tradition, as it emerges from the Middle Ages that, personally applied, turns Giovanni of Correggio into "prophet" Mercurio, or Guillaume Postel into a prophet of a new revelation, or John Dee and Edward Kelley into prophets "sanctified by the Lord," or make people believe Johann Valentin Andreae's *ludibrium* (serious game) of a "fraternity R.C." could convince people that Rosicrucian adepts were effecting a new age, or why a fictional Enoch in the Scottish Rite's 13th Degree can make ordinary men perform extraordinary rituals?

The case of Mormon Church of Jesus Christ of Latter-Day Saints founder, Joseph Smith (1805–1844)—believed a prophet today by over eight million followers—is another case in point. We may recall Edward Kelley used a crystal shew-stone as medium for seeing and taking instruction from angels. Young Joseph Smith in rural New York State and elsewhere used a seer-stone to seek valuable underground deposits, and for receiving (or projecting) angelic instruction. An autodidact, Smith wrote his own extensions to parts of the Bible, known to followers as the "Joseph Smith Translation," though no translation was involved (as we ordinarily understand the word) since the King James Version was sufficient to stimulate his imagination to mimic its style and revise its contents.[1] Enoch appears in Smith's "Book of Moses," taken from the first chapters of Genesis in the "Joseph Smith Translation." Smith's book of Moses is included in a work dubbed "The Pearl of Great Price," canonized by Smith's church after his death. It consists of random texts of scripture elaborated upon by Smith.

Smith's Bible revision began, according to scholar Jared Ludlow, in June 1830, some nine years after Laurence's first edition of 1 Enoch. The parts dealing with Enoch were completed within three years.[2] The passages regarding Enoch in Smith's book of Moses, however, show no

Fig. 19.1. Painting of Joseph Smith by unknown painter, ca. 1842.

Fig. 19.2. Daguerrotype attributed to Mormon photographer Lucian Rose Foster (1806–1876), and thought to be of Joseph Smith in 1844; discovered in an inherited locket in 2020 by Daniel Larsen, Smith's great-great-grandson.

reliance on the English version of 1 Enoch, any more than the Scottish Rite's 13th Degree did. We appear to be dealing with Smith's own extrapolation of the Genesis story and the Epistle of Jude's fragment—Smith's Enoch is largely *his* Enoch. While Smith and brother Hirum became 3rd-Degree Master Masons, there's no evidence to prove he drew on experience of the (numerically) higher Scottish Rite degrees, though Smith may well have heard of the 13th Degree legend as many Masons completed their first three degrees within the Scottish Rite. That Rite's 13th Degree resonates more with Smith's account of the circumstances and furniture involved in writing the Book of Mormon than with Smith's fairly conservative treatment of Enoch. Furthermore, the Masonic notion taken from Genesis of Cain's son Enoch building the first city seems to have inspired the Mormon ideal of building a new Zion for the faith more than 1 Enoch, which is oblivious to a Cainite Enoch.

During the 1840s, Mormons who investigated Laurence's English translation of 1 Enoch interpreted its prophecies as applying to events surrounding the persecution of the Church of Jesus Christ of Latter-Day Saints. When they read of Enoch's provision of books for posterity, they saw it as prescient of Smith's provision of the Book of Mormon and ancillary texts, as evinced in the Latter-Day Saints' paper *Millennial Star* 1.3 (July 1840, 61–62).[3] The convergence of Smith's Enoch and 1 Enoch sealed a specific identification of Smith's church with the patriarch. While valued for its supposed prophecies of Mormon experience, however, 1 Enoch was never canonized, despite its role as confirmatory scripture. The image of translating the righteous to a heavenly city beyond hostile powers has been an abiding inspiration for Smith's followers, convinced the church's founder deserved a place among God's prophets. It is belief in Smith's own powers of revelation, rather than Enoch's prophecies, that have proved the principal driving force in the Mormon movement.

The Hermetic Order of the Golden Dawn and Aleister Crowley

While John Dee's reputation was very mixed during his lifetime, with his last years stymied by neglect, his reputation after death in 1608 was blackened. Widely ridiculed as deluded necromancer and dupe of devils, Enlightenment commentators dismissed Dee as fallen magus. Despite efforts by defenders like Elias Ashmole and antiquarian John Aubrey, Dee's brilliance and value lay in mud: relics of superstitious ignorance. Centuries later, a curious vindication came when the very practice that had most damaged him—angel magic with Edward Kelley—attracted serious commitment from intelligent British Rosicrucian-inspired Freemasons.

William Westcott, Samuel Mathers, and William Woodman were determined to bust out of the theosophical straitjacket enveloping occultism in Europe and America and re-establish what they considered the essence of true Rosicrucianism, which for them meant a holy system of white magic with practical access to heavenly states of mind and an ultimate goal in apotheosis. Their Hermetic Order of the Golden Dawn, which began functioning discreetly in 1888, promised a complete training in Western Magic open to men and women. Intended to synthesize white magical systems, including the tarot, astrology, alchemy, Egyptian magic (as they understood it), and rites of evocation of spirits and demons, and invocation of gods and angels, with much magical lore of other kinds, the Order's greatest contribution to practical magic came only to those invited into the Second Order of the Ruby Rose and Cross of Gold. Initiates to the Adeptus Minor grade in this Second Order were taught "skrying in the spirit vision," as Kelley had apparently practiced.

In fact, "Enochian" words of power were already features of the original cipher manuscripts from which the Order drew its authority. Until 1900, members did not know these manuscripts were forgeries, suggesting approval came from a Nuremberg Rosicrucian Order descended from Frater R.C., imagined as perfect adept.

A late arrival to a skein of the original Order, psychologist Israel Regardie (1907–1985) collected most of the Order's manuscripts on Enochian magic. In some 70,000 words, they comprised nothing less than "a thoroughgoing and comprehensive synthesis of the entire magical system of the Golden Dawn."[4] The Order's British founders had concentrated every item of knowledge and practice within the scope of the inherited angelic tablets from Dee's magical records. Regardie, who made efforts to work the magic, referred to "this noble system."

Nevertheless, while Regardie reckoned the magic deduced from MSS Sloane 3189–91 in the British Library was rudimentary compared to what Mathers and Westcott brought to it, Hal Sundt, a contributor to Regardie's study of the Golden Dawn's rites and ceremonies, believed Mathers and company had not grasped the subtleties and scope of what Dee believed to be the same angelic knowledge given to patriarch Enoch, knowledge that enabled him to traverse the heavens. Sundt reckoned the Golden Dawn reduced all occult symbology to an "Elemental Bias," combining elemental attributions in a mechanical manner to create their own system, thinking it an exposition of Dee and Kelley's system.[5] This they considered valid on the basis that the Fraternity R.C. actually existed and that they were spiritual and magical inheritors of it, and if they could project it into a new era then so much the better.

Like first mentor Aleister Crowley (for whom Regardie worked as secretary for three years), Regardie was immensely impressed by what he took to be, not an ad hoc invention of Kelley's deviousness, but a remarkable discovery of inner plane experience that really opened one up to heavens of sublime powers and a plenitude of cosmic revelation.

Regardie imagined Dee at his table with pages depicting over one hundred large squares 49 inches by 49 inches, whose square grids were mostly filled with letters. Kelley would sit by the holy table, its four legs resting on wax seals. On its surface were magical pentacles and a large crystal, or shew-stone, in which Kelley saw an angel pointing to, say, column four, rank 29. Initially, this was how angels communicated the Calls that preceded spiritual ingress to the Aethyrs or Aires, inner plane worlds. The resulting message would be written backward because its magical power demanded indirect contact. Regardie had no doubt the Calls brought access to realities, not Kelley's imagination. Regardie believed the planes transcended even the individual's astral plane, extending to divine planes of consciousness as well. Regardie's testimony, and that of modern Enochian magic practitioner, John DeSalvo, are adamant in this, and that the sigil-like "Enochian" or angelic alphabet is a true language, whatever its origin.

However it was done, Regardie believed Kelley and Dee had stumbled, perhaps through some curious unconscious blip, into some possibly pre-Sanskrit root tongue. While this is not the view of modern philologists who've analyzed "Enochian," I found some elucidation of a vexed subject in John DeSalvo's very readable *The Lost Art of Enochian Magic* (2010), which explains how to practice the magic for oneself, how to pronounce the language, and what one might expect, with due practice, caution, and sincerity. DeSalvo makes no claims that Dee and Kelley actually got close to Enoch's mind, but one ought to consider what kind of inner road was trodden by the authors of 1 Enoch, 2 Enoch, and the *Sefer Hekhalot* in the first place. Is there some psychic magic in common to generate such visions, visions we now take for granted because printed?

Aleister Crowley's approach to the "Enochian Calls" was imbued with the Golden Dawn system, but his mentality was mostly that of the experimenter. If he found a system that worked, he would repeat it in the scientific interest and establish some ground rules by recording the experience systematically. Crowley experienced the first two of the thirty Enochian Aethyrs, called TEX (the thirtieth) and RII (twenty-ninth) in August 1900 in Mexico City, but found the experience too forbidding to proceed further, not resuming experimentation with the remaining twenty-eight until he took poet Victor Neuburg across Algerian deserts between November 23 and December 19, 1909. First published in Crowley's journal *The Equinox*, Crowley left people to assess for themselves. Numerous biographers have described the experience he and Neuburg endured, but the best thing is to study Crowley's *The Vision and the Voice*, published by Hymenaeus Beta with Samuel Weiser in 1998.[6] Neuburg told Jean Overton Fuller over twenty years after the events that he and Crowley pioneered their own methods to get results.

As Regardie observed, Crowley's Aethyrs are *Crowley's* Aethyrs, and the things he envisioned frequently relate to his own magical aspirations and his belief in the authenticity of *The Book of the Law* dictated, he believed, by an angel—or discarnate messenger—in Cairo in April 1904. Crowley's "Enochian" visions add prophetic encouragement to establishing his religion of Thelema, while indicating his personal

Fig. 19.3. Aleister Crowley in 1929.

spiritual destiny. John DeSalvo believes Crowley's and Neuburg's approach to the Enochian Calls hindered them from receiving what the beings encountered might have had to communicate for their benefit. DeSalvo suspects Crowley brought "too much of his own furniture" into his visionary landscape as he gazed into the topaz at the center of his hand-sized "rosy cross" amid Algerian sands.[7]

As far as I know, Crowley took no interest in the publication in 1912 (three years after his Algerian experiences) of R. H. Charles's revised translation of 1 Enoch. Had he read it, I expect it would have reminded him of the Book of Revelation which his parents pummelled into his boyhood mind until, as he put it, he was so sick of heaven he felt sympathetic to heaven's enemies. For Crowley the idea of eternal torture even for the wicked Watchers would have highlighted his moral objection to his parents' religion. Could eternal torture ever be justified from the creator of all? If Crowley took too much of his personal furniture to his encounter with the angels of Dee and Kelley's system, Crowley might argue that there was too much human vengefulness taken into the visionary experiences of the original creators of Enochic apocalypses.

It is not surprising that Crowley suspected Edward Kelley was a previous incarnation, believing as he did that Kelley was likely on the cusp of not only envisioning, but enacting the new Aeon of Horus that Crowley himself felt compelled to prophesy. He would rationalize Kelley's contribution as preparing spiritual ground for the "real" event, and what Crowley felt was fulfillment of the long expected new age in his reluctantly accepting the role as prophet of Thelema. That he was truly reluctant to accept the role is arguably Crowley's best card for meriting attention, but as Regardie diagnosed, Crowley labored under a conflicted subconscious.

PART FOUR

Enoch and
Christian Origins

TWENTY

The Son of Man
and Gospel Echoes

I saw in the night visions, and, behold, one like a son of man came
with the clouds of heaven, and came to the Ancient of days, and
they brought him near before him. And there was given him dominion, and glory, and a kingdom, that all people, nations, and languages, should serve him: his dominion is an everlasting dominion,
which shall not pass away, and his kingdom that which shall not be
destroyed.

   (Daniel 7:13–14)

And there I saw One who had a head of days,

And His head was white like wool,

And with Him was another being whose countenance had the
appearance of a man,

And his face was full of graciousness, like one of the holy angels.

And I asked the angel who went with me and showed me all the hidden things, concerning that Son of Man, who he was, and whence
he was, (and) why he went with the Head of Days?

And he answered and said unto me:

This is the Son of Man who hath righteousness,

With whom dwelleth righteousness,
And who revealeth all the treasures of that which is hidden,
Because the Lord of Spirits hath chosen him,
And whose lot hath the pre-eminence before the Lord of Spirits in
uprightness for ever.
And this Son of Man whom thou hast seen
Shall raise up the kings and the mighty from their seats,
    (1 Enoch 46:1–4a)

For the son of man shall come in the glory of his Father with his
angels; and then he shall reward every man according to his works.
Verily I say unto you, There be some standing here, which shall not
taste of death, till they see the son of man coming in his kingdom.
    (Matthew 16:27–28)

And he began to teach them, that the son of man must suffer many
things, and be rejected of the elders, and of the chief priests, and
scribes, and be killed, and after three days rise again.
    (Mark 8:31)

The Enochic Parables (1 Enoch 37–71) are remarkable chiefly because
their imagery anticipates eschatological gospel sequences where Jesus
envisions, and at times identifies himself with, the son of man who
comes *into the world* either on high in judgment or, finding no home
on earth,* to suffer. Enoch actually beholds this figure before the Lord
of Spirits' throne: one *like* a man in appearance but not man, or born
of man. In Parables the Son of Man is identified, through his role,
with "the Elect one," the "anointed" heavenly messiah who "shall arise,
And he shall choose the righteous and holy from among them: For the
day has drawn nigh when they shall be saved" (1 Enoch 51:2, 5a).

In Parables, Daniel's angelic figure resembling a man achieves
definition by title: one *like* a son of man becomes *the* Son of Man.
Intimations of this development perhaps occur in Daniel 10 where,

---

*cf. Matthew 8:20 and the plight of "Wisdom" in 1 Enoch 42:1–3.

in a vision, Daniel is raised from weakness by "one like the appearance of a man" (v.18) who then departs to "fight with the prince of Persia" after which he opposes a "prince [*archon* = ruler] of Grecia [the Seleucids]" (Daniel 10:20). The being says Michael is *Daniel's* "prince," so we may take Israel's *enemy* "princes" as rogue spirits, or fallen angels *behind* worldly powers (cf. Luke 10:18; Isaiah 14:12), as John J. Collins does in his chapter "The Apocalyptic World-View of Daniel."[1] We find a tellingly similar use of *prince* in John 12:31–32: "Now is the judgment of this world: now shall the prince [*archōn*] of this world be cast out. And I, if I be lifted up from the earth, will draw all men unto me." The gospel narrator says the latter indicates crucifixion, but when the "people" retort that the "law" maintained the *anointed* would live forever, they ask: "The son of man must be lifted up? Who is this son of man?" (v.34) Jesus answers, perhaps like a "son of light" of sectarian provenance, with a hint of Enoch "hidden" from the world till final judgment is nigh (1 Enoch 12:1): "Yet a little while is the light with you. Walk while ye have the light, lest darkness come upon you: for he that walketh in darkness knoweth not whither he goeth. While ye have light, believe in the light, that ye may be the children of light. These things spake Jesus, and departed, and did hide himself from them" (vv.35–36). Strange to think of Jesus *hiding*, isn't it?—but then, was not Enoch "hidden with the Watchers," as was the Son of Man in Parables (1 Enoch 12:1; cf. 48:6)?

Of superhuman nature, the Elect one of Parables is glorified by God to defeat spiritual forces responsible for evil, something no mortal messiah could do. While Boccaccini has noted "striking parallels with the development of early Christology,"[2] the Parables' Elect One does *not* become mortal flesh; such is not prophesied. Humanity is not accented; the glorified one is glorious, visionary.

In 1976, Milik's *The Books of Enoch* concluded that Parables' absence from Qumran indicated it was Christian—doubtless convenient from the Catholic point of view: Christianity owed nothing to the "Qumran sect." George W. E. Nickelsburg and Paolo Sacchi's reassessments were vindicated at the 2005 Enoch Seminar at Camaldoli when an overwhelming number of specialists confirmed Parables was late first century BCE (Herodian) or, at the latest, early first century CE. Its anticipation of Christian ideas ought not to surprise, since Jesus's religion was 100 percent Jewish, presented as prophecy fulfilled, possibly including Enoch's prophecies (though unstated, except for Jude).

Parables bears no reference to Moses, Torah, Abraham, Exodus, Sinai, or temple, but we do find elements of the pre-existent Sophia or Wisdom (42:1–3), companion of the Lord (see Proverbs 8), praised by Jesus (Matthew 11:16–19), a characteristic of Alexandrian speculation. 1 Enoch 48:2–3 ascribes pre-existence to the Son of Man who "shall be a staff to the righteous whereon to stay themselves and not fall, And he shall be the light of the Gentiles, And the hope of those who are troubled of heart. All who dwell on earth shall fall down and worship before him, And will praise and bless and celebrate with song the Lord of Spirits" (48:4–5). "And the wisdom of the Lord of Spirits has revealed him to the holy and righteous" (v.7). In the Elect One "dwells the spirit of wisdom" (49:3).

Son of Man and Hermetic Poimandrēs

Parables' eschatological foes are the rich and mighty, the proud who fail to extol the Lord of Spirits: a message that resonates with Mary's song-celebration "Magnificat" (Luke 1:46–55), though Mary's "Lord" is called in Parables "Lord of Spirits," a title that may have resonated in Egypt—which thought makes me wonder whether the Son of Man figure influenced the name of the wisdom-revealer to Hermes Trismegistos—Poimandrēs, long considered derived from "shepherd (*poimēn*) of men," which may be compared to the role of shepherd in 1 Enoch. The idea of Poimandrēs being the sovereign Mind (*nous*) of God in Hermetic libellus 1 resonates also with the divine, pre-existent *Logos* (word) = Hokhma (wisdom) equation of Philo of Alexandria, again giving us a possibly Jewish-Egyptian source for Parables. Furthermore, as Orlov has observed, the Son of Man's proximity to God's throne in Parables gives the figure a kind of proto-Merkaval aspect, and if we don't find the figure in later beliefs about Metatron, it's arguable that the Metatron figure *is* a Son of Man figure. There is also resonance with the Gnostic primal, heavenly Man, or *Anthrōpos*, called *Phōs*, that is: *light*. Is not Simeon's long-expected one the *light* of the Gentiles and the *glory* of thy people Israel? (Luke 2:32).

Gilles Quispel believed the Phōs was God's *glory*.[3] *Phōs* derives from an obsolete Greek verb, meaning "to make manifest," "shine," or "bring to vision." God's manifestation or reflection is humanlike in form, hence: "God created man in his own image" (Genesis 1:27). Alexandrian playwright Ezekiel Tragicus's second-century BCE play *Exagōgē* has Moses dream of a heroic man or Phōs on a throne in Sinai.

The idea of the divine image was worked cleverly into the Hermetic "fall" of man, arguably analogous to the Watchers falling for human women. The Anthrōpos sees his image reflected below in earthly waters. Attracted, he descends into the waters where nature spirits (female) entice and entrap him, like Narcissus. The heavenly man fell for the image, not the source: the cardinal Hermetic sin. So we can say in Parables, that the glory comes to restore the glory, of which restoration Enoch is a type.

It's very interesting indeed that St. Paul never employs the term "son of man" as the gospels do. His "second Adam" ("son" of Adam [Man], as it were?) in 1 Corinthians 15 is also pre-existent, being with God from the beginning, ready for redemption of the first Adam, through whom came sin (and Fall via female temptation) and death. After Paul, the title that apparently meant so much to Jesus himself slowly fades from Christology, absent from all creeds—perhaps too tricky, too esoteric, and *who knew what it really meant?* We're far from certain today. Had the term enjoyed an opportunity to invite controversy like that over "Son of God," Nicene Christology may have looked very different. Besides, the relationship between Jesus on earth and heavenly Son of Man is an enigma in all canonical gospels. In Parables, Enoch's *ascending* is more pronounced than his descending (to inform Methuselah and posterity of what is coming), that is, it is only through *ascent* that Enoch is granted vision of the Son of Man; there's no hint of incarnation. The Son of Man *raises* the elect.

It is also interesting that in the light of Paul's silence or arguably, reinterpretation, the gospels still retained so many son of man references. Indeed, the notion of the son of man acting as a human being on earth seems unique to the memories of the Jesus movement reflected in the gospels, and constitutes another argument why Milik was wrong to think Parables a Christian text or a Jewish text rendered Christian, since any *kerygma* (proclaiming) of incarnation is absent; the emphasis is on apotheosis, an idea taken *ne plus ultra* in 2 Enoch, which probably predates the earliest gospel, Mark, by several decades.

We learn in Parables 49 that the Elect One "standeth before the Lord of Spirits" and that "in him dwells the spirit of wisdom" (vv.2–3); "For wisdom is poured out like water" (v.1). In John 19:34, when a soldier pierces Jesus crucified, blood and water pour forth. One wonders whether the Enochic-Parables wisdom symbolism is at work here. While the world offers vinegar, Christ offers blood and water. Is this the new wine? We are reminded of the first sign or miracle in John 2 when Jesus at Cana orders servants to fill six stone jars with water. When tasted, it is wine, and the feast's ruler says: "thou hast kept the good wine till now" (v.10). The miracle, it is said, "manifested forth his glory" (v.11). Parables 49:1—where wisdom issues like water—concludes: "And *glory* faileth not before him for evermore" (my italics). Is mystical blood the water of wisdom, that is, the new wine of the eschaton? (see Isaiah 27:2, 6).

Parables involves a definite sense of two worlds, with the heavenly world more real to Enoch, for there he truly *sees* what to men is invisible; he sees that the Elect One embodying wisdom "shall judge the secret things" (Parables 49:4). The heavenly kingdom is all vision, all light, all revelation; the earth dim where darkness is invisible.

The secret not revealed even to Enoch, as far as the gospels go, is that the son of man will suffer death on earth. Parables had nothing direct to influence the gospels where the son of man's suffering was concerned, but Matthew, in particular, shows a palpable influence from Parables' throne language. However, as Daniel Boyarin points out in his chapter "Was the Book of Parables a Sectarian Document?," to talk of a Jewish Book of Parables, or pre-Christian Jewish traditions influencing

Christian usage, may be quite misleading: "Once we fully take in that Christianity is simply part and parcel of ancient Judaism, this very way of posing the issue becomes immaterial, in my humble opinion."[4]

Paolo Sacchi, concluding his summary of "Prospects for Future Research" after the 2005 Camaldoli Seminar on the Parables of Enoch wrote that tracing the Enochic tradition into Jesus's milieu involved "profound implications even for the contemporary religious landscape. The search for Christian origins is also a search for the nature of both Christianity and Judaism and the origin and values of our modern society."[5]

The seventh Enoch Seminar, held at Camaldoli in July 2013, generated fresh papers on 1 Enoch's relations to Matthew, Mark, and Luke. While taking off from R. H. Charles's old statement that the world had yet to see how influential 1 Enoch's contents were on the New Testament, scholars avoided listing apparent quotation parallels such as Charles corralled to his cause in 1912.

In Loren T. Stuckenbruck and Gabriele Boccaccini's introduction to the published papers (*Enoch and the Synoptic Gospels: Reminiscences, Allusions, Intertextuality*, 2016), entitled "1 Enoch and the Synoptic Gospels: The Method and Benefits of a Conversation," they highlighted now-established connections between the Son of Man in Parables and Matthew,[6*] and outlined how chapters by Henryk Drawnel (on Demonology) and Archie Wright's (on Mesopotamian incantations) illuminated possible links between Jesus's exorcisms and the tradition of demons being disembodied spirits of Giants: "This narrative throws the activity of Jesus, as presented in the Synoptic Gospels, into the spot-

---

*However, note that Lester Grabbe in "'Son of Man': Its Origin and Meaning in Second Temple Judaism" concludes that the expression in gospel traditions is not *equivalent* to 1 Enoch, and this is not not merely a result of borrowing from Daniel; "it is precisely for its titular (and messianic) use that the Enochic Parables provide evidence" (*Enoch and the Synoptic Gospels*, 15). This insight explains, by the way, why I tend to use capitals for Enochic "Son of Man" references (except where Nickelsberg and VanderKam's translation indicates otherwise), while preferring lowercase for gospel references, the majority of our earliest gospel manuscripts using lowercase Greek for "son of man."

light as one who does not destroy unclean or evil spirits at any time, relocating them instead to a position where they can be managed or remain remote."[7]

I should add Jesus's insight that it is what comes from *inside* man that defiles him (Mark 7:20; Matthew 15:11); that is to say: Does the saying imply inherited corruption from antediluvian times? Is there a link here with the imperative to be "born again" (John 3:3) to escape effects of miscegenation, or inherited evil? One could comprehend, in this context, why Paul stressed observance of Mosaic law was inadequate and, by itself, hopeless, for some.

Boccaccini's *Paul's Three Paths to Salvation* (2020) recognizes Paul's joining the messianic movement involved accepting eschatology as a solution to the power of evil. Evil's corruption makes humans sin's slaves, defenseless. The remedy, Paul believed, was Jesus. According to Boccaccini, Paul saw justification by faith and forgiveness of sins graciously *added* to the paths of salvation. The Law remains a path for the righteous of Torah. Another path is righteousness by natural law. The gracious path is justification by Christ, remedy for those unable to fulfill the law because of evil's power. Evil, not Law, was Paul's problem, for evil fatally frustrates the will. Thus, Parables 50 can be seen as preparing the ground by indicating three subjects of judgment: righteous, unrepentant, repentant. For victims of sin, opportunity to repent is an act of mercy. Christ's crucifixion justifies *sinners*, whom Christ came to heal. Thus, Boccaccini suggests Paul enlarged, not restricted, the boundaries of salvation to include sinners and Gentiles as well as the Torah righteous. In his talk about his book at the Enoch Seminar Webinar from June 26–29, 2023, Boccaccini concluded: "Paul is an answer to an Enochic problem."

Mark 3:30 has Jesus's enemies accusing him of having "an unclean spirit." Does this idea stem from spiritual defilement in 1 Enoch; is Jesus born of the "holy spirit" to contrast with unclean spirits in ordinary men and women?[8] A similar tack is pursued in Amy Richter's chapter "Unusual Births: Enochic traditions and Matthew's infancy narrative," where she ponders whether awareness of unclean births in Watchers made Matthew emphasize the birth of righteousness without sex.[9]

1 Enoch sheds light on Jesus's role in the defeat of evil.* In 1 Enoch, evil's defeat is prefigured from the beginning; Jesus furnishes precise *signs* of an impending or present end-time, a program arguably enriched by the Enochic view of evil part-defeated, afterward managed.[10]

David Gurtner's chapter comparing "The Revelatory Experiences of Enoch and Jesus," resists claiming 1 Enoch "influenced the Synoptic Gospels directly; instead, they underscore the common socio-cultural and religious framework within which the traditions present the figures of Enoch and Jesus, respectively."[11]

Likewise keen to avoid what he calls "parallelomania," Leslie Baynes's chapter "The Parables of Enoch and Luke's Parable of the Rich Man and Lazarus" notes how the Epistle of Enoch, Parables of Enoch, and Luke's parable (16:19–31) all condemn the wealthy with eternal torment while the poor receive comfort. Only the Enochian and Lukan parables highlight a rejected plea for relief from hellish torment in the first person.[12] This poses questions about the use of Enoch's Parables in Mary's Canticle where the "rich hath been sent empty away" (Luke 1:53), though it also echoes Psalm 49 where those who die trusting in wealth die like the beasts that perish.

In 1 Enoch 62–63, the poor are exalted, the rich feed fire. The parable subsists in comparing rich and poor. Unlike the rich man of Luke's parable, Lazarus reclines in "Abraham's bosom," which may suggest the messianic banquet. Textual evidence from studying the Ge'ez "provides little foundation for an argument for verbal dependence between Parables of Enoch and Luke 16:19–31."[13] There is however a striking verbal link in 1 Enoch 63:10 where the rich and mighty admit "our lives are full of ill-gotten wealth [*newayā 'ammaḍā*], but it does not prevent our descending into the flame of the torment of Sheol." The Ge'ez *newayā 'ammaḍā* (literally "wealth of unrighteousness") is an identical

---

*In Mark, Jesus's authority ("not as the scribes") manifests in his power of exorcism. As Nicholas A. Elder (University of Dubuque Theological Seminary, Iowa) maintained in his article "Scribes and Demons: Literacy and Authority in a Capernaum Synagogue (Mark 1:21–28)," presented at the Enoch Seminar paper webinar, June 28, 2023, Jesus doesn't compete with the scribes, having his own authority.

phrase to Luke 16:9's Greek *mamōna tēs adikias* in the parable of the steward, the Greek being unique to that instance. It doesn't prove literary dependence but it does link them.

Baynes compares Mary's hymn of praise in Luke 1:52–3 with Hannah's prayer in 1 Samuel 2:1–10, but only Mary reverses the status of the poor and the rich.[14] While Hannah gives strength to the king and the "horn of the Lord's anointed," Mary adds the overthrow of kings. Mary is closer to 1 Enoch than to 1 Samuel. Modestly, Baynes thinks that if he's right, the Enoch Seminar's dating consensus concerning Parables is supported. It's fair to conclude Luke had an affinity with the sentiments in Parables.

Enoch, Priesthood, and Jesus

Before we proceed to focus more upon the figure of Jesus, it's worthwhile consulting Joseph L. Angel's chapter "Enoch, Jesus, and Priestly Tradition," where Angel finds Enoch and other Dead Sea Scrolls illuminate Jesus as eschatological revealer of divine wisdom, as expressed in Matthew 11:25–30.

Angel admits that demonstrating direct influence is difficult, but "striking points of contact suggest that the traditions surrounding the figure of Enoch could have provided early Christians with a significant model for interpreting the person and work of Jesus Christ."[15] Its significance "underappreciated," the model is Jewish priesthood,[16] whose most pertinent sacerdotal functions are atoning for and forgiving/removing sin, and teaching Torah/divine wisdom. Angel sees Enoch and Jesus representing "complex and multifaceted ideal figures of the Second Temple period."[17] He notes Manchester University theologian Philip Alexander's observation that Enoch in Jubilees in the second century BCE is a high priest whose intercession for the Watchers is "most naturally" understood as a priestly function. This is set against contrary views of James D. G. Dunn (Durham University) and Göttingen University's Jürgen Becker who both dismiss any significant identity of Jesus and Jerusalem's priesthood.[18] Angel attributes such apparent prejudice to Jesus's attitude to the temple and his not being a Levite.

Challenging these assumptions, Angel finds "numerous Second Temple period texts that ascribe these sacerdotal functions on a cosmic scale to exalted and/or eschatological priestly figures" more relevant to the Synoptic image of Jesus. For example, archangel Michael in 1 Enoch 10 "likely serves as high priest when he is ordered to "cleanse the earth . . . from all impurities" so that "all the sons of men will become righteous." While the Book of the Watchers doesn't ascribe atonement to Enoch, he does intercede for the Watchers so "that they might have forgiveness" for their sins (1 Enoch 13:4–7). Bearing in mind Exodus 30:7–10 and Numbers 16:46–48, Jubilees 4's having Enoch offer "the incense of the sanctuary" suggests an intercessory and atoning role, while in 2 Enoch 64, the patriarch, made high priest in chapter 18, is located at the site of the eschatological temple (akhuzan), and described as "the one who carried away the sins of humankind."[19]

Of the Second Temple sources, Angel finds the fragmentary Aramaic Apocryphon of Levi (4Q541) the most significant. From about 100 BCE, it describes construction of an eschatological temple. Related to other traditions about Levi important to Enochic sources, fragment 9 refers to an eschatological savior: "[and he will transmit to them] his [wi]sdom. And he will atone for all the children of his generation; and he will be sent to all the children of his [peop]le. His word is like a word of the heavens, and his teaching is like the will of God. His eternal sun will shine; and fire will burn in all the ends of the earth. And on the darkness it will shine; then the darkness will disappear [fr]om the earth and the cloud from the dry land. They will speak many words against him, and a number of [lie]s. and they will invent fables against him, and they will speak all manner of infamies against him. Evil will overturn his generation. . . . will be; and because falsehood and violence will be its setting, and the people will go astray in his days; and they will be confounded."

The text's eschatological setting, its striking parallels with the Testament of Levi (chapter 18 in particular), and the atoning role of line 2, all encourage scholars to agree that here is described a messianic priest, with some seeing signs of a suffering messiah in pre-Christian Judaism. If so, the link to priesthood is remarkable. Supporting this is the atoning and sending sequence reminiscent of Leviticus 16:6 and 20–22, where the dismissal of the scapegoat is preceded by atonement. Like Isaiah 53's suffering servant, the priest appears to have taken on the people's sins and is "making atonement through his person."[20]

Another relevant Qumran text is the so-called "self-glorification hymn" (SGH) wherein the teacher claims "no teaching is like my teaching," and the teacher must suffer for it. Angel asks whether the servant imagery applied to Jesus, and Jesus as son of man, might also be "tinged with a priestly background."[21] That is, despite Jesus's not being a Levite, Jewish traditions already existed of a messianic priest-servant role associated with figures with extra-earthly teaching, or knowledge of the heavens. Do such "in some way lie beneath the understanding of Jesus's identity and purpose in certain New Testament writings"?[22] Angel refers particularly to Hebrews, John, Luke through Acts, and Mark.*

We come to forgiving. Angel notes that since the authority given "one like the son of man" in Daniel 7:13–14 does not obviously apply to forgiving sins on earth, some have argued that Mark 2:10, where Jesus says the "son of man hath power on earth to forgive sins," marks a radical interpretation of the tradition, one supposedly arising after Jesus's death. Angel finds comfort, however, in Gloucestershire University's Crispin Fletcher-Louis's view that at the time of Jesus, the Daniel figure "would have been perceived as Israel's true messianic high priest: his coming to God with the clouds evokes the day of atonement when the high priest enters God's presence surrounded by clouds of incense."[23] "Again," writes Angel, "it seems that pre-Christian priestly tradition lies in the background of the Gospel's portrayal of Jesus."[24]

Angel does not deny substantial differences between Matthew and the Qumran texts, and accepts it cannot be shown that

---

*Regarding the sending of goat *Azazel* (translated "scapegoat") into the desert (Leviticus 16:8) is there not resonance here with Matthew 4:1: "Then Jesus was led by the Spirit into the wilderness to be tempted by the devil (Matthew 4:1)? Being tempted was Jesus's *intention*. Is he casting himself in the role of the condemned goat, with the people's sin upon him? And does he not reverse the roles and lead *Satan* to be tempted (to kill him)?

Matthew 11:25–30 drew directly from any Qumran fragments mentioned. He also recognizes no obvious intention in Matthew to portray Jesus as priest (if Matthew was compiled after 70 CE, as is thought, it would have made such a relatively ordinary role redundant). What Angel does show, or hope to show, is that lines of contact between the texts show Matthew 11:25–30 comfortable in Second Temple traditions that treat of divine wisdom revealed eschatologically by a priestly figure rejected by other teachers despite his serving God.

Furthermore, neither Jesus nor Enoch are identified as Levites (though Hebrews identifies Jesus with the "order of Melchizedek" claimed by the Maccabee Levites—see Psalm 110:4; Hebrews 7). If therefore perfection were by the Levitical priesthood (for under it the people received the law) what further need was there that another priest should rise after the order of Melchizedek, and not be called after the order of Aaron (Hebrews 7:11)?

Angel concludes that "in line with the specific concern of the Gospels to spotlight other aspects of Jesus's identity, the priestly elements attributed to Jesus remain beneath the surface."[25]

TWENTY-ONE

Enoch and Christian Origins II

....

Jesus

In March 2021, Amy-Jill Levine, Rabbi Stanley M. Kessler distinguished professor of New Testament and Jewish Studies at Hartford International University for Religion and Peace, and Gabriele Boccaccini, professor of Second Temple Judaism and Christian Origins in the Department of Near Eastern Studies, University of Michigan, participated in an online conversation entitled "The Historical Jesus in His Historical Context" with questions fielded by Jeremiah Cataldo, associate professor, Frederik Meijer Honors College, Grand Valley State University.

Cataldo began by asking Amy-Jill Levine what kind of a Jew Jesus was. "If we get Second Temple Judaism wrong," she replied, "we get Jesus wrong." "He is a different kind of Jew," she said. He was concerned with the kingdom of heaven, the kingdom of God, with separating families, and the younger generation. He was popular, a storyteller, healer, exorcist.

Gabriele Boccaccini emphasized that Jesus's time was not, as people once thought, a time of decadence after a great age of prophets. Archaeology suggests otherwise—to which Levine added that the idea of Judaism as a spent force reliant on strict legalism, not spirit, and that "Jesus comes and changes it," was untrue. The image comes from ret-rojection of rabbinic sources from later, played back against statements of Jesus. All this falsely represents Second Temple Judaism. We need to look at the 20s and 30s CE in Galilee and Judea.

Boccaccini dissented from the inherited idea of Jesus coming to "destroy Judaism." Scholarship emphasizes the diversity of Second Temple Judaism. Jesus belonged to Judaism, "but did it in his own way." Jesus's contribution to Jewish thought is now debated: his ethical teaching, about forgiveness and love.

Professor Levine added: "We think the [Dead Sea] Scrolls were written by Essenes, but can't prove it." Jesus was not a peasant. Levine thought him an artisan, storyteller. There was openness in his stories; "he doesn't tell animal stories."* Jesus's answers to questions were spontaneous. *Love your enemies . . .* "he's the only person who says this." To be *alive* to people, even after death: "he must have had *charisma.*"

Boccaccini emphasized the *originality* in the package; it wasn't a case of single elements: it was a living synthesis. Boccaccini compared the situation to his childhood pleasure in Lego: the same bricks are used by all children; they play with the same elements, but *the building* is what makes the difference.

"We have interesting documents from [the] period, including *Enoch.*" Professor Levine thought these interesting documents can help us to to understand . . . there's Paul, Enoch, the Parables, the Testament of Abraham, 4 Ezra, 2 Baruch: the response to the temple's destruction. The gospels. There've been excavations of Magdala. They've found a table on which the Torah could be read . . . purity practices . . . coin hordes.

Levine lamented that many Jews don't know their history post-Maccabean to the Mishnah (ca. 200 CE). Boccaccini added that Jews needed to reclaim the Judaism of the Second Temple.

---

*I think Professor Levine, in the heat of the moment, forgot Jesus's lament that the foxes have holes and the birds have nests, but the son of man had nowhere to lay his head (Matthew 8:20); also, the parables about lost sheep and the dogs that eat crumbs from the master's table; never mind the birds that neither toil nor spin but are fed by their heavenly father.

Levine said we needed different, alternative terms for "Christian." Why not "Jesus-centered" or "messianic Judaism"?

"Why," asked Boccaccini, "did Jesus and Paul give birth to a separate religion?"

It was, he said, vital to get all this right, rather than transmit anti-Jewish stereotypes. It was important to avoid violent bigotry. People, especially churches and seminaries, are ignorant of the work that has been done on this whole field. They don't know or understand the diversity of Second Temple Judaism.

"Source-criticism is back on the table. The Gospel of John's back on the table." *Matthew*, it transpires, was the most popular gospel among second century *Gentiles*, not just Jewish Christians, as received wisdom has it. Proclaiming the messiah happened when there was no peace on earth. Some Jews might have signed on with Jesus, and after some years, went back home. Jesus's followers were now turning from paganism to the God of Israel. The Christian message resonated in the religious marketplace: more Gentiles, less Jews. Jews were carrying on with the Law. The messianic age became something for Gentiles without the halakah. Suddenly "Jews stand out." Christians lost their sense of Jewish roots. And Jews who hadn't, would not convert.

At which point, Jeremiah Cataldo interjected. He agreed on understanding the diversity of the Second Temple period; there was too much homogenization of sources. "We overlook the social and political aspects of texts in favour of theological issues," he said. "How do we get over the theological baggage that Jesus entails in the modern situation?"

Professor Levine observed that Herod Antipas was "OK" in Galilee. There were no Roman soldiers in Galilee. Jesus was not worried about Rome, but evil . . . Satan.

Boccaccini said it was difficult to distinguish Jesus from other rabbis' attitudes in his time. Jesus was the first to be "rabbbi." Later rabbis can be distinguished from Christianity. Even messianic beliefs varied from rejection to different understandings. We have the burden of centuries of theological hostility. "We have to avoid anachronisms."

Levine said: "Gentile" was the most neutral term. The alternative was "pagan." Boccaccini added that not all Gentiles were polytheists.

Jesus was a charismatic leader, like John the Baptist. The rabbinic period drew back from the charismatic leader. When the leader dies, it all changes without the charismatic leadership.

Boccaccini said the destruction of the temple was extremely important. It began the need to rethink Judaism. Groups lost their common house. The first followers of Jesus were attending the temple. Money was still collected for the temple after 70 CE. The Bar Kokhba rebellion, over sixty years later, was traumatic—from that point, "they cannot rebuild the temple."[1]

The Parables of 1 Enoch suggests Jesus grew up amid intense speculation regarding the nature of the messiah, interest reflected in Matthew's story of the star of Bethlehem allegedly marking the messiah's birth (Matthew 2:1–12). If the core is historical, and we dismiss supernatural elements, astronomical analysis supports dating Jesus's birth to 7 BCE, for three times that year Jupiter (indicating kingship) and Saturn (justice) were conjoined in Pisces (sign of Israel) within one degree of separation, a fact significant to contemporary astrologers (*magoi*).[2]

Historical reasons for dating Parables around this same period give us insight into the world Jesus had entered. First clue comes in 1 Enoch 56:5–7.

> And in those days the angels shall return
> And hurl themselves to the east upon the Parthians and Medes:
> They shall stir up the kings, so that a spirit of unrest shall come upon them,
> And they shall rouse them from their thrones,
> That they may break forth as lions from their lairs,
> And as hungry wolves among their flocks.
> And they shall go up and tread under foot the land of His elect ones,
> [And the land of His elect ones shall be before them a threshing floor and a highway:]
> But the city of my righteous shall be a hindrance to their horses.

Such an invasion occurred in 40 BCE, recorded by Josephus, when Parthian king's son Pacorus, along with Parthian satrap Barzaphranes, occupied Syria while Hasmoneans Antigonus II and Hyrcanus II waged civil war in Judea. When the Parthians moved on Judea, Herod the Great and brother Phasael engaged them. Hyrcanus and Phasael fell prisoners to the Parthians, but Herod escaped to Masada while the Parthians plundered Jerusalem (*Antiquities* 14.344). Herod eventually triumphed and was declared king of the Jews by the Roman Senate that year. The event seems fresh in the writer's memory, with Jerusalem's walls providing hindrance to the Parthians' equestrian flair.

Fig. 21.1. On the obverse of this coin's sun symbol
are the Greek words *BASILEŌS HRŌDON* ("KING HEROD").

Charlesworth has found another clue to dating. In the first Parable (38:4), we read of "that time those that possess the earth shall no longer be powerful and exalted"—note *those that possess the earth* may be translated "landowners." In the second Parable (45:5): "I will transform the earth and make it a blessing: And I will cause Mine elect ones to dwell upon it: But the sinners and evil-doers shall not set foot thereon." In 48:8: "In these days shall the kings of the earth have become downcast in countenance, And the strong who possess the dry ground because of the works of their hands;" a condemnation repeated in 62:3–6 when "all the kings and the mighty and the exalted, and those who possess the earth" or "the land," will suffer in the judgment. In 62:9, the mighty kings, and the exalted, "and those who rule the dry ground" will fall to worship the Most High, setting their hopes on the Son of Man—rather like the wicked Watchers who petitioned God for clemency with tears, but, like the Watchers, the angels of punishment send "the mighty kings who possess the dry ground" to torments in Sheol (63:1–10). "Thus spake the Lord of Spirits: 'This is the ordinance and judgment with respect to the mighty and the kings and the exalted and those who possess the earth before the Lord of Spirits'." (63:12).

Charlesworth accepts the "kings of the earth" are Roman emperors, but notices the oppression of the rich over the *dry land*. He ponders who caused Jews to suffer by control of dry land.[3]

Oppression in Galilee?

Old Israel was divided between dry, cultivatable land and wetlands, marshes. Swamps were found west of the Kinneret and the Hulah Valley: thirty miles of swamp used to stretch from Paneas (Dan) to Capernaum, northern Galilee. Jews did labor on the dry land, producing vines and cereals, but the best went to the *owners*, while *their* lands were swampy, and if drained, taken by the rich. Parables promises hell for the "mighty landowners" (48:8). They're going to burn "like grass in the fire"—fitting punishment; one can feel the anguish in these judgments. Jews are toiling on land no longer theirs. Kings, governors, high officials, landlords: these are the guilty sinners (62:1, 3, 6). Charlesworth imagines an "Enochic community," presumably in Galilee, suffering under the Herodian yoke.[4] The old Hasmonean order was being bulldozed away as parts of God's country began to resemble a series of Helleno-Roman building sites, dedicated to Herod's patron: Caesar. Thus Paneas-Dan would soon become Caesarea Philippi. Land taxes were raised, old estates were forfeited. Rome wanted its own taxes; a notable tax was raised in 8 BCE.

Concerned about competing claims, Herod ordered all aristocratic genealogies destroyed, which further removed rival claimants to the throne. He really *was* interested in anyone being born to be king he or one of his wives didn't know about. Absentee foreign landlords became commonplace. By the time of Herod's death, Charlesworth tells us Herod and his supporters possessed two-thirds of the country's fertile land. Herod's finance minister Ptolemy owned an entire village—small compared to wealthy Eleazar of Jerusalem: he owned a thousand.[5] Herod's taxation was so severe he even had to remit portions, as Josephus reported in *Antiquities* (15.365; 16.64). His son Archelaus's reign collapsed amid complaints of ruinous taxation leading to lost farmland. Hideous when presented as news, one can feel the tremors echoing in Parables. Hearers of the prophecy would have known intimately what was being prophesied, and the news would be welcome: good news indeed for the poor and those struggling to improve things for others. Meanwhile, the rich got richer and the poor poorer. When would deliverance come to Abraham's children? Parables speaks to them, with promise that the chosen or elect one would restore the ground as a blessing to those living on it.

This all makes Charlesworth particularly confident Parables was composed fairly soon after the Parthian invasion of 40 BCE and before Herod's death in 4 BCE (37–4 BCE), certainly no later than 20 CE. As for place, Charlesworth concluded that his "dry land" hypothesis makes a *Galilean* source for Parables more likely, with the phrase "Son of Man" known there before Jesus used it; indeed, he may have absorbed it after his father, according to Matthew's account, settled the family in Galilee after Herod's death. Could the wicked Watchers' tears, wept at "Abelsjail" (1 Enoch 13:9) west of Dan, have referred to the swampy marshland, a daily reminder of the stakes?

Charlesworth's "dry land" hypothesis finds support in Princeton University scholar Jolyon Pruszinski's paper "To Measure for Me the Place of the Chosen: Phenomenologies of Dwelling in the Parables of Enoch," delivered to the Enoch Seminar on June 28, 2023. Studying the theme of "dwelling" in the Parables, Pruszinski notes how apocalyptic literature oft compares ideal spaces with experienced reality. Ultimate dwellings of the righteous compensate for life's harshness (e.g. 39:4–5, 39:8, 41:2, 41:5, 45:5–6, 51:5b, 61:12, 70:3–4, 71:16). Pruszinski recognizes in Parables features typical to literatures of marginal "dwelling" described by French philosopher Gaston Bachelard in *La poètique de l'espace*. Employing a "topoanalysis" based in Bachelard's work, Pruszinski surmises a background to Parables of community displacement and consignment to marginal, subsistence living. Flood waters rising may represent rising of resistance. The righteous oppressed dwell in watery areas that to Pruszinski suggest the Hula Valley, close to Dan in Upper Galilee.

Rev. Darrell D. Hannah's article "The Book of Noah, the Death of Herod the Great, and the Date of the Parables of Enoch" offers insight into a third clue for dating Parables in Herod's reign.[6] 1 Enoch 67:8–13 refers to healing waters turning dangerous. They have been linked to Herod the Great's seeking remedial treatment for terrible skin afflictions at Callirrhoe's hot springs on the Dead Sea's northwest coast (*Antiquities* 17.168–72; *War* 1.656–58):

> But those waters shall in those days serve for the kings and the mighty and the exalted, and those who dwell on the earth, for the healing of the body, but for the punishment of the spirit; now their spirit is full of lust, that they may be punished in their body, for they have denied the Lord of Spirits and see their punishment daily, and yet believe not in His name. And in proportion as the burning of their bodies becomes severe, a corresponding change shall take place in their spirit for ever and ever; for before the Lord of Spirits none shall utter an idle word. For the judgement shall come upon them, because they believe in the lust of their body and deny the Spirit of the Lord. And those same waters will undergo a change in those days; for when those angels are punished in these waters, these water-springs shall change their temperature, and when the angels ascend, this water of the springs shall change and become cold. And I heard Michael answering and saying: "This judgement wherewith the angels are judged is a testimony for the kings and the mighty who possess the earth." Because these waters of judgement minister to the healing of the body of the kings and the lust of their body; therefore they will not see and will not believe that those waters will change and become a fire which burns for ever.

While there were other medicinal hot springs in the country, such as near Macherus and Tiberias, only Tiberias and Callirrhoe earned Pliny's attention, the latter attracting people for "the celebrity of its waters" (*Natural History* 70–72). The site's archaeology is Herodian.

Hannah gives good reasons for showing the Parables passage was written by whoever interpolated material from a separate apocryphon of Noah into the work. In trying to join the materials, the interpolator adopted phrases from Parables proper, but included a sin of the "kings and the mighty" to be punished not earlier mentioned, namely *lust*,[7] a notorious sin of Herod, and of his family from ten wives and concubines (*Antiquities* 15.319–22). Like the royal figures in 1 Enoch 67, Herod's final hideous illness was regarded as divine punishment for licentiousness, and other crimes. In the latter half of March, 4 BCE, a desperate Herod visited the springs, probably not for the first time. If fresh in hearers' memories, the prophetic allusion would have scored a direct hit: the pits of subterranean liquid fire reserved for wicked angels were ready for sinful kings and mighty oppressors; seeking solace in warming waters, they'd find scorching disfigurement instead. The target, if Hannah and other scholars are right, was the man Matthew tells us tried to murder the infant Jesus, having heard Micah 5:2: "But thou, Bethlehem Ephratah, though thou be little among the thousands of Judah, yet out of thee shall he come forth unto me that is to be ruler in Israel; whose goings forth have been from of old, from everlasting."

Yeshua ben Yosef (a Hypothesis)

Taking in all we have learned about the Enochic milieu, we can now approach the life and worldview of the person known first to his countrymen as Yeshua ben Yosef: two ordinary Jewish names of son and presumed father.* We shall, I hope, see accounts enriched and leavened by knowledge of Enochic and sectarian contexts.

According to Romans 1:3, the messiah Yeshua was "made of the seed of David according to the flesh," meaning *as far as the flesh is concerned*:

---

*Some of what follows was pre-empted by studies undertaken for *The Missing Family of Jesus* (2010) and *The Mysteries of John the Baptist* (2012). In the first I examined every scrap of evidence concerning Jesus's relatives and their descendants. The second presented an impartial analysis of all historical records, including the Qumran Scrolls, relevant to the historical reality of John and his relations with Jesus. These studies yielded numerous insights, not least among them the best date for Jesus's crucifixion (Passover 37 CE). Further study, however, has revealed a few minor errors in the latter work that this book corrects. Those books and this one constitute an interrelated trilogy pertinent to Christian origins.

the flesh or "seed of David" came from Yosef. Matthew's genealogy also shows Yosef as King David's descendant, of the tribe of Judah, although temple slave-girl (*hē doulē*) Myriam, or Maryam, "was found with child of the Holy Spirit" (Matthew 1:18). Pious virgin girls were regularly dedicated to Temple slavery. Rabbinic sources note the sons or daughters of the house of Rechab (the Rechabites) did service at the altar, while priests could find wives from virgin Israelites (Ezekiel 44:22). Once a temple slave girl had "known" a man, freedom from temple slavery was redeemed through rededication to husbands. Yosef may have been one such priest.

Fragmentary text in what Geza Vermes calls "The Book of War" (4Q285, 11Q14) describes Levites blowing trumpets to archangel Michael and "the Prince of the Congregation," identified as the "Branch of David" (fragments 4 and 7) who will enter into the judgment of the wicked by slaying the leader of the "Kittim" (in this context, Romans), assisted by "a Priest of renown." In related Commentaries on Isaiah (4Q161–65, 3Q4), the famous Isaiah 11:1–3 prophecy of "a rod from the stem of Jesse" wherefrom "a Branch shall grow out of its roots" was interpreted as the Branch of David "who shall arise at the end" (line 15). "God will uphold him . . . a throne of glory and a crown of [holiness] and many-coloured garments . . . [He will put a scepter] in his hand and he shall rule over all the [nations]." "One of the Priests of renown shall go out, and garments of . . . shall be in his hands."

Romans are not sole targets for judgment; "Scoffers in Jerusalem" are also condemned. Dated by Vermes to the first century BCE,[8] these were fresh texts when Yeshua entered the world, though sectarians omitted Isaiah 1:6: "and a little child shall lead them." Yosef surely knew of expectations laid upon the "Branch." Did he also know Isaiah 7:14? "Therefore the Lord himself shall give you a sign; Behold, a virgin shall conceive, and bear a son, and shall call his name Immanuel." *Matthew* knew it, viewing Yosef's shock discovery that his betrothed was already pregnant as prophecy fulfilled.

Who was Yosef—other than descendant of King David, of the house from which the Branch would spring?

Matthew 13:55 (uniquely) has opponents in Nazareth call Jesus "the son of the *tektōn*," which could mean architect-mason, or builder in wood or stone. Possibly a side-trade reputation (as Saul was "tent-maker" [Acts 18:1–4]), it could have been a sectarian insult, for in the Damascus Document (4:15–20), a reference to Ezekiel 13:10 accuses "the builders of the wall" of following "Precept" (see Isaiah 28:7, 13), a priest and "Spouter" who, in violating marital law, profaned the temple. (I shall here resume calling Yeshua "Jesus" and Yosef "Joseph" for clarity's sake.)

In Mark 12:10, Jesus, in the temple, when presumably referring to John, quotes Psalm 118:22 to the chief priests and scribes, that the "stone the builders rejected" is now temple cornerstone, "the builders" having connived in the death of God-sent John, *zaddik*, or righteous one. Herod's profane family were involved not only in John's death, but in a long construction spree.

Luke sets Joseph's betrothal to Mary around Mary's "kinswoman" (*syngenis*) Elizabeth "of the daughters of Aaron," (priestly family) whose husband Zachariah is of priestly division Abijah ("Jahveh is father"), granted eighth lot to burn incense at the temple altar, with a house in Judean hill country (Luke 1:5, 39). There may be a messianic hint here, for the ninth, or *next* lot was given to "Jeshua," (or Yeshua = "God is salvation"). Certainly, Jesus's reported life is often physically centered on the temple. Luke has bar-mitzvah Jesus impressing temple teachers with scriptural mastery when "about his Father's business" (Luke 2:49). At Mary's purification, Jesus is celebrated by Jerusalem notable Simeon (possibly an Essene: "just and devout, waiting for the consolation of Israel"—and a predictor of the future*) and by widowed prophetess Anna, called a "daughter of Phanuel" (Luke 2:36).

Phanuel appears elsewhere *only* in Parables: an archangel with Gabriel, Michael, and Raphael. These four will "on that great day" cast the "hosts of Azaz'el" into the "abyss of complete condemnation" (1 Enoch 54:6). His name meaning "face" or "presence of God," Phanuel is "set over the repentance unto hope of those who inherit eternal life"

---

*According to Josephus, Essene prophet Simon (or Simeon, a common name) interpreted a dream of Archelaus in 4 BCE that Archelaus would succeed his father in Judea and reign for ten years, which he did.

(40:9). Luke has Anna leave her temple home to speak "of him [Jesus] to all people that looked for redemption in Jerusalem," a phrase in strict keeping with Phanuel's Enochic function. Anna, incidentally, is of the tribe of Asher, one of the ten *lost tribes* from Galilee's Tyrian coast, west of Dan.

Cousin John (*Johanan* = "Jahveh provides protection") would certainly have been raised to priesthood, and it's possible Jesus was too, especially if Joseph was himself a priest (the period saw resistance to the tradition that priesthood was exclusive to Levites; see Hebrews 7:28— and Joseph Angel's chapter, page 322).

Why is this significant?

We have traced the Enochic influence through accounts of rival priests in the Second Temple period, particularly in a rift between richer, high priestly factions politically tolerant of foreign influence, and poorer priests concerned with a prophetic new covenant with spiritual priorities opposed to dominant priests. If Jesus's background matches these distinctions, we may explain why the Epistle of Judas sees the Book of the Watchers as prophetically authoritative and why Judas's brother (?) James's epistle speaks of oppression of Jesus's followers by the rich: "Do not rich men oppress you and bring you before the judgement seats?" (James 2:6). There are indications in Josephus's *Antiquities* book 20 of a Sadducean plot to wipe out "Nazoreans," in which Saul-Paul participated before conversion, whereafter he severely disrupted the messianic party on returning to Damascus (Galatians 1:17–18).

Dated 140–170 CE, with a Syriac version considered older than the Greek, the Infancy Gospel (or *protoevangelium*) of James contains suggestive, if late, data about an allegedly priestly context for Jesus's birth. Its supposed authority is James, seen as Jesus's half-brother from a previous marriage of Joseph, whom Jewish-Christian historian Hegesippus, writing in about 170 CE, described as Jesus's brother without caveat, and as "the righteous," a temple priest "holy from his mother's womb" (*Commentaries on the Acts of the Church*, book 5, paraphrased in Eusebius, *Ecclesiastical History* 2.23). In the Protoevangelium, Mary's father Joachim (*Yehoyaqim* = "raised by Jahveh"), husband of temple slave girl Anna, wears a priest's miter. Aged twelve, orphaned Mary is adopted by a priest called Zadok. Zechariah advises on marriage after her stepmother dies. Instructed by an angel, Zechariah summons a gathering of "widowers of the people"—in the Greek—and men of the house of David—in the Syriac—at which a temple dove lands on Joseph's rod and head: a sign. Mary and Joseph are each children of the other's uncle. The Syriac implies Mary becomes ward of Joseph's wife (also called Mary), given wifely status to protect her name when a child is conceived.

Matthew maintains Joseph had to protect Mary from possible scandal as an unmarried pregnant girl (the Protoevangelium says she was sixteen). Ezekiel 44:22 lays down ordinances for priests: "Neither shall they take for their wives a widow, nor *her that is put away* [my italics]: but they shall take maidens of the seed of the house of Israel, or a widow that had a priest before." If Joseph was a priest, which would fit the Protoevangelium picture, he knew it forbidden to take for a wife a girl already pregnant; something scandalous had occurred.

Josephus's account of Sadducee High Priest Ananus's murderous attack on Jesus's brother (or half-brother) James the Righteous (62–63 CE), in *Antiquities* 20.9.1, does not indicate James was a priest but makes clear his support from "the most equitable of the citizens" who objected to Ananus's summoning a Sanhedrin court to have him stoned for lawbreaking. Herod Agrippa and Procurator Lucceius Albinus had Ananus deposed for the deed. According to Hegesippus:

James, the Lord's brother, succeeded to the government of the Church, with the apostles. He has been called the Righteous by all men, from the days of the Lord down to the present time. For many bore the name of James; but this one was holy from his mother's womb. He drank no wine or other intoxicating liquor, nor did he eat flesh; no razor came upon his head; he did not anoint himself with oil, nor make use of the bath. He alone was permitted to enter the sanctuary: for he did not wear any woollen garment, but fine linen only. And alone he used to go into the temple: and he used to be found kneeling and praying, begging forgiveness for the people, so that the skin of his knees became horny like that of a camel's, by reason of his constantly bending the knee in adoration to God, and begging forgiveness for the people.

(ca. 170 CE, Hegesippus, *Commentaries on the Acts of the Church*, book 5 paraphrased in Eusebius, *Ecclesiastical History* 2.23)

When the Sadducees beg James mount a temple battlement to tell people at Passover to cease believing Jesus is messiah by putting the question to him openly: "What is the door of Jesus?" Hegesippus's account has James using "son of man" language to answer (with lower case Greek for the title): "Why do you ask me concerning the son of man? He is sitting in heaven on the right hand of the great power, and he will come on the clouds of heaven." Many believe, crying "Hosanna to the Son of David"—at which "scribes and pharisees" pull James down and begin stoning him on the temple steps. Hegesippus recounts how priests (*note*) of the "sons of Rechab" cried out: "Stop! What are you doing? The Righteous one is praying for you."

A Kenite tribe adopted into Israel (1 Chronicles 2:55; Jeremiah 35:19), Jeremiah praised Rechabites for keeping their father Jonadab's commandments. He insisted they live in tents, resist wine, vineyard ownership, and cities. At this period, however, the term might have been a group moniker for persons frustrated with priestly corruption. Josephus refers to hymn-singing Levites taking to wearing the linen of the priesthood, appalled at profanation of the sacerdotal office— perhaps not alone among lesser religious persons in adopting the linen.

The Epistle of James was likely composed during this trying period, at the eve of his own murder: "Do not rich men oppress you and bring you before the judgement seats?" Josephus reports that it was the ruling high priests' wealth that allowed them to overthrow poorer priests' plans.

Statements in James's epistle make sense in the context of a Sadducean plot to wipe out Nazoreans: "behold the judge standeth before the door [note that "door" reference again]. Take, my brethren, the prophets, who have spoken in the name of the Lord, for an example of suffering affliction and of patience. Behold, we count them happy which endure. Ye have heard of the patience of Job, and have seen the end of the Lord" (James 5:9). The Messiah will return.

Shortly after James's death, Herod Agrippa enflamed Judean opposition when beautiful artifacts from Judea were transported for rebuilding Caesarea Philippi (Dan), to be renamed Neronias, in honor of *Nero*. Then, Jesus son of Damneus (Agrippa's replacement for Ananus), was succeeded by *another* Jesus, son of moderate *Pharisee* Gamaliel, an appointment outraging high priests, igniting what Josephus calls "a sedition."

The high priests gathered their own rowdy supporters, as rival parties threw stones at one another, causing a tumult quelled only by Ananias who, having more money, injected more muscle. Josephus's next statement well reflects Jerusalem's internal politics wherein the Jesus movement assembled:

> Costobarus also, and Saulus, did themselves get together a multitude of wicked wretches, and this because they were of the royal family; and so they obtained favour among them, because of their kindred to Agrippa: but still they used violence with the people, and were very ready to plunder those that were weaker than themselves. And from that time it principally came to pass, that our city was greatly disordered, and that all things grew worse and worse among us. (*Antiquities* 20.9.4)

We know little of the real causes for this infra-priestly disruption. It's most unlikely the Herodian "Saulus" was apostle Paul, since Agrippa II (Galilee's ruler 54–68) knew it was the "*chief* priests and elders" who hated Paul (Acts 25:13–26), but Paul had pro-Jesus factional opposition too. The period marks the beginning of the slide that, with the arrival of new and very severe procurator Gessius Florus, would lead to the Jewish Revolt and collapse of the world familiar to the first Nazoreans. We also see yet another twist on a now centuries-old chasm in "Zadokite" leadership, with Enochic influence on the Nazorean side.

Joseph and his family's precise place in similar sacerdotal fissures may partly underlie Matthew's account of family exile from Bethlehem to

Egypt driven by angelic prediction that Herod would "seek the young child to destroy him" (2:13). Omitting the supernatural element, the story is plausible.

A fragmentary letter to one Aristides from Christian geographer and historian Julius Africanus (ca. 170–245) in Eusebius's *Ecclesiastical History* attempts to reconcile two genealogies concerning Joseph's father using information provided by *desposunoi*, that is, Jesus's family descendants (a *desposunos* is one "belonging to the master or lord"). Julius tells Aristides that while Jews had maintained lineage records for generations, Idumean Arab Herod the Great's jealousy of Jewish nobility overcame him. His claim to rule, other than Rome's approval, was second marriage to Hasmonean princess Mariamne. He executed her for alleged adultery in 29 BCE. Their sons Aristobulus and Alexander were executed for alleged treason in 7 BCE.* Herod thought to make himself more noble than the old nobility by burning their genealogical records while claiming descent from the patriarchs or proselytes and those mingled with them, so-called *geiōras*: a Hellenized form of a Hebrew word for "stranger."

All was not lost, according to Julius:

> Now a few who were careful, however, having private records for themselves, either remembering the names or otherwise deriving them from copies, gloried in the preservation of the memory of their good birth; among these were those mentioned above, called *desposunoi*, because of their relation to the family of the saviour, and from the Judean villages of *Nazarōn* [which can be transliterated from the Greek as *Nazara*] and *Kōchaba* [or *Cochaba*], they traversed the rest of the land and expounded the preceding genealogy of their descent, and from the Book of Days [*Chronicles*] as far as they went. (*Ecclesiastical History* 1.7)

So, despite the gospels' apparent disinterest in Jesus as rival political claimant—the *eschaton* would settle the kingdoms of *this* world—

---

*Some have speculated Herod's executing his children lies behind the story of the "massacre of the innocents," as it occurred contemporaneously to Jesus's birth.

Herod, himself very much of this world, had every reason to annihilate at birth any supposed messiah, especially if succored by opponents of his Sadducean supporters.

Had Herod known a perceived rival was in Egypt, he had means to assassinate him. When Aelius Gallus was Rome's second prefect in Egypt (26–24 BCE), Herod contributed five hundred of his personal guard to Gallus's disastrous invasion of Arabia Felix (*Antiquities* 15.9.3 [317]). Herod's payback financed a magnificent gold and marble palace in Jerusalem, into which he desired to indulge the pleasure of Mariamne, "the most beautiful woman of that time," daughter of Jerusalem citizen, Simon. Avoiding condemnation as violent tyrant should he abuse Mariamne, Herod opted for marriage. Sensitive to Simon's inferior dignity as ally and father-in-law, Herod raised that dignity by giving Simon the high priesthood, depriving Jesus, son of Phabet, of the role: an idea perhaps inspired by Simon's father Boethus's being, according to Josephus, "a citizen of Alexandria, and a priest of great note there."

The only Jewish temple in Egypt was of course founded by Onias III or Onias IV in the Heliopolitan nome. Perhaps Josephus had it in mind when writing of how, sixty-six years later in 41 CE, Herod Agrippa replaced High Priest Theophilus with Simon's son, Simon *Cantheras*:* "Simon therefore had the Priesthood, with his brethren, and with his father; in like manner as the sons of Simon [I], the son of Onias [I], who were three [presumably Simon I's son Onias II; Onias II's son Simon II; and Simon II's son Onias III] had it formerly under the government of the Macedonians [Seleucids]" (*Antiquities* 19.6:2).

So Simon, son of Egypt-based priest Boethus, was high priest when (or if) Joseph took Jesus to Egypt in or after 7 BCE, but Simon was not so when (or if) the family left on Herod's death, for in 4 BCE—commonly supposed year of Herod's death—Simon's daughter Mariamne II was implicated in a plot against a sick Herod and brother Pheroras, led by Antipater, Herod's son from first wife Doris. Antipater was executed, Mariamne was divorced, and her and

---

*Probably from the Greek *Kantharos*: a drinking cup, a probable swipe at winebibbing excesses; Pharisees despised Boethusian priests, "in" with Sadducees.

Herod's son Herod II was removed from the succession.* Mariamne's father Simon was replaced as high priest by Matthias. By the year's end, however, Simon's *son* Joazar was high priest, quickly replaced by brother Eleazar (Latin *Lazarus*). In 3 BCE Eleazar was superseded by Jesus (or Joshua) ben Sie, with Joazar restored sometime before eventual deposition by Ananus (or Annas) ben Seth in 6 CE at Roman legate Quirinius's instigation when establishing Judaea province under direct Roman rule.

Whatever religious proclivities might have motivated Simon's father Boethus in Egypt, by the time Simon lost the high priesthood, he and his sons were firmly associated with ruling Sadducees when Joseph returned to "Israel" (Matthew 2:19–23) after an angel's reassurance that "*they*" who sought the child's life were dead ("they" could include executed Antipater or possibly Simon). According to Matthew, however, Joseph *still* feared "to go thither" on hearing Archelaus had succeeded to the throne.

After Herod's heir Antipater's execution, Herod Antipas stood next in line, but Herod changed his will shortly before his death, making son Archelaus from fourth wife Malthace, a Samaritan, ethnarch of Judea, with Archelaus's brother Antipas and half-brother Philip tetrarchs over Galilee, Peraea, Gaulanitis, Trachonitis, Batanaea, and Paneas. Perhaps Joseph heard of the will-change after leaving Egypt. Matthew's explanation for a plan change that took Joseph "into the parts of Galilee" where "he came and dwelt in a city called Nazareth" (Matthew 2:23) was that Judea held dangers, and followed a dream-warning to head north. Joseph's reliance on oneiromancy for decisions is, incidentally, reminiscent both of Enoch at Dan, and Essene expertise in interpreting dreams.

Apparently, Joseph had found the prospect of Antipas ruling Judea acceptable, proceeding to Galilee knowing Herod Antipas was now ruler there. Since Archelaus had not yet launched his bloody decade as ethnarch, could Joseph's issue have been one of Antipas and Archelaus supporting different priestly factions? Archelaus inherited massive tem-

---

*Having married half-sister Herodias, Herod II fathered Salome, instrumental in John the Baptist's beheading (Mark 6:14–29).

ple protests instigated by anti-Sadducean protestors. These dissolved into punitive carnage. Were there relations between Joseph's family, or religious associates, and Antipas's supporters? Luke 8:3 refers to one Joanna, wife of Chuza, Herod Antipas's steward. Joanna financially supported Jesus's mature operation in Galilee. Some connection with Antipas's administration existed. Jesus was not molested by Antipas; later opposition came chiefly from Jerusalem.

More to Nazareth than Meets the Eye

Matthew 2:23 tells us destination Nazareth was to fulfill prophecy that the messiah "shall be called a Nazarene." No such prophecy exists. Its closest kin is Judges 13:2–7, referring to Samson's miraculous birth: "the child shall be a Nazarite unto God from the womb: and he shall begin to deliver Israel out of the hand of the Philistines," which has nothing to do with a *place* but with the Nazarite vow. Nazarites' holy practices included attending the "door of the tabernacle of the congregation" (i.e. Jerusalem's temple; Numbers 6:1–21), fasting, abstaining from wine, and not cutting hair. Furthermore, it's extremely doubtful Nazareth was established, let alone a city at the time. Archaeology indicates mid-*second*-century structures; Nazareth's not mentioned in Jewish scripture, nor even by Josephus, who fortified Galilean towns in the revolt. In Mark 6, when Jesus comes to his "own country," Nazareth is not mentioned. Luke 4:16 on the other hand, supposedly based on Mark, *adds* Nazareth to an expanded story. If Luke's (?) Acts 24:5 is factual, a lawyer for high priest Ananias (46–58 CE) accused Paul as "ringleader of the sect of the Nazarenes"—the Greek *Nazōraiōn* almost certainly derived from transliterating the Hebrew *Natzarim*, though Acts' author probably thought it referred to Nazareth; but why should a group of messianists name themselves, or be called, after an unknown *place*? Besides, Jesus was of *Bethlehem*, house of Judah, son of David! An acceptable nickname would reference *self*-perception, which, on analysis, is what we find.

We've heard Julius Africanus refer to a "Nazara," apparently in Judea and home for *desposyni*. Nazara suggests the Hebrew *netzer*

(English transliteration of nun, tzadi, resh = *ntzr*), which means "sprout" or "root," commonly translated "branch"—messianically promising! Ntzr+*artz* (aleph, resh, tzaddi ="land") gives "Branchland": a good place to put down roots, especially to plant the root and raise the "Branch" (Isaiah 11:1)?

Another contender: *nezer* (Hebrew: nun, zayin, resh), referring to something consecrated, dedicated, separated, hence the Nazarite vow: something rendered holy to God. It can mean "crown," as sign of consecration, or "hair" in like mode (see Exodus 28:36). It suggests both consecrated kingship and priesthood (the high priest's miter = *nezer hakodesh*: "the holy crown" in Leviticus 8:9, with its golden *tzitz* inscribed with the words: HOLY TO JAHVEH (Exodus 28:36). Nzr+artz gives "consecrated land" or even "crown land."

The key difference between these cognate roots is in "nzr" the "z" or "s" sound is a zayin (ז) and in "ntzr" a tzadi (צ). Tzadi is in the name "Nazareth" today: nun, tzadi, resh, tav ("Natseret"). It seems to me such associative pun value would have been unmissable to messianically minded contemporaries. Be that as it may, it's most likely the original word transliterated as "Nazarene" or "Nazorean" from Greek *Nazōraiōn* (Acts 24:5) indicated primarily not a place, but a dedicated ideal, purposeful action—and one is close, for Hebrew verb *natzar* (or *natsar* = nun, tzadi, resh—again!) means to *watch*, guard, preserve, or keep. Its scriptural incidents include keeping God's covenant; the Lord preserving them; watching (as in watchmen from a tower); keeping loving kindness; keeping mercy; keeping His commandments. From this verb we find our collective noun in *natzarim*, or natsarim (נצרים), which we find—with another meaningful pun, *perfectly placed*—in Jeremiah 4:15–17:

> For a voice declareth from Dan [!], and publisheth affliction from mount Ephraim [between Bethel and Shechem]. Make ye mention to the nations; behold, publish against Jerusalem, that *watchers* [natzarim] come from a far country, and give out their voice against the cities of Judah. As keepers of a field are they against her round about; because she has been rebellious against me, saith the LORD.

While Jeremiah's original prophecy refers to Nebuchadnezzar's army's impending descent on Judea and Jerusalem, with advance spies (?), this text may well have spoken volumes to the first century too. These "watchers," apparently the reverse of 1 Enoch's wicked Watchers (Aramaic: *iyrin*; see also Daniel 4:13, 17, 23), are rather *agents of God's judgment*, for Nebuchadnezzar is but God's instrument. These watchers from a "far country" (Dan?) are literally "legal guardians" of a field, come to redeem the owner's rights. Yes, one immediately recalls Jesus's parable, aimed at "pharisees and chief priests" in the temple, of the wicked husbandmen (Matthew 21:33–46). Indeed, Jeremiah reveals Jesus's mature operation in a nutshell. He and the twelve will descend as "watchers from a far country" on Jerusalem and prophesy doom. The Natzarim are the Watchers, the Keepers, or the Guardians: a fine collective name for an enterprise launched from Galilee. In John 11:54, after raising Lazarus, knowing his enemies' plot to kill him, Jesus takes the disciples to *Ephraim* "near to the wilderness," before final (?), fateful return to Bethany and Jerusalem.

We may note the significance to contemporary messianists of the watchtower in the Damascus Document, where it is written of the endtimes: "But when the age is completed, according to the number of those years, there shall be no more joining the house of Judah, but each man shall stand on his watchtower: The wall is built, the boundary far removed [Micah 7:11: 'In the day that thy walls are to be built, in that day shall the decree be far removed']." In Mark's overtly apocalyptic 13:33–37, Jesus repeats the imperative "Watch" *four* times: "lest coming suddenly he ['the son of man'] find you sleeping" (v.36).

According to Matthew, Jesus's father was familiar to Galilean locals as *tektōn*, meaning builder in stone and/or wood. I should like to suggest he constructed his "natzaret," his keeper-land or watcher-land, in a high place, with a view on the Jordan Valley south, with Tel Megiddo southwest, Mount Gilboa southeast toward the Ephraim mountains—and beyond, unseen, Judah and destiny. Alternatively, there was already something of a camp or priestly dacha there, and sympathetic people, possibly Essenes or "New Covenanters" of Enochic hue. Joseph may have added to it, which is to say *Nazareth* may originally have been a noun associated with the cause of *natzarim*: a holy enclave, a separated and consecrated place, no city or town, but a neo-Zadokite camp established or joined in Galilee by Joseph and familial associates to further plans concerning the son of David. Such would explain much, including confusion over Jesus as Nazarite, separated for holiness, and Jesus's followers as so-called Nazarenes.

After the temple's destruction in 70 CE, priests appear to have retired to sympathetic communities. A Galilean "natzeret" might have provided sanctuary. A third- or fourth-century fragmentary Hebrew inscription, discovered at Caesarea in 1962, refers to a priestly (kohanim) family of the Hapizzez, or eighteenth of the twenty-four priestly courses, from after Bar Kokhba's last-ditch Zealot revolt of 132–135 CE and expulsion of Jews from Jerusalem. The family settled in "Natzareth," Galilee. That the eighteenth Kohen clan lived at "Nitzrat" or "Nitzrath" (נצרת) is supported by Galilean poet Eleazar Kalir, writing between the sixth and tenth century CE. After the expulsion, the site may have attracted hoi polloi settlers, with a town emerging on or close to the site, whose original referent was forgotten, pronunciation garbled. Such would fit the archaeology.

TWENTY-TWO

Further Enochic
Adventures in Galilee

David Suter's article "Why Galilee?"[1] explores relations between
the upper Jordan valley and 1 Enoch 6–16. It builds on George
Nickelsburg's "Enoch, Levi, and Peter: Recipients of Revelation in
Upper Galilee,"[2] which observed a Galilee distinguished for revelations, particularly in 1 Enoch 12–16, the Testament of Levi, and
Peter's confessing Jesus as Christ near or at Dan, around Philip's new-
built Caesarea Philippi (Mark 8:29). Comparing a spiritually shadowy
Jerusalem with traditional sacred place Dan, Nickelsburg wondered
whether the Damacus Document's "land of Damascus" suggested a
new-covenant group linked to Dan's ancient sanctuary. Similarly, Suter
sees the Book of the Watchers' *original* authors—of Judean scribal and
priestly origin—at odds with Jerusalem's Zadokite establishment.[3] He
asks whether their Watchers story reflected Syro-Phoenician divination
and incubation oracles (1 Enoch 13–14) prevalent in the region of lost
tribes Naphtali and Asher (whence came Anna, "daughter of Phanuel").

Archaeology suggests Roman-era Galilee was populated by
Judeans,[4] though Paneas's "Paneion" indicates pagan Hellenism from
the Ptolemaic era persisted, with Herod dedicating a sanctuary there to
Augustus Caesar.

Dan's geography in relation to Mt. Hermon and waters to Hermon's
southwest (Tel Dan's once blindingly gushing Jordan source by the

Fig. 22.1. "Pan's cave" at today's "Banias" (Paneas) by a main tributary of the Jordan. The river originated in ancient times at Pan's cave before it was blocked by earthquake.
(Photo: gugganij)

Fig. 22.2. Ancient remains of the sanctuary to Pan at Baneas.

Damascus road) accurately frames the Watchers drama. Suter identifies 1 Enoch 13's "Abel Mayya," where the Watchers weep (Abel's root means to weep), with Abel Mayim, an alternative name for Tel Abel-beth-Ma'akah, some four miles west of Dan, a mound yielding much mid–Iron Age stonework and Phoenician pottery.

Fig. 22.3. Canaanite Gate at Tel Dan, preserved by the Council for the Conservation of Heritage Sites in Israel. (Photo: Hanay)

Suter wonders if meteorological "powers" falling on Hermon shaped folk myths, along with the Jordan's "descent" from the mountain, recalling a version of the Watchers story in Syncellus where Hermon is finally cursed for the Watchers' oath by conflagrations of frost, snow, ice, and dew.[5] Suter also notes a pagan temenos and stone circle around Hermon's southernmost third peak, where French archaeologist Clermont-Ganneau (died 1923) found an inscription at a nearby cave associated with god Ba'al Hermon: "By order of the greatest and holy god, those who swore—from here"—linking it to 1 Enoch 6–12.[6]

Possible Syro-Phoenician coloring to Enoch's sleeping at Dan's waters to receive a vision of the Watchers' end is significant. The Greco-Roman world was dotted with deity sanctuaries where visitors were encouraged to obtain revelations by dreaming at the site (incubation oracles). Springs were ideal because of the underworld link. Archaeologist Vassilios Tzaferis sees adjacent sites of Dan and Paneas as linked, with the latter, built up under Ptolemy II, declining with Paneas's growth under the Seleucids, consistent with Antiochus III's victory at Paneas (see pages 117-19). Antiochus's forebear Seleucus I (died 281 BCE) had erected a temple to Pythian Apollo at Daphne, outside Antioch, suitable for dream purposes.* Suter notes how writing dream-questions and writing dream *experiences* was an important scribal task in the Hellenistic world, reflected perhaps in Enoch's scribal role for Watchers holy and wicked.[7] Interestingly, 2 Samuel 20:18 has "a wise woman" crying out from besieged "Abel of Bethmaachah" that the city was a place for "counsel": "Then she spake, saying, They were wont to speak in old time, saying, They shall surely ask counsel at Abel: and so they ended the matter." She called this oracle "an inheritance of the Lord," to be preserved.

Suter sees evidence indicating a Hellenized cult of the "God who is in Dan" (a phrase from an oracular inscription at nearby Kedesh) plus oneiromantic oracle linked to the "waters of Dan." This idea would add force to Jeremiah 4:15's news broadcast from Dan of impending *judgment*. Suter's question "Why Galilee?" would "thus be answered in part by appeal to the policies of the Ptolemaic empire in establishing a sanctuary at the site of the ancient Israelite sanctuary as an instrument of social control in a frontier region in the empire, and perhaps in choosing or recruiting a priesthood to serve it."[8] While further observing that Hermon's inspiring grandeur made a better source than Jerusalem for the heavenly ice-and-fire sanctuary of 1 Enoch 14, he also emphasizes the links to divination, vision, and revelation may have contributed more to apocalyptic literature's themes of heavenly ascent than any presence of apocalyptic "circles" or even a New Covenanted community in or near Damascus.[9]

---

*Note that 2 Maccabees 4:33–34 has Onias III seeking "sanctuary" there before his murder.

Joseph made a sound, if fateful, decision bringing his Judean family to Galilee.

The Hypothesis Continued

What Jesus learned, and who and where he learned it from, may only be guessed at, but one may ask whether so-called sectarian documents lodged at Qumran were as exclusive in their time as commentators imagine. For example, a text Vermes calls a "Messianic Apocalypse" (4Q521) systematically lists the signs of the messianic kingdom the righteous will perceive: the recognition of the pious, the calling of the righteous by name, the renewal of the Lord's poor and faithful by his spirit, the glorification of the pious on "the throne of the eternal kingdom," the liberation of captives, the restoration of sight to the blind, the straightening of the bent, the doing of glorious things never seen before, the healing of the wounded, the leading of the uprooted, the feeding of the hungry, the giving of good news to the poor, and the revival of the dead, when "the Life-giver will raise the dead of his people."

In Luke 7 is a curious scene where John the Baptist sends "two disciples" to ask if Jesus is the expected one (v.19). Jesus has just raised the widow of Nain's son from the dead in v.15. Notwithstanding, "in that same hour [as John's disciples ask] he cured many of their infirmities and plagues, and of evil spirits; and unto many that were blind he gave sight" (v.21). He then says John should be told how the blind see, the lame walk, the lepers cleansed, the deaf hear, dead are raised and "to the poor the gospel is preached" (v.22). Practically every box of the listed signs to the righteous are ticked, and all remaining signs are fulfilled elsewhere. Jesus operates according to an *existing itinerary*.

In like manner, it's impossible to ignore priorities from Qumran's Community Rule (8:1–15) reflected in Jesus's Galilean operation in assembling a new, holy community to prepare the way of salvation:

In the Council of the Community there shall be twelve men and three Priests, perfectly versed in all that is revealed of the Law, whose works shall be truth, righteousness, justice, loving-kindness, and humility. They shall preserve the faith in the Land with steadfastness and meekness and shall atone for sin by the practice of justice and by suffering the sorrows of affliction. They shall walk with all men according to the standard of truth and the rule of the time. When these are in Israel, the Council of the Community shall be established in truth. It shall be an Everlasting plantation, a house of holiness for Israel, an Assembly of Supreme Holiness for Aaron. They shall be witnesses to the truth at the Judgment, and shall be the elect of Goodwill who shall atone for the Land and pay to the wicked their reward. It shall be that tried wall, that precious cornerstone, whose foundations shall neither rock nor sway in their place [Isaiah 28:16]. It shall be a Most Holy Dwelling for Aaron, with everlasting knowledge of the Covenant of justice, and shall offer up sweet fragrance. It shall be a House of Perfection and Truth in Israel that they may establish a Covenant according to the everlasting precepts. And they shall be an agreeable offering, atoning for the land and determining the judgment of wickedness and there shall be no more iniquity. When they have been confirmed for two years in perfection of way in the Foundation of the Community, they shall be set apart as holy within the Council of the men of the Community. And the Interpreter shall not conceal from them, out of fear of the spirit of apostasy, any of those things hidden from Israel, which have been discovered by him. And when these become members of the Community in Israel according to all these rules they shall separate from the habitation of unjust men and shall go into the wilderness to prepare there the way of Him; as it is written, Prepare in the wilderness the way of . . . make straight in the desert a path for our God [Isaiah 40:3.] This (path) is the study of the Law, which He commanded by the hand of Moses, that they may do according to all that has been revealed from age to age, and as the prophets have revealed by His Holy Spirit.

As for "three priests," my book *The Mysteries of John the Baptist* advances the thesis that Jesus's operation was coordinated with John's at some point, with John a priest, garbed by gospel writers as Elijah. If Jesus's brother James was a priest, and Jesus too, you have the three. Otherwise, the gospels maintain there was an inner group of three, usually John, James, and Peter. Paul famously ridicules Cephas (Peter), John, and James as men "who seemed to be pillars," that is *so-called pillars* (Galatians 2: 9, 11–13). However the twelve-and-three is played out, a template existed already. Even Isaiah 40:3 appears in Mark 1:3 to announce John the Baptist.

The Community Rule recommends members enter the wilderness to study the Law. Certainly we have vivid accounts of John and Jesus in the wilderness confronting their destinies, though the Rule suggests communal entry. John is said to have attracted multitudes, and Jesus, in the wilderness after baptism, is ministered to by "angels," appropriate company for purified members of a religious community. As young men, John and Jesus would be familiar with alternatives to Jerusalem's urban priesthood, and there's little doubt they shared much with literature advocating a pact made "in the land of Damascus," and paid the price, opposed and spied on by divers Pharisees, Sadducees, and scribes over doctrine and politics. Jesus's self-perception would prove the stumbling block.

Another aspect of the Galilean experience emerges in Matthew 15:21–28. After bitter exchanges with scribes and Pharisees in Jerusalem, Jesus heads far northwest to the Syro-Phoenician coast of Tyre and Sidon (the old land of Israel's lost tribe of Asher), due west of Dan, where a "Canaanite woman" hails him as "Lord" and "Son of David," begging Jesus exorcize a demon from her daughter. When the disciples brush her aside, Jesus says: "I am not sent but unto the lost sheep of the house of Israel," (v.24) apparently having a message for the lost tribes separated from Judea when the northern kingdom of Israel fell to Assyria in the eighth century. The religio-political meaning of this message seems to have got lost in Pauline Christianity. *Jesus wants to re-unite the remnant of faith*, even among folk such as Samaritans whom Judean leaders rejected. It may explain why Jesus's supposed purse-bearer was Judas *Iskariōtes* (Greek) which may indicate a link to "Issachar," lost tribal area just south of Naphtali (see Genesis 49:14–15; 1 Chronicles 12:32). The image of sheep needing a good shepherd reflects 1 Enoch 89, inspired by Ezekiel 34: "I will bring them [the sheep] out from the nations and gather them from the countries, and I will bring them into their own land. I will pasture them on the mountains of Israel, in the ravines and in all the settlements in the land. . . . I will search for the lost and bring back the strays. I will bind up the injured and strengthen the weak, but the sleek and the strong I will destroy. . . . I the Lord will be their God, and my servant David will be prince among them" (vv.13; 16, 24).

Jesus's Anti-Demon Operation

Many modern commentators struggle to understand Jesus's belief in demonic possession and exorcism. Enoch's confrontation with the wicked Watchers may illuminate Jesus's view (as also proposed by Henryk Drawnel, page 316). Evil spirits remained when the Giants' bodies were destroyed because they derived from immortal Watchers and humans, living on earth until the end. Jesus *sees* them, as does Enoch.

> Evil spirits have proceeded from their [the giants'] bodies, because they are born from men, and from the holy Watchers in their beginning and primal origin; they shall be evil spirits on earth, and evil spirits they shall be called . . . and these spirits shall rise up against the children of men and against the women. (1 Enoch 15:9)

In the gospels, Jesus teaches his disciples how to cast out evil spirits. Everyone remembers the madman *chained* (cf. the fate of the evil Watchers) whose "Legion" of evil spirits hop into the Gadarene swine to plunge suicidally into the sea (Mark 5:1–13). Jesus's operation mirrors Enoch's progressive condemnation of Azaz'el: "Now is the judgment of this world: now shall the prince of this world be cast out" (John 12:31). In John 14, Jesus declares the "prince of this world" has no hold over him, a boast made by Enoch dealing with Azaz'el.

The "prince of this world" is the gospels' *Satan*—not a name; *Satan* means the "adversary." In the book of Job, "ha-satan" plays prosecution counsel in God's own court, where he is not "fallen," or ungovernably evil, but God's servant responsible for exposing human evil. Temptation can be a divine test, so the Satan has governance of evil spirits. The first century sees full convergence of the two ideas, arguably under Persian dualist influence, and Enoch's wicked Watchers.

Enoch regards the Watchers and evil spirits' final end as an ancient secret, stored in the heavenly tablets. The gospels' salvation itinerary is similarly regarded as a secret concealed from the beginning. Jesus forgives enemies in the gospels when he sees their wickedness as instruments of a spiritual power they don't perceive, uprootable only by divine action; the crucifiers "know not what they do" (Luke 23:34). God's enemies are fundamentally spiritual enemies who play humans like puppets. Humans think they have a will, but do the will of powers of which they are unconscious, unless they repent and accept God's will—a doctrine with contemporary resonance.

Ethics and Vision

Jesus's ethics conform to the highest standards advocated in Enochic texts: righteousness in what is owed to God, mercy in what is owed to human beings. There is a space for repentance (see pages 57, 61, 69) and a distinct note in Jesus's ethical teaching of refraining from judging others without judgment of oneself; God is judge. Such spectacular generosity finds resonance with behavior both Philo and Josephus attribute to Essenes: sharing of personal property; simplicity of diet and clothing; restraint from revenge, violence, fornication, personal vanity, profiteering. Loving kindness is advocated; feeding the poor; visiting the sick and needy; selflessness; courage in adversity; truthfulness; the virtue of peacemaking, loving God and one's neighbor as oneself. Jesus's proscription on oath-taking (Matthew 5:34–37) resonates with Essene practice. The same goes for fearlessness concerning the body, with fearfulness reserved for losing the soul or presence of God. Like the Essenes, the way of Jesus calls men away from their families, but as with some Essenes, there is tolerance of female participation, though this seems more pronounced of Jesus in the gospels (especially Luke). Jesus apparently doesn't share Essene fastidiousness over bodily purity, washing, and toilet practice. His teaching that that which defiles a man comes from the heart, not via flesh, would severely qualify any notion of physical impurity being close to evil, and would upset Essenes generally, and outrage more separatist New Covenanters.

Essene ambivalence with regard to the temple appears shared with Jesus; indeed, he prophesies its destruction without regret (Matthew 24:2). Another distinct aspect of Jesus's practical ethics is a profound condemnation of hypocrisy: acting as to appear virtuous but hiding the heart's true state. Above all, Jesus's conception of the kingdom of heaven is an *inward*, perception-opening reality, subsisting on a heavenly counterpart; the *rock* is that link that outlives the world. The inspiration here would be Jeremiah and Ezekiel's idea of the new covenant written in the heart, where lies the true "circumcision" of divine dedication. Furthermore, the gospel Jesus is more interested in the spirit in which the law is fulfilled than the externally observed letter. If the spirit is at risk, the letter must be re-examined in the light of the spiritual call. Jesus's famous sabbath teaching is axiomatic (Mark 2:27). We cannot be sure Essenes would have accepted Jesus's embellishments on the law in Matthew 5:21–22, 27–28, 31–34, 38–39, 43–44. Jesus upholds the law absolutely in Matthew 5, but it must be *fulfilled*, that is, seen and acted upon in its spiritual totality (did he have in mind the "heavenly tablets" of Jubilees?). The "righteousness" of the Pharisees and scribes is inadequate (Matthew 5:20). Perfection is the aim, nothing less. Whoever attains not perfection has no right to judge others (Matthew 5:48). One senses there would have been Essenes whose eyes would have been opened by Jesus's teaching on the Torah, and who would have recognized it as fruit of the new covenant prophesied by Ezekiel and Jeremiah. Matthew 7:29: "For he taught them as one having authority, and not as the scribes." Evil makes one blind to true authority.

The cornerstone of the ethical consciousness lies in vision, in *seeing things as they really are*. Those in the kingdom of heaven have been granted *perception*. This insight is vital to Enochic ascended awareness, and arguably its chief legacy. Opening the eyes of the blind is not only a theme of Jesus's healing works but signifies his spiritual gift to his closest disciples: "Unto you it is given to know the mystery of the kingdom of God: but unto them that are without, all these things are done in parables: That seeing they may see, and not perceive; and hearing they may hear, and not understand; lest at any time they should be converted, and their sins should be forgiven them" (Mark 4:11–12).

Vision is vital, crucial: "The light of the body is the eye: if therefore thine eye be single, thy whole body shall be full of light" (Matthew 6:22). Opening the eyes of the sheep dominates 1 Enoch 89 where the sheep's blindness is the principal issue: "but the sheep began to be blinded and to wander from the way which he had showed them," (v.32) "And sometimes their eyes were opened, and sometimes blinded, till another sheep arose and led them and brought them all back, and their eyes were opened" (v.41). "And after that I saw that when they forsook the house of the Lord and His tower [note!] they fell away entirely, and their eyes were blinded," (v.53) "And as touching all this the eyes of those sheep were blinded so that they saw not, and (the eyes of) their shepherds likewise; and they delivered them in large numbers to their shepherds for destruction" (v.74). Sight is what "darkness" denies. The "light" Jesus bestows is the power to discriminate light from darkness, to perceive directly the spiritual world, or kingdom of heaven. Jesus sees men and sees right through them to the reality that is spiritual, to which ordinary or ungodly minds are blind: "that seeing they may not see." They *think* they see; they *think* they know, but they neither see nor know; they have no authority. To see Satan clearly, Jesus has to enter the wilderness to experience a sensorium undistracted by objects and people, where existence is stark: earth, heaven; light, darkness; life, death; truth, lies.

When Enoch ascends to heaven, he rises above ordinary man's perception of earth, and sees the "many mansions," so to speak, of the heavenly realms; when Satan tempts Jesus, he can only show him earthly kingdoms, where he holds sway. As Jesus sees beyond this, he sees the root of the tempter's tactics and overcomes them.

Enoch scholar Andrei Orlov has also observed that Enoch's otherworldly knowledge inversely mirrors illicit revelations of the fallen Watchers. Enoch then offers this transcending perspective to his posterity. As we shall see, Jesus takes his closest disciples to Mount Hermon for visionary experience. Orlov's book chapter "Ocular Epistemology and the Watchers' Lost Perception" in his book *Divine Mysteries in the Enochic Tradition* (2023), shows how the Watchers forsook access to heavenly knowledge in the process of their rebellion: the reverse of Enoch's destiny. Orlov shows how important visual knowledge is to Enoch's illumination. Enoch is *shown* the Son of Man. He *sees* the throne. He beholds the heavens. His ocular perception is enhanced to the ultimate.[10] He *sees* also in dreams what is coming; the visionary plane is open to him, for he "walks with God."

Acquiring this faculty is of the essence of Jesus's teaching. The parables are pictures one must look *through*, as with a true "ikon." The image is what meets the eye; the eye must meet the mind, or source and spirit of vision. What Enoch sees, no man has ever seen before: "For since the beginning of the world men have not heard, nor perceived by the ear, neither hath the eye seen, O God, beside thee, what he hath prepared for him that waiteth for him" (Isaiah 64:4). Jesus's enemies see him; but they don't see *him*, and so know not what they do. Enochic vision seems embedded in Jesus's understanding, although it's worth noting we never hear of Jesus dreaming or interpreting a dream. Did his whole consciousness have the character of a perfectly lucid dream?—for his "reality" can hardly have been identical with that of others: he *saw* spiritual reality. Disciples were called out of the world to enter his reality of inspirited consciousness. When Raphael is told in 1 Enoch 10:4–5 to bind Azaz'el, he is told to cover Azaz'el's face "and let him not see the light." This is hell indeed: covered in darkness. This is the dwelling place of the "father of lies," whose blindness corrupts the earth.

Enoch sees the light in heaven; Jesus is presented in the gospels as bringing it back to earth, for those who see it.

Back to Dan with the Son of Man— the Profound Ascent

Hidden under the Herodian rename of "Caesarea Philippi," the significance of Dan-Paneas has been lost to Christian tradition. Yet it is here that Jesus puts the key question to his disciples: "Whom do men say that I am?" (Mark 8:27–29). In Mark they say John the Baptist, Elijah, or "one of the prophets" (did someone suggest Enoch?). Matthew 16:14 adds Jeremiah. Peter says Jesus is the messiah, and while praised, is told to keep it secret. Jesus then tells of the sufferings the son of man must undergo before rising again "after three days," which all upsets Peter so much he grabs Jesus and rebukes him. Jesus rebukes him back, calling him "Satan," for seeing things the way men see them, not as God. Satan doesn't see; the son of man does.

Fig. 22.4. Roman bridge at Baneas today. The Via Maris connecting Heliopolis to Damascus—the famous "road to Damascus"—leads eastward via Herod Agrippa II's palace at Caesarea Philippi, renamed Neronias by Agrippa. (Photo: Andrew Abado)

Six days later (Luke says eight, but see Exodus 24:16), Jesus takes the three (James, Peter, and John) to the "high mountain"—surely highly visible Mount Hermon (none higher)—and shows them what *seeing* means. He's transfigured before them in a scene reminiscent of 1 Enoch's Parables, with raiment "exceeding white as snow, so as no fuller on earth can white them" (Mark 9:3), or as Matthew 17:2 puts it: "his face did shine as the sun, and his raiment was white as the light." The three saw Moses (the Law) and Elijah (the Prophets) talking with Jesus. Scared stiff are the three, hearing a voice from a cloud declaring they must listen because this was His "beloved son" (Mark 9:7).

Fig. 22.5. Mount Hermon.

Nobody familiar with 1 Enoch 71 can avoid a comparison with what happened when "my [Enoch's] spirit was translated. And it ascended to the heavens: And I saw the holy sons of God. They were stepping on flames of fire: Their garments were white [and their raiment], And their faces shone like snow" (v.1). After translation to the "heaven of heavens" (v.8) Enoch sees the four archangels, including Phanuel, "And with them the Head of Days, His head white and pure as wool, And His raiment indescribable" (v.10). Overwhelmed, Enoch falls on his face. Matthew 17:6 has the disciples react in *exactly* the same way to the voice proclaiming the "beloved Son": "And when the disciples heard it, they fell on their face, and were sore afraid." Enoch is comforted: his whole taut body becomes relaxed, whereupon his "spirit was transfigured," (v.11) and is shown "the Son of Man who is born unto righteousness" who proclaims to Enoch "peace in the name of the world to come" while the righteous will "not be separated from him for ever and ever" (v.16).

In order to *see*, the three had to ascend the mountain with Jesus. The idea of ascension for vision is central to Enochic dynamics. The wicked

Watchers' sin was in descending. The completion of the son of man's work in the gospels requires he "rise again," but accounts differ as to what was involved.

Luke, in Acts 1 (presuming Luke wrote it) harmonizes to a degree with his gospel account where the resurrected Christ leads the disciples to Bethany (southeast slope of Mt. Olivet), lifts his hands, blesses them, and is "parted from them, and carried up into heaven" (Luke 24:51). Acts 1:12 has the disciples returning "unto Jerusalem from the mount called Olivet, which is from Jerusalem a sabbath day's journey" immediately after Jesus "was taken up; and a cloud received him out of their sight. And while they looked steadfastly toward heaven as he went up, behold, two men stood by them in white apparel; Which also said, Ye men of Galilee, why stand ye gazing up into heaven? this same Jesus, which is taken up from you into heaven, shall so come in like manner as ye have seen him go into heaven" (Acts 1:9–11).

Matthew knows nothing of any Mt. Olivet or Bethany ascension. In Matthew 28:16–20 "the eleven disciples went away into Galilee, into a mountain where Jesus had appointed them. And when they saw him, they worshipped him: but some doubted. And Jesus came and spake unto them, saying, All power is given unto me in heaven and in earth. Go ye therefore, and teach all nations, baptizing them in the name of the Father, and of the Son, and of the Holy Ghost: Teaching them to observe all things whatsoever I have commanded you: and, lo, I am with you always, even unto the end of the world. Amen."

That final valediction seems closely inspired by 1 Enoch 71:16 where the Son of Man comforts Enoch with the knowledge that the righteous need never fear separation from him. It is also significant, I think, that for this, the disciples have to travel north again to Galilee "into a mountain where Jesus had appointed them." The Greek etaxo (from tassō = to appoint or assign, on one's own authority or by agreement) means Jesus had chosen the site specifically; the place was arranged in advance; they had a date. Matthew says that before Jesus's arrival, they "worshipped him." Could this have been at one of the three tabernacles Peter had enthusiastically proposed to commemorate the vision Jesus commanded be kept secret until he was "raised" (Matthew 17:4)? A tabernacle is a place of dwelling; in the Bible a tent or hut for spiritual communion. In the wilderness of Sinai, it was where God could be encountered (see Exodus 25:8; 26:30: "And thou shalt rear up the tabernacle [for the Ark of the Covenant] according to the fashion thereof which was shewed thee *in the mount*" (my italics). For *six* days the glory of the Lord abode upon Mt. Sinai (Exodus 24:16), and a cloud covered it.

In which case, according to Matthew, Jesus departed from their vision on Mt. Hermon, not Mt. Olivet. The Watchers descended; Jesus ascended. It makes Enochic sense, doesn't it?—a new covenant fulfilled, in the land of Damascus.

It's a thought.

A Personal Coda

It is generally held that the crushing of the Bar Kokhba Jewish Revolt by six Roman legions after its leader's death in 135 CE marked the end of the radical apocalyptic message whereby God's messiah would imminently save Israel from foreign domination to institute a new world for the righteous. The lines of Jews sold into slavery after the revolt vividly demonstrated that God did not lift a finger to help the Zealots. For many Jews, Emperor Hadrian's expelling them or their countrymen from Jerusalem, and imperial imposition of a temple to Jupiter over a levelled Temple Mount, tolled the bitter end of the messianic prophetic promise, whose scheme had manifestly failed. *It* hadn't happened; no messiah had come, or, if Jesus was expected, no messiah had *returned* in clouds of power to turn wrong to right. The "new Jerusalem" that replaced the old was a pagan abomination, a wasteland.

I remember philosopher Hans Jonas telling me rather gingerly about a somewhat visceral conflict played out between himself and Gershom Scholem over 1800 years later, when in Jerusalem in the 1950s the two scholars stood opposed over the Jewish component of Gnosticism. While Jonas in the 1930s had seen a creative element in gnostic antinomianism, that is, that despite what he called Gnostics' ritual "wildness" (especially sexual wildness or libertinism), the practices were intended to free the spirit from the zodiacal fate-system controlled by ignorant archons—an idea that appealed to Scholem in that decade—Jonas, who fought in the British Army's Jewish Brigade against the Nazis, was suspicious of Scholem's expression "Jewish gnosticism." Scholem's "Jewish gnosticism" was quietly shorn of Gnosticism's most controversial aspects to highlight hekhalot and kabbalist written traditions that might equally be called Jewish Neoplatonism; the (for Jonas) definitive radicalism, or as he put it to me, "the things that make the flesh creep," were absent.

Missing from Scholem's "Jewish gnosticism" was the radical gnostic denial of the personal creator-God of the Tanakh (the disposable universe being fashioned by a subordinate, ignorant demiurge far beneath an "unknown God"), and outright rejection of Mosaic law. While Christian Gnostic authors condemned by church fathers as heretics used Jewish source material, Gnostic works were, Jonas believed, saturated with antisemitism, so Scholem's "Jewish gnosticism" linked to a "metaphysical antisemitism" within Gnosticism constituted for Jonas a dangerous error.[11]

Meanwhile, Dutch scholar Gilles Quispel was considering whether Gnosticism was fostered in radical *Jewish* circles in Alexandria in reaction to the catastrophe of Hadrian's enforced diaspora. Jonas disagreed, insisting no patriotic Jewish community could tolerate annihilation of divine authority in scripture and tradition; Jahveh created the world "and saw that it was good." Quispel's position was, I recall from our conversation, based on the question "Who else *cared* about the issues?" Quispel believed there had occurred among some Jews a traumatic loss of faith in any restitution *in this world*. On this basis, however, one could also point to Gentile Christians impressed already by Paul's doctrine that salvation need not depend on Mosaic law but on Christ's conquest of sin into which the believer could be baptized and thus freed from Satan's worldly dominion.

Jonas's overall view emphasized seeing Gnostic religion within the history of *ideas*: Gnosticism, he believed, testified to an epoch-marking protoexistentialist rift between human beings and the world of nature, with man *alienated* from confidence in natural processes or of a good creation, overwhelmed by a cosmic nihilism that drained value from the world, inviting a response of antinomian cynicism in order to be liberated from the cosmos.

Gnostic systems accounting for prevalence of evil in nature *did* appear following the Bar Kokhba revolt. While many seeds had been planted before, the intense growth period of "Gnosticism" that so alerted church fathers was between roughly 130 and 160 CE, a phenomenon predominantly impacting on and within Christian doctrine, having at its core a redeemer figure called, in the main, "Jesus" (or "the great Seth").

We should then also recognize another sense of traumatic disappointment. Throughout the 40s, 50s, and 60s, apostles James, Paul, Judas, Peter, and their colleagues preached that the messiah had come and would return with clouds of power in judgment at a time of God's choosing, but the Lord *would* return, probably in the lifetime of the oldest followers (Mark 9:1). The temple's destruction in 70 CE must have seemed a sign of imminence to many, but the messiah did *not* reappear, neither on Olivet nor Hermon.

We must presume, however, that Enochic scripture still circulated and was doubtless scoured for indications to explain the delay. As we have seen in chapter 11, the Book of the Watchers was used in the third century by Egyptian Zosimos to justify warnings about demonic influence. Can we avoid supposing the book had a formative effect on gnostic mythology, presenting as it does, a world corrupted by wicked angels? How big a step was it between positing a world corrupted by evil angels and, in the absence of an eschaton, a world *created by* evil angels, from which the only salvation required an ascension that took Enoch, Elijah, and Jesus *out of this world* into a higher world of dazzling light and knowledge. The deduction was clear enough: those figures came *not* to save the *world*, but to save the light, to redeem it to its true source above. When *that* was accomplished, the residue of matter and unredeemed soul could be discarded (the end of the world). In effect, the fallen angel was now Man, or in alchemical terms, salvation was evaporation followed by distillation.

What then stopped people from waking and rising? Answer: the evil angels (archons), who being divorced from it themselves, opposed the spirit. The whole effort of Gnostic mythology is to explain how this divorce came about (a myth of Wisdom falling into the world, prefigured in 1 Enoch's Parables), and to furnish the rising spirit after death with knowledge to enable passage through archontic checkpoints to divine realms beyond. One *can* see Gnosticism as born from disappointment in the apocalyptic scheme—even though formulated from the scheme's shattered fragments.

Tearing itself from Jewish roots, Gentile Christianity could have gone the "Gnostic" way, and doubtless a significant number took that road, but among orthodox interpreters of its apocalyptic elements, it was not dependent on the fate of Jewish territory, and the apocalyptic hope could persist, despite the dénouement being ever projected forward, giving history its religious meaning. Enoch's transcending, spiritual hope in a timetable of unearthly glory-in-waiting still had legs, because it bore a valid mystical idea within it: "my kingdom is not of this world" (cf. John 18:36). One could ascend to heaven, depending on the life well lived, and faith kept. The saints at least could glimpse heaven in this life, and this life still offered vital religious opportunity. Christ would come when the word was preached to every part of the world. The flame of righteousness could burn brightly when the church through Christ triumphed over the wicked world, so it becomes "on earth as it is in heaven," and this gift of mysticism, vouchsafed by Enoch in Christian, Jewish, and later, Islamic mysticism, has enabled salvation mythology to be reenacted through time at the individual level.

Good does not always triumph in this world, but often it does, and can, and ultimately—will; such anyway is the hope Enoch brought to Methuselah's posterity. In Enoch's vision, the Son of Man is one reflecting the Glory; present with the righteous evermore. The alternative, as we see by analogy in unchained politics, is resignation to an eternal opposition.

Chronology

538 BCE. Persian king Cyrus permits exiled Jews in Babylon to return to Jerusalem and build a temple: beginning of Second Temple period.

332 BCE. Alexander the Great conquers Egypt.

323 BCE. Alexander dies; his generals (Diadochi) fight for control of his empire.

301 BCE. Ptolemy I Soter, Macedonian general, now king of Egypt, conquers Judea.

201–200 BCE. Ptolemaic forces sack Jerusalem for supporting Seleucids (descendants of Diadochi general Seleucus I).

201–198 BCE. Seleucid King Antiochus III the Great fights Ptolemy V of Egypt in Galilee and Judea. Decisive battle at Paneas, northern Galilee, ca. 200–198 BCE, ousts Ptolemaic rule from Judea.

197 BCE. Onias III high priest, under initially benign Seleucid rule.

175 BCE. Antiochus IV Epiphanes forces Onias III from high priesthood in favour of pro-Hellenist, Jason. Onias III afterward seeks Ptolemy VI Philometor's protection. Ptolemy subsequently permits a Jewish tower-temple established in the Heliopolitan nome.

172 BCE. Extreme Hellenizer Menelaus high priest.

Ca. 171 BCE. Onias III possibly murdered (according to 2 Maccabees).

167 BCE. Temple desecrated by Antiochus IV; Judaism banned; Hasmonean Judas Maccabeus leads brothers in revolt.

165 BCE. Temple rededicated after Judas Maccabeus retakes Jerusalem.

Ca. 164 BCE. Book of Daniel.

161/160 BCE. Judas Maccabeus killed; brother Jonathan "Apphus" takes over.

153–143 BCE. Jonathan high priest. According to Josephus, sects of Sadducees, Pharisees, and Essenes active. Seleucid King Diodotus Tryphon executes Jonathan in 143 BCE.

142–135 BCE. Simon Thassi (Jonathan's brother), king and high priest.

135–104 BCE. John Hyrcanus I, king and high priest, after murder of father Simon Thassi.

Ca. 100 BCE. Most books of 1 Enoch (except Parables) have probably appeared in some form.

103–76 BCE. Alexander Jannaeus king of Judea.

96 BCE. Alexander Jannaeus falls out with Pharisees.

Ca. 100–50 BCE. First archaeological evidence for buildings at Qumran.

63 BCE. Roman general Pompey conquers Jerusalem.

Ca. 47 BCE. Idumean Antipater (trusted by Julius Caesar), makes son Herod provincial governor of Galilee, tax-farming for Rome and defeating "bandits." Sanhedrin condemns his brutality.

40 BCE. Parthians enter Jerusalem and impose Antigonus on Hyrcanus II's throne, against Herod's interest. Roman Senate appoints Herod king of the Jews (40 or 39 BCE).

37 or 36 BCE. Herod replaces Hasmonean dynasty—though he marries Mariamne, Antigonus's niece; Antigonus sent by Herod to Mark Antony for execution.

29 BCE. Mariamne executed for alleged plot to kill husband.

7 BCE. Possible birth of Jesus (Yeshua ben Yosef) in Bethlehem.

4 BCE. Herod the Great dies. Sons from marriage to Samaritan Malthace inherit: Archelaus ethnarch of Judea; Herod Antipas tetrarch of Galilee, and so on. According to Matthew, Jesus's father Joseph takes family from Egyptian refuge not to Judea, as intended, but to Galilee.

BCE/CE. By early first century CE; Parables has probably appeared.

Ca. 1–70 CE. 2 Enoch probably appears.

36 CE. John the Baptist executed.

37 CE. Jesus crucified.

62 CE. Stoning to death of James, brother of Jesus, on temple steps by order of high priest Ananus, for insisting Jesus was messiah.

70 CE. Jerusalem temple destroyed by Romans.

73–74 CE. Jewish temple in Heliopolitan nome closed by Romans.

81–96 CE. Emperor Domitian sees House of David as threat to Roman rule; interrogates grandsons of Jesus's brother, Judas ("Jude").

Ca. late 130s CE. Epistle of Barnabas cites Enoch as scripture; Justin Martyr also.

Ca. 176. Athenagoras cites Enoch as scripture.

Ca. 200. Tertullian cites Enoch as scripture, but indicates some Christian communities don't accept it as genuine, along with Jewish rabbis, who suspect its use in Christian propaganda.

Ca. 200–800. 3 Enoch.

Ca. 210–250. Origen indicates some Christian communities don't accept Enoch as scripture.

Ca. 300. Zosimos of Panopolis employs account of Book of the Watchers, calling it scripture, and links it to writings of Hermes Trismegistos.

367. Bishop Athanasius of Alexandria includes Epistle of Jude in Christian canon; Book of Enoch not included.

Ca. 410–30. Augustine of Hippo rejects authenticity of Book of Enoch.

Late sixth / early seventh century. Probably date of Greek Book of the Watchers (Codex Panopolitanus), discovered at Akhmim 1886–87.

Late eighth / early ninth century. George Syncellus in Constantinople transcribes Greek passages from Book of Enoch in his *Chronographia*.

Ninth century. Byzantine chronicle *Palaea Historica* ascribes to Enoch building of pillars in Egypt ascribed to "Sethites" in Josephus, and invention of writing.

Mid- to late ninth century. Baghdad-based scholar Abu Ma'shar in *The Thousands* identifies Enoch with Hermes Trismegistos.

Late thirteenth century. Rabbi Moses de León's kabbalist text the *Zohar* refers to a Book of Enoch.

Fifteenth century. Earliest known copies of Enoch the prophet in Ge'ez, in Ethiopia.

1484. Giovanni "Mercurio" da Correggio arrives in Rome as "Pymander." He dubs disciple Lodovico Lazzarelli (author *Epistola Enoch*) "Enoch."

1486. Pico della Mirandola identifies Enoch with Metatron.

1551. Guillaume Postel's *De Etruriae regionis* insists the Book of Enoch's prophecies are canonical in Ethiopia. English mathematician and polymath John Dee learns of the Book of Enoch through Postel; it inspires him to learn what Enoch learned from angels.

1606. Joseph Justus Scaliger publishes Enoch extracts from Syncellus in his *Thesaurus Temporum* (Leiden, 1606).

1638. Dr. Robert Fludd's *Philosophia moysaica* identifies "Mettatron" with Christ and anima mundi.

1710. First commentary on 1 Enoch by Pompeo Sarnelli.

1723. Rev. James Anderson's *Constitutions of the Free-Masons* refers to "Enoch's pillars."

Late 1760s–1783. The 13th Degree of "Morin's Rite": basis for the Ancient & Accepted Scottish Rite of Freemasonry introduces what is called in England the "Royal Arch of Enoch."

1773. James Bruce returns to Europe from Ethiopia with the Book of Enoch.

1820. Daniele Manin's study of Enoch (Venice).

1821. Richard Laurence's English translation of the Book of Enoch published.

1888. John Dee and Edward Kelley's "Enochian" angel-magic revived in the Hermetic Order of the Golden Dawn; after 1898 inspires Aleister Crowley to occult experimentation.

1893. R. H. Charles's first translation of 1 Enoch published.

1949. Eleazar L. Sukenik first relates Dead Sea Scrolls to Essenism (first scrolls discovered at Qumran in 1946–47).

1952. Józef Milik identifies first fragment of Book of Enoch at Qumran, Jordan.

2001. First meeting of Enoch Seminar.

Notes

One. Bruce

1. Bruce, *Travels to discover the source of the Nile*, 620.
2. Schmidt, *The Books of Jeu and the Untitled Text in the Bruce Codex*, 29.
3. Boccaccini, "James Bruce's 'Fourth' Manuscript," 237–63. Ted M. Ehro's paleographical analysis has confirmed Boccaccini's identification of the Rome manuscript as Bruce's; see Hessayon, Reed, and Boccaccini, *Rediscovering Enoch?*, 101n.
4. Boccaccini, "Earliest Commentaries on 1 Enoch before Laurence," in Hessayon, Reed, and Boccaccini, *Rediscovering Enoch?*, 150–51.
5. Quote from Vat. Et. 71 (Giorgi to Antonelli), in Hessayon, Reed, and Boccaccini, *Rediscovering Enoch?*, 102.
6. Hessayon, Reed, and Boccaccini, *Rediscovering Enoch?*, 104.
7. Ehro, "James Bruce's Illusory 'Book of Enoch the Prophet,'" in Hessayon, Reed, and Boccaccini, *Rediscovering Enoch?*, 183–208.
8. Hessayon, Reed, and Boccaccini, *Rediscovering Enoch?*, 184.
9. Hessayon, Reed, and Boccaccini, *Rediscovering Enoch?*, 198.
10. Hessayon, Reed, and Boccaccini, *Rediscovering Enoch?*, 202.
11. Hessayon, Reed, and Boccaccini, *Rediscovering Enoch?*, 207.
12. Cited from Bruce, *Travels to discover the source of the Nile*, "vol ii, octavo edition," 425–26 in Laurence, *The Book of Enoch the Prophet: An Apocryphal Production*, vi.
13. Laurence, *The Book of Enoch the Prophet*, "Preliminary Dissertation," iv.
14. Laurence, *The Book of Enoch the Prophet*, iv.
15. Hessayon, "James Bruce and His Copies of Ethiopic Enoch," in Hessayon, Reed, and Boccaccini, *Rediscovering Enoch?*, 233.
16. Hessayon, "James Bruce and His Copies of Ethiopic Enoch," in Hessayon, Reed, and Boccaccini, *Rediscovering Enoch?*, 237.
17. See Murray, *Account of the Life and Writings of James Bruce*, 254–60, cited

by Boccaccini, "Earliest Commentaries on 1 Enoch before Laurence," in Hessayon, Reed, and Boccaccini, *Rediscovering Enoch?*, 103.

18. Hessayon, "James Bruce and His Copies of Ethiopic Enoch," in Hessayon, Reed, and Boccaccini, *Rediscovering Enoch?*, 241.

19. Hessayon, "James Bruce and His Copies of Ethiopic Enoch," in Hessayon, Reed, and Boccaccini, *Rediscovering Enoch?*, 244.

20. Hessayon, "James Bruce and His Copies of Ethiopic Enoch," in Hessayon, Reed, and Boccaccini, *Rediscovering Enoch?*, 254.

21. Hessayon, "James Bruce and His Copies of Ethiopic Enoch," in Hessayon, Reed, and Boccaccini, *Rediscovering Enoch?*, 254.

Two. A Long Time Coming

1. Laurence, *The Book of Enoch the Prophet*, "Preliminary Dissertation," a2.

2. Fabricius, *Codex Pseudepigraphus Veteris Testamenti*, 1:209–11.

3. Fabricius, *Codex Pseudepigraphus Veteris Testamenti*, 1:222–23.

4. Boccaccini, "Earliest Commentaries on 1 Enoch before Laurence," in Hessayon, Reed, and Boccaccini, *Rediscovering Enoch?*, 91–101.

5. Boccaccini, "Earliest Commentaries on 1 Enoch before Laurence," in Hessayon, Reed, and Boccaccini, *Rediscovering Enoch?*, 95.

6. Boccaccini, "Earliest Commentaries on 1 Enoch before Laurence," in Hessayon, Reed, and Boccaccini, *Rediscovering Enoch?*, 103.

7. Boccaccini, "Earliest Commentaries on 1 Enoch before Laurence," in Hessayon, Reed, and Boccaccini, *Rediscovering Enoch?*, 104.

8. Laurence, *The Book of Enoch the Prophet*, "Preliminary Dissertation," xii.

9. Laurence, *The Book of Enoch the Prophet*, xiv.

10. Laurence, *The Book of Enoch the Prophet*, xviii.

11. Laurence, *The Book of Enoch the Prophet*, xxii–xxiii.

12. Laurence, *The Book of Enoch the Prophet*, xxxviii–xxxix.

13. Laurence, *The Book of Enoch the Prophet*, xliv.

Three. I Enoch

1. Boccaccini, *Beyond the Essene Hypothesis*, xiii, 12.

2. Boccaccini, *Beyond the Essene Hypothesis*, xiii, 12.

3. Nickelsburg, *1 Enoch 1*, 119.

4. Milik, *The Books of Enoch*, 153–54.

5. Koch, "History as a Battlefield of Two Antagonistic Powers in the Apocalypse of Weeks and in the Rule of the Community" in Boccaccini, *Enoch and Qumran Origins*, 185.

6. Nickelsburg, *1 Enoch 1*, 440–41.

7. Nickelsburg, *1 Enoch 1*, 434.

8. Nickelsburg, *1 Enoch 1*, 446.

9. Nickelsburg, *1 Enoch 1*, 542.

10. Nickelsburg, *1 Enoch 1*, 554.

Four. The Book of Enoch 2

1. Nickelsburg and VanderKam, *1 Enoch 2*, 32, 33.

2. Nickelsburg and VanderKam, *1 Enoch 2*, 41.

3. Nickelsburg and VanderKam, *1 Enoch 2*, 153.

4. Nickelsburg and VanderKam, *1 Enoch 2*, 214.

5. Nickelsburg, *1 Enoch 1*, 83.

6. Nickelsburg and VanderKam, *1 Enoch 2*, 44–45.

7. Nickelsburg and VanderKam, *1 Enoch 2*, 47.

8. Nickelsburg and VanderKam, *1 Enoch 2*, 311.

9. Nickelsburg and VanderKam, *1 Enoch 2*, 327.

10. Nickelsburg and VanderKam, *1 Enoch 2*, 322.

11. Nickelsburg and VanderKam, *1 Enoch 2*, 328.

12. Nickelsburg and VanderKam, *1 Enoch 2*, 328.

Five. Further Adventures of I Enoch

1. Laurence, *The Book of Enoch the Prophet*, xxxiv–xxxvi.

2. Laurence, *The Book of Enoch the Prophet*, xlvii–xlviii.

3. Laurence, *The Book of Enoch the Prophet*, xlvii–xlviii.

4. Charles, *The Book of Enoch*.

5. Charles, *The Book of Enoch*, xcv.

6. Charles, *The Book of Enoch*, xcv–ciii.

7. Burkitt, *Jewish and Christian Apocalypses*, 21; cited in Charles, *The Book of Enoch*, xxviii.

8. Baynes, "The Parables of Enoch and Luke's Parable of the Rich Man and Lazarus," in Stuckenbruck and Boccaccini, *Enoch and the Synoptic Gospels*, 129.

9. Stuckenbruck and Boccaccini, "1 Enoch and the Synoptic Gospels: The Methods and Benefits of a Conversation," in *Enoch and the Synoptic Gospels*, 1.

10. Stuckenbruck and Boccaccini, "1 Enoch and the Synoptic Gospels: The Methods and Benefits of a Conversation," in *Enoch and the Synoptic Gospels*, 6.

11. Stuckenbruck and Boccaccini, "1 Enoch and the Synoptic Gospels: The Methods and Benefits of a Conversation," in *Enoch and the Synoptic Gospels*, 6.

12. Nickelsburg, *1 Enoch 1*, 112.

13. Charles, *The Book of Enoch*, chap. 20, "Theology" [of 1 Enoch], ciii–civ.

14. Charles, *The Book of Enoch*, chap. 20, "Theology" [of 1 Enoch], ciii–civ.

15. Scholem, *Major Trends in Jewish Mysticism*, 175.

16. Scholem, *Major Trends in Jewish Mysticism*, 43.

Six. Amazing Discoveries

1. Boccaccini, *Enoch and Qumran Origins*, 298.

2. Milik, *The Books of Enoch*, 5.

3. Milik, *The Books of Enoch*, 6–7.

4. Magness, *The Archaeology of Qumran and the Dead Sea Scrolls*; Humbert, "L'éspace sacré a Qumran: Proposition pour l'archéologie," 161–214.

5. Dimant, "The Qumran Manuscripts: Contents and Significance," in Dimant and Schiffman, *Time to Prepare the Way in the Wilderness*, 57–58.

6. Nickelsburg, *1 Enoch 1*, 114.

7. Nickelsburg, *1 Enoch 1*, 65.

8. Nickelsburg, *1 Enoch 1*, 67.

9. Boccaccini, *Enoch and Qumran Origins*, 204.

10. Boccaccini, *Enoch and Qumran Origins*, 65.

11. Philo of Alexandria, *Hypothetica* 11.14; Colson, *Philo, in Ten Volumes*, 9:442.

12. Philo of Alexandria, *Hypothetica* 11.14; Colson, *Philo, in Ten Volumes*, 9:442.

13. Philo of Alexandria, *Hypothetica* 11.14; Colson, *Philo, in Ten Volumes*, 9:442.

14. Pliny, *Natural History*, trans. H. Rackham, 2:277.

15. Regev, "Jubilees, Qumran, and the Essenes," in Boccaccini and Ibba, *Enoch and the Mosaic Torah*, 209.

16. Boccaccini, *Enoch and Qumran Origins*, 373–83.

17. Boccaccini, *Enoch and Qumran Origins*, 376.

18. Boccaccini, *Enoch and Qumran Origins*, 378–80.

19. Boccaccini, *Enoch and Qumran Origins*, 346.

20. Boccaccini, *Enoch and Qumran Origins*, 347.

21. Boccaccini, *Enoch and Qumran Origins*, 350.

22. Charles, *The Book of Enoch*, chap. 20, "Theology" [of 1 Enoch], civ.

23. Boccaccini, *Beyond the Essene Hypothesis*, 12.

24. Boccaccini, *Beyond the Essene Hypothesis*, 185.

25. Boccaccini, *Beyond the Essene Hypothesis*, 98.

26. Boccaccini, *Beyond the Essene Hypothesis*, 26.

27. Boccaccini, *Beyond the Essene Hypothesis*, 34.

28. Vermes, *The Complete Dead Sea Scrolls in English*, 129.

29. Boccaccini, *Beyond the Essene Hypothesis*, 113.

30. Boccaccini, *Beyond the Essene Hypothesis*, 202.

31. Vermes, *The Complete Dead Sea Scrolls in English*, 221.

32. Boccaccini, *Beyond the Essene Hypothesis*, 116.

33. Vermes, *The Complete Dead Sea Scrolls in English*, 221.

34. Boccaccini, *Beyond the Essene Hypothesis*, 120.

35. Taeubler, "Jerusalem 201 to 199 BCE on the History of the Messianic Movement," *Jewish Quarterly Review*, n.s., 37, no. 1 (July 1946): 1.

36. Taeubler, "Jerusalem 201 to 199 BCE on the History of the Messianic Movement," *Jewish Quarterly Review*, n.s., 37, no. 3 (Jan. 1947): 251–61.

37. Taeubler, "Jerusalem 201 to 199 BCE on the History of the Messianic Movement," *Jewish Quarterly Review*, n.s., 37, no. 2 (Oct. 1946): 125.

38. Taeubler, "Jerusalem 201 to 199 BCE on the History of the Messianic Movement," *Jewish Quarterly Review*, n.s., 37, no. 2 (Oct. 1946): 130.

39. Vermes, *The Complete Dead Sea Scrolls in English*, 128.

40. Freedman, *Eerdmans Dictionary of the Bible*, 61.

41. Boccaccini, *Beyond the Essene Hypothesis*, 171.

42. Charlesworth in *Enoch and Qumran Origins*, 438-40.

43. Charlesworth in *Enoch and Qumran Origins*, 441.

44. Charlesworth in *Enoch and Qumran Origins*, 441.

Seven. Enoch Received I

1. James C. VanderKam, "The Manuscript Tradition of Jubilees," in Boccaccini and Ibba, *Enoch and the Mosaic Torah*, 3.

2. Boccaccini, "Preface: The Enigma of Jubilees and the Lesson of the

Enoch Seminar," in Boccaccini and Ibba, *Enoch and the Mosaic Torah*, xiv.

3. Charles, *The Book of Jubilees*, lix, lxxiii.

4. Boccaccini, "Preface: The Enigma of Jubilees and the Lesson of the Enoch Seminar," in Boccaccini and Ibba, *Enoch and the Mosaic Torah*, xvi.

5. Boccaccini, "Preface: The Enigma of Jubilees and the Lesson of the Enoch Seminar," in Boccaccini and Ibba, *Enoch and the Mosaic Torah*, xvi.

6. Boccaccini, "Preface: The Enigma of Jubilees and the Lesson of the Enoch Seminar," in Boccaccini and Ibba, *Enoch and the Mosaic Torah*, xvi.

7. Orlov, "The Heavenly Counterpart of Moses in the Book of Jubilees," in Boccaccini and Ibba, *Enoch and the Mosaic Torah*, 131–32.

8. Orlov, "The Heavenly Counterpart of Moses in the Book of Jubilees," 134.

9. Orlov, "The Heavenly Counterpart of Moses in the Book of Jubilees," 138.

10. Orlov, "The Heavenly Counterpart of Moses in the Book of Jubilees," 139.

11. Orlov, "The Heavenly Counterpart of Moses in the Book of Jubilees," 143.

12. Orlov, "The Heavenly Counterpart of Moses in the Book of Jubilees," 144.

13. Orlov, "The Heavenly Counterpart of Moses in the Book of Jubilees," 144.

14. Boccaccini, "From a Movement of Dissent to a Distinct Form of Judaism," in Boccaccini and Ibba, *Enoch and the Mosaic Torah*, 193–94.

15. Boccaccini, "From a Movement of Dissent to a Distinct Form of Judaism," in Boccaccini and Ibba, *Enoch and the Mosaic Torah*, 196.

16. Boccaccini, "From a Movement of Dissent to a Distinct Form of Judaism," in Boccaccini and Ibba, *Enoch and the Mosaic Torah*, 197.

17. Boccaccini, "From a Movement of Dissent to a Distinct Form of Judaism," in Boccaccini and Ibba, *Enoch and the Mosaic Torah*, 199.

18. Boccaccini, "From a Movement of Dissent to a Distinct Form of Judaism," in Boccaccini and Ibba, *Enoch and the Mosaic Torah*, 201.

19. Boccaccini, "From a Movement of Dissent to a Distinct Form of Judaism," in Boccaccini and Ibba, *Enoch and the Mosaic Torah*, 202.

20. Sacchi, *The History of the Second Temple Period*, 404.

21. Boccaccini and Ibba, *Enoch and the Mosaic Torah*, 205–7.

22. Boccaccini and Ibba, *Enoch and the Mosaic Torah*, 209.

23. Charles, *The Testaments of the Twelve Patriarchs*, xvii.

24. Boccaccini, *Beyond the Essene Hypothesis*, 141

25. Stuckenbruck, "The Book of Enoch," 16. Regarding the reference to the Testament of Zebulun 3:4, Stuckenbruck adds a footnote: "Since the passage is drawing on Deuteronomy 25:5–10 in support of Levirate marriage, it

is not clear whether Mosaic tradition is being attributed to Enoch or Enoch should be emended to read 'Moses.' On the problem, see H. W. Hollander and M. de Jonge, *The Testaments of the Twelve Patriarchs: A Commentary*, SVTP 8; Leiden, 1985, 68; J. J. Collins, *The Apocalyptic Imagination* (2nd ed.; Grand Rapids, 1998), 152."

26. Stuckenbruck, "The Book of Enoch," 16.

Eight. The Epistle of Jude

1. Charles, *The Assumption of Moses*, lvii.
2. Polczer, "Papyrus 72: An Introduction," text no longer available online.
3. Wasserman, "Papyrus 72 and the Bodmer Miscellaneous Codex," 140.
4. Nongbri, "The Construction of P.Bodmer VIII and the Bodmer 'Composite' or 'Miscellaneous' Codex," 410.
5. Strickland, "The Curious Case of P72," 788.
6. Robinson, *The Nag Hammadi Library in English*, 16–22. See also Robinson, "The Pachomian Monastic Library at the Chester Beatty Library and the Bibliothèque Bodmer," 19–21.
7. Paul Davidson, "The Book of Enoch as the Background to 1 Peter, 2 Peter, and Jude." Is That in the Bible? (website), August 20, 2014.
8. Jones, "The Bodmer 'Miscellaneous' Codex and the Crosby-Schøyen Codex MS 193," 18.

Nine. 2 Enoch

1. Charles, *The Book of the Secrets of Enoch*, viii.
2. Orlov, "The Pillar of the World," 119–35; see also Orlov, Boccaccini, and Zurawski, *New Perspectives on 2 Enoch*.
3. Charles, *The Book of the Secrets of Enoch*, xxi–xxii.
4. Charles, *The Book of the Secrets of Enoch*, xxvi.
5. Charles, *The Book of the Secrets of Enoch*, xx.
6. Orlov, *From Apocalypticism to Merkabah Mysticism*, 135–36.
7. Orlov, Boccaccini, and Zurawski, *New Perspectives on 2 Enoch*, 8.
8. Orlov, Boccaccini, and Zurawski, *New Perspectives on 2 Enoch*, 13.
9. Orlov, Boccaccini, and Zurawski, *New Perspectives on 2 Enoch*, 37–67.
10. Orlov, Boccaccini, and Zurawski, *New Perspectives on 2 Enoch*, 58.
11. Orlov, Boccaccini, and Zurawski, *New Perspectives on 2 Enoch*, 60.

Ten. Testimony to Enoch from
Church Fathers, or . . . *Enoch Gets Around*

1. Stuckenbruck, "The Book of Enoch," 17–18.
2. Stuckenbruck, "The Book of Enoch," 18.
3. Stuckenbruck, "The Book of Enoch," 18.
4. Reed, "Enoch Lost and Found? Rethinking Enochic Reception in the Middle Ages," chap. 1 in Hessayon, Reed, and Boccaccini, *Rediscovering Enoch?*, 19–49.
5. British Library Additional manuscript 12,172, foll. 79–134; letters in Syriac by Jacob of Edessa. The Syriac text of epistle 13 was published by Wright, "Two Epistles of Mār Jacob, Bishop of Edessa," 430–33.
6. Adler, "Jewish Pseudepigrapha in Jacob of Edessa's Letters and Historical Writings," 49.
7. Adler, "Jewish Pseudepigrapha in Jacob of Edessa's Letters and Historical Writings," 49.

Eleven. Panopolis: Zosimos,
Enoch, and Hermes Trismegistos

1. See facsimile edition of Codex Panopolitanus published in Bouriant and Lods, *L'Évangile & l'Apocalypse de Pierre*.
2. Dugan, "Enochic Biography and the Manuscript History of 1 Enoch," 113–14.
3. Dugan, "Enochic Biography and the Manuscript History of 1 Enoch," 122.
4. Dugan, "Enochic Biography and the Manuscript History of 1 Enoch," 125.
5. Dugan, "Enochic Biography and the Manuscript History of 1 Enoch," 134.
6. Dugan, "Enochic Biography and the Manuscript History of 1 Enoch," 137–38.
7. Litvinau, "A Note on the Greek and Ethiopic Text of 1 Enoch 5:8," 28–35.
8. Litvinau, "A Note on the Greek and Ethiopic Text of 1 Enoch 5:8," 34–35.
9. Lewis, "Death on the Nile," 161.
10. Krause, "Die Texte von Nag Hammadi," 243.
11. Lewis, "Death on the Nile," 173.
12. *The Chronography of George Synkellos*, 18–19.

13. Berthelot and Duval, *La Chimie au Moyen Age*, vol. 2, *L'Alchimie Syriaque*, 2.8.1, 238–39.

14. Berthelot and Ruelle, *Collection des Anciens Alchimistes Grecs*, vol. 2, 3.51.7, 234–35.

Twelve. Hermes Trismegistos and Enoch

1. Pingree, *The Thousands of Abu Ma'shar*, 14–15.
2. *Manetho*, with an English translation by W. G. Waddell, 208–11.
3. Copenhaver, *Hermetica*, xv.
4. Vassiliev, *Anecdota Graeco-Byzantina*, 196–98.
5. Taylor, "Evidence for the Zadokite Temple of Onias," 299.
6. Taylor, "Evidence for the Zadokite Temple of Onias," 305.
7. Taylor, "Evidence for the Zadokite Temple of Onias," 311.
8. Taylor, "Evidence for the Zadokite Temple of Onias," 316–18.
9. Piotrkowski, "Priests in Exile," 169; the author cites: "Horbury and Noy, JIGRE, 90 (inscription no. 38)."
10. Piotrkowski, "Priests in Exile," 165.
11. Piotrkowski, "Priests in Exile," 170.
12. Piotrkowski, "Priests in Exile," 174.
13. Piotrkowski, "Priests in Exile," 175.
14. Piotrkowski, "Priests in Exile," 176.
15. Piotrkowski, "Priests in Exile," 177.
16. Piotrkowski, "Priests in Exile," 178–79.
17. Piotrkowski, "Priests in Exile," 179.

Thirteen. Ethiopia

1. Nickelsburg and VanderKam, *1 Enoch 2*, n16, 106–8.
2. Stuckenbruck, "The Book of Enoch," 22.
3. Stuckenbruck, "The Book of Enoch," 30.
4. Stuckenbruck, "The Book of Enoch," 30–31.
5. Stuckenbruck, "The Book of Enoch," 33.
6. Lee, "The Reception and Function of 1 Enoch in the Ethiopian Orthodox Tradition," 316.
7. Lee, "The Reception and Function of 1 Enoch in the Ethiopian Orthodox Tradition," 317–24.

8. Stuckenbruck, "The Book of Enoch," 37.

9. Lee, "The Reception and Function of 1 Enoch in the Ethiopian Orthodox Tradition," 325.

Fourteen. 3 Enoch: Enoch-Metatron, Hero of Jewish Mysticism

1. Odeburg, *3 Enoch or The Hebrew Book of Enoch*, 17 (introduction).

2. Karr, "Notes on the Study of Merkabah Mysticism and Hekhalot Literature in English with an Appendix on Jewish Magic," (2022 update), 2.

3. Odeberg, *3 Enoch or The Hebrew Book of Enoch*, 38 (introduction).

4. Schiffman, "III Enoch and the Enoch Tradition," in Boccaccini, *Enoch and Qumran Origins*, 153.

5. Schiffman, "III Enoch and the Enoch Tradition," 155.

6. Schiffman, "III Enoch and the Enoch Tradition," 156.

7. Schiffman, "III Enoch and the Enoch Tradition," 156.

8. See Orlov, *From Apocalypticism to Merkabah Mysticism*, 136.

9. Orlov, *From Apocalypticism to Merkabah Mysticism*, 143.

10. Odeberg, *3 Enoch or The Hebrew Book of Enoch*, 125.

11. Milik, *The Books of Enoch*, 129–30.

12. Milik, *The Books of Enoch*, 132.

13. Gruenwald, *Apocalyptic and Merkavah Mysticism*, 192.

14. Milik, *The Books of Enoch*, 133–34.

15. Gruenwald, *Apocalyptic and Merkavah Mysticism*, 191.

Fifteen. Enoch in Medieval Islamic Traditions

1. Van Bladel, *The Arabic Hermes*, 137–38.

2. Atanasova, "Enoch as Idrīs in Early Modern Ottoman Sufi Writings," in Hessayon, Reed, and Boccaccini, *Rediscovering Enoch?*, 399–400.

3. Nasr, *An Introduction to Islamic Cosmological Doctrines*, 35.

4. Wheeler, *Prophets in the Quran*, 47.

5. Wheeler, *Prophets in the Quran*, 47.

6. Atanasova, "Enoch as Idrīs in Early Modern Ottoman Sufi Writings," 401.

7. Nasr, *An Introduction to Islamic Cosmological Doctrines*, 13n28.

8. Atanasova, "Enoch as Idrīs in Early Modern Ottoman Sufi Writings,"

402; citing her own translation of Muhyī al-dīn ibn 'Arabi, *Fuṣūṣ alḥikam* (Beirut, n.d.), 75.

9. Atanasova, "Enoch as Idrīs in Early Modern Ottoman Sufi Writings," 412.

10. Atanasova, "Enoch as Idrīs in Early Modern Ottoman Sufi Writings," 404–12.

Sixteen. "Holy Enoch" and the Renaissance

1. Busi, "Giovanni Pico della Mirandola, Enoch, and Hermetism," in Hessayon, Reed, and Boccaccini, *Rediscovering Enoch?*, 67.

2. Busi, "Giovanni Pico della Mirandola, Enoch, and Hermetism," 68, citing Giovanni Pico della Mirandola, *Commentary on a Canzone by Benivieni*, 147.

3. Recanati, *Perush 'al ha-Torah*, vol. 1, *Be-re'shit*, 147. Cf. G. Corazzol, "Le fondi 'caldaiche' dell'Oratio: Indagine sui presupposti cabbalistici della concezione pichiana dell'uomo," *Accademia* 15 (2013): 9–62, especially 28–29. Cited in Busi, "Giovanni Pico della Mirandola, Enoch, and Hermetism," 70.

4. Busi, "Giovanni Pico della Mirandola, Enoch, and Hermetism," 70.

5. Wirszubski, *Pico della Mirandola's Encounter with Jewish Mysticism*, 231.

6. Busi, "Giovanni Pico della Mirandola, Enoch, and Hermetism," 72.

7. Hanegraaff, *Lodovico Lazzarelli and the Hermetic Christ*, 19.

8. Hanegraaff, *Lodovico Lazzarelli and the Hermetic Christ*, 24.

9. Hanegraaff, *Lodovico Lazzarelli and the Hermetic Christ*, 31.

10. Hanegraaff, *Lodovico Lazzarelli and the Hermetic Christ*, 34.

11. Hanegraaff, *Lodovico Lazzarelli and the Hermetic Christ*, 39–40.

12. Hanegraaff, *Lodovico Lazzarelli and the Hermetic Christ*, 41.

13. Hanegraaff, *Lodovico Lazzarelli and the Hermetic Christ*, 81–82.

14. Hanegraaff, *Lodovico Lazzarelli and the Hermetic Christ*, 82.

15. Idel, "Hermeticism and Judaism," 60.

Seventeen. John Dee, Guillaume Postel, and the Book of Enoch

1. Reed, "Enoch Lost and Found? Rethinking Enochic Reception in the Middle Ages," in Hessayon, Reed, and Boccaccini, *Rediscovering Enoch?*, 42.

2. Reed, "Enoch Lost and Found? Rethinking Enochic Reception in the Middle Ages," in Hessayon, Reed, and Boccaccini, *Rediscovering Enoch?*, 42.

3. Whitby, "John Dee's Actions with Spirits," vol 1, commentary on British Library MS Sloane 3188, fol. 5A, 1–42, 191; vol. 2, 8–9.

4. Whitby, "John Dee's Actions with Spirits," folio 101b, vol 2, 378.

Eighteen. A Rosicrucian Fludd and Freemasonry

1. McIntosh and McIntosh, *Fama Fraternitatis* 1614–2014, 46.

2. Fludd, *Philosophia Moysaica*, 304.

3. Fludd, *Mosaicall Philosophy*, 151–52.

4. Churton, "Enoch and the Genesis of Freemasonry," in Hessayon, Reed, and Boccaccini, *Rediscovering Enoch?*, 119–29.

5. Boccaccini, "Earliest Commentaries on 1 Enoch before Laurence," in Hessayon, Reed, and Boccaccini, *Rediscovering Enoch?*, 76.

6. Sarnelli, *Annotazioni sopra il libro degli Egregori del s. profeta Henoch*, 43–44.

7. Sarnelli, *Annotazioni sopra il libro degli Egregori del s. profeta Henoch*, 55–56.

8. Sarnelli, *Annotazioni sopra il libro degli Egregori del s. profeta Henoch*, 65.

9. Sarnelli, *Annotazioni sopra il libro degli Egregori del s. profeta Henoch*, 85.

10. Sarnelli, *Annotazioni sopra il libro degli Egregori del s. profeta Henoch*, 117–18.

11. Sarnelli, *Annotazioni sopra il libro degli Egregori del s. profeta Henoch*, 151.

12. Sarnelli, *Annotazioni sopra il libro degli Egregori del s. profeta Henoch*, 152.

13. Sarnelli, *Annotazioni sopra il libro degli Egregori del s. profeta Henoch*, 180–82.

14. Boccaccini, "Earliest Commentaries on 1 Enoch before Laurence," in Hessayon, Reed, and Boccaccini, *Rediscovering Enoch?*, 109.

15. Churton, *Freemasonry: The Reality*, 313–49.

16. Vassiliev, *Anecdota Graeco-Byzantina*, 196–98, cited after Orlov, "Overshadowed by Enoch's Greatness," 137–58.

17. British Library Add. MS 23, 198; British Library MS Sloane 3848.

18. Speth, *Quatuor Coronatorum*, Part 1, Facsimile and Transcript, "Matthew Cooke Manuscript" (BL Add. MS 23,198), lines 140–50.

19. Ariel Hessayon summarizes medieval and early modern references to Enoch in *Scripture and Scholarship in Early Modern England*, 21, 22, 24, 28, 36, 39, 40. On Abu Ma'shar and the Harranian Sabians, see Green, *The City of the Moon God*, 137.

20. Grafton, "Protestant versus Prophet," 78–93.

21. Anderson, *Constitutions of the Free-Masons*, 2–3.

22. Anderson, *Constitutions of the Free-Masons*, 3n.

23. Anderson, *New Book of Constitutions*, 3.

24. Dermott, *Ahimon Rezon*, 47.

25. Jackson, *Rose Croix*, 25–26.

Nineteen. Prophets and Magic Galore

1. Ludlow, "Enoch in the Tradition of the Church of Jesus Christ of Latter-Day Saints (Mormonism)," in Hessayon, Reed, and Boccaccini, *Rediscovering Enoch?*, 162–63.

2. Ludlow, "Enoch in the Tradition of the Church of Jesus Christ of Latter-Day Saints (Mormonism)," 163.

3. Ludlow, "Enoch in the Tradition of the Church of Jesus Christ of Latter-Day Saints (Mormonism)," 177–78.

4. Regardie, *The Golden Dawn*, 624.

5. Regardie, *The Golden Dawn*, 625.

6. Crowley, *The Vision and the Voice*.

7. DeSalvo, *The Lost Art of Enochian Magic*, 145–48.

Twenty. The Son of Man and Gospel Echoes

1. Boccaccini, *Enoch and Qumran Origins*, 61.

2. Boccaccini, *Enoch and the Messiah Son of Man*, 9.

3. Quispel, "Hermes Trismegistus and the Origins of Gnosticism," 1–19.

4. Daniel Boyarin, "Was the Book of Parables a Sectarian Document?," in Boccaccini, *Enoch and the Messiah Son of Man*, 385.

5. Boccaccini, *Enoch and the Messiah Son of Man*, 512.

6. See Charlesworth and Bock, *Parables of Enoch*, 373–90.

7. Stuckenbruck and Boccaccini, *Enoch and the Synoptic Gospels*, 7.

8. Stuckenbruck and Boccaccini, *Enoch and the Synoptic Gospels*, 9.

9. Stuckenbruck and Boccaccini, *Enoch and the Synoptic Gospels*, 45–73.

10. Stuckenbruck and Boccaccini, *Enoch and the Synoptic Gospels*, 8.

11. Stuckenbruck and Boccaccini, *Enoch and the Synoptic Gospels*, 13.

12. Baynes, "The Parables of Enoch and Luke's Parable of the Rich Man and Lazarus," 129.

13. Baynes, "The Parables of Enoch and Luke's Parable of the Rich Man and Lazarus," 142.

14. Baynes, "The Parables of Enoch and Luke's Parable of the Rich Man and Lazarus," 144.

15. Angel, "Enoch, Jesus, and Priestly Tradition," in Stuckenbruck and Boccaccini, *Enoch and the Synoptic Gospels*, 285.

16. Angel, "Enoch, Jesus, and Priestly Tradition," 286.

17. Angel, "Enoch, Jesus, and Priestly Tradition," 289.

18. Angel, "Enoch, Jesus, and Priestly Tradition," 293–94.

19. Angel, "Enoch, Jesus, and Priestly Tradition," 297.

20. Angel, "Enoch, Jesus, and Priestly Tradition," 298.

21. Angel, "Enoch, Jesus, and Priestly Tradition," 303.

22. Angel, "Enoch, Jesus, and Priestly Tradition," 304.

23. Angel, "Enoch, Jesus, and Priestly Tradition," 306.

24. Angel, "Enoch, Jesus, and Priestly Tradition," 307.

25. Angel, "Enoch, Jesus, and Priestly Tradition," 316.

Twenty-One. Enoch and Christian Origins II: Jesus

1. Padnos Public Engagement on Jewish Learning Event, "The Historical Jesus in His Jewish Context," YouTube (website), March 12, 2021.

2. Following Kepler's 1603 analysis, Sheffield astronomer Prof. David Hughes calculated the Magi thought a king of the Jews was born on September 15, 7 BCE; see Hughes, *The Star of Bethlehem Mystery*.

3. Boccaccini, *Enoch and the Messiah Son of Man*, 459–61.

4. Boccaccini, *Enoch and the Messiah Son of Man*, 462.

5. Boccaccini, *Enoch and the Messiah Son of Man*, 463.

6. Boccaccini, *Enoch and the Messiah Son of Man*, 469–77.

7. Boccaccini, *Enoch and the Messiah Son of Man*, 474.

8. Vermes, *The Complete Dead Sea Scrolls in English*, 497.

Twenty-Two. Further Enochic Adventures in Galilee

1. Suter, "Why Galilee?," 167–212.

2. Nickelsburg, "Enoch, Levi, and Peter," 575–600.

3. Suter, "Why Galilee?," 6. For notes 3-9, page numbers refer to original article.

4. Suter, "Why Galilee?," 8.

5. Suter, "Why Galilee?," 19.

6. Suter, "Why Galilee?," 23.

7. Suter, "Why Galilee?," 33–34.

8. Suter, "Why Galilee?," 44.

9. Suter, "Why Galilee?," 47.

10. Orlov, "Ocular Epistemology and the Watchers' Lost Perception," in *Divine Mysteries in the Enochic Tradition*, 54–55.

11. See Cahana-Blum, "Jonas, Scholem, and the Taubeses in Jerusalem," 949.

Bibliography

Anderson, James. *Constitutions of the Free-Masons*. London, 1723.

———. *New Book of Constitutions*. London, 1738.

Berthelot, Marcellin, and C. E. Ruelle. *Collection des Anciens Alchimistes Grecs.* 3 vols. bound in 2. Paris: Georges Steinheil, 1888.

Berthelot, Marcellin, and Rubens Duval. *La Chimie au Moyen Age*. 2 vols. 1893. Reprint, Osnabruck, Germany: Otto Zeller, 1967.

Boccaccini, Gabriele. *Beyond the Essene Hypothesis: The Parting of the Ways between Qumran and Enochic Judaism*. Grand Rapids, MI: W. B. Eerdmans, 1995.

———, ed. *Enoch and the Messiah Son of Man—Revisiting the Book of Parables*. Grand Rapids, MI: W. B. Eerdmans, 2007.

———, ed. *Enoch and Qumran Origins: New Light on a Forgotten Connection*. Cambridge, UK: W. B. Eerdmans, 2005.

———. Paul's Three Paths to Salvation. Grand Rapids, MI: Eerdmans, 2020.

Boccaccini, Gabriele, and Giovanni Ibba, eds. *Enoch and the Mosaic Torah: The Evidence of Jubilees*. Grand Rapids, MI: W. B. Eerdmans, 2009.

Bouriant, M. Urbain, and Adolphe Lods. *L'Évangile & l'Apocalypse de Pierre. Le texte grec du Livre d'Énoch, Mémoires publiés par les membres de la Mission Archéologique Française au Caire*. Paris: Ernest Leroux, 1893.

Bruce, James. *Travels to discover the source of the Nile, in the years 1768, 1769, 1770, 1771, 1772, and 1773*. Vol. 4. Edinburgh: J. Ruthven, for G.G.J. and J. Robinson, 1790.

Burkitt, F. C. *Jewish and Christian Apocalypses*. London: Oxford University Press for the British Academy, 1914.

Charles, R. H., trans. *The Assumption of Moses*. London: A&C Black, 1897.

———, trans. *The Book of Enoch*. Introduction by W.O.E. Oesterley. 1917. Reprint, London: S.P.C.K., 1994.

———. *The Book of Jubilees, or The Little Genesis*. London: A&C Black, 1902.

———, ed. *The Book of the Secrets of Enoch Translated from the Slavonic.* Translated by W. R. Morfill. Oxford: Clarendon Press, 1896.

———. *The Testaments of the Twelve Patriarchs, with Introduction, Notes, and Indices.* London: Adam and Charles Black, 1908.

Charlesworth, James H., and Darrell L. Bock, eds. *Parables of Enoch: A Paradigm Shift.* JCTCRS 11. London: Bloomsbury T&T Clark, 2013.

Churton, Tobias. *Freemasonry: The Reality.* Hersham, UK: Lewis Masonic, 2007.

———. *The Lost Pillars of Enoch.* Rochester, VT: Inner Traditions, 2021.

———. *The Missing Family of Jesus.* London: Watkins, 2010.

———. *The Mysteries of John the Baptist.* Rochester, VT: Inner Traditions, 2012.

Collins, J. J. *The Apocalyptic Imagination.* 2nd ed. Grand Rapids, MI: Eerdmans, 1998.

Colson, F. H., trans. *Philo, in Ten Volumes.* Vol. 9. Cambridge, MA: Harvard University Press, 1985.

Copenhaver, Brian B., trans. *Hermetica.* Cambridge, UK: Cambridge University Press, 1997.

Crowley, Aleister. *The Vision and the Voice, with Commentary and other Papers.* Edited by Hymenaeus Beta. Boston: Weiser, 1998.

Dermott, L. *Ahimon Rezon.* London, 1756.

DeSalvo, John. *The Lost Art of Enochian Magic.* Rochester, VT: Destiny Books, 2010.

Fabricius, Johannes Albertus. *Codex Pseudepigraphus Veteris Testamenti.* Vol. 1. Hamburg: Christiani Lieberzeit, 1713.

Fludd, Robert. *Mosaicall Philosophy.* London, 1659.

———. *Philosophia Moysaica.* Gouda, Netherlands: Petrus Rammazenius, 1638.

Freedman, David Noel, ed. *Eerdmans Dictionary of the Bible.* Amsterdam, Netherlands: Amsterdam University Press, 2000.

Green, T. M. *The City of the Moon God: Religious Traditions of Harran.* Leiden: Brill, 1992.

Gruenwald, Ithamar. *Apocalyptic and Merkavah Mysticism.* Leiden: Brill, 1980.

Hanegraaff, Wouter J. *Lodovico Lazzarelli and the Hermetic Christ: At the Sources of Renaissance Hermetism.* Tempe, AZ: Arizona Center for Medieval and Renaissance Studies, 2005.

Hessayon, A., and N. Keene, eds. *Scripture and Scholarship in Early Modern England.* London: Ashgate, 2006.

Hollander, H. W., and M. de Jonge. *The Testaments of the Twelve Patriarchs: A Commentary.* SVTP 8. Leiden: Brill, 1985.

Hughes, David. *The Star of Bethlehem Mystery*. London: J.M. Dent & Sons, 1979.

Jackson, A. C. F. *Rose Croix: A History of the Ancient and Accepted Rite for England and Wales*. Hersham, UK: Lewis Masonic, 1980.

Lafitaga, Elekosi F. *Apocalyptic Sheep and Goats in Matthew and 1 Enoch*. Emory Studies in Early Christianity 24. Atlanta: SBL Press, 2022.

Laurence, Richard, trans. *The Book of Enoch the Prophet*. Introduction by Charles Gill (anon.). London: Kegan Paul & Trench, 1883.

———. *The Book of Enoch the Prophet: An Apocryphal Production, supposed to have been lost for ages; but discovered at the close of the last century in Abyssinia; now first translated from an Ethiopic Ms. In the Bodleian Library*. Oxford: Oxford University Press, 1821.

Magness, Jodi. *The Archaeology of Qumran and the Dead Sea Scrolls*. Grand Rapids, MI: Eerdmans, 2002.

Manetho. *Manetho*. With an English translation by W. G. Waddell. Cambridge, MA: Harvard University Press, 1964.

McIntosh, Christopher, and Donate McIntosh, trans. *Fama Fraternitatis 1614–2014*. N.p.: Vanadis Texts, 2014.

Milik, J. T., ed. *The Books of Enoch: Aramaic Fragments of Qumran Cave 4*. With the collaboration of Matthew Black. Oxford: Clarendon Press, 1976.

Murray, Alexander. *Account of the Life and Writings of James Bruce*. Edinburgh: George Ramsay, 1808.

Nasr, Seyyed Hossein. *An Introduction to Islamic Cosmological Doctrines*. Albany: SUNY Press, 1993.

Nickelsburg, George W. E. *1 Enoch 1: A Commentary on the Book of 1 Enoch*. Edited by Klaus Baltzer. Hermeneia series. Minneapolis, MN: Fortress, 2001.

Nickelsburg, George W. E., and James VanderKam. *1 Enoch 2: A Commentary on the Book of 1 Enoch*. Hermeneia series. Minneapolis, MN: Fortress, 2012.

Odeburg, Hugo, ed. and trans. *3 Enoch or The Hebrew Book of Enoch*. London: Cambridge University Press, 1928.

Orlov, Andrei A., "1.6 Ocular Epistemology and the Watchers' Lost Perception" in *Divine Mysteries in the Enochic Tradition*, Ekstasis vol. 11; Berlin; New York, De Gruyter, 2023.

———. *From Apocalypticism to Merkabah Mysticism*. Leiden: Brill, 2007.

———. "The Pillar of the World: The Eschatological Role of the Seventh Antediluvian Hero in 2 (Slavonic) Enoch." Henoch 30, no. 1 (2008): 119–35.

Orlov, Andrei A., Gabriele Boccaccini, and Jason Zurawski, eds. *New Perspectives on 2 Enoch: No Longer Slavonic Only*. Leiden: E. J. Brill 2012.

Pico della Mirandola, Giovanni. *Commentary on a Canzone by Benivieni.* Translated by Sears Jayne. New York: Peter Lang, 1984.

Pliny. *Natural History.* Vol. 2. Translated by H. Rackham. Loeb Classical Library. Cambridge, MA: Harvard University Press, 1942.

Recanati, Menahem. *Perush 'al ha-Torah.* Edited by A. Gros. Vol. 1, *Be-re'shit.* Tel Aviv: n.p., 2003.

Regardie, Israel. *The Golden Dawn.* St. Paul, MN: Llewellyn Publications, 1989.

Robinson, James M., ed. *The Nag Hammadi Library in English.* 3rd ed. New York: HarperCollins, 1977.

Sacchi, Paolo. *The History of the Second Temple Period.* London: T&T Clark International, 2004.

Sarnelli, Pompeo. *Annotazioni sopra il libro degli Egregori del s. profeta Henoch.* Venezia: Antonio Bortoli, 1710.

Schmidt, Carl, ed. *The Books of Jeu and the Untitled Text in the Bruce Codex.* Translation and notes by Violet MacDermot. Nag Hammadi Studies, edited by R. McL. Wilson, vol. 13. Leiden: EJ Brill, 1978.

Scholem, Gershom. *Major Trends in Jewish Mysticism.* New York: Schocken Books, 1961.

Stewart, Tyler A. *The Origin and Persistence of Evil in Galatians.* Tübingen, Germany: Mohr Siebeck, 2022.

Stuckenbruck, Loren T., and Gabriele Boccaccini, eds. *Enoch and the Synoptic Gospels: Reminiscences, Allusions, Intertextuality.* Atlanta: SBL Press, 2016.

Synkellos, George. *The Chronography of George Synkellos. A Byzantine Chronicle of Universal History from the Creation.* Translated by W. Adler and P. Tuffin. Oxford: Oxford University Press, 2002.

Van Bladel, Kevin. *The Arabic Hermes: From Pagan Sage to Prophet of Science.* Oxford: Oxford University Press, 2009.

Vassiliev, A. *Anecdota Graeco-Byzantina.* Moscow: Universitatis Caesareae, 1893.

Wheeler, B. *Prophets in the Quran: An Introduction to the Quran and Muslim Exegesis.* New York: Bloomsbury, 2002.

Whitby, Christopher Lionel. "John Dee's Actions with Spirits: 22 December 1581 to 23 May 1583," in 2 vols. PhD diss., University of Birmingham, UK, October 1981. Available at the University of Birmingham, E Theses website.

Wirszubski, C. *Pico della Mirandola's Encounter with Jewish Mysticism.* Cambridge, MA: Harvard University Press, 1989.

Sources from Academic Journals, Bound Series, and Collections

Adler, William. "Jewish Pseudepigrapha in Jacob of Edessa's Letters and Historical Writings." In *Jacob of Edessa and the Syriac Culture of His Day,* edited by Bas Ter Haar Romeny, 49–65. Monographs of the Peshitta Institute 18. Leiden: Brill, 2008.

Angel, Joseph L. "Enoch, Jesus, and Priestly Tradition." In Stuckenbruck and Boccaccini, *Enoch and the Synoptic Gospels: Reminiscences, Allusions, Intertextuality.*

Atanasova, Kameliya. "Enoch as Idrīs in Early Modern Ottoman Sufi Writings, Two Case Studies." Chap. 16 in Hessayon, Reed, and Boccaccini, *Rediscovering Enoch?*

Baynes, Leslie. "The Parables of Enoch and Luke's Parable of the Rich Man and Lazarus." In Stuckenbruck and Boccaccini, *Enoch and the Synoptic Gospels: Reminiscences, Allusions, Intertextuality*, 129.

———. "James Bruce's 'Fourth' Manuscript: Solving the Mystery of the Provenance of the Roman Enoch Manuscript (Vat. et. 71)." *Journal for the Study of the Pseudepigrapha* 27, no. 4 (2018): 237–63.

Boccaccini, Gabriele. "Preface: The Enigma of Jubilees and the Lesson of the Enoch Seminar," in *Enoch and the Mosaic Torah.*

———. "Earliest Commentaries on 1 Enoch before Laurence: Pompeo Sarnelli (1710) and Daniele Manin (1820)." In *Rediscovering Enoch? Studia in Veteris Testamenti Pseudepigrapha*, Eds.: Ariel Hessayon, Annette Yoshiko Reed, Gabriele Boccaccini, Vol. 27, chapter four, Leiden: Brill, 2023, 150–51.

———. "From a Movement of Dissent to a Distinct Form of Judaism: The Heavenly Tablets in Jubilees as the Foundation of a Competing Halakah." In *Enoch and the Mosaic Torah.*

Boccaccini, Gabriele and Loren T. Stuckenbruck. "The Methods and Benefits of a Conversation." In *Enoch and the Synoptic Gospels: Reminiscences, Allusions, Intertextuality*. Atlanta: SBL Press, 2016.

Busi, Giulio. "Giovanni Pico della Mirandola, Enoch, and Hermetism." Chap. 3 in Hessayon, Reed, and Boccaccini, *Rediscovering Enoch? Studia in Veteris Testamenti Pseudepigrapha*, Eds: Ariel Hessayon, Annette Yoshiko Reed, Gabriele Boccaccini, Vol. 27, chapter three, Leiden, Brill, 2023.

Cahana-Blum, Jonathan. "Jonas, Scholem, and the Taubeses in Jerusalem: From Metaphysical Antisemitism to a Jewish Gnostic Conspiracy." *Religions* 13, no. 10 (2022): 949.

Churton, Tobias. "Enoch and the Genesis of Freemasonry." Chap. 5 in Hessayon, Reed, and Boccaccini, *Rediscovering Enoch?* 111–35.

Davidson, Paul. *Is That in the Bible?* (website). "The Book of Enoch as the Background to 1 Peter, 2 Peter, and Jude."

Dimant, Devorah, and Lawrence H. Schiffman, eds. *Time to Prepare the Way in the Wilderness: Papers on the Qumran Scrolls by Fellows of the Institute for Advanced Studies of the Hebrew University, Jerusalem,* 1989–1990. Leiden: Brill, 1995.

Dugan, Elena. "Enochic Biography and the Manuscript History of 1 Enoch: The Codex Panopolitanus Book of the Watchers." *Journal of Biblical Literature* 140, no. 1 (2021): 113–38.

Ehro, Ted M. "James Bruce's Illusory 'Book of Enoch the Prophet.'" Chap. 8 in Hessayon, Reed, and Boccaccini, *Rediscovering Enoch?*, 183–208.

Grafton, A. "Protestant versus Prophet: Isaac Casaubon on Hermes Trismegistus." *Journal of the Warburg and Courtauld Institutes* 46 (1983): 78–93.

Hessayon, Ariel, "James Bruce and His Copies of Ethiopic Enoch," in *Rediscovering Enoch?*, 2023.

Humbert, Jean-Baptiste. "L'éspace sacré a Qumran: Proposition pour l'archéologie." *Revue Biblique* 101, no. 2 (1994): 161–214.

Idel, M. "Hermeticism and Judaism." In *Hermeticism and the Renaissance*, edited by Ingrid Merkel and Allan Debus. Washington, London: Folger Shakespeare Library; Associated University Presses, 1988, 59–76.

Jones, Brice C. "The Bodmer 'Miscellaneous' Codex and the Crosby-Schøyen Codex MS 193: A New Proposal." *Journal of Greco-Roman Christianity and Judaism* 8 (2011): 9–20.

Karr, Don. "Notes on the Study of Merkabah Mysticism and Hekhalot Literature in English with an Appendix on Jewish Magic." *Jewish Studies* 52 (2017): 35–112; updated 2022.

Koch, Klaus. "History as a Battlefield of Two Antagonistic Powers in the Apocalypse of Weeks and in the Rule of the Community." In Boccaccini, *Enoch and Qumran Origins.*

Krause, Martin. "Die Texte von Nag Hammadi." In *Gnosis: Festschrift für Hans Jonas*, edited by Barbara Aland. Göttingen, Germany: Vandenhoeck and Ruprecht, 1978.

Lee, Ralph. "The Reception and Function of 1 Enoch in the Ethiopian Orthodox Tradition." Chap. 12 in Hessayon, Reed, and Boccaccini, *Rediscovering Enoch?*

Lewis, Nicola Denzey. "Death on the Nile: Egyptian Codices, Gnosticism, and Early Christian Books of the Dead." In *Practicing Gnosis: Ritual, Magic,*

Theurgy and Liturgy in Nag Hammadi, Manichaean and Other Ancient Literature, edited by April D. DeConick, Gregory Shaw, and John D. Turner, 161–80. Nag Hammadi and Manichaean Studies 85. Leiden: Brill, 2013.

Litvinau, Fiodar. "A Note on the Greek and Ethiopic Text of 1 Enoch 5:8." *Journal for the Study of the Pseudepigrapha* 29, no. 1 (2019): 28–35.

Ludlow, Jared W. "Enoch in the Tradition of the Church of Jesus Christ of Latter-Day Saints (Mormonism)." Chap. 7 in Hessayon, Reed, and Boccaccini, *Rediscovering Enoch?*

Nickelsburg, George W. E. "Enoch, Levi, and Peter: Recipients of Revelation in Upper Galilee." *Journal of Biblical Literature* 100, no. 4 (1981): 575–600.

Nongbri, Brent. "The Construction of P.Bodmer VIII and the Bodmer 'Composite' or 'Miscellaneous' Codex." *Novum Testamentum* 58, no. 4 (2016): 394–410.

Orlov, Andrei A. "The Heavenly Counterpart of Moses in the Book of Jubilees." In Boccaccini and Ibba, *Enoch and the Mosaic Torah*.

———. "Overshadowed by Enoch's Greatness: 'Two Tablets' Traditions from the Book of Giants to Palaea Historica." *JSJ* 32 (2001): 137–58.

Pingree, David. *The Thousands of Abu Ma'shar*. Studies of the Warburg Institute, vol. 30. London: Warburg Institute, 1968.

Piotrkowski, Meron M. "Priests in Exile: On the Identity of the Oniad Jewish Community of Heliopolis." In *A Question of Identity: Social, Political, and Historical Aspects of Identity Dynamics in Jewish and Other Contexts*, edited by Dikla Rivlin-Katz, Noah Hacham, Geoffrey Herman, and Lilach Sagiv. Berlin: Walter de Gruyter, 2019.

Quispel, Gilles. "Hermes Trismegistus and the Origins of Gnosticism." *Vigiliae Christianae* 46, no. 1 (March 1992): 1–19.

Reed, Annette Yoshiko. "Enoch Lost and Found? Rethinking Enochic Reception in the Middle Ages." In *Rediscovering Enoch? Studia in Veteris Testamenti Pseudepigrapha*, edited by Ariel Hessayon, Annette Yoshiko Reed, Gabriele Boccaccini, vol. 27, chapter 1, 19–49. Leiden: Brill, 2023.

Regev, Eyal. "Jubilees, Qumran, and the Essenes." In Boccaccini and Ibba, *Enoch and the Mosaic Torah*.

Robinson, James M. "The Pachomian Monastic Library at the Chester Beatty Library and the Bibliothèque Bodmer." *Occasional Papers of the Institute for Antiquity and Christianity* 19. Claremont, CA: Claremont Graduate School, 1990.

Schiffman, Lawrence H. "III Enoch and the Enoch Tradition." In Boccaccini, *Enoch and Qumran Origins*.

Schrader Polczer, Elizabeth. Assistant Professor of New Testament at Villanova University. "Papyrus 72: An Introduction." n.p.: n.d. Text no longer available online.

Speth, G. W., ed. *Quatuor Coronatorum, Masonic Reprints*, vol. 2. Margate: 1890.

Strickland, Philip David. "The Curious Case of P72: What an Ancient Manuscript Can Tell Us about the Epistles of Peter and Jude." *Journal of the Evangelical Society* 60, no. 4 (2017): 781–91.

Stuckenbruck, Loren T. "The Book of Enoch: Its Reception in Second Temple Jewish and in Christian Tradition." *Early Christianity* 4, no. 1 (2013): 7–40.

Suter, David W. "Why Galilee? Galilean Regionalism in the Interpretation of 1 Enoch 6–16." *Henoch* 25, no. 2 (2003): 167–212.

Taeubler, Eugene. "Jerusalem 201 to 199 BCE on the History of the Messianic Movement." *Jewish Quarterly Review*, n.s., 37, no. 1 (July 1946): 1–30.

———. "Jerusalem 201 to 199 BCE on the History of the Messianic Movement." *Jewish Quarterly Review*, n.s., 37, no. 2 (Oct. 1946): 125–37.

———. "Jerusalem 201 to 199 BCE on the History of the Messianic Movement." *Jewish Quarterly Review*, n.s., 37, no. 3 (Jan. 1947): 249–63.

Taylor, Joan E. "Evidence for the Zadokite Temple of Onias." *Journal for the Study of Judaism in the Persian, Hellenistic, and Roman Period* 29, no. 3 (1998): 297–321.

Vermes, Geza, trans. *The Complete Dead Sea Scrolls in English*. Rev. ed. London: Penguin, 2004.

Wasserman, Tommy. "Papyrus 72 and the Bodmer Miscellaneous Codex." *New Testament Studies* 51, no. 1 (2005): 137–54.

Wright, W. "Two Epistles of Mār Jacob, Bishop of Edessa." *Journal of Sacred Literature and Biblical Record* NS vol. 10 (1867): 430–33.

Presentations from the Enoch Seminar

Bokhorst, Mirjam Judith. "Opportunities and Limitations of a Synoptic Approach in Editing and Translating, Exemplified by 1 Enoch 22." Paper presented at the Enoch Seminar, Online, June 26, 2023.

Carlson, Stephen C. "The Reception of the Watchers Tradition in Tertullian with regard to 1 Cor 11:2–16" (2022). Article presented at the Enoch Seminar, Online, June 28, 2023.

Dugan, Elena. "New Philology and the Discovery of New Works: Enoch in the First-Century CE." Paper presented at the Enoch Seminar, Online, June 26, 2023.

Elder, Nicholas A. "Scribes and Demons: Literacy and Authority in a Capernaum Synagogue (Mark 1:21–28)" (2021). Article presented at the Enoch Seminar, Online, June 28, 2023.

Esler, Philip. "Heaven in 1 Enoch 1–36 as a Royal Court." Paper presented at the Enoch Seminar, Online, June 27, 2023.

Gieschen, Charles A. "The Importance of the Parables of "1 Enoch" for Understanding the Son of Man in the Four Gospels" (2020). Article presented at the Enoch Seminar, Online, June 26–29, 2023.

Hessayon, Ariel. "Richard Laurence and Ethiopic Enoch." Paper presented at the Enoch Seminar, Online, June 29, 2023.

Kreps, Anne. "The 'Lost' Book of Enoch and Christian Vernacular Fundamentalism." Paper presented at the Enoch Seminar, Online, June 29, 2023.

Lee, Ralph. "Christian Commentary on 1 Enoch: The Gunda Gunde Commentary." Paper presented at the Enoch Seminar, Online, June 28, 2023.

———. "Little Known Giants Traditions in Ethiopian Literature" (2021). Article presented at the Enoch Seminar, Online, June 27, 2023.

Litvinau, Fiodar. "Reception of Hellenistic Traditions in Jewish Pseudepigrapha: Examples from 1 Enoch 69:8 and Apocalypse of Abraham 5." Paper presented at the Enoch Seminar, Online, June 28, 2023.

Nir, Rivka. "Sexual Desire in the Book of the Watchers (1 Enoch 6–36) and the New Testament Exhortation to Sexual Abstinence" (2021). Article presented at the Enoch Seminar, Online, June 28, 2023.

Papaioannou, Kim. "The Sin of the Angels in 2 Peter 2:4 and Jude 6" (2021). Article presented at the Enoch Seminar, Online, June 26-29, 2023.

Pruszinski, Jolyon. "'To Measure for Me the Place of the Chosen': Phenomenologies of Dwelling in the Parables of Enoch." Paper presented at the Enoch Seminar, Online, June 28, 2023.

Schumann, Daniel. "Making Sense of Silence: How to Read the Lack of Covenantal Terminology in Early Enochic Literature in a 3rd and 2nd Century BCE Judean Context." Paper presented at the Enoch Seminar, Online, June 28, 2023.

Williams, Logan. "Debating Daniel's Dream: The Synoptic Gospels and the Similitudes of Enoch on the Son of Man" (2020). Article presented at the Enoch Seminar, Online, June 26–29, 2023.

———. "Temple and Cosmos in the Book of Watchers: Reassessing the Evidence." Paper presented at the Enoch Seminar, Online, June 27, 2023.

Index